D1705574

2€
Avec enveloppe
CARTIPLUS
Fabrication
Française
Heureux Anniversaire
JOYEUX
Joyeux Anniversaire
BON
Joyeux
Anniversaire
Joyeux
Anniversaire
Joyeux
Anniversaire
Heureux Anniversaire

PARIS

LOUIS VUITTON
CITY GUIDE

ABOUT THE CITY GUIDES

Louis Vuitton has selected its favourite places in destination cities around the world. The aim is to offer a good balance of addresses, from time-honoured classics to fashionable new establishments. Well known or offbeat, exclusive or unassuming, they are invariably fascinating, each conveying in its own way something of the essence of the city. Given the speed at which cities evolve, between the time when the guide was researched and its publication some addresses may have closed, others may have emerged and prices may have changed. A renowned chef may have taken his talents to another restaurant, a fashion store may have moved or a museum closed temporarily for renovation. Such changes will be incorporated in the next edition of the Louis Vuitton City Guide.

LOUIS VUITTON AND TRAVEL

Travel is a multifaceted art. It is something that is imagined, envisioned and savoured. As for the journey itself, it cannot be totally improvised. It requires planning and organization.

Louis Vuitton and the history of luggage

Right from its foundation in 1854, Maison Louis Vuitton stood out for its creativity, highlighted by a series of inventions and innovations that revolutionized the art of travelling. Representing three generations, Louis, Georges and Gaston were the three men who, at the turn of the 20th century, built the reputation of a house whose savoir-faire went well beyond simple luggage. Each had his own way of meeting travellers' expectations, ranging from the manufacturing of trunks to the design of lightweight, refined bags, as the craftsman's skill and the styling of the object came together in the service of the idea. Witness the unpickable lock invented in 1890 and still valuable today, and the famous Keepall, the first duffel-type (*polochon*) bag, which inaugurated the era of supple bags.

Extraordinary luggage for unique travellers

Travellers and explorers demanded the impossible. A bed-trunk to withstand the humid heat of the jungle for Pierre Savorgnan de Brazza, a trunk-cum-secretaire to house his precious scores for the conductor Leopold Stokowski and a luxurious chest for the Maharajah of Baroda's tea service. The famous wardrobe, designed so that travellers would never have to unpack, was followed by a host of creations, from the supremely surprising to the last word in luxury. Witness the "driver bag", designed when the motor car was in its infancy, capable of holding spare tyres and inner tubes, as well as the driver's effects, but also usable as a shower tub! Also extraordinary is the extreme refinement of the toiletry set in crocodile, tortoiseshell and cut crystal designed for the opera singer Marthe Chenal. Over the years, Louis Vuitton has continued to invent the most beautiful luggage for the most fabulous journeys.

Moving on: the spirit of travel

Beautiful luggage plays its part in departure reverie. But, ultimately, travellers' dreams are born of encounters. Encounters with cities, to which those other travel essentials, the Louis Vuitton City Guides, hold the key. Redesigned as individual volumes, the Louis Vuitton City Guides know no bounds. Revisited and transformed in 2013 (to mark their fifteenth birthday), the guides explore destination cities the world over. Today, twenty-nine cities covering all continents are celebrated by the Louis Vuitton City Guides. Discovering these cities has been made even simpler thanks to the digital version of the City Guides. Available for iPhone and iPad, the app offers a compact vision of all these exciting destinations, which look to the future while cherishing their past.

A mirror and setter of trends

Readers will discover the subtle cocktail of offbeat finds, classics and dependable addresses that have made the Louis Vuitton City Guides such a success. The guides are served by a team of talented journalists and writers from various countries and backgrounds. Sharp-eyed and informed chroniclers of the transformations at work in the heart of the city, they offer unexpected perspectives on fashion, well-being, interior design, contemporary art, gastronomy and culture, capturing the essence of each metropolis. Always open-minded, they are prepared when necessary to omit the obvious address in favour of some little-known new find, following a discerning trail from the finest hotels to the best chocolatiers and from the hippest fashion addresses to spaces showcasing art. Their contributions, combined with those of renowned artists, designers, business people and gallerists, make the City Guides unique mirrors and setters of trends, astute witnesses to urban vitality. The original photographs illustrating the Louis Vuitton City Guides complement the vision that these unique books offer of each destination.

CONTENTS

DOMINIQUE PERRAULT, GUEST

PORTRAIT

As an architect he works with shape, meaning, dynamism, knowledge and energy – in short with the spirit of place. His buildings engage with all these dimensions.

A master of materials

He dresses in black, of course with a hint of navy blue, just for fun. As the protagonist of his own tale of ethical and social engagement, Dominique Perrault writes each chapter with audacity, intelligence and pragmatism. He is one of the most widely acclaimed French architects in the world, from Spain to Australia. He is also one of the most surprising – fundamentally down-to-earth with just a touch of subtle utopian irony in his use of materials and space. He's also extremely versatile. Exercising a deliberate reticence when it comes to the media, his conceptual hedonism is accompanied by an enthusiasm and sense of mischief punctuated by an enthusiastic taste for puns and word play. He was born in Clermont-Ferrand in 1953; His mother was a housewife and his father, uncle and cousins all engineers. He entered the School of Architecture in 1973, graduating from Paris's École des Beaux-Arts five years later as a qualified architect.

From books to the TGB

While establishing his first agency in 1981, Perrault continued his explorations in urbanism and history. After a few well-received projects, he took part in the international competition launched by President François Mitterrand to design the French National Library in Paris – a competition he won in 1989 as a complete outsider. As a way of managing this ambitious and highly symbolic project, which became known as the "Très Grande Bibliothèque", or TGB, he designed an ultra-modern industrial building on the edge of the site, where he set up office in order to be nearer to the construction site. The Hôtel Industriel Jean-Baptiste-Berlier garnered a slew of awards, including the famous Équerre d'Argent. Since then, Dominique Perrault has been overwhelmed with prestigious prizes, ultimately being awarded the Légion d'Honneur in 2012. In 2015, the Japanese named him a Living Treasure as winner of the Praemium Imperiale in the architecture section, and in 2016 he was made a member of the Institut at the Académie des Beaux-Arts.

A protean architect

Opened in March 1995 by President François Mitterrand, the TGB paved the way for the rebirth of Paris's eastern districts in the 13th arrondissement. Meanwhile, Dominique Perrault headed for Berlin, Luxembourg, Madrid and Seoul. Further projects took him to cities as far flung as Milan and Sofia via Osaka, Albi, Vienna, Naples and Zürich. Bridges, factories, towers, thermal baths, universities, museums, offices, theatres, Olympic swimming pools, courts of justice: Perrault's work demonstrates a protean quality, whatever the sector, be it private, industrial, tertiary, sports or residential. Perrault set up local offices in Berlin, Naples, Madrid, Seoul and Groningen through collaborations with local architects who became his network of friends, and through publications – some fifty to date, including many written by Gilles de Bure, a late and much missed friend. With his muse, Gaëlle Lauriot-Prévost, Perrault has taken on the challenge of interior design, furniture and lighting.

On the road

Perrault is the proud father of three children – two sons and a daughter – from a previous marriage. All three demonstrate that the fruit never falls far from the tree. One son, who studied at a business school, then urban planning at Columbia University in New York, works as a cartographer and urban planner in San Francisco. After studying in London, the other son worked as an architect in London, Los Angeles and Berlin, and is a member of the artistic collective Ayr. Perrault's daughter dreams of becoming a painter, and is currently studying at the École Cantonale d'Art in Lausanne. As a proud father, Perrault is still conscious of the weight his name carries. An incessant traveller, he lives where he works, at present in the 11th arrondissement of Paris, in a former electrical fittings factory for the aviation industry whose basement still harbours a wooden flight-simulation cockpit. Perrault has turned it into a ship, known as the "tanker", on which his faithful crew redesigns the future of our cities – and Paris above all.

MY CITY

"Ever since my first project in Paris, the engineering school ESIEE in Marne-la-Vallée, I've approached Paris from the east, in concentric circles. There's no plan, just pure chance – but one that is aiming to come up with a strategy and create a geography of meaningful projects." Dominique Perrault

Paris – away and back again

Then there was the Hôtel Industriel Berlier, plonked in the middle of nowhere, on a scrap of land in the 13th arrondissement, wedged between a junction with Paris's ring road, the Quai d'Ivry, the Austerlitz railway tracks and Rue Bruneseau – completely out in the sticks. That's where I set up my office during the construction phase of the National Library in 1990, and where I spent fifteen years of my life! I returned to town in 2007 with the "tanker" in the 11th arrondissement, still in the east. The following year, I became more a part of central Paris with the exhibition that the Centre Pompidou devoted to my work. I was still travelling around the world. In 2011, I was in Versailles, having won the international competition for the redevelopment of the Dufour pavilion, which François Hollande opened in 2016.

In the meantime, I was drawn back to Paris one again, but – unusually – to the west, more precisely by the Citylights towers (formerly the Pont de Sèvres towers), in Boulogne-Billancourt, by the Pascal towers at La Défense, and by Longchamp racecourse, the setting for the Prix de l'Arc de Triomphe.

Journey to the centre of Paris

I'm now back in the centre, not far from Les Halles, working on the redevelopment of La Poste du Louvre on Rue du Louvre. Even more central is my Île de la Cité project, in the very heart of Paris, which former President François Hollande entrusted to me. The Île de la Cité is a monument that promises the future. This Parisian island bore witness to my early days when, thanks to an ad in *Le Figaro*, I rented an attic room on Place Dauphine. The owner was none other than Ida Chagall, the daughter of the great painter. And the controlled rent was very cheap. My window looked out over the square, towards the house occupied by Simone Signoret and Yves Montand. I stayed there for several years during my studies at the École des Beaux-Arts on Quai Malaquais, which I could reach on foot. It made a change from riding the suburban train to Paris.

Then I moved into my first apartment: it was in Les Halles, when the district was one big hole in the ground. I watched Marco Ferreri filming his absurdist Western, *Don't Touch the White Woman!* By then I'd graduated, so I turned my apartment into my studio. In the evening, I dined at the Royal Mondétour, a restaurant run by an authentic family from the Auvergne – a real Paris favourite. Ricardo Bofill, the star architect in charge of creating the new Forum des Halles, and a member of the Catalan group known as the "Divine Left", booked a permanent table there for himself and his team.

The Paris playground

My first job in Paris's urban planning department did not stop me working on personal projects in the evening and winning competitions. If I needed space, there was a mezzanine available, again on Place Dauphine. Highly discreet, almost clandestine meetings were organized here by Christo and his wife, Jeanne-Claude, on their project to wrap the Pont Neuf, which was just a stone's throw away. I loved this Parisian focus. I soaked it all up like a sponge, meeting and exchanging ideas with incredible artists. It was a period that seemed fragmented, intense and intimate.

After that, I have always lived where I worked, and vice versa. Of necessity, but also for pleasure, I've driven along Paris's ring road thousands of time: in my probably provocative but also convinced opinion, it's the most beautiful avenue in Paris. It gives you a real tour of twentieth-century architecture: Le Corbusier's Cité Universitaire and Swiss Pavilion, buildings by Claude Parent, the Parc des Princes by Roger Taillibert, Jean Nouvel's Philharmonie, and so on.

When on foot in town, one of my favourite strolls is to admire the town halls in each arrondissement, with their Romanesque republican architecture. I also love the Orgues de Flandres, in the 19th arrondissement, with their cantilevered tiled volumes designed by German architect Martin Schulz van Treeck. By contrast, I also love climbing to the top of the Arc de Triomphe de l'Étoile to relish the views created by the main axes, especially the road that runs towards the Bois de Boulogne.

THE CITY AND ITS NEIGHBOURHOODS

Paris has been growing in concentric circles ever since it was founded. This process reached completion in 1860, when the city was divided into twenty arrondissements, or districts, winding like an escargot around the first one, in the centre, and increasing in size as the city annexed suburbs, farmland, parts of neighbouring communities and former villages and hamlets, among them Auteuil, Passy, Grenelle, Montmartre and Belleville. When Parisians say they live in, for example, the 3rd or the 14th arrondissement, they usually add a qualifier – "in the Marais" or "on Boulevard Raspail". They will often give the nearest metro station, too – "near Denfert (Rochereau)" or "at Abbesses" – even if, like many Parisians, they ride a scooter or a bicycle.

In everyday life and at work, whether they are talking about shopping, appointments, social life or leisure activities, Parisians generally refer not to arrondissements but to neighbourhoods, whose borders shift at their convenience – in other words, depending on their own address. And Parisians never describe their neighbourhood as a "village". This sometimes desperate description is used only by former Parisians who have left for the suburbs and cling to this urban legend to justify their desertion of the city. For many Parisians, it is better to live in the provinces than to commit such an ignominious act as moving to the suburbs.

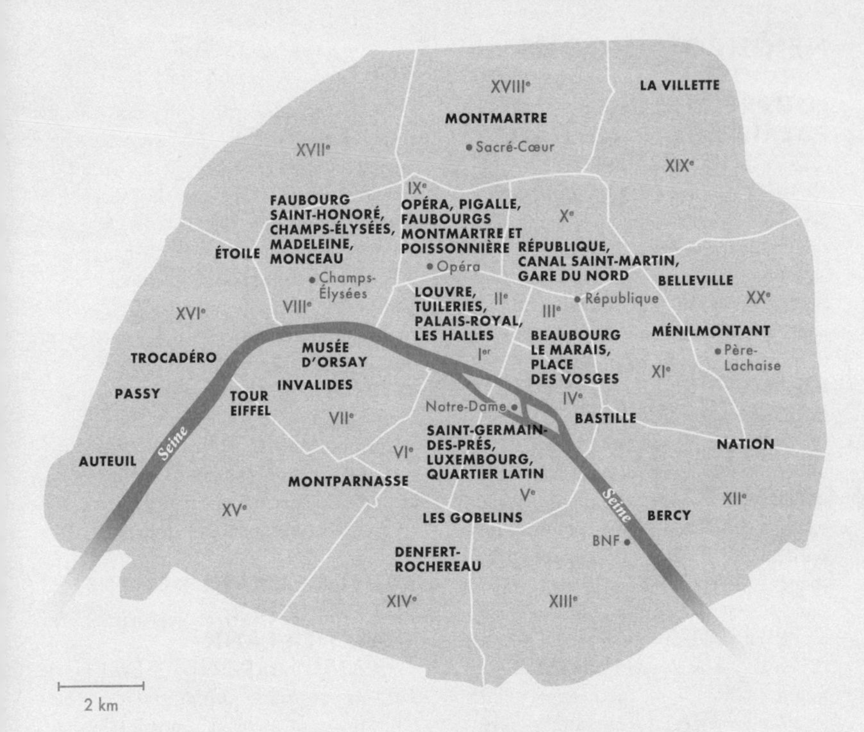

LOUVRE, TUILERIES, PALAIS-ROYAL, LES HALLES
1ST & 2ND ARRONDISSEMENTS
Royal residences & top shopping

BEAUBOURG, LE MARAIS, PLACE DES VOSGES
3RD & 4TH ARRONDISSEMENTS
Historic landmarks & arty strolls

SAINT-GERMAIN-DES-PRÉS, LUXEMBOURG, QUARTIER LATIN
5TH & 6TH ARRONDISSEMENTS
Literary lights & chic lifestyle

MUSÉE D'ORSAY, INVALIDES, TOUR EIFFEL
7TH ARRONDISSEMENT
Fashionable living & ministerial elites

FAUBOURG SAINT-HONORÉ, CHAMPS-ÉLYSÉES, MADELEINE, MONCEAU
8TH ARRONDISSEMENT
Gilded neighbourhoods & luxury labels

OPÉRA, PIGALLE, FAUBOURGS MONTMARTRE AND POISSONNIÈRE
9TH ARRONDISSEMENT
Saucy streets & bohemian chic

RÉPUBLIQUE, CANAL SAINT-MARTIN, GARE DU NORD
10TH & 11TH ARRONDISSEMENTS
Working-class areas & bobo strongholds

BASTILLE, NATION, BERCY
12TH ARRONDISSEMENT
Outliers & countercurrents

LES GOBELINS, DENFERT-ROCHEREAU, MONTPARNASSE
13TH, 14TH & 15TH ARRONDISSEMENTS
Greenery & family life

AUTEUIL, PASSY, TROCADÉRO, ÉTOILE
16TH & 17TH ARRONDISSEMENTS
Nobility & urban elegance

MONTMARTRE, LA VILLETTE, BELLEVILLE, MÉNILMONTANT
18TH, 19TH & 20TH ARRONDISSEMENTS
Old Paris & modern nostalgia

NEIGHBOURHOODS

LOUVRE, TUILERIES, PALAIS-ROYAL, LES HALLES
1ST & 2ND ARRONDISSEMENTS
Royal residences & top shopping

The 2nd arrondissement may be the smallest, but the first is the least populated, with two-thirds taken up by the Louvre and the Jardin des Tuileries. Crowds tend to concentrate in Rue Saint-Honoré between the Palais-Royal and Rue Cambon.
Rue Saint-Honoré, between Saint-Roch, the most "artistic" parish in the city, and the Polish church on Place Maurice Barrès, bisects a vast network of fashion and jewellery shops and grand hotels as it runs south-east to the Louvre, which was a royal residence until Louis XIV abandoned it to move to Versailles. The Palais-Royal, once the fief of the dukes of Orléans, is a patrician residential bastion that is much in demand. The elegant clothing and fragrance shops lining the arcades conjure an air of nostalgia for the era of the great courtesans. The less upmarket Les Halles area seems to be reviving, despite the controversial Canopée, with the opening of new cocktail bars and a famous chef's brasserie, the transformation of the former Bourse du Commerce into an exhibition space for the Pinault Foundation, and the conversion of the old Louvre post office into a hotel, residences and shops by architect Dominique Perrault, who has also been asked by the president's office to reflect on the future of the Île de la Cité (Hôtel-Dieu, etc.).

BEAUBOURG, LE MARAIS, PLACE DES VOSGES
3RD & 4TH ARRONDISSEMENTS
Historic landmarks & arty strolls

When it opened in 1977, the Centre Pompidou saved the area from bleak decay. The Marais followed its arty lead.
The conspicuous centre of gay life and commerce, the Marais has become a cult neighbourhood. The first gallery owners, architects and advertising and press agencies to settle in the area have since migrated northward, passing into the 3rd arrondissement well beyond the Musée Picasso to create the Haut (Upper) Marais, a pure real-estate concept. Further south, in the 4th arrondissement, the shops on Rue des Francs Bourgeois, which runs to the Place des Vosges, stay open on Sunday. Finally, the Île Saint-Louis, a floating museum between the two banks of the Seine, is also part of the 4th arrondissement. The city of Paris is considering melding these four first arrondissements into one entity.
It's unlikely to happen soon, though.

SAINT-GERMAIN-DES-PRÉS, LUXEMBOURG, QUARTIER LATIN
5TH & 6TH ARRONDISSEMENTS
Literary lights & chic lifestyle

The 5th arrondissement is mostly taken up by the Quartier Latin, home of the Sorbonne, founded in 1257 and paved with the cobblestones that served as weapons during the demonstrations of May 1968. It shares a playground, the Jardin du Luxembourg, with its neighbour, the more sought-after 6th arrondissement, home to the Saint-Germain-des-Prés area. If the fifth is a learned and scholarly place, with all its universities and students, the sixth is more worldly and literary, with a weakness for fashion and luxury. Today, though distinguished chocolate-makers and pastry cooks have joined the fashion and luxury boutiques, there are still enough print sellers, bookstores and unusual boutiques to delight both collectors and casual strollers. From Jussieu to Saint-Germain, the fifth and sixth are also still home to a number of Parisian publishing houses and most of the city's ninety arthouse cinemas, some of which, like the Champo, are listed as monuments, while others have been stylishly modernized.

MUSÉE D'ORSAY, INVALIDES, TOUR EIFFEL
7TH ARRONDISSEMENT
Fashionable living & ministerial elites

The 7th arrondissement is rightly regarded as the most elegant and exclusive on the Left Bank. It is justifiably proud of the two best perspectives in the city: the Champ-de-Mars and the Esplanade des Invalides, which are flanked by peaceful, tree-lined avenues whose residents are never seen, except when the city's best chocolate-maker, Jean-Paul Hévin, is out of stock. The residential seventh resents the close proximity of the 15th, considered ersatz, but loves rubbing up against the literary and fashion gentry of the sixth. What else? Nothing less than the Seine, with its finest quays; the Eiffel Tower, the symbol of Paris; the Musée d'Orsay; and the National Assembly.

FAUBOURG SAINT-HONORÉ, CHAMPS-ÉLYSÉES, MADELEINE, MONCEAU
8TH ARRONDISSEMENT
Gilded neighbourhoods & luxury labels

The 8th arrondissement is a concentration of financial and political power – beginning with the Élysée Palace – but especially of luxury, whether the luxury shopping bags on Rue du Faubourg Saint-Honoré and Avenue Montaigne or the luxury of the presidential suites in the many five-star hotels and great restaurants located there. From the colossal sanctity of the Madeleine church, surrounded by posh food stores, to the foliage of the Parc Monceau, the stomping ground of high society during the Second Empire, the eighth is superb. It is home to the Champs-Élysées, an avenue built for triumphal parades if ever there was one, and to the Grand Palais and Petit Palais, where many blockbuster art exhibitions are held. It is intersected by beautiful avenues studded with unusual museums in sumptuous mansions. Full of grandeur, the eighth becomes less so farther north towards the Europe quarter and the recently modernized Gare Saint-Lazare, where every day thousands of commuters arrive to fill the area's office buildings.

OPÉRA, PIGALLE, FAUBOURGS MONTMARTRE AND POISSONNIÈRE
9TH ARRONDISSEMENT
Saucy streets & bohemian chic

The Opéra Garnier, Place Saint-Georges and Pigalle have lost little of the artistic and decadent liveliness they were known for in the 19th century. For many, this is the real Paris, with the department stores on Boulevard Haussmann, Trinity church and the bright lights of Place de Clichy, crowded at night with fun-seekers. It is also home to the Drouot auction house, several covered passageways and many theatres, and it has the provincial charm of the Cité Treviso and Cité Bergère. Pigalle, that "antechamber of vice and lust", with its scandalous traditions, memories of a now legendary underworld and promises of sex for pay, is still open for business, but it has lost its swagger. Amid all this, between Rue de La Rochefoucauld, Rue Saint-Lazare and Rue des Martyrs (now part of SoPi, or "South Pigalle"), the Neoclassical ninth cherishes the memory of the time when it was known as Nouvelle Athènes, a bucolic, out-of-the-way neighbourhood where the artistic elite of the 19th century lived, among them Alexandre Dumas, George Sand and Frédéric Chopin, as well as the painters Ary Scheffer and Gustave Moreau, whose homes are now museums. These places are all haunted by the memory of a world of bohemians, *grisettes* (young women of loose morals, personified by Mimi Pinson in Alfred de Musset's poem of that name) and courtesans, all living in their garrets. The livelier streets nearby, encompassing the Folies Bergère and Rues du Faubourg Montmartre and Faubourg Poissonnière, have become a new urban epicentre in the past few seasons with the renewal of the hotel, bar and bistro scene. From Rue Trévise to Rue Hauteville, the 9th arrondissement is starting to overflow into the 10th, proof of porous borders within Paris.

RÉPUBLIQUE, CANAL SAINT-MARTIN, GARE DU NORD
10TH & 11TH ARRONDISSEMENTS
Working-class areas & bobo strongholds

Parisians think of the Place de la République as the starting or arrival point of major demonstrations that follow the Nation-Bastille-République route. This huge, recently renovated square was created by Haussmann during the Second Empire, at the junction of three arrondissements – the 3rd, 10th and 11th. Place de la République is also the unofficial entry point to the Boboland that is the Upper Marais. While the original bobos set up barricades around Boulevard Voltaire, the neo-bobos have taken up residence in the much riskier areas around Boulevard Magenta and the Gare du Nord.
They set the tone and the rest of the area followed. The Gare du Nord, historically linked to northern cities – Arras, Lille, Valenciennes – now also serves London via Eurostar and Cologne, Brussels, Antwerp and Amsterdam via Thalys. Along with the new station in Berlin, the Gare du Nord is the largest in Europe. Its little sister, the Gare de l'Est, serves Reims, Strasbourg, Nancy and Metz by TGV. Much more romantic, and often even melancholy, the Canal Saint-Martin, inaugurated by King Charles X, flows peacefully over 4 kilometres, from the Bassin de l'Arsenal at Bastille, now a pleasure port, to the Bassin de la Villette.

BASTILLE, NATION, BERCY
12TH ARRONDISSEMENT
Outliers & countercurrents

The Bastille area, the buffer between the Marais and the suburbs, encompasses three arrondissements: the 4th, 11th and 12th. Parisians from other parts of town think of the Bastille as just a nightmarish intersection, but those who live or work in the area know that it is circumscribed by Boulevard Richard Lenoir – the Boulevard Beaumarchais is so very Marais – and the first part of Rue du Faubourg Saint-Antoine as far as Square Trousseau. Running towards Place de la Nation, the Faubourg Saint-Antoine, which still lives up to its nickname "Furniture Row", is the long street separating the 11th and 12th arrondissements. Along the way, it offers culinary delights from around the world at the Marché d'Aligre, while Faidherbe's Rue Paul Bert, with its commendable bistros and provincial charm, is a haven of relaxed creativity. The Bercy area, Paris's first village, is signalled by the Gare de Lyon's clock tower. The former centre of the wine trade still has warehouses and wine sheds, which have been turned into shops and restaurants, and is home to the Ministry of Finance building, an indoor arena and the Cinémathèque Française, housed in a building by Frank Gehry.

LES GOBELINS, DENFERT-ROCHEREAU, MONTPARNASSE
13TH, 14TH & 15TH ARRONDISSEMENTS
Greenery & family life

Bordering the brainy, university-filled 5th arrondissement, the Gobelins neighbourhood stretches towards the 13th, the Parisian Chinatown. To the east, the new Tolbiac quarter, with the four towers of the Grande Bibliothèque, designed by the architect Dominique Perrault, gives this side of the river a hint of modern Berlin. The 14th is another story. With the statue

Lion de Belfort, by Frédéric Bartholdi, who also sculpted the Statue of Liberty, France's gift to New York, the residential Denfert-Rochereau area is home to Rue Daguerre, with its gourmet delights, as well as the Fondation Cartier and the École Camondo. Very soon, it will welcome the new head office of the Centre National du Cinéma. With the Observatoire, Parc Montsouris, hidden private gardens and the chestnut trees along Boulevard Arago, this southern part of Paris is truly green, both politically and in reality. The 15th looks very stately with its long streets and eclectic architecture, but toughens up when you reach the towers of the Beaugrenelle area. Typical of 1970s urban planning, this Seine-side development has a new look, designed by the architects Valode & Pistre. When you look to the west, you will see, on the tip of the Île aux Cygnes, a replica of the Statue of Liberty. The circle is complete.

AUTEUIL, PASSY, TROCADÉRO, ÉTOILE
16TH & 17TH ARRONDISSEMENTS
Nobility & urban elegance

Symbols of chic, opulent Paris, these large neighbourhoods were built on the leafy western side of Paris, where the air was pure, far from the smoke and pollution of the factories in the poor eastern quarters. The 16th has the Bois de Boulogne and the Bagatelle for gardens; beautiful, wide avenues radiating from Place de l'Étoile; and Trocadéro and its breathtaking view of the Eiffel Tower. It has retained its tasteful elegance and shows off its cultural riches with the Cité de l'Architecture, the Palais de Tokyo, the Musée Guimet and other museums. The Fondation Louis Vuitton, designed by architect Frank Gehry, is another spectacular example, of course. It billows like a ship made of glass in the Jardin d'Acclimatation. The 17th is full of contrasts. On the Villiers side, it retains its grand-bourgeois, Haussmann character, but the Batignolles area – a former village and site of a convent, once populated by workers and shopkeepers and home to the painter Édouard Manet – forms a border between two worlds and is influenced by the spirit of Montmartre. Though surrounded by the Clichy, Rome and Pereire neighbourhoods, it still feels like a village.

MONTMARTRE, LA VILLETTE, BELLEVILLE, MÉNILMONTANT
18TH, 19TH & 20TH ARRONDISSEMENTS
Old Paris & modern nostalgia

Montmartre was among the villages absorbed by Paris in 1860. The Butte Montmartre, 131 metres high and crowned by Sacré Cœur, teems with visitors night and day. Parisians love to hate the church, nicknaming it the Meringue. On the northern slope of the hill, the quiet, chic Avenue Junot and the Fémis film school make you forget the Abbesses neighbourhood, very lively in the high season when both visitors and Montmartre residents crowd the café terraces and fill the shops. In the 19th, La Villette, once the site of slaughterhouses, is now home to the Cité des Sciences et de l'Industrie, the Géode and the Conservatoire National de Musique. The far end of the 19th, up against the Boulevard Périphérique, or ring road, is finally getting interesting, even on the other side, in the suburb of Pantin, which has become trendy since a couple of pioneering art galleries opened spaces there. Who knows, it may yet become a Parisian-style Brooklyn overtaken by ad agencies. Belleville, with its highest point at 128.5 metres, is traversed by a steep street and a boulevard with a food market. Once a proletarian area, it now has a multi-ethnic population yet still manages to retain a bit of its Parisian soul. Celebrated in song by Maurice Chevalier, Ménilmontant, a rough working-class neighbourhood before the Second World War, climbs up to 118 metres on the eastern side of the city.

THE ESSENTIALS

Visitors from around the world associate Paris with all sorts of more or less imaginary pleasures. In this multicultural city, knowledge and tradition are cultivated like orchids in greenhouses until they become brand images exported with much panache throughout the world. Its glowing reputation as the City of Light may not be new, but Paris still shines with thousands of lights: intellectual, electrical, artistic and worldly.

The city is a photogenic metropolis where film, music and literature reign. It is also, and always will be, the capital of haute couture, fashion and luxury, where designers from around the world contribute to a vibrant Tower of Babel bristling with talent. Curious travellers will make it a point of honour to be in the know and show off their knowledge. You don't have to live in Paris to be a Parisian.

What follows is a broad portrait of the city, drawn with touches of humour and full of practical information. It sums up the soul of the city, its good and bad sides, highlights and idiosyncrasies. It will also help you understand the inhabitants and will give you everything you need to feel as Parisian as they are.

ARRIVING IN THE CITY

AIRPORT FORMALITIES

How quickly you arrive at passport control depends on whether you land at Paris–Charles-de-Gaulle ("Roissy" to Parisians) or Orly Airport. Orly Sud and CDG Terminal 1 can be exhausting, with their moving walkways out of order more often than not. As for the controls themselves, the wait varies depending on how crowded the airport is and any possible security issues that may arise. In all situations, remain neutral and friendly – in spite of your jet lag – and do not try to change queues, except when asked to by staff. Baggage carousels are always clearly indicated, and unless a strike is on, luggage sometimes arrives mysteriously fast.

Time to the passport control area: 10–40 mins
Controls: 35–90 mins

GETTING TO THE CITY

TRAIN

RER Line B is the least glamorous and least expensive way into town. It directly connects Paris to the two main airports, but it can be an uncomfortable experience. Breakdowns are not uncommon. People arriving in Paris for the first time or laden with luggage might be better off opting for another solution. From Orly, take the Orlyval train to Antony, then RER Line B4 to Paris. From Paris-CDG, RER Line B3 trains leave every 10 minutes, 5am to midnight. From Orly, Orlyval trains leave every 4-7 minutes, 6am to 11pm.

RER Line B3, Paris-CDG Airport to Paris, 50 mins, €9.25
Orlyval and RER Line B4 to Antony and Paris, 40 mins, €12.05

www.ratp.fr
www.orlyval.com
www.aeroportsdeparis.fr

BUS

A slightly less stressful way to get to Paris is by RoissyBus, OrlyBus or the Air France coach. The latter offers the most comfort and premium service, with a baggage handler at each stop. The buses have varying stops in central and residential neighbourhoods (Denfert-Rochereau, Porte Maillot, Invalides, Opéra, etc.).

Buses leave every 10 to 30 mins, from 6am to 11pm
From Roissy: 60 mins, €10.50 to €17.50
From Orly: 30 mins, €7.50 to €12.50

www.aeroportsdeparis.fr
www.ratp.fr
www.lescarsairfrance.com

TAXI

It's very simple: there is one queue for taxis to Paris and another for the suburbs. Never try to choose a taxi: you are expected to take the next one in the queue, unless driver does not accept payment by credit card, which often happens at Orly. For a family of four with luggage, book a "grand taxi" (a minivan, or *monospace* in French) with the company G7, which specializes in this niche. It is customary to ride in the back seat and, when you are alone, opposite the driver's side. Once you have arrived, pay while still in the car and ask for a receipt, mandatory for fares over €25. A surcharge of about 15 percent is added from 7pm to 7am and on Sundays and holidays. Tipping is at the discretion of the customer. To counter competition from VTCs (chauffeured car services like Uber, LeCab, etc.), since 1 March 2016, Parisian taxis have been legally required to apply the same flat rates to and from the airports, no matter what the time of day or traffic conditions (special lanes are reserved for them on the A1 and A6 motorways). And a Paris Taxis app (iPhone and Android) is available.

Orly-Left Bank: €30 (Right Bank: €35)
CDG-Right Bank: €50 (Left Bank: €55)
Taxis G7: 01 47 39 47 39, www.G7.fr
Taxis Bleus: 01 49 36 10 10,
www.taxis-bleus.com
Alpha Taxis: 01 45 85 85 85,
www.alphataxis.fr

MOTORCYCLE TAXI

The motorcycle taxi is the fastest way into town, but is only an option for solo travellers with one carry-on bag. You must reserve in advance, since they are not allowed to pick up passengers who hail them on the street, even at airports. A helmet and other accessories and passenger insurance are included in the price, which varies depending on whether it is a motorcycle or a super-scooter. Fast, but not very pleasant when it rains.
From Paris-CDG: from €65
From Orly: from €50
Urban Driver: tel 01 75 60 15 06,
www.urban-driver.com

CHAUFFEUR-DRIVEN CAR

Booking a limousine with chauffeur has more benefits than just the VIP cachet. Someone will welcome you at the door of the plane, you'll be able to jump the queue at passport control, your luggage will be taken care of, and you will be escorted to the car by a multilingual driver. The vehicles are comfortable, and you can even order things like champagne and flowers.
Limousines Laisser Passer:
tel 01 49 70 70 10,
www.laisserpasser.fr
Paris Airport Limousines:
www.parisairportlimousines.com
Paris Major Limousine:
tel 01 44 52 50 00,
www.1st-limousine-services.com

37 bridges

30 million visitors every year

2.27 million population of central Paris

105 km^2 area of Paris

FIRST IMPRESSIONS

Whether you arrive in Paris from Orly or Charles-de-Gaulle, you won't see the landscape of the Île-de-France at its best during the drive into town. Oddly enough, even when the weather is nice, everything looks grey. Motorway works often add to frequent traffic problems. Unless a miracle occurs, your first impression will probably be of a traffic jam. Paris is permanently blocked up. This is not a thrilling way to be introduced to the city. Once you have arrived in town, you will pass through multi-ethnic outer arrondissements before encountering the urban harmony of the centre, dominated by 19th-century "Haussmannian" buildings. Everything is still grey, however, from the zinc rooftops to the Parisians' coats. Unlike many capitals, there is no abrupt change of landscape or sign of chaos (except the traffic). Then, suddenly, you find yourself in the midst of a picture postcard – or a game of deluxe Monopoly – surrounded by monuments, palaces, museums and shops. You will ask yourself: Will I measure up? Will I become a Parisian?

GETTING AROUND THE CITY

TAXIS

A Paris taxi is usually black and might be a large Skoda sedan or a Toyota Prius to economize on fuel. The Taxis Bleus company recently introduced a flat fare of €10 on weekends between midnight and 5am. The new Paris Taxis app (iPhone and Android), perfect for anyone who understands this fearsome and complex world, has fare schedules that would give a migraine to a computer.

Average fare: €15
Minimum fare: €7
Tipping: 10% of the fare (optional, but recommended)

To ring the nearest taxi rank:
tel 01 45 30 30 30
Taxis Bleus: tel 01 49 36 10 10 or 3609
Taxis G7: tel 01 47 39 47 39

ON FOOT

Walking is the best way to discover the city. The many pedestrian and shopping streets encourage exercise, while the narrow pavement on most side streets complicates the task by forcing walkers to step off the curb as soon as a pram, bicycle, granny with a shopping bag or military tank approaches. In Paris, where everyone walks all over everyone else anyway, the best way to proceed is to walk on eggshells. It's a question of etiquette, although Parisians prefer those who put their foot in their mouth over those who step into the gutter...

THE METRO

The metro is the fastest and least expensive way to get around. Parisians make a point of trying to get into the metro carriage that will be closest to the exit when they reach their destination. They put their heads down and rush ahead. The pleasantest line is number 6, serving the posh neighbourhoods in the west. It runs between Nation and Étoile and part of it is elevated. The busiest is line 4, between Porte d'Orléans and Mairie de Montrouge, ending at the Saint-Ouen flea market. A small group of students has drawn up a map that purports to predict Parisians' income based on their metro stop. It must be biased, however, since those who live in the 7th, 8th, 16th and 17th arrondissements and in Neuilly do not (often) take the metro.

Runs daily from 6am to 12:30am (until 2am on Friday and Saturday)
Single ticket: €1.90 (€14.50 for 10)
Mobilis card: from €7.30 (1 day)
Paris Visite card: from €11.65 (1 day) to €37.25 (5 days)
Weekly Pass Navigo card: from €19.25

www.ratp.fr

BUSES

The bus is the preferred means of transport for those who do not like the idea of going underground like a mole to get around. At bus stops, with their new, poorly designed shelters (open to the winds and rain), electronic signs indicate the waiting time – often as long as 10–20 minutes – before the next bus will arrive. Metro tickets are valid on buses; time-stamp the ticket in the validator when you get on the bus. However, tickets purchased on the bus are not valid on the metro. Fare-dodging can be expensive: €45, payable on the spot; otherwise it's the damp straw of the dungeons for the offender.

Price of ticket purchased on the bus: €2

www.ratp.fr

TRAMWAY

The Citadis 402 model of the electric tram, running along the Boulevards des Maréchaux (also known as the Petite Ceinture), has been put into service by sections. The latest will close the loop in the north of the city. The Paris tram

17,702 taxis

runs around the city's periphery and does not go into the centre, but its stations are connected to tram lines serving the surrounding communities and beyond. Same ticket as for the Metro or bus
www.tramway.paris.fr

4,360 metres
– the length of Rue de Vaugirard, the longest street in Paris

BIKES

Paris, which is not a flat city that is easy to cycle in, waited a long time before creating a network of more than 350 kilometres of cycle paths created along existing streets and pavements. The bike share scheme, Vélib, was introduced in 2007 and has been pretty popular. The current generation of ugly, heavy bikes are on their way out. In 2018, new Vélibs provided by Smoove will take their place in the form of more intelligent, solar-powered machines. The changeover will require the 300,000 scheme members to accept new terms and conditions and pay a higher annual fee. Many Parisians, however, have chosen to buy their own bikes so they can be totally independent, though there are many thefts and occasional accidents. It is important that cyclists learn the basic traffic rules. Riding a motor-free vehicle is not a licence to flout the law, even though bikes are granted breathtaking liberty to be reckless. Jumping red lights, cycling on pavements, not stopping for pedestrian crossings, talking on the phone while cycling – it's all banned. Before they grumble about motorists, Parisian cyclists must also learn to behave well. For occasional cyclists, guided tours are organized by Paris Bike Tour, but watch out for guides who do not know the Highway Code.
Vélib': €1.70 (for a day), €8 for 7 days, €29 (annual subscription)
Paris Bike Tour: from €32
www.velib.paris.fr
www.parisbiketour.net

BOATS

The Batobus riverboat line operates throughout the year, with nine stops serving tourist sites from Beaugrenelle port to the Jardin des Plantes – Cité de la Mode.
Batobus: €17 (one-day pass) and €19 (two-day pass), €60 (1 year)
www.batobus.com

CAR

Since 1 July 2016, the circulation of petrol- and diesel-fuelled vehicles dating from before 1997 has been forbidden between 8am and 8pm, somewhat unfortunate for the admittedly small number of Youngtimer owners. If you defy the ban you risk a fine and having your vehicle immobilized (one wonders how and where). Cars, motorbikes and scooters all need to display a Crit'Air sticker (corresponding to 1 of 6 levels of pollution). The fine for non-compliance is 68 euros. Traffic lanes are being made narrower, causing additional traffic congestion, and service stations are being shut down as efforts are made to curb car use in Paris. Maybe the best idea is to hire a big black limo with chauffeur to drive you around.
www.certificat-air.gouv.fr
www.agencevipcar.fr
www.avischauffeur.fr
www.cinq-s.com

OFFBEAT TRANSPORT

The Autolib' is the automotive version of the Vélib' bike-rental system.
To sign up, all you need is a valid licence, an ID and a credit card. Another option, the Parisian "tuk tuk", can carry up to three passengers. Produced by Piaggio, these white Ape Calessinos brighten up grey Paris but usually are only seen in purely touristic spots.
www.autolib.eu
www.tuktukparisiens.fr

PRACTICAL MATTERS

COMMUNICATIONS

TELEPHONE

To reach Paris from abroad, dial the international access code, then the code for France **(33)**, followed by the 9-digit phone number without the first 0.
To call abroad from Paris, first dial **00**.
To call Paris from anywhere else in France, dial the 10-digit number. There are four mobile operators in France: Bouygues Telecom, Orange, SFR and Free.
Mobile numbers begin with **06** or **07**.

EMAIL/INTERNET

Wifi is not free in all hotels, to the dismay of many travellers. Even the most luxurious hotel may charge for it. Restaurants, cafés, fast-food restaurants and cocktail lounges are more generous, and many of them stay open quite late. Free connections are available in some public parks when they are open. Signs are posted at the entrance and in the exact locations.

POST

Stamps are sold in post offices and tobacco shops, and cost €0.85 for a first-class letter weighing up to 20 grams for France, €1 for other EU countries or €1.25 for the United States, Asia, Australia, etc. Prices increase depending on weight and size.

Post offices: Monday–Friday 8am to 7pm, Saturday until noon
24/7 post office: 16, rue Étienne Marcel, 2nd, metro Étienne Marcel, tel 36 31, www.laposte.fr

CURRENCY AND BANKS

EURO (€)

EXCHANGE RATE

€1=$1.10 / €1=£ 0.83

ATMs connected to the Visa and MasterCard systems can be found on almost every street corner, but American Express is not accepted everywhere. Small amounts can now be paid by card.
If your card is lost or stolen, report it immediately to your bank and the police.

Banks: Monday to Friday or Tuesday to Saturday, 9am to 5pm
Lost credit card: tel 0892 705 705 (24/7)
Lost chequebook: tel 0892 68 32 08 (24/7)

AVERAGE PRICE INDEX

PROPERTY PRICE

From €6,390 (in the 19th arrondissement) to €12,150 (in the 6th arrondissement)

MONTHLY NET WAGE

€2,750 per household

A CINEMA TICKET

€12

A BAGUETTE

Between €0.80 and €1.70

AN ESPRESSO IN A CAFÉ

€1.50 at the counter (can go as high as €8 on the Champs-Élysées)

CLIMATE/GEOGRAPHY

WEATHER

Temperate summers and relatively mild winters characterize the Paris Basin, which is subject to both oceanic and continental influences. Although it rains one day out of two on average, the Île-de-France is one of the driest regions in France.

SUNRISE AND SUNSET

MARCH 6am to 6pm
JUNE 4am to 8pm
SEPTEMBER 5:30am to 6pm
DECEMBER 7:30am to 4pm

TIME ZONE

GMT/UTC + 1
GMT/UTC + 2 (French summertime)

ALTITUDE

The lowest point in Paris is the average level of the Seine, 26 metres; the highest point is in Montmartre, at 131 metres.

2½ hours time it takes to cross Paris on foot from north to south

RIVER

"Under the Mirabeau Bridge flows the Seine", wrote the poet Guillaume Apollinaire. UNESCO has classified the river's quays and thirty-seven bridges as a World Heritage Site. The Seine flows for 13 kilometres through the city and has three islands: Île Saint-Louis, Île de la Cité (the historic heart of Paris) and Île aux Cygnes. Parisians measure the flood levels of the Seine by the statue of the Zouave on the Pont de l'Alma – the waters reached his shoulders in 1910. In June 2016, they reached his belt.

PUBLIC HOLIDAYS

1 JANUARY New Year's Day
LATE MARCH/APRIL Easter Monday
1 MAY Labour Day
8 MAY V.E. Day 1945
LATE MAY Ascension
LATE MAY/EARLY JUNE Whit Monday
14 JULY Bastille Day
15 AUGUST Assumption
1 NOVEMBER All Saints' Day
11 NOVEMBER Armistice of 1918
25 DECEMBER Christmas Day

KEEP IN MIND

HOTEL TAXES

Recently become steeply higher, a tax of between €0.99 (for a two-star hotel) and €4.40 (for a palace) is usually included in the price per person per day. Children under 18 are exempt.

ANIMALS

European Union citizens must be in possession of a "European pet passport" issued by a veterinarian within five days prior to departure and certifying the good health of a pet. If a pet is from a country outside the European Union, the pet owner must be able to show an international health certificate. In France, only a rabies vaccine is required. Pet animals must have identification tattoos or microchips. Four-legged friends weighing less than 6 kilos are allowed in public transport when carried in a basket or bag.
Hotels that accept pets sometimes charge a fee for them.
Customs information
Tel 0811 20 44 44 (from France)
+33 1 72 40 78 50 (from abroad)

TOURIST OFFICE

Paris Convention and Visitors Bureau
25, rue des Pyramides, 1st, metro Pyramides,
www.parisinfo.com
Open daily 10am to 7pm, May to October from 9am, closed 1 May

IMPORT/EXPORT

A tax refund is available for non-EU citizens over the age of 15 on purchases of more than €175 made in the same store in a period of less than three months. Fill out the "Tax-free Shopping France invoice", available in the store, then have it stamped by customs at the airport and send it in within three months. Luxury products purchased in duty-free shops are already duty free.

EMERGENCY NUMBERS

Phone **17** for police, **15** for ambulance, **18** for fire
24-hour pharmacies:
5, place de la République, 3rd, metro République, tel 01 47 00 18 08
84, avenue des Champs-Élysées, 8th, metro George V, tel 01 45 62 02 41
6, place de Clichy, 9th, metro Place de Clichy, tel 01 48 74 65 18
52, rue du Commerce, 15th, metro Avenue Émile Zola, tel 01 45 79 75 01
Lost property: tel 0821 00 25 25

HISTORICAL AND MUST-SEE SITES

ARC DE TRIOMPHE

Standing at the end of the Champs-Élysées, this monument commissioned by Napoleon to commemorate his victories plays its role to perfection. On it are 128 names of battles and 660 of officers and generals. At its foot is the Tomb of the Unknown Soldier, which symbolizes all the soldiers killed in the First World War. From the 50-metre-high terrace, visitors have a 360-degree view that extends for 7 km, but not as far as Marengo, where Napoleon won one of his victories. Arc de Triomphe, www.paris-arc-de-triomphe.fr

ARÈNES DE LUTÈCE

This vestige of the Gallo-Roman period dating from the end of the first century AD was unearthed in the 19th century and restored in 1917. The arena could accommodate 17,000 spectators for gladiatorial combats, chariot races, and bear and lion fights. 49, rue Monge, 5th

COLONNE DE JUILLET

The Colonne de Juillet stands in the Place de la Bastille in memory of the victims of the French Revolution of 1830. Made of hollow bronze, it weighs 174 tons, and at 47 metres high, it is topped by a 5-metre-high gilt-bronze statue, the *Génie de la Liberté*. Parisians enjoy perilously circling it in their cars. Place de la Bastille, 4th

COLONNE AND PLACE VENDÔME

Commissioned in 1686 by the Marquis de Louvois, Louis XIV's secretary of state for war, and lined with stately mansions built in the early 18th century, Place Vendôme is the most sumptuous square in Paris. An equestrian statue of the Sun King, destroyed during the Revolution, once stood in its centre. The first Colonne Vendôme, erected in 1810 by Napoleon in honour of the soldiers who fought at Austerlitz, was made of bronze from enemy cannons. It was pulled down during the Commune on the suggestion of painter Gustave Courbet, who thus was charged with the cost of its restoration. It was re-erected in 1873. Place Vendôme, 1st

HÔTEL DES INVALIDES

Founded by Louis XIV in 1670 to care for disabled soldiers, this institution encompasses the Musée de l'Armée, the Musée des Plans-Reliefs, the Église du Dôme, the Église Saint-Louis des Invalides, Napoleon's sarcophagus, and the tombs of Maréchal de Vauban and Rouget de Lisle, author of the *Marseillaise*.
www.musee-armee.fr/lhotel-des-invalides.html

NOTRE-DAME DE PARIS

Built on the orders of Maurice de Sully, bishop of Paris, beginning in 1163 (the work took almost two centuries), the cathedral was highly romanticized by Victor Hugo. To mark its 850th anniversary in 2013, its five bells were replaced. Over 13 million visitors enter it each year. Île de la Cité, 1st

PALAIS DU LUXEMBOURG

Marie de Médicis, widow of Henri IV, built this palace for the young regent, Louis XIII, so he could hunt wild boar in the Luxembourg garden. The work on the Florentine-style building began in 1615. It became the headquarters of the French Senate in 1801. Boar hunting may have been a tradition in Corsica, but Napoleon put an end to it and turned the garden into one for children. The marionettes are still there. 19, rue de Vaugirard, 6th

PANTHÉON

Laid out like a Greek cross, the Panthéon (1791) is dedicated to "great men by a grateful nation". Among the great men (and one great woman) are Victor Hugo, Émile Zola, Voltaire, Jean-Jacques Rousseau, Jean Jaurès, Pierre and Marie Curie, Jean Moulin and André Malraux. Place du Panthéon, 5th

PLACE DE LA CONCORDE

Built by Louis XV as a site for his equestrian statue and completed in 1772, Paris's largest square soon underwent radical changes, becoming a place for revolutionary head-chopping rather than royal splendours. Once the guillotine was gone, King Louis-Philippe elegantly remodelled the octagonal square, with, in the centre, the famous 230-ton obelisk from the temple of Ramses II, a gift to the king from the viceroy of Egypt, Muhammad Ali. Erected in 1836 (not without difficulty), the obelisk is flanked by two monumental fountains. The Marly horse statues are copies. Place de la Concorde, 8th

PLACE DAUPHINE

Another fine example of Paris under Henri IV, the first French king interested in urban planning, Place Dauphine was the second royal square he built. It was named in honour of the dauphin, the future Louis XIII. Its triangular shape caused Surrealist poet André Breton to call it "Paris's vagina". Celebrated in song by Jacques Dutronc and once inhabited by the couple Yves Montand and Simone Signoret, the square has appeared in innumerable films. Place Dauphine, 1st

PLACE DES VOSGES

Built in the heart of the Marais in 1605–12 on orders from Henri IV and finished during the reign of his son, Louis XIII, the Place des Vosges, a favourite of Parisians, is composed of thirty-six pink-brick and beige-stone pavilions with arcades, neatly laid out in the style of royal squares. Madame de Sévigné and Victor Hugo lived there, as did the bishop and theologian Jacques-Bénigne Bossuet, and Théophile Gautier and Georges Simenon. Place des Vosges, 4th

PONT NEUF

The Pont Neuf is the oldest but not necessarily longest bridge in Paris, and it is certainly the most handsome, and as soon as it was opened in 1607 during the reign of Henri IV, it was the most modern, since it was not lined with houses, as was then the custom. It has long been a symbol of Paris, seen in the cinema in Leos Carax's *The Lovers on the Bridge,* wrapped by Christo and Jeanne-Claude, and covered with flowers by Kenzo. Pont Neuf, 1st

SACRÉ CŒUR

This neo-Byzantine-style basilica, consecrated in 1919, boasts a 19-ton bell called the Savoyarde, nestled in its campanile. The Sacré Cœur, dubbed "the Meringue" by Parisians, who love to hate it, is the highest point in Paris, after the Eiffel Tower. "Climb up on it, and you'll see Montmartre," they used to sing in the cabarets. 35, rue du Chevalier de la Barre, 18th

SAINTE-CHAPELLE AND THE CONCIERGERIE

The Sainte-Chapelle, a masterpiece of 13th-century Gothic art built on the orders of Saint Louis to house the Crown of Thorns, is part of a complex that includes the Palais de Justice and the Conciergerie, a vestige of a Capetian palace converted into a prison where Marie-Antoinette, Danton and others were held before being taken to the scaffold. 4, boulevard du Palais and 1, quai de l'Horloge, 1st

TOUR EIFFEL

With seven million visitors a year, the Eiffel Tower, the world's most famous monument, is worth an estimated €434 billion, according to a recent study. In spite of its burden of millions of girders, rivets and bolts, the pressure it exerts on the ground is equal to that of a woman in high heels. It has grown from 312 metres to 324 metres in height, which just goes to show that one can grow at any age. Three floors can be visited, with the third, at a height of 276 metres, accessible by lift or stairs, depending on the condition of your calf muscles. www.toureiffel.paris

EVENTS CALENDAR

JANUARY

LAST WEEK
Men's Fashion Week & Haute Couture shows.
www.modeaparis.com

LATE JANUARY
Chinese New Year in the streets of the 13th.
www.nouvel-an-chinois.com

FEBRUARY

EARLY FEBRUARY
Rétromobile. Vintage cars, Porte de Versailles.
www.retromobile.com

LATE FEBRUARY–EARLY MARCH
International Agricultural Show at Porte de Versailles.
www.salon-agriculture.com
Paris Fashion Week
www.modeaparis.com

MARCH

LATE MARCH
Paris Book Fair at the Porte de Versailles.
www.salondulivreparis.com

APRIL

Mois de la Photo du Grand Paris.
www.mep-fr.org

EARLY APRIL
Paris Marathon. One of the five largest in the world (40,000 runners).
www.parismarathon.com

LATE APRIL–EARLY MAY
Foire de Paris. Food, wine, homes and gardens at the Porte de Versailles.
www.foiredeparis.fr

MAY

3RD SATURDAY
La Nuit Européenne des Musées. www.nuitdesmusees.culture.fr

LATE MAY–EARLY JUNE
French Open tennis at Roland Garros.
www.rolandgarros.com

JUNE

EARLY JUNE–LATE JULY
Paris Jazz Festival at the Château de Vincennes.
www.parisjazzfestival.fr

21 JUNE
Fête de la Musique.
www.fetedelamusique.culture.fr

LAST WEEK
Men's Fashion Week.
www.modeaparis.com

JULY-AUGUST

FIRST WEEK
Haute Couture shows.
www.modeaparis.com

LATE JULY–MID AUGUST
Paris Plage. The Seine river banks turn into a resort.

LATE JULY–LATE AUGUST
Cinéma en Plein Air at the Parc de la Villette.
www.villette.com

SEPTEMBER

MID-SEPTEMBER–LATE DECEMBER
Festival d'Automne. A multidisciplinary arts festival.
www.festival-automne.com

3RD WEEKEND
European Heritage Days. Monuments open to the public. www.journeesdupatrimoine.culture.fr

4TH WEEKEND
Fête des Jardins. The city's secret gardens open to all.

LATE SEPTEMBER–EARLY OCTOBER
Paris Fashion Week.
www.modeaparis.com

OCTOBER

1ST SATURDAY
Nuit Blanche. Night-time arts events held all over the city.

LATE OCTOBER
FIAC international contemporary art fair at the Grand Palais.
www.fiac.com

LATE OCTOBER–EARLY NOVEMBER
Salon du Chocolat at Porte de Versailles.
www.salonduchocolat.fr

NOVEMBER

END NOVEMBER
Christmas decorations are lit on the Champs-Élysées.

DECEMBER

EARLY DECEMBER
Salon Nautique International at the Porte de Versailles.
www.salonnautiqueparis.com
Salon de la Moto at Porte de Versailles.
www.lesalondelamoto.com

MID-DECEMBER–EARLY MARCH
Two ice rinks (1,635 square metres) are set up in front of the Hôtel de Ville.

WHEN THE CITY SHUTS DOWN

Unlike New York, Paris is not a city that never sleeps. Paris loves to sleep. Constantly demanding that any noise that might keep them awake be banned, Parisians get bored and wonder what to do with themselves on Sundays and public holidays and during holiday periods. No need to worry, however: the city never completely closes down, especially now that shops are allowed to stay open on 12 Sundays per year.

KEEP FIT

Go walking, jogging or biking in the parks (Montsouris, Luxembourg, Buttes Chaumont) or woods (Boulogne and Vincennes) or along the Canal Saint-Martin or the banks of the Seine (both river and canal are reserved for pedestrians on Sunday). Boating on the lakes of the Bois de Vincennes or the Bassin de la Villette is a good way to stimulate the appetite and open the chakras.

FILL YOUR SHOPPING BASKET

On Sunday morning, take a walk on rues Daguerre, Poncelet, Mouffetard or de Buci, or in the Marché d'Aligre, and be tempted by the stalls and shops selling exotic fruits, farm cheeses, bread, etc. Or check out the organic market on Boulevard Raspail, where you can empty your wallet by decorating your basket with a single plum and radish.
http://marches.equipements.paris.fr

DAWDLE

Like a good tourist, take a ride in a Bâteau-Mouche or the Balabus, then go up to Saint-Pierre-de-Montmartre, descend into the Catacombs, stroll through the Marais (where everything is open), photograph Parisian doors (closed, of course), etc.

GO ANTIQUING

Browse the flea market in Saint-Ouen, which is open all day, or at Porte de Vanves, open only in the morning (and closed on holidays). Check out the calendar for the occasional flea markets and junk sales held around the city and in the suburbs. Every Parisian is a rag-and-bone man at heart.
www.marcheauxpuces-saintouen.com
www.pucesdevanves.typepad.com

SHED A TEAR

Take a moment to reflect at the graves of the famous in Père-Lachaise, Montmartre or Montparnasse cemeteries, which are never closed – except at night.
www.pere-lachaise.com

SAVOUR THE FLAVOUR

Have Sunday brunch in a Parisian bistro in eastern Paris, dig into a seafood platter at La Rotonde, sample all the cakes at the Pâtisserie du Panthéon, drink cocktails in hotel bars in Pigalle, feast on choucroute at Wepler.
105, boulevard du Montparnasse, 6th
www.sebastien-degardin.com
www.wepler.com

GET A BIT OF CULTURE

Enjoy Sunday visiting the Paris museums, which are closed on either Monday or Tuesday. The Louvre is free on the first Sunday of each month.
www.paris.fr/musees

SPLASH OUT

Go window-shopping in the Marais, where almost all the shops are open. At Christmas time, check out the beautifully decorated windows at Printemps and Galeries Lafayette.

LIVING LIKE A LOCAL

"Métro-boulot-dodo" (train-work-sleep) goes a favourite Parisian saying that sums up the daily grind. There is some truth to that, but a Parisian's day is organized according to a well-established ritual that allows for regular breaks. The key is to always look overwhelmed, and, as a result, impatient and grumpy.

UP AND RUNNING

Parisians not riding two-wheeled vehicles run day and night. Or, at least, walk very fast while carrying bags of all kinds. They dress in black or dark colours out of laziness and "because the city is dirty". When it is nice out, they wear beige and crow about walking around Paris, a polite way of saying they are not working. Ditto for those who say they adore taking the metro; translation: their driving licence has been revoked, their bike or scooter stolen, or they are broke.

Pressed, stressed and overwhelmed, the majority of Parisians are single Parisiennes who like to look fearless in their helmets – yes, they also ride scooters. "Being from Paris does not necessarily mean that you have seen the light there but rather that you have seen clearly," according to Sacha Guitry. In other words, sunglasses for everyone, even when there is no sun – especially when there is no sun. It's a way of saying, "My nights are more beautiful than your days."

2,300 champagne bottles opened every night in the cabarets

THE WORKING DAY

Parisians who are not morning people (i.e., who don't wake up at 5am to go to the gym or meditate while stirring organic granola mixed with dwarf-goat yogurt) wake up late. They do not eat breakfast, but gulp down their coffee at the café counter. They never sit for breakfast, except the white-collar types, who love business breakfasts at a hotel, even if it is just coffee and a brioche (it is difficult and not very polite to talk business with croissant crumbs between your teeth).

At the office, the day starts around 9:30am at the coffee machine.
Lunch runs from 12:30pm to 3pm, depending on one's profession, obligations and business. Some replace lunch with cardio training at the gym, frequented with great fanfare from September to November and then forgotten until April, when Parisians' thoughts turn to how they will look in a bathing suit at the beach the following summer.

Parisians work hard in the afternoon, unless they have the day off, work part-time, are procrastinators or have an appointment outside the office on the other side of town. Executives tend to work very late – they have to make up for those three-hour lunches.

THE EVENING

Parisians often go straight from the office to the theatre or a restaurant, which explains why they are generally dressed casually at the opera or a concert. Only tourists and retirees dress up for the opera or theatre.

Though happy hour is popular with younger people, the pre-prandial drink is often neglected by thirty-somethings, who see no advantage in trying in vain to get a few peanuts to go with a Perrier with lemon slice at the price of a glass of fine wine.

Dinner is the Parisian sport par excellence. For Parisians worthy of the name, a real dinner is a cancelled dinner – at the last minute, because of an 8:30pm meeting, another Parisian sport. A different trend has been observed among youthful fifty-somethings who have passed the age of workaholism: dinner at 8pm, "like the Germans", so they can go to bed earlier. Explanation: "At that hour, there are still tables available in the restaurants." Real reason: "At least we will see people other than these odious bobos who are everywhere now." This early dinner hour is becoming more common, even for dinner at the home of friends. And herbal tea is replacing the *digestif*.

Parisians go out on Tuesday, which is calm both day and night. They avoid going to the cinema on Wednesday, the day when new films are released; hop from one gallery opening to another on Thursday evening, which has become the usual opening night; and leave for the country on Friday, returning late Sunday evening. Basically, Parisian social life is concentrated in the three evenings from Tuesday to Thursday. An emerging trend: a quick dinner on Monday with close friends "to start the week on the right foot".

THE WEEKEND

Those who stay in Paris spend the weekend catching up on their culture by going to exhibitions, flea markets or the cinema at 10am or noon. Many lunch informally on a croque-monsieur with friends on Saturday between 1:30pm and 2pm. On weekend evenings, only suburbanites are out in Paris; Parisians stay at home. If they do go out, it is to the home of friends, but only if they live in the same neighbourhood, so they can avoid the stress of returning home amidst a rowdy crowd of revellers.

30% of Parisians were born in the city

11,000 restaurants, approximately

8,000 cafés with terraces

On Sundays, a day that is despised if there ever was one, Parisians go to the market as religiously as some go to church, and make faces at the heirloom vegetables. Unless, of course, they are lunching at their parents' home on a leg of lamb with beans, a practice that is more common than you might expect. Others are still going out to brunch, the last desperate attempt to socialize among recomposed families with collapsible strollers and "single-hipster" cyclists with tweed jackets and vasectomies. The latest Sunday fad is the afternoon snack. It is cheaper than lunch or dinner and reminds Parisians of their childhood as they gobble up slices of cake.

During the school holidays (Christmas, February, Easter, July and August), the city literally empties out: traffic flows easily, restaurants have tables available and those who stay in the city are miraculously nicer and more attentive.

Between May and September, Parisians like to jump on the TGV to "weekend" with their cousins in Cap Ferret or Marseille. The return trip usually takes twenty-two hours because of a vandalized train, strikes or floods. Those who stay in Paris have a good laugh – Parisians love to mock each other.

ETIQUETTE AND GOOD TASTE

As everyone knows, Parisians are fanatical individualists, and individualism does not predispose one to politeness. Rebels at heart and full of the spirit of contradiction, Parisians favour inner politeness, which frees them from following rules honoured in another age.

TIPPING

In Paris, service is included, but you can still tip the waiter in a café (round up to the nearest euro), the taxi (ditto: tell the driver to keep the change), hairstylist (between €5 and €10), delivery person (€5 minimum) or tour guide (at your discretion). In a restaurant, add between 5 percent and 10 percent of the bill. At a hotel, give a tip to the porter, concierge and maid (leave a €20 bill in an envelope on the pillow or bedside table). When Parisians, who tend to be stingy anyway, are not happy with the service, they leave the miserly sum of 10 centimes.

DRESS CODE

For women, the total look and layering have never been popular, but accessorizing according to the situation and time of day is strongly encouraged. It is even the very basis of the inimitable, enviable and never-inappropriate Parisian style. For men, coquetry is back. Out between 8am and 11pm, a period during which they rarely go home to change, Parisians rely on the versatility of a basic wardrobe that is acceptable in all circumstances. For cocktail parties and openings, they go all out to be elegant and always try to subvert the formality required by the invitation so they will not be confused with the servers, their greatest fear. Wedding invitations, seen as a major pain in the neck, plunge Parisians into a deep state of annoyance. Men go out and buy a dark suit – never a tuxedo! Women wear a hat and gloves. They attend the ceremony, give at least €10 when the collection is taken up, congratulate the newlyweds, do not criticize anyone and, when they leave, do not honk their horns. *Tenue décontractée* ("casual dress") means that nothing special is required. But avoid being too casual (sweatshirts, leggings, nylon windcheaters, etc.). *Tenue de ville* means a cocktail dress for her and a suit for him. If *tenue habillée* is requested, women should wear long dresses and men tuxedos.

THANK YOU

For many Parisians, politeness can be summed up as "BAM" (*bonjour-au revoir-merci*, or hello-goodbye-thank you), a formula that is perfect for the supermarket and equivalent to minimum service at the post office on a strike day. The Parisians generally offer a terse, almost pinched or condescending *merci*. *Merci beaucoup* is reserved for foreigners whom Parisians have decided to be friendly to. A rather whiny *merciiiiiii* and *Oh! Merci* (translation: "You shouldn't have!") are affectionate and quickly followed by *Je t'adore* ("I adore you"), usually after an invitation for a drink or a meal or the presentation of an unexpected gift. The peremptory *S'il vous plaît, merci* is used to close a transaction or pay a bill. The speaker is in a hurry but remains polite.

THE RIGHT ATTITUDE AT THE RIGHT TIME

Even if they pretend not to care, Parisians pride themselves on observing the rules of etiquette in social situations. A playful *Bonjouuur* is reserved for professional circles. To the *Comment allez-vous?* ("How are you?") that follows, they expect only good news. *Ça vaaah?* means that one is aware of the worries and problems of the other, who then has

108 Wallace fountains
223 Morris columns

permission to talk about them. Parisians greet those they do not know with a firm handshake while stating their own name. The problem is that they usually mumble it, so it's impossible to understand. Only salespeople or yokels would use their family name when introducing themselves.

Parisians automatically kiss everyone, even those they hate. Two kisses – one on each cheek – are de rigueur in the city. In the provinces, it's three; in the suburbs, four. In recent years, men have started giving the *bise* (cheek kiss) to each other, punctuating it with an ironic "Hello, darling" so no one will think they are gay (a gay man would kiss on the mouth). The bear-hug trend, borrowed from North Americans, seems to be dying out. The worst greeting if all is *Tiens tu es là, toi ?* ("Oh, you're here?") conveying both disdain and social banishment.

WHAT NOT TO DO

Never arrive on time for an appointment with a friend or for a dinner party; you are expected to be a quarter of an hour late. If you arrive for an 8:30 dinner at 8:45, no apology is needed.

Never kiss someone you met only recently at a meeting or conference, even if you got on famously. It would be embarrassing or even offensive. One person's politeness is another's rudeness.

Never give someone your calling card if you have not been asked for it. At a meeting, do not place your card on the table and point to your name and position. If there is a formal exchange of cards, it is as rude to immediately examine the person's card as it is to turn over your plate to look for the name of the manufacturer as soon as you sit down at the dinner table.

Never forget to thank the person who holds a door open for you. Parisians moan incessantly about the rudeness of those around them and heap with insults anyone who does not thank them for this service on the rare occasions when they kindly condescend to offer it.

A man should never let a woman enter a restaurant first. Along with climbing stairs, this is a rare exception to the golden rule stating that a man should always let a woman go ahead of him.

ON TIME

Parisians don't "eat", they "lunch" or "dine". They arrive at a restaurant between 12:45pm and 1:30pm for lunch and between 8:30pm and 9pm for dinner. At a café in the morning, they drink espresso or *café crème* until 11am, after which they will be chased away by servers setting the tables for lunch. After 4pm, they drink tea, lemonade or Perrier with a slice of lemon. Cocktail receptions last from 7pm to 8:30pm.

Invitations to dinners at home are issued from three to five weeks ahead of time. Late invitations are accepted on Monday for the following Thursday, but then you know that it will be potluck. After dinner, a reasonable departure time is around 11:30pm, after discussing private hire vehicle apps.

HERE AND NOWHERE ELSE

Except for monuments, museums and cultural sites, the fabric of Parisian cultural life is woven of traditions, exclusives, secret addresses, details and unique initiatives. "Here and nowhere else" applies to Parisian gastronomy, culture, zeitgeist and moods. And to snobbery with a scent of insincerity.

BOUQUINISTES

Open four days a week,
the 250 railway-green (the official colour since 1952) wooden bookstalls along the quays of the Seine are stocked with 300,000 used books, creating an open-air bookstore that is unique in the world.
www.paris.fr
www.bouquinistedeparis.com

CITROËN 2CV: MADE ON QUAI DE JAVEL

Take a ride in an old 2-horsepower Citroën manufactured on Quai de Javel, with a chauffeur who is also a guide and interpreter. The fleet of vintage models owned by the company 4 Roues Sous un Parapluie, the first to offer this service, has received special dispensation from the City of Paris, which has banned the use of vehicles predating 1997 from the roads during the daytime. This is your chance…
4roues-sous-1parapluie.com

MONA LISA'S SMILE

The* Mona Lisa *is at the Louvre.
It may be tightly guarded and under glass for protection, but the world's most famous painting is here, and nowhere else.

ALMOND CROISSANTS

The almond croissant is the invention of Parisian bakers who were forbidden to raise the price of croissants. In other words, these revised croissants encompass two Parisian reflexes: the art of using leftovers (almond croissants are made from day-old croissants) and the art of taunting the tax authorities.

FLEA MARKETS

The Saint-Ouen flea market,
on the northern edge of the city, was granted protection as an Urban and Rural Architectural Heritage Conservation Area in 2001. It groups together more than a dozen separate markets with literally thousands of stalls. The best day for bargain seekers is generally thought to be Monday, when crowds are smaller.
www.marcheauxpuces-saintouen.com

WINE

An independent municipality, Montmartre has its own vineyard,
Clos Montmartre, and celebrates the harvest in mid-October with great fanfare, including concerts, fireworks and balls. At another ceremony, single people are honoured by the mayor of the 18th arrondissement – nothing to do with marriage for all, however.
www.fetedesvendangesdemontmartre.com

HECTOR GUIMARD'S METRO ENTRANCES

And other decorations on metro station entrances, sometimes with pure Art Nouveau floral motifs and enamel plaques. See the entrances at the Tuileries, Louvre-Rivoli, Ternes and Porte-Dauphine stations, which also feature a glass canopy.

6 million skeletons in the catacombs

300 fashion shows organized each year

THE CITY IN WORDS, FILM AND MUSIC

The following list, while not exhaustive, encompasses a wide range of what cultivated Parisians are reading, watching and listening to: newspapers, magazines, novels, non-fiction, books and albums you might want to discover before coming to Paris or after, as well as cult films and songs whose melodies still drift through the streets of the City of Light.

NEWSPAPERS AND MAGAZINES

Le Figaro. Founded in 1826, this is the right-leaning morning paper. Its *Figaroscope* supplement, launched in 1987 and published every Wednesday, is a full guide to what is happening in the city: new restaurants, trends, shows, exhibitions. www.lefigaro.fr, scope.lefigaro.fr

Le Monde. Founded in 1944 by Hubert Beuve-Méry, with a readership in both Paris and the provinces, *Le Monde* is the left-of-centre evening paper. Its weekend supplement, *M*, gets more hits online than any other of its type. www.lemonde.fr

Le Parisien. Founded in August 1944, three days before the Liberation of Paris, this is the leading Paris daily paper. It is popular, comprehensive and informative. Parisians love to flip through it while leaning against a café counter and sipping their morning coffee. www.leparisien.fr

Libération. Co-founded in 1973 by Jean-Paul Sartre and then directed by Serge July, "Libé" remains resolutely left-wing, but also offers offbeat cultural reporting and a very opinionated approach to the news. The monthly supplement *Next* appears on the first Saturday of the month. www.liberation.fr

Soixante-Quinze. This monthly magazine founded in 2016 offers reports on Paris and its suburbs. Smart, modern and realistic. A nice breath of fresh air. www.soixantequinze.paris

BOOKS

The Hunchback of Notre Dame, Victor Hugo (1831). The ultimate French Gothic historical novel, starring Quasimodo and his hump, Esmeralda and her goat, Archdeacon Frollo, Gringoire, the Court of Miracles and Notre Dame's gargoyles.

The Belly of Paris (1873) and ***The Ladies' Paradise*** (1883), Émile Zola. The former takes place in Les Halles food market with its Baltard pavilions, the latter in the Bon Marché department store. Two great novels all about the little people.

Paris Sketchbook, Ronald Searle and Kaye Webb (1950). A poetic delight, with drawings by one of the darkest, most playful illustrators ever.

Zazie in the Metro, Raymond Queneau (1959). Made into a rebellious, humorous and libertarian film by Louis Malle, this cheeky burlesque novel invented an entire neo-French language.

Les Parisiennes. The delightful illustrator Kiraz has published a number of exquisitely joyous albums: *Les Parisiennes* (1963), *Les Parisiennes au volant* (1966) and *Les Parisiennes se marient* (1994), with a preface by Carla Bruni. As sparkling and enchanting as champagne.

A Moveable Feast, Ernest Hemingway (1964). In this memoir written in 1956–60 and published posthumously in 1964, Hemingway meets F. Scott Fitzgerald, Ezra Pound and Gertrude Stein, and frequents La Closerie des Lilas and the Deux Magots in 1920s Paris. A real treat.

Paris tendresse, Brassaï and Patrick Modiano (1990). Five years after publishing *Quartier perdu,* the quintessential poisonous Parisian novel, Modiano casts a tender, nostalgic eye on Paris in a text inspired by the black-and-white photos of Brassaï (Paul Morand did the same) taken in the 1930s.

25,000 artists live in Paris

2,800 songs have been written about Paris since the late 19th century

FILMS

Hôtel du Nord, Marcel Carné (1938). With Annabella, Jean-Pierre Aumont, Arletty, Louis Jouvet. Based on the novel by Eugène Dabit and entirely shot in the studio, this classic is a legend. Plenty of *atmosphère* on the Canal Saint-Martin.

Quai des Orfèvres, Henri-Georges Clouzot (1947). With Louis Jouvet, Suzy Delair, Bernard Blier, Simone Renant. The cast of characters includes a lecherous old man who is murdered, a flashy singer, her jealous pianist husband and a lesbian photographer. Christmas Eve holds no gifts for Inspector Jouvet as he navigates between the restaurant La Pérouse and the Quai des Orfèvres. A timeless masterpiece.

An American in Paris, Vincente Minnelli (1951). Starring Gene Kelly, Leslie Caron, Georges Guétary. The most fabulous series of postcard shots of Paris ever seen was filmed in a studio and later showered with Oscars. A perpetual delight.

Moulin Rouge, John Huston (1952). José Ferrer plays Henri de Toulouse-Lautrec in a magnificent reconstruction of his world. You are thrown into the heart of his work and the frenzied cabaret atmosphere.

The Trip Across Paris (La Traversée de Paris), Claude Autant-Lara (1956). With Jean Gabin, Bourvil, Louis de Funès. Adapted from a novel by Marcel Ayme. Set in Paris during the Occupation, when the black market was in full swing, this film features superstars like Gabin, thanks to whom Rue Poliveau (5th) is etched in our memories.

Breathless (À bout de souffle), Jean-Luc Godard (1960). Starring Jean-Paul Belmondo and Jean Seberg. The ultimate New Wave film, with Seberg's famous line: "What is *dégueulasse?*"

Irma la Douce, Billy Wilder (1963). Starring Shirley MacLaine and Jack Lemmon. The 1956 musical comedy by Alexandre Breffort and Marguerite Monnot triumphed in London and on Broadway. The non-musical film version is set in Paris but was shot in a studio with sets by Alexandre Trauner representing Baltard's Halles and the Rue Saint-Denis.

Six in Paris (Paris vu par...) (1965). Six short films made by New Wave directors Éric Rohmer, Jean-Luc Godard, Claude Chabrol, Jean Rouch, Jean Douchet, and Jean-Daniel Pollet, and shot in Saint-Germain-des-Prés, La Muette, Montparnasse, and other places.

What's New Pussycat?, Clive Donner (1965). Starring Peter O'Toole, Peter Sellers, Woody Allen, Romy Schneider. Written by Woody Allen and packed with stars, the plot is pure Parisian delirium and remains exciting right up to the climax in the legendary Château Chantelle. The Tom Jones song is another bonus.

Last Tango in Paris, Bernardo Bertolucci (1972). Starring Marlon Brando and Maria

Schneider. What hasn't already been said about this film? Perhaps that the apartment in the 16th arrondissement overlooking Pont Bir Hakeim and the Passy metro station is a cult destination, unfortunately for the privacy of the building's inhabitants. Redecorated, it has been featured in the magazine *Côté Paris.*

Two Days in Paris, Julie Delpy (2007). Starring Julie Delpy, Adam Goldberg, Daniel Brühl. This film was made after *Before Sunset,* which also took place in Paris and starred Delpy and Ethan Hawke. For this movie, Delpy wrote the screenplay, composed the music, directed and edited. A nice surprise bristling with rewards.

Midnight in Paris, Woody Allen (2011). Starring Owen Wilson, Rachel McAdams, Adrien Brody. A gentle, nostalgic film inspired by *A Moveable Feast.* Carla Bruni has a small role.

Lost in Paris, directed by and starring Dominique Abel and Fiona Gordon (2016). With Emmanuelle Riva and Pierre Richard. The search for an elderly aunt lost in Paris sets off a hilarious chase.

MUSIC AND SONGS

April in Paris, performed by Frank Sinatra, Sarah Vaughan, Helen Merrill, Billie Holiday, Lisa Ekdahl, Blossom Dearie, etc.

Le Poinçonneur des Lilas, Serge Gainsbourg (1958).The singer-songwriter's first hit, from his album *Du chant à la une!...,* was praised by Boris Vian. Fans paying their respects at Gainsbourg's tomb in the Montparnasse Cemetery often leave a metro ticket, since the song is about a ticket puncher. In 2010, a park named after him was opened at Porte des Lilas.

Il n'y a plus d'après à Saint-Germain-des-Prés, Guy Béart (1961). Performed by Juliette Greco, muse of the neighbourhood and of the time. Existentialist, of course.

Ah les P'tites Femmes de Paris, Brigitte Bardot and Jeanne Moreau (1965). A single from the soundtrack to the film *Viva Maria!* A great way to revive the spirit of Old Pigalle.

Il est 5 heures, Paris s'éveille (1968). By Jacques Lanzmann and Jacques Dutronc, with Roger Bourdin on flute, this delightful song is one of the best in forty-five years. *"Les camions sont pleins de lait, les balayeurs sont pleins de balais..."* Pure nostalgia.

Paris mai, Claude Nougaro (1968). May 1968 and its turmoil inspired the singer from Toulouse to write this percussive song, which was banned from the airwaves when it was released.

Paris Paris, Catherine Deneuve (1994). This gem of a conceptual double album by Malcolm McLaren also includes songs by Françoise Hardy. Cult trash.

J'aime plus Paris, Thomas Dutronc (2007). Nearly forty years after his father's cult song *Il est 5 heures, Paris s'éveille,* Thomas Dutronc sings of his disenchantment with the city. He plays guitar in Django style.

La Seine, duo between – M – Matthieu Chedid and Vanessa Paradis (2011). Declaration of love to the river in Paris.

Paname, Slimane (2016). A song of conquest by the winner of The Voice. An exultant summer hit.

THE GREAT AND THE GOOD

SAINTE GENEVIÈVE (423–512)

PATRON SAINT OF PARIS

A unique destiny was reserved for Geneviève, called to serve God when she was only nine years old. Heir to her father's seat on the Paris city council, she was a spirited woman. It was she who urged the panicked Parisians to resist the attacks of the Huns in 451. Attila himself could not get into the city. Geneviève was at it again a few years later, when Childeric I besieged the city. The patron saint of Paris, Geneviève gave her name to an abbey, which is now the Lycée Henri IV, and to a historical library located on the Place du Panthéon. Her reliquary, desecrated during the Revolution, is kept in the Saint-Étienne-du-Mont Church on the Montaigne Sainte-Geneviève in the fifth arrondissement. Her statue, which stands on the Pont de la Tournelle, was made in 1928 by Paul Landowski.

MOLIÈRE (1622–73)

PLAYWRIGHT AND ACTOR

Born Jean-Baptiste Poquelin in Paris, Molière was baptized in Saint-Eustache and died at home on Rue de Richelieu on 17 February 1673. Considered the best comic actor and writer in the kingdom during his lifetime, he was catapulted to the rank of literary genius by posterity and was credited with founding the Comédie-Française, thanks to the universality of his troupe. The greatest actors in France still perform his plays, and his writing has become the standard for the French language. In Parisian slang, a "molière" is a 500-franc bill (from days gone by) bearing his likeness.

ROSE BERTIN (1747–1813)

MILLINER

Born Marie-Jeanne Bertin, she is considered to be the first fashion designer. Nicknamed "Minister of Fashion" by Marie-Antoinette, who swore by her work, Mademoiselle Bertin invented hairstyles with names like *à la belle poule, pouf aux sentiments, à la Montgolfier* and *à la Philadelphie.* She had the good fortune not to lose her head during the Revolution, which, for a hat-maker, would have been a disaster.

GEORGES EUGÈNE, BARON HAUSSMANN (1809–91)

ADMINISTRATOR, POLITICIAN

Appointed prefect of the Seine in 1853, he left a huge urban legacy after transforming Paris into a "healthy, liveable, breathable and enviable city". He left his mark on stations, gardens, parks, forests, boulevards and traffic patterns. He also joined towns including Passy, Auteuil, Montmartre, Grenelle and Vaugirard to Paris. In the process, he contributed to the destruction of archaic, pestilential old Paris. Ennobled by Emperor Napoleon III, who placed his blind trust in him, he was despised by Empress Eugénie, who accused him of profiting from the largesse of the Empire.

JACQUES OFFENBACH (1819–80)

COMPOSER, CELLIST

Jacques Offenbach was the musical director of the Comédie-Française, the great master of comic opera and operetta, and the big shot of the Opéra-Comique, the Bouffes-Parisiens and the Variétés. Author of *La Vie Parisienne, The Tales of Hoffmann* and other memorable and oft-performed musical works, he was the artificer of the "imperial fête" and the long-time lover of the flamboyant soprano Hortense Schneider, for whom he wrote, among other operettas, *La Grande Duchesse de Gérolstein.* Offenbach, who is buried in Montmartre Cemetery, was played by Pierre Fresnay in the film *La Valse de Paris* in 1950, while Schneider was played by Yvonne Printemps, a great Parisian singer and actress of the first half of the 20th century, known as the "nightingale of Paris."

BONI DE CASTELLANE (1867–1932)
POLITICIAN, COLLECTOR, DANDY

His family was one of the most titled in France. A count, then a marquis, and above all a dandy right down to his detachable collar, Marie Ernest Paul Boniface "Boni" de Castellane married the unattractive American heiress Anna Gould for her fortune. It was unkindly said of her that she was "beautiful when seen from her dowry". They had the famous Pink Palace built for them, but he never took advantage of it. Boni de Castellane was the talk of the town until his death and published the highly enjoyable *L'Art d'Être Pauvre (The Art of Being Poor)*. A true Parisian.

PAUL POIRET (1879–1944)
COUTURIER

Paul Poiret, a pure Parisian who was the son of a cloth merchant, was the couturier who "killed the corset" and invented (after Charles Frederick Worth) the intricacies of French haute couture. He was the most illustrious designer of his time. In the early 1920s, Poiret asked Gabrielle Chanel who she was in mourning for, since she was wearing a black dress. She retorted, "For you, sir." After glory came decline. Poiret was ruined, forgotten and indigent. A photo shows him sharing his crust of bread with pigeons on the Promenade des Anglais in Nice, where he had gone to flee the German occupation.

JEAN COCTEAU (1889–1963)
NOVELIST, POET, FILMMAKER

Writer, playwright, filmmaker, poet and painter, Jean Cocteau would go to great lengths to find the perfect one-liner. Bard of the moderns and confessed opium addict, he did not hide his homosexuality – his affair with the actor Jean Marais was notorious but never tarnished his reputation or Marais' popularity. A neighbour of Colette, Cocteau was one of the illustrious residents of the Palais-Royal and the friend of all artists of his time and beyond.

MARIE-LAURE DE NOAILLES (1902–70)
PATRON, WRITER

Born Marie-Laure Henriette Anne Bischoffsheim, a descendant of the Marquis de Sade, Marie-Laure De Noailles became a viscountess through her marriage in 1923. This patron, collector, artist and writer formed with her husband the ultimate Parisian couple, flirting with all that was avant-garde, transgressive and controversial. They even stormed the 1968 barricades in his Rolls. She was painted by Dalí, Balthus, Matisse, Man Ray, etc. A Parisian legend.

SERGE GAINSBOURG (1928–91)
SINGER, SONGWRITER, PIANIST

Born Lucien Ginsburg in Paris's fourth arrondissement, Serge Gainsbourg died on Rue de Verneuil in the seventh. Composer, lyricist, singer, actor, filmmaker, artist and many other things, he wrote for Juliette Gréco, Marianne Faithfull, France Gall, Zizi Jeanmaire, Françoise Hardy, Brigitte Bardot, Dani, Petula Clark, Jane Birkin, Catherine Deneuve, Vanessa Paradis and his own daughter, Charlotte Gainsbourg. His alter ego Gainsbarre was capable of all types of provocation, and the man with a cabbage head who scored so many successes now rests in Montparnasse Cemetery. In 2010, he was played by Éric Elmosnino in a biopic directed by Joann Sfar.

CATHERINE DENEUVE (B. 1943)
ACTRESS

Catherine Deneuve was born Catherine Dorléac in Paris, the younger sister of actress Françoise Dorléac, who died tragically in 1967. Star of French cinema since the 1960s, she is now an icon who dares to take radical roles in auteur films. On-screen and in real life, her image and style were fashioned by her friend Yves Saint Laurent. She lives in the 6th arrondissement and is *la Parisienne* par excellence. Her fans are careful not to bother her in the street.

24 HOURS IN THE CITY

TWELVE UNBEATABLE EXPERIENCES

8AM

Get up on the right side of the bed after sleeping comfortably at Le Saint (page 66), ideally located between Saint Germain and the Louvre. To go running in the Tuileries Garden, just cross the Pont des Arts.

LE SAINT
www.lesainthotelparis.com

10AM

Have coffee at the Flore (page 143). Make sure you sit inside on the main floor – never on the terrace! Watch the parade of celebrities sans make-up and of intellectuals carrying the morning papers under their arm.

CAFÉ DE FLORE
www.cafedeflore.fr

11AM

Wander around the Drouot auction house (page 239) to see what objects, furniture, paintings and other curiosities will be auctioned off in the afternoon. Notice that half of Paris's antiques dealers are present, stalking hot finds. Once you have made your choice, you can bid online.

DROUOT-RICHELIEU
www.drouot.com

NOON

Sip a tomato juice at the bar of Loulou (page 90) on the first floor in the Musée des Arts Décoratifs. On sunny days, sit on the huge terrace in the gardens of the Louvre.

LOULOU
www.loulou-paris.com

1PM

Have lunch at one of the shared tables at Bel Ordinaire (page 133), the fashionable deli-cum-restaurant invented by Sébastien Demorand, where all the dishes are made from ingredients on sale in the store (whether fresh or in jars or tins).

LE BEL ORDINAIRE
www.lebelordinaire.com

3PM

Take a stroll through the Palais-Royal. Wander among the Buren columns, do a bit of designer window shopping under the arcades, then cross the garden diagonally to reach the store of perfumer Serge Lutens (page 218), whose heady scents are sure to intoxicate you.

PALAIS ROYAL – SERGE LUTENS
www.sergelutens.com

4PM

Go for some colour therapy at the Musée National Picasso (page 285). Nearly 400 works are on show in the recently refurbished Hôtel Salé, one of the finest mansions in the Marais. Enchanting

MUSÉE NATIONAL PICASSO

www.musee-picasso.fr

5PM

Now try retail therapy at Bazartherapy (page 227) on Rue Beaurepaire in the 10th arrondissement, picking up nostalgia-loaded retro souvenirs, trinkets and baubles that will gratify your eye and lift your spirits.

BAZARTHERAPY

www.bazartherapy.com

6PM

Go to Place Vendôme and take a spin through the revolving door of the recently renovated Ritz (page 63), a repository of Parisian history. Check to make sure that the Hemingway Bar is still there. It is, along with its star bartender. Breathe a sigh of relief.

RITZ PARIS

www.ritzparis.com

9PM

Stay tuned in at the Philharmonie de Paris (page 260), the superlative concert hall, blessed with outstanding acoustics, designed by architect Jean Nouvel. The best orchestras in the world perform there.

PHILHARMONIE DE PARIS

www.philharmoniedeparis.com

11PM

Dine at La Rotonde (page 95), following in the footsteps of President Emmanuel Macron and so many other politicians, intellectuals, theatricals, journalists and architects. Classic dishes include steak tartare, *sole meunière* and seafood platter.

LA ROTONDE

105, boulevard du Montparnasse, 6th

1AM

Make a beeline for chic nightspot Yeeels (page 171), and enjoy one of the sophisticated cocktails whipped up by Aurélien Fleury.

YEEELS

www.yeeels.com

HOTELS

FIVE-STARS TO OFFBEAT HIDEOUTS: WHERE TO STAY IN THE CITY

Paris's highly varied hotel scene – with some 1,500 establishments and 80,000 rooms, and rankings as high as five stars, along with a few "palace" rankings – is in constant evolution as new hotels open and old ones reopen. Renovations are constantly taking place at both quirky independent establishments and the most prestigious grand hotels like the Ritz, Crillon, Lutétia and Samaritaine-Cheval Blanc. And Parisian hotels now have to cope with competition from fresh new concepts, like that of the Okko, which opened in 2017.

Otherwise, the Paris hotel scene is characterized by a wealth of establishments that are either independent or belong to small enterprising groups that dare to try out new concepts. Some are ridiculous or unsuccessful, while others hit the mark with a concept that fits the zeitgeist and, more importantly, offers top-level design, hospitality, service and amenities. This is especially true for three-star hotels. This phenomenon is most evident in the 2nd and 9th arrondissements, where most of these hotels are located, on or around Rue de Trévise, Place Blanche and Place Favart, but the Left Bank also has its share of successful new establishments.

The good news is the almost total abandonment of gadgets associated with fake digital modernity and the reintroduction of the traditions guests really want. The new Paris hotels offer distinctive character, comfort and good food.

ARMÉE DU SALUT

LOUVRE, TUILERIES, PALAIS-ROYAL, LES HALLES

1ST & 2ND ARRONDISSEMENTS

Royal residences & top shopping

GRAND HÔTEL DU PALAIS ROYAL

4, rue de Valois, 1st
Metro Palais-Royal–Musée du Louvre
Tel 01 42 96 15 35
www.grandhoteldupalaisroyal.com
68 rooms and suites, €390 to €3,400

PARISIAN CHIC

This extension of the former Palais-Royal opera house, built in the 18th century, is a historic monument with a listed facade and staircases. Entirely renovated by Pierre-Yves Rochon, who has redone many a Paris hotel in good taste, the hotel pays tribute to the composer Jean-Baptiste Lully, superintendent of Louis XIV's royal music and composer of French operas. His name has been given to the charming restaurant, where breakfast and lunch are served on weekdays. This wonderful secret spot has a small terrace in summer on the Place de Valois, where time seems to have stood still. The panoramic duplex suite on the top floor of the dome is irresistible: 70 square metres of space with a rooftop solarium and private lift. Chic and cosy, the Grand Hôtel attracts the type of people who make Paris attractive. Atelier Cologne products can be found in the bathrooms, and the hotel has a Technogym fitness centre, a Carita spa (by appointment), an adorable Kure Bazaar hair and manicure salon and, as a bonus, a large hammam.

HÔTEL REGINA

2, place des Pyramides, 1st
Metro Tuileries
Tel 01 42 60 35 58
www.leshotelsbaverez.com
99 rooms and suites, €350 to €3,400

LISTED CLASSIC

The hotel's sumptuous lobby, dating from 1898, has lost none of its authentic charm. This five-star hotel, renovated in 2015, has been run for four generations by descendants of Constant Baverez, who opened it for the 1900 World's Fair. It looks like a film set, and the Paris scenes in many films, among them *Nikita* and *Jason Bourne*, were indeed shot here. The rest of the hotel has period furnishings, mosaics, cornices and mouldings, and the extra-large rooms are much more generous than those in the average Paris hotel. We loved the woody charm of the alcove suite with its king-size bed and marquetry desk. Other highlights include the Belle Époque stained-glass windows by master glassmaker Jacques Galland and the wonderful view of the Tuileries Garden and the statue of Joan of Arc (duplicates have been made for Melbourne and Portland). A typical English bar is located on the arcade side, and the hotel has plans to open a spa.

NOLINSKI

16, avenue de l'Opéra, Ist
Metro Pyramides,
Palais-Royal–Musée du Louvre
Tel 01 42 86 10 10
www.nolinskiparis.com
45 rooms and suites, €410 to €2500

FRENCH BUT WILD

Jean-Louis Deniot decorated this five-star hotel where all the furniture is for sale. The contemporary Art Deco decor, without being overdone, is in tune with the times: the designer borrows Montaigne grey from the bourgeois apartments of the 8th arrondissement to spiff up this less-formal neighbourhood. Special details include quadruple glazing on the avenue-side windows to ensure a good night's

SPOTLIGHT

LEFT LUGGAGE

Major hotels offer a "storage" service that no one ever mentions and that doesn't even have a name, yet it makes good sense and is almost compulsory in luxury hotels. At the George V, Plaza Athénée and other leading hotels, guests can leave their personal belongings behind for their next trip to Paris. At the Plaza Athénée, the housekeeper is responsible for a secret storeroom with four aisles filled with travellers' personal effects: coats, furs, suits, lots of shoes, favourite pillows, embroidered towels, curling irons, children's games, etc., all carefully labelled and waiting for the return of their owner, which may never happen. Some will have to wait for years. To avoid annoying anyone, the hotel has a golden rule: to prevent awkward situations, never contact a person who has left an object behind in a room – the confidentiality of guests and their friends must be preserved. On their return, some guests have even denied ownership. "It's not mine!" "Never seen it before!" Then it goes back into storage, now classified as a lost object. Some treasures are extremely valuable; watches and jewellery are kept in a safe. The customer must make a specific request to the hotel for it, unless he or she is a regular. If this is not the case, after three months and one day, the object moves to the lost and found section. When clients return, everyday objects are automatically sent to their room. Spirits and perishables are also kept for reasonable periods of time, as are closed suitcases. How long? Maybe for eternity – there is no expiry date. One guest even arrived with his own wheeled chest with scented drawers. Luxury hotels may not have that many guests, but the ones they do have certainly own a lot of things!

sleep, D-Vine wine-tasting machines in the suites, Samsung smartphones at the disposal of guests, Marshall Bluetooth speaker, Toto toilets, handsome Louis Vuitton books and braided leather headboards. The focus is on service: VIP reception for children and pets, shoeshine service with La Cordonnerie Anglaise products, Dringme concierge in the room, etc. The La Colline spa offers a good list of treatments for both men and women, and has a beautiful 16-metre swimming pool with a mirror on the ceiling. On the street side, the **RÉJANE** brasserie has a real brass counter and a neighbourhood feel – it is open to the public all day long for snacks. The pastry chef, Yann Brys, is a holder of the Meilleur Ouvrier de France distinction, and the tea comes from Pascal Hamour. For a more peaceful setting, we recommend the library-salon, complete with piano.

PARK HYATT PARIS-VENDÔME

5, rue de la Paix, 2nd, Metro Opéra
Tel 01 58 71 12 34
parisvendome.park.hyatt.com
153 rooms and suites, €810 to €14,000

PALACE, FASHIONABLE

The Park Hyatt has redecorated all of its rooms. The revamped lobby is now adorned with black granite and serpentine stone, and the rooms boast a sober contemporary style in black and mahogany, with cutting-edge technology. The marble and granite bathrooms have Japanese Toto toilets. The real luxury here is space, always hard to find in the heart of Paris: the best rooms measure 35 square metres. The hotel has gone all out with the presidential suite, a renovated 180-square-metre duplex on the sixth floor with a piano, a fireplace, a private terrace and a glass ceiling in the bathroom so that make up can be applied in the light of day. It even has a hairdresser's sink and a massage table. The hotel's fitness centre has been enlarged, and its sublime mineral spa has everything needed to keep guests in top form: La Mer treatments and Martine de Richeville slimming programmes. The Nail Suite is run by Kure Bazaar, while superstar hairdresser John Nollet offers an incredible hair salon experience in Suite 101, which should be tried at least once. In the kitchen, chef Jean-François Rouquette offers gourmet cuisine in the restaurant **PUR'** and a light menu in **ORCHIDÉES**, located in pleasant spaces in the centre of the hotel on either side of a double-sided fireplace. Desserts are by Jimmy Mornet, a pastry chef worth watching.

RITZ PARIS

15, place Vendôme, 1st
Metro Tuileries, Madeleine
Tel 01 43 16 30 30
www.ritzparis.com
142 rooms and suites, €1,000 to €28,000

THE HEIGHT OF LUXURY

All dressed up in its new clothes, the Ritz has lost nothing of its former grandeur, in spite of what some critics say. The Salon Proust in the main gallery holds a French tea ceremony presided over by a "tea sommelier" every day at 2:30pm. We love the five suites with terraces, designed by Jean Mus, that have been added on the garden side. They are more contemporary and streamlined, especially no. 119, with a large terrace-solarium on the roof, unseen by prying eyes. In this empire of Parisian opulence, there is no check-in or checkout time. If you reserve a suite, the hotel will pick you up at the airport gate (a great way to zip through the formalities). If you want to go out to dinner, the Ritz's blue Bentley courtesy car is at your disposal, although everything you need is available right there in the hotel on Place Vendôme: the gourmet restaurant **L'ESPADON**, the realm of chef Nicolas Sale and pastry chef François Perret, both indoors with a glass ceiling and outdoors in the courtyard; the **BAR VENDÔME** brasserie; and the **RITZ BAR** – hidden across from the **HEMINGWAY BAR** – where lunch is served every day, with specials starting at €30 and cocktails and tapas in the evening. In the **RITZ CLUB**, a 1,400-square-metre cocoon, the legendary pool has been restored to its former glory, with music broadcast under the water and wellness cocktails created by the bartender of the Hemingway Bar, Colin Field. The spa treatments are by Chanel, which has a boutique next to the state-of-the-art fitness centre, and a hairdressing salon is run by another star, David Mallett. The Ritz was the height of modernity when it opened – it was the first hotel to have bathrooms and electricity in all rooms in 1898 – but today it has a vintage spirit: "keys" serve as switches in the room and chains can be pulled to call the "maid" or "butler" (just a question of sex) in case of an accident in the bathroom. Eighty percent of the historic furniture has been restored, so don't expect any revolution in the decor. One might be tempted to sell one's soul for a night in the black-and-white Coco Chanel suite, the Chopin suite (a historic monument) or the Imperial Suite, with its wood-panelled bathroom, a replica of Marie Antoinette's bedroom at Versailles. If you want the same decor at home, you can order replicas of the Coco Chanel screen, as well as the woodwork, bed and light fixtures. In the gallery are several fancy shops, including the house concept store, selling such souvenirs of Paris as the Ritz Monopoly game. The Ritz-Escoffier cooking school offers courses in French-style savoir-vivre, complete with a diploma.

ALSO IN THIS NEIGHBOURHOOD

HÔTEL SQUARE LOUVOIS

12, rue Louvois, 2nd
Metro Quatre Septembre
Tel 01 86 95 02 02
www.hotel-louvois-paris.com
50 rooms, €170 to €550

ELEGANT, COMFORTABLE

Le Square Louvois takes its cue from the neighbouring national library, with a book-filled lounge where workshops on such topics as "honeyology" or writing are held. Newspapers and music on headphones are supplied in the breakfast area, and free snacks are available from 4pm to 6pm. Something extra: an 8-metre-long heated swimming pool in a beautiful vaulted room.

BEAUBOURG, LE MARAIS, PLACE DES VOSGES

3RD & 4TH ARRONDISSEMENTS

Historic landmarks & arty strolls

LE PAVILLON DE LA REINE

28, place des Vosges, 3rd
Metro Saint-Paul, Chemin Vert
Tel 01 40 29 19 19
www.pavillon-de-la-reine.com
56 rooms and suites, €385 to €1,330

LUXURIOUS HIDEAWAY

This hotel is not called "the queen's pavilion" for nothing. Located in a listed 16th-century building where Anne of Austria lived before her marriage to Louis XIII, this luxury hotel is a favourite refuge of American stars visiting Paris. Discretion and charm are guaranteed by the Chevalier family, who opened Le Pavillon des Lettres (8th) in 2010 near the Élysée Palace and bought the Hôtel du Petit Moulin (3rd) in 2012. Renovated by architect Didier Benderli and Antoine Delaire, the setting is elegant and flowery, and the service delightful. In the rooms, the hotel remains faithful to the style of its surroundings with period furniture and paintings, oak panelling, etc. In winter, the mansarded rooms on the fourth floor are the most charming; in summer, opt for those looking out on the flower-filled courtyard, their windows framed by an exuberant vine. The duplex overlooking the main courtyard is particularly desirable. Whatever the season, the hotel is always romantic, even in the pouring rain. The products in both the Spa de la Reine and the rooms are provided by Codage,

"When spring comes to Paris the humblest mortal alive must feel that he dwells in paradise." **Henry Miller, *Tropic of Cancer*, 1934**

which has a shop nearby in the Marais. The small fitness centre, two treatment rooms, a unisex steam room and jacuzzi are also open to those who are not guests of the hotel. City bikes are available, and there is a luxury brasserie next to the bar. The car park is free, and valet parking is available, a big plus in this area.

LES BAINS

7, rue du Bourg L'Abbé, 3rd
Metro Étienne Marcel
Tel 01 42 77 07 07
www.lesbains-paris.com
39 rooms and suites, €490 to €1,700

FASHIONABLE

Owner Jean-Pierre Marois, a former film producer, hired Tristan Auer to decorate the rooms in this hotel in a former public bath house. The ones on the south side have balconies and sometimes very large courtyard terraces. The light-filled penthouse suite attracts fashion designers, who stay for months – and the rest of the world follows. The past is honoured without false nostalgia by such touches as vintage telephones and large bottles of Les Bains Guerbois 1885 eau de Cologne by Michel Almairac. The rooms are chic, spacious and comfortable. The spirit is rock-and-roll (the place was long home to a popular club), but without the clichés. Breakfast and lunch (international cuisine) are served until 6pm, the lights are low in the restaurant all day long, dinner is served until 2am, party evenings are held three times a month, and there is a DJ in the restaurant Wednesday to Saturday from 8pm. The club in the well-soundproofed basement is open Wednesday to Sunday. Smaller than it used to be, it has a stage for concerts and a bar. What is less well known is that when these baths were built in 1885, François-Auguste Guerbois equipped them to provide such rituals as Turkish and Russian baths, hydrotherapy, massages and sulphur steam showers. Opposite the hotel, the shop serves Les Bains coffee, roasted by the Brûlerie de Belleville, vegetable milks and homemade pastries from 8am. Products on sale include Descamps bathrobes, Pierre Hardy leather goods and Thierry Lasry sunglasses – nice souvenirs to take home, as is the house honey (the hives are on the roof) at €15 a jar. And there is always the swimsuit printed with the "Les Bains" logo.

ALSO IN THIS NEIGHBOURHOOD

HÔTEL JULES & JIM

11, rue des Gravilliers, 3rd
Metro Arts et Métiers
Tel 01 44 54 13 13
www.hoteljulesetjim.com
23 rooms, €240 to €400

COSY, FASHIONABLE

This hotel offers a warm welcome, a fireplace and, in the courtyard, a wall of plants. The rooms, even the smallest (13 square metres; this is the Marais after all) are cleverly arranged, and Molton Brown products are used in the bathrooms. The elegant decoration is based on wood, glass, leather and rough concrete. We liked the village feel of the rooms on the courtyard, the charm of the attic rooms, and the family spirit fostered by owner Geoffroy Sciard.

SAINT-GERMAIN-DES-PRÉS, LUXEMBOURG, QUARTIER LATIN

5TH & 6TH ARRONDISSEMENTS

Literary lights & chic lifestyle

HÔTEL RÉCAMIER

3 bis, place Saint-Sulpice, 6th
Metro Saint-Sulpice
Tel 01 43 26 04 89
www.hotelrecamier.com
24 rooms, €290 to €850

LEFT BANK CHARM

Good taste and erudite elegance characterize this hotel. The distinguished owner, Sylvie de Lattre, who also owns the Hôtel Thérèse in the 1st arrondissement, has turned the Récamier into a cosy hideout. The decor, by Jean-Louis Deniot, is warm and refined, with Madame Récamier represented on every floor. On the ground floor, the mini-garden terrace is located next to the bar-reading room and the guest room preferred by poet and novelist Michel Butor. Little extras and attentive service make up for the lack of space. There is no fitness centre, but the hotel can lend you a Ram & Row folding rowing machine to use in your room; the concierge always has tickets for big exhibitions; and you can check in on a tablet. With a lovely view of the church, the Récamier has a strategic position in this corner sheltered from the winds of Place Saint-Sulpice. Every afternoon, complimentary tea is served with madeleines, pastries, jam and Provençal honey. In summer 2016, mother and son crossed the Seine to the Cité Rougemont in the 9th arrondissement, just behind the Musée Grévin, to open a hotel in two neighbouring buildings decorated by Stéphane Poux. Called the **HÔTEL ADÈLE & JULES** (2 and 4 bis, cité Rougemont, 9th, tel 01 48 24 60 70), it offers four-star accommodation.

LE SAINT

3, rue du Pré aux Clercs, 7th
Metro Rue du Bac
Tel 01 42 61 01 51
www.lesainthotelparis.com
54 rooms, apartments and suites
€350 to €850

CHARMING

Bertrand Plasmans runs Le Saint, for which he has annexed the former Lenox, the favourite hotel of stars seeking anonymity in the 1980s. The architect Vincent Bastie has paid homage to Left Bank charm in the decoration. The rooms and suites are delightful cocoons with furniture and objects found at auctions and antiques shops, all adorned with photographs by Pierre-Élie de Pibrac. Particularly sought after are the duplex Junior Suite, the 504, apartment 101 with its teak terrace and the corner suite with view of the Rue de l'Université. The bathrooms, all marble and mosaics, offer toiletries by Barnabé Fillion, who also created the room fragrance. The basement houses a gym and steam room. Bicycles are available. On arrival, guests can choose the flowers they prefer from a selection in pots, which are then sent to their room. Three green running courses are suggested: in the Tuileries, the Champs de Mars and the Jardin du Luxembourg, with maps showing you where to go. Restaurant-bar **KULT** is open to all in the morning for a great breakfast and for lunch and dinner prepared bistro style. In the afternoon, deluxe snacks are available, including a wonderful club sandwich and fine cocktails when the time comes.

L'HÔTEL

13, rue des Beaux-Arts, 6th
Metro Saint-Germain-des-Prés
Tel 01 44 41 99 00
www.l-hotel.com
20 rooms and suites, €325 to €1,000

INTIMATE, LUXURIOUS

Opened in 1827, this little five-star wonder, redecorated by Jacques Garcia, has survived with grace. This is where Oscar Wilde lived "beyond his means" before he died. Reopened in 1967, it welcomed such musical celebrities as the Beatles, the Rolling Stones, Jim Morrison and Serge Gainsbourg. The latter lived there for two years, composing *Melody Nelson* and letting his daughter Charlotte jump into the fountain on the patio. Renovated in 2000, the rooms are still wildly charming. The bathrooms are hidden in veiled marble boxes, the Marco Polo room is papered with period chinoiseries, the Oscar Wilde and Mistinguett rooms are full of relics from the past, and the apartment on the top floor measures nearly 60 square metres and has a stunning view. You can have a massage on the edge of the small counter-current pool in the basement, which you can rent for yourself for one hour. Le Restaurant is run with distinction by award-winning chef Julien Montbabut and his wife, Joana, the pastry chef. With only twenty-eight covers, it offers high visual and gustatory quality.

RELAIS CHRISTINE

3, rue Christine, 6th
Metro Saint-Michel, Odéon
Tel 01 40 51 60 80
www.relais-christine.com
48 rooms and suites, €330 to €1,300

ROMANTIC CHIC

The favourite hotel of visiting Americans was completely redone by decorator Laura Gonzalez during a two-month closure. The new decor in pastel shades includes lots of passementerie and toile de Jouy. One of the first luxury boutique hotels in Paris, the Relais Christine has four rooms with terraces overlooking the garden, ideal for sunbathing on beautiful days in Saint-Germain – especially no. 14. There are also four rooms with private access from the courtyard, allowing guests to imagine that they are staying in their own Left Bank apartment; one of them is a charming 52-square-metre ground-floor suite on the Rue Christine side. The revamped spa in the 13th-century vaulted cellars, which once belonged to the Grands-Augustins, has two treatment rooms (open to non-guests), a sauna, a jacuzzi and a fitness area. Other features: goodies from Angelina, an honesty bar, two salons with panoramic tapestries that can be rented for private events, and a menu of light meals available throughout the day. Free parking.

ALSO IN THIS NEIGHBOURHOOD

HÔTEL BAUME

7, rue Casimir-Delavigne, 6th
Metro Odéon
Tel 01 53 10 28 50
www.hotelbaume.com
35 rooms and suites, €170 to €720

UPSCALE

This boutique hotel near the Odéon Théâtre de l'Europe and a number of publishing houses, cleverly decorated by Thibaut Fron and Thierry Martin (T&T agency), is an absolute gem with the good taste to remain discreet. It has eight categories of rooms and suites, and the same number of Art Deco-influenced decors, with a view of Odéon or the indoor garden. A snack buffet provided by the house of Méert is available in the afternoon. This is the perfect pied-à-terre in Paris.

GOING IT ALONE

SLEEPING ON THE WATER

Currently the only floating hotel in Paris is a 58-room barge with four suites. The rooms are fairly large, whether on the upper or lower deck. The bar, terrace and marina overlook a swimming pool (not heated year-round). Atelier Cologne products are found in the bathrooms. Great location right next to the Cité de la Mode et du Design, by architects Jakob & Macfarlane. Open to the public for drinks year-round. **OFF PARIS SEINE** 86, quai d'Austerlitz, 13th, metro Gare d'Austerlitz, Gare de Lyon, tel 01 44 06 62 65, www.offparisseine.com, 58 rooms and suites, €120 to €325

SLEEPING IN A WOOD CABIN

This comfortable wood cabin can be reached by crossing a bridge, like a boat's gangway, in the back of the courtyard garden of the 9 Hotel Montparnasse. The exterior is in red cedar and the interior in chestnut. Wheelchair accessible, it was opened in 2016 and boasts a king-size bed, a double shower, light therapy and a Japanese toilet. The bedside table is a swing, the roof is a garden and breakfast (included) is served on a private terrace under the trees. The "nine deadly sins" option consists of nine naughty accessories to be tested (or not) by a couple. **9 HOTEL MONTPARNASSE** 76, rue Raymond Losserand, 14th, metro Pernéty, tel 01 40 52 12 40, www.9hotelmontparnasse.fr, 1 cabin, €199 to €259

SLEEPING IN A BOOKSTORE

In 2016, David Lécuiller (formerly of L'Oréal) and his associates had the idea of taking over Paris boutiques that had closed and transforming them into suites with services. In this one, the shop window on the ground floor looks like a bookstore (there are actually 4,500 books inside), but it is really a room decorated in excellent taste with rough stone and wood. It's a good way to experience the spirit of Paris through its now-disappearing authentic shops. Coming soon: a wine cellar, a fine grocery in the Bastille area and many others. Concierge service from 7am to 11pm, practical bathroom and kitchenette with microwave. **PARIS BOUTIK** 12, rue Caffarelli, 3rd, metro Temple, Filles du Calvaire, tel 01 75 43 29 26, www.parisboutik.com, 1 suite, €320 to €390

HÔTEL DA VINCI

25, rue des Saints-Pères, 6th
Metro Saint-Germain-des-Prés
Tel 01 55 35 41 88
www.hoteldavinciparis.com
24 rooms, €320 to €420

BAROCOCO

This small refurbished hotel pays tribute to the Italian Renaissance. The room called the "Adorateur" is where the man who stole the *Mona Lisa* in 1911 found refuge before giving himself up to the authorities. In the attic, you'll find exposed beams and a fake *Mona Lisa*. The toiletries are by Roberto Cavalli. Best for short stays (with few suitcases), since the rooms are so small, although still liveable, even at 12 square metres. Ask for the Privilege room (510), which is not listed on any website. And, as soon as you arrive, reserve private time in the pretty relaxation pool under a starry vault.

MUSÉE D'ORSAY, INVALIDES, TOUR EIFFEL

7TH ARRONDISSEMENT

Fashionable living & ministerial elites

HÔTEL DE LA RUE DE LILLE

40, rue de Lille, 7th
Metro Rue du Bac, RER Musée d'Orsay
Tel 01 42 61 29 09, www.hoteldelille.com
15 rooms, €320 to €600

WRITER'S HAVEN

A scented candle, a photo of Françoise Sagan, a little jazz music: everything is just right in this hotel renovated in October 2015, from the vaulted cellar that serves as the breakfast room to the tablet in your room, the courtyard, the Clarins bathroom products and personalized ideas for activities, such as jogging routes or family treasure hunts in the city. Even the smallest spaces have a warm ambience thanks to the contemporary decor, free of any excess. Each room is dedicated to an illustrious person who lived in the neighbourhood, complete with exhaustive information in video, audio and digital form. The Sagan room contains a real treasure: the writer's own typewriter. The charming, spacious Modiano suite is in the attic.

LE CINQ CODET

5, rue Louis Codet, 7th, metro École Militaire
Tel 01 53 85 15 60, www.le5codet.com
68 rooms and suites, €249 to €3,000

NEW YORK STYLE

Built in a pure industrial style in the early 1930s, Le Cinq Codet once housed France Télécom's directory services. The building was converted into a low-key hotel after a restoration project overseen by architect Jean-Philippe Nuel (who also transformed the Molitor swimming pool into a luxury hotel). Nuel is unrivalled when it comes to juggling past and present. Like the prow of an ocean liner anchored near the Champ de Mars, the Cinq Codet is a spectacular, light-filled sixty-eight-room hotel. Everything has a New York feel: the lobby, the salon, which looks like a sculptor's studio, and the rooms – the best being the duplexes with a view of the Invalides dome. Book the 83-square-metre Prestige Suite here; it has a terrace and a jacuzzi. In the restaurant-bar, which include a pleasant patio, food is served all day. The wine cellar can be seen from the restaurant, and the cool thing here is to dine at the chef's table. Car park, laptops on loan, spa with Sundari products, outdoor jacuzzi, fitness centre and herbal tea round out this pleasant experience. In the age of smartphones, buildings of this type seem prehistoric.

LE NARCISSE BLANC

19, boulevard de La Tour Maubourg, 7th
Metro Invalides
Tel 01 40 60 44 32, www.lenarcisseblanc.com
37 rooms and suites, €330 to €900

ELEGANT

The idea of the owners of Maison Favart and the Domaine de la Soucherie in the Loire Valley, this five-star hotel was inspired by the life of the dancer Cléo de Mérode, who was painted, sculpted and loved during her lifetime by many artists, from Toulouse-Lautrec to Klimt, and who was known as the "pretty little narcissus". The spirit of the muse does indeed haunt the hotel, represented by blown-glass flowers found in the bathrooms and public spaces. It's chic, feminine, discreet, elegant and Parisian, and it smells great! Room 501 has a terrace and is decorated in six beige and pastel shades, an indication of the hotel's high standards. In the basement are a Carita treatment room and a beautiful swimming pool (13 metres long) with sun beds, a steam room, a nice fitness centre, a jacuzzi and massaging waterfalls. The salon (which can be hired for private events) and the restaurant under the veranda are intimate and discreet. The wine list was put together by Olivier Poussier, named

the best sommelier of the world in 2000. In short, an ideal base for visiting this chic part of town, which has been spared by hipster mania.

THOUMIEUX

79, rue Saint-Dominique, 12th
Metro La Tour Maubourg
Tel 01 47 05 79 00, www.thoumieux.fr
15 rooms, €250 to €450

FASHIONABLE

An accumulation of colours, prints and tapestries gives Thierry Costes' reassuring four-star hotel a surprising, shimmering neo-vintage style, designed by India Mahdavi. The rooms on the courtyard side are amazingly quiet – a miracle in the heart of Paris. The room-service food and breakfasts are the work of Sylvestre Wahid, the multitalented chef with an unlimited imagination who runs the gourmet restaurant Sylvestre on the first floor and the Thoumieux brasserie on the ground floor, which has been there since 1923. The hotel reception desk is in the restaurant, as in the inns of yesteryear. Before you leave, make a stop at the house pastry shop, located across from the hotel, where you will find madeleines, "travel cakes" and Paris-Brests with sesame to prolong the pleasure of a stay in a hotel with a view of the Eiffel Tower.

ALSO IN THIS NEIGHBOURHOOD

LE PETIT CHOMEL

15, rue Chomel, 7th, metro Sèvres-Babylone
Tel 01 45 48 55 52, www.lepetitchomel.com
23 rooms, €150 to €300

CHARMING, FAMILY FEEL

This three-star family-run hotel ideally located near the Bon Marché department store is small, comfortable, newly renovated and decorated like a real home, full of souvenirs. It is a godsend in this neighbourhood, which has few reasonably priced hotels.

FAUBOURG SAINT-HONORÉ, CHAMPS-ÉLYSÉES, MADELEINE, MONCEAU

8TH ARRONDISSEMENT

Gilded neighbourhoods & luxury labels

FOUR SEASONS HOTEL GEORGE V

31, avenue George V, 8th
Metro George V
Tel 01 49 52 70 00
www.fourseasons.com/paris
244 rooms and suites, €1,200 to €22,500

PRESTIGIOUS, OPULENT

Built in 1928 by an American entrepreneur, the George V has never lost a whit of its international fame. The first hotel to have an air-taxi service (from London to Berlin) when it opened, it is still playing in the big leagues. The Canadian Four Seasons group spared no effort when it came to restoring this legendary hotel to its place among the grandest in the French capital. The sumptuous decoration is by Pierre-Yves Rochon, with nods to Second Empire opulence. The hotel offers vast spaces, fabulous bedding (which can be purchased online) and large bathrooms stocked with Bulgari and Sodashi products, along with perfumed pellets of Skinjay essential oils in the shower. The 150-square-metre penthouse has three terraces and a breathtaking view of Paris. The ten apartments make ideal pieds-à-terre for stays of six months or more. Room no. 824 is a 180-square-metre penthouse with terraces and sun deck invisible to prying eyes and a romantic roof terrace with a 360-degree view, while the 250-square-metre Royale has a large family dining room and can be connected to five additional rooms all in a row. The showers are also steam rooms, and the faucets, doors and chandeliers are made of Baccarat crystal – just so you know. In the vaulted cellars 14 metres underground in an old quarry (whose stones were used to build the Trocadéro), sommelier Éric Beaumard, known as "The Legend", gives thrilling guided tours of the 50,000-bottle treasure trove by candlelight. At lunchtime, a club sandwich at the bar is an absolute must, and the pastries served at teatime are enough to make you lose your head – and your figure. The multi-starred **LE CINQ** gourmet restaurant, run by chef Christian Le Squer, offers numerous culinary surprises; one example: the frozen-milk dessert with a yeasty flavour, which was inspired by the sails of Frank Gehry's architecture for the Louis Vuitton Foundation. With an Italian-Mediterranean restaurant, **LE GEORGE**, presided over by Italian chef Simone Zanoni, and, across from it, **L'ORANGERIE**, featuring the refined cuisine of David Bizet, the George V is the only hotel with three starred chefs. Their restaurants share the inner courtyard in summer. The globetrotting art director, Jeff Leatham, who has worked for the hotel for seventeen years, is now in demand around the world and decorates the whole hotel with flowers every season. The **POP-UP SPA** (with Sodashi, Carita and Swiss Perfection products) is located on the fourth floor, along with a hairdressing salon and a 110-square-metre gym, where the chefs work out every day. The permanent spa, designed by Pierre-Yves Rochon, will open in the summer of 2018 with a sublime 18-metre infinity pool.

HÔTEL DE CRILLON

10, Place de la Concorde, 8th
Metro Concorde
Tel 01 44 71 15 00
www.rosewoodhotels.com/en/hotel-de-crillon
124 rooms and suites, €1,200 to €25,000

HIGH-END LUXURY

Originally a royal palace designed for Louis XV in 1758 by architect Ange-Jacques Gabriel and long owned by the Comte de Crillon, the Hôtel de Crillon was transformed into a "traveller's hotel" in 1909. This jewel on the Place de la Concorde, a picture postcard of Parisian luxury and French-style glamour, now belongs to the American group Rosewood. It reopened with great pomp on 5 July 2017, after a colossal overhaul that took four (long) years and the input of the very best talents in Paris. The architect Richard Martinet (also responsible for the George V, the Shangri-La and the Peninsula), a specialist in the restoration of historic buildings, made the most of the history of this emblematic building and supervised its renovation alongside artistic director Aline Asmar d'Amman (Culture in Architecture) and interior decorators Tristan Auer (for the lobby, reception area, brasserie, cognac shop and cigar lounge), Chahan Minassian (bar, gourmet restaurant, spa) and Cyril Vergniol (rooms and suites), supported by 147 artisans. The original frescoes in the former chapel and the historic coach gate have been restored. The green spaces were designed by Louis Benech, a famous landscape artist who has, among other things, worked on the Tuileries Garden and the Théâtre d'Eau grove at Versailles. Among the most prestigious suites are the "Grands Appartements" (two suites and a room) designed by Karl Lagerfeld, an enthusiast of the 18th century. The three new artists' studios in the attic are sure to attract travellers looking for novelty. The body and facial treatments at **SENSE, A ROSEWOOD SPA** are provided by EviDenS de Beauté and Maison Caulières, and the swimming pool is illuminated by a skylight. One discordant note is the presence of the Barbière de Paris, not the best barbershop in the city. The travel-inspired menu of the gourmet restaurant **L'ÉCRIN** (28 covers) was created by Christopher Hache, while **LA BRASSERIE D'AUMONT** is run by chef Justin Schmitt. Jérôme Chaucesse (Meilleur Ouvrier de France, 2015) makes the delightful pastries on offer in the **JARDIN D'HIVER**. Another Meilleur Ouvrier de France, head bartender Christophe Davoine, officiates at the bar **LES AMBASSADEURS**. A thoroughly Parisian touch: in addition to the usual Maybach and Range Rover courtesy vehicles, the Crillon has a 1973 Citroën DS 23 Pallas, the property of Tristan Auer, who has created a custom interior to turn it into a "luxury flying carpet".

HÔTEL SPLENDIDE ROYAL

18, rue du Cirque, 8th
Metro Franklin D. Roosevelt, Miromesnil
Tel 01 43 87 10 10
www.splendideroyal.fr
12 suites, €445 to €2,300

DOLCE VITA

Opened in December 2016 in an impeccable Haussmannian building dating from 1897, the Splendide Royal has only twelve suites. This small luxury hotel has an Italian identity: it belongs to the Naldi family, a hotel dynasty for three generations. The hotel's director is Max-Michel Grand, former managing director of the Hanae Mori couture house. The spacious suites in this five-star hotel are family-friendly and feature a rococo decor with handsome marble bathrooms, perfectly regulated subdued lighting, heated floors and mirrors, room fragrance by Lorenzo Villoresi, king-size beds, a well-stocked wine cellar and a kitchenette with microwave oven. The smartphone lent to guests during their stay has an app for calling a driver. The glassware is by Christofle, the champagne by Arlaux and the dishes by Deshoulières. The dressing tables are leather-covered, and creamy shades soothe the eye and spirit.
On request, a sports coach, Pilates/yoga teacher or relaxation therapist will be sent to you to help prevent lost sleep caused by jet lag. The house butlers will take care of that for you. On the ground floor, guests have direct access to the hotel's Italian bistro, opened in 2017 and owned by Michelino Gioia.

LE PLAZA ATHÉNÉE

25, avenue Montaigne, 8th
Metro Alma-Marceau
Tel 01 53 67 66 65
www.dorchestercollection.com
208 rooms and suites, €950 to €28,000

OPULENT LUXURY

Reopened in the summer of 2014, the Parisian couture hotel par excellence (opened in 1911) is still terribly elegant. Marie-José Pommereau decorated the rooms and suites, as well as six spectacularly large new apartments located above the Harry Winston jewellery shop, all fitted out like private homes, with huge white Carrara marble bathrooms. The great attention to detail and excellent service will make you feel at home, only better, with tablets in the rooms containing the restaurant menus, and relaxing lavender and chamomile spray by ThisWorks for the pillows to help you fall asleep. Breakfast is served in the restaurant **ALAIN DUCASSE AU PLAZA ATHÉNÉE**, where the atmosphere changes between lunch and dinner thanks to giant polished-stainless-steel bells that serve as cocoons, a reference to service bells. A shower of crystal falls from the ceiling, and a cabinet of curiosities appears in the evening. Chef Romain Meder works behind the scenes in the multi-starred restaurant, decorated, like the **BAR**, by Patrick Jouin and Sanjit Manku. On the menu, no more meat, just "naturalness", with cereals, fish, vegetables and, above all, a great deal of talent and poetry. The **RELAIS PLAZA**, an Art Deco temple dating from 1936, overseen by

Werner Küchler, offers chic brasserie food and is always a good bet. The walls of the **COUR JARDIN**, redecorated by Bruno Moinard, like all the communal spaces, are covered with vines; from May to the end of September, the courtyard serves as a terrace, and in winter it becomes an ice rink. In **LA GALERIE**, where one goes to see and be seen, pastry chef Angelo Musa – world pastry champion and Meilleur Ouvrier de France – makes the goodies for afternoon tea. Light meals are also served throughout the day. The **DIOR INSTITUT** supplies "made in Montaigne" couture quintessence.

MARQUIS FAUBOURG SAINT-HONORÉ

8, rue d'Anjou, 8th
Metro Madeleine, Concorde
Tel 01 44 80 00 00
www.marquisfaubourgsainthonore.com
15 suites, €680 to €1,380

COSY, LUXURIOUS

With a lavish design by Michele Bönan, the official designer of the Ferragamo Group's luxury hotels, the Marquis has been restored to its noble status in one wing of the former Marquet de Bourgade hotel. The Marquis de Lafayette lived here (and died in the other wing, now home to the restaurant 1728, date of the year it was built), on this street formerly called Rue des Morfondus. This wonderful hotel is discreet, cosy and intimate – you won't even want to go outside. Located in a luxury shopping area, it is decorated with beautiful materials in a Florentine style. The suites are spacious, and a fitness room is hidden in the vaulted cellar.

ALSO IN THIS NEIGHBOURHOOD

AMASTAN

34, rue Jean-Mermoz, 8th
Metro Saint-Philippe-du-Roule
Tel 01 49 52 99 70
www.amastanparis.com
24 rooms, €260 to €770

FASHIONABLE

Created by the Paris agency Nocc, this boutique hotel has reasonable prices, which makes it a bargain in the area. It has an arty spirit, exemplified by Jan Kath's floor-to-ceiling carpet. Byredo, Sachajuan and Korres toiletries are used in the bathrooms, and the hotel has a bar and plant-filled courtyard terrace. Ask for room no. 21 for its very large bathroom, or 63 for its balcony with a view.

HÔTEL VERNET

25, rue Vernet, 8th, metro George V
Tel 01 44 31 98 00, www.hotelvernet.com
50 rooms and suites, €300 to €2,200

CHIC, LUXURIOUS

The nine suites in this five-star hotel near the Champs-Élysées offer spacious accommodations for this neighbourhood. It was renovated in 2014 with a contemporary decor by François Champsaur and is scented with the odour of precious woods. The restaurant, under the recently renovated glass ceiling by Gustave Eiffel, is worth a visit, as is the bar, which features custom-made cocktails.

OPÉRA, PIGALLE, FAUBOURGS MONTMARTRE AND POISSONNIÈRE

9TH ARRONDISSEMENT

Saucy streets & bohemian chic

GRAND PIGALLE HOTEL

29, rue Victor Massé, 9th
Metro Pigalle
Tel 01 85 73 12 00
www.grandpigalle.com
37 rooms and suites, €140 to €450

COMFORTABLE, INTIMATE

The first hotel opened in 2015 by the Experimental Group (before the Henrietta opened in London in the spring of 2017), the Grand Pigalle hosts a clientele of insiders and artists. The mattresses are handmade in Brittany, cement tiles are a large part of the decoration and the coffee is organic. The restaurant menu, devised by Giovanni Passerini (who now has a restaurant on Rue Traversière in the 12th arrondissement), lists 200 Italian wines, which are also available in the rooms. The cocktails in the minibars are house-made (e.g., the Negroni old-fashioned) and are accompanied by the hotel's own cocktail book. And where there are cocktails, there are also healthy breakfasts: reparations must be made after a night of drinking. The granola, cakes and spreads are also homemade. If you are wondering why there is a pineapple on every door, it's because it is a symbol of welcome in the English tradition. The reception desk is located in the middle of a mutant lobby, which also serves as a bar and cocktail lounge; the staff is dressed by the Parisian brand FrenchTrotters; and the house car is a Citroën DS that commutes between the group's different establishments (Experimental Cocktail Club, Prescription, Beef Club & Ballroom, etc.).

HÔTEL BIENVENUE

23, rue Buffault, 9th
Metro Cadet
Tel 01 48 78 32 18
www.hotelbienvenue.fr
40 rooms, €120 to €250

ATMOSPHERIC

The latest creation of the Parisian hotelier Adrien Gloaguen – following the Paradis and Panache and before the upcoming Barbizon – is in an old hotel (the Villa Fénelon) that luckily had not been damaged by bad renovations. There are two buildings – one city style, the other country – with a pretty 100-square-metre inner courtyard decorated by artist Julien Colombier. Referring to traditional family inns, the street side is decorated in monochrome pastels, while the courtyard side has flowered wallpaper, both designed by Chloé Nègre, who used to work with India Mahdavi and has now accomplished her first full hotel design. We like the two wheelchair-accessible ground-floor rooms on the courtyard for a taste of the countryside in the middle of Paris, and no. 505, a vast space on the top floor with a large bathroom with double sinks and a playlist to entertain guests in the shower/steam bath. The menu of light meals was created by Bogato, and pastry classes are offered for children, open to non-guests during the day in the gallery and restaurant.

HÔTEL DE NELL

7-9, rue du Conservatoire, 9th
Metro Grands Boulevards
Tel 01 44 83 83 60
www.hoteldenell.com
33 rooms and suites, €250 to €1,200

DISCREET LUXURY

In this five-star hotel, owned by the same people as the Benkirai in Saint-Tropez, Jean-Michel Wilmotte has designed everything except the canvas furniture. His converging lines and soothing style, stony and streamlined, is easily recognizable. Nothing is superfluous, nothing lacks a purpose. The details were meticulously thought out by seventy-two tradespeople, including an acoustic engineer who had only one objective: to ensure that the doors make no noise when they close. That may seem unnecessary, but it is actually essential for city hotels. The same high standards apply to the pillows: guests can choose feather, ergonomic, ecological or relaxation. The hotel, whose listed facade overlooks the church of Saint Eugène-Sainte Cécile, offers its guests Olympian calm and comfortable spaces with an unpretentious reception. This contemporary yet timeless hotel avoids the superficiality of the fashionable. A Nuxe spa can be found in the vaulted stone basement, and the bar serves cocktails made with aged spirits. The house restaurant is none other than **LA RÉGALADE**, always a safe bet.

LE PANACHE

1, rue Geoffroy Marie, 9th
Metro Grands Boulevards, Cadet
Tel 01 47 70 85 87
www.hotelpanache.com
40 rooms and suites, €120 to €450

STYLISH

Located between the Drouot auction house and the Folies-Bergère, this is one of several hotels owned by Adrien Gloaguen (others include the Paradis and the Bienvenue, which was decorated by Chloé Nègre). All the rooms are different in this four-star establishment decorated by Dorothée Meilichzon with retro-Parisian accents. Welcoming and unpretentious, the Panache pampers families with its colouring gazette with crayons from the Petite Papeterie Française, tepees set up in the (larger) rooms and even a miniature golf course in the hallway. Another gag (there are two joke shops located nearby) is a fortune cookie instead of a chocolate on the pillow, which tells guests whether or not they will have the good fortune to win a free night. The Panache offers Bonne Nouvelle beauty products and has a stylish bistro on the ground floor. The generous, healthy breakfast, with cakes from Noglu, the gluten-free restaurant in the Passage des Panoramas, is also served in the restaurant. In the rooms, the minibars are full of chocolates from À La Mère de Famille, the oldest chocolate maker in Paris, located nearby. In short, there is no need to leave the hotel if you want to feel part of the Parisian scene.

MAISON SOUQUET

10, rue de Bruxelles, 9th
Metro Blanche
Tel 01 48 78 55 55
www.maisonsouquet.com
20 rooms and suites, €375 to €1,230

OPULENT, INTIMATE

A former bordello at the foot of the Butte Montmartre, owned by Madame Souquet from 1905 to 1907, inspired this hotel designed by Jacques Garcia for the group Maisons Particulières in 2015. The daring, testosterone-charged atmosphere is full of fragrance, beginning in the lobby. Three salons in a row follow the old-fashioned codes of love: the Moorish salon was reserved for "discussions" between men, the Empire lounge was for small pleasures and the winter garden for the last drink. The house cocktails and rooms are named after famous courtesans. You'll find antique furniture, fine fabrics, designer backgammon games, an impressive library, Hermès products in the bathrooms and a Louis Vuitton trunk on the doorstep. The swimming pool (10 metres long) and steam bath decorated in gold leaf can be privately rented for one hour a day, even on your departure day.

ALSO IN THIS NEIGHBOURHOOD

1ER ÉTAGE SOPI

34, rue Jean-Baptiste-Pigalle, 9th
Metro Pigalle, Saint-Georges
Tel 06 49 76 18 84
www.1eretagesopi.com
7 rooms, €150 to €250

B&BOURGEOIS

After the 1er Étage Marais and the 1er Étage Opéra, the 1er Étage SoPi (South Pigalle) opened at the beginning of 2017 in a renovated townhouse with a new Pop decor. A few rooms are distributed around the main room, a living room with a fireplace and five listed frescoes. Breakfast is also served there in what was once the music room of the 19th-century composer Benjamin Godard. The hotel, located on the ground, first and second floors, has a kitchen and rooms ranging in size from 19 to 25 square metres, decorated with 1950s furniture. A good option in the neighbourhood.

MONSIEUR CADET

4, rue Cadet, 9th
Metro Le Peletier
Tel 01 76 76 69 26
www.monsieurcadet.com
31 rooms and suites, €199 to €239

ART DECO

This hotel has a retro piano bar, velvet banquettes and a small outdoor terrace on a pleasant pedestrian street where a permanent market is held. It's a prime spot for observing the new Parisian tribes with a Roaring Twenties spirit. Bonuses: a Le Tigre spa and mosaic-lined steam bath with a starry ceiling.

RÉPUBLIQUE, CANAL SAINT-MARTIN, GARE DU NORD

10TH & 11TH ARRONDISSEMENTS

Working-class areas & bobo strongholds

HÔTEL PROVIDENCE

90, rue René Boulanger, 10th
Metro Strasbourg-Saint-Denis
Tel 01 46 34 34 04
www.hotelprovidenceparis.com
18 rooms, €190 to €650

SMALL, LUXURIOUS

A providential address opened by Élodie and Pierre Moussié (who took over the Barbès Brasserie in 2015), ideally located near train stations, the theatres on the Grands Boulevards and Place de la République. It has a real café and participates in the life of the neighbourhood, offering a close-up on Right Bank chic. The restaurant-bar, the heart of the hotel, serves a variety of dishes and food cooked in a wood-fired oven from 7am to 2am (last order at midnight). The staff wears uniforms by the Parisian label Proêmes de Paris. The bar's offerings can be also be found in the rooms, each of which has its own zinc "minibar" with all the ingredients to make a favourite cocktail. The walls are covered in stretched fabrics and House of Hackney wallpaper, with prints galore, and the furniture comes from flea markets. The quiet rooms have a certain charm and a view of a very Parisian pedestrian street, site of the stage entrance to the Porte Saint-Martin theatre – so *West Side Story*. Our favourites are the rooms with balconies and the mansarded suite on the top floor.

LES GOBELINS, DENFERT-ROCHEREAU, MONTPARNASSE

13TH, 14TH & 15TH ARRONDISSEMENTS

Greenery & family life

HÔTEL HENRIETTE

9, rue des Gobelins, 13th
Metro Les Gobelins
Tel 01 47 07 26 90
www.hotelhenriette.com
32 rooms and suites, €89 to €299

FASHIONABLE

This charming hotel with a paved courtyard full of greenery and light has been renovated into a three-star hotel by Vanessa Scoffier, former fashion editor for the magazines *Elle* and *Marie-Claire,* with highly Instagrammable results. On the courtyard side, a gluten-free breakfast is laid out with grandma's porcelain and organic teas on a marble bar under the glass roof. The bouquets are created in-house. The quiet street side is furnished with flea-market finds. Nuxe toiletries are used in the bathrooms. The rooms are filled with light, and one wonderful single room is saved by its magazine-style decoration. The biggest rooms are in the attic.
Every detail has been carefully thought out, from the choice of fabrics to the retro door handles, enamelled glasses in the bathrooms and tote bags given to guests on arrival.

AUTEUIL, PASSY, TROCADÉRO, ÉTOILE

16TH & 17TH ARRONDISSEMENTS

Nobility & urban elegance

HÔTEL RAPHAEL

17, avenue Kléber, 16th
Metro Kléber
Tel 01 53 64 32 10
www.raphael-hotel.com
83 rooms and suites, €400 to €4,750

LUXURIOUS, TRADITIONAL

This townhouse dating from 1925 was designed for long stays and has retained a considerable advantage from the past: space. While the Paris hotel industry juggles with increasingly smaller rooms, the Raphael luxuriates in all those square metres. The wear and tear of time has not harmed this majestic place where the past reigns supreme: the sculpted-wood elevator still has its velvet bench, for example. The spirit of Serge Gainsbourg also floats in the hotel (he stayed in room 501-502 for several months, preparing his album for Vanessa Paradis and going behind the bar to pass on his cocktail recipes to the staff and clients of the **BAR ANGLAIS**). But the Raphael's real hidden treasure can be found on its roof: **LA TERRASSE**, totally renovated in the summer of 2017, is a discreet restaurant with a view of Paris, open from May to September. Its tables are scattered among trees and open to non-guests from noon to 11pm. The menu now offers a vegan dish, and pastry chef Sébastien Reul makes gluten-free goodies for teatime.
The owners, Madame Baverez and her daughter, Véronique Beauvais-Valcke, also own the **VILLA & HÔTEL MAJESTIC** (30, rue La Pérouse, 16th, tel 01 45 00 83 70), redecorated by Paul Sartres and also recommended.

SAINT JAMES PARIS

24, avenue Bugeaud, 16th
Metro Victor Hugo, Porte Dauphine
Tel 01 44 05 81 81
www.saint-james-paris.com
49 rooms and suites, €385 to €1,690

LUXURIOUS, FUN

What could be more charming than a château in the heart of Paris, with a verdant central courtyard and plashing fountain, an ideal setting for the ballet of limousines belonging to its members? The hotel begins in the courtyard: two triplex 70-square-metre pavilions, located on either side of the gate, are connected by an underground corridor. The first one houses a spa with jacuzzi and steam bath in the basement, while the other has a private cinema. This very courtyard was once used as a launch pad for early hot-air balloons; later the building was transformed into a boarding school by the widow of the forgotten president of the Third Republic, Adolphe Thiers. Today, it is owned by the Bertrand group. Non-guests of the hotel must cough up an annual membership fee of €1,800, plus a €1,000 fee for access to the restaurant, bar (until 7pm), gym and meeting rooms. Dinner from Monday to Saturday and brunch on Sunday are open to the public. Chef Jean-Luc Rocha, a Meilleur Ouvrier de France who used to work at Cordeillan-Bages in Pauillac, runs the restaurant. His delicate dishes (croque-caviar canapé with chicken mousse, fried ravioli with honey and goat cheese, lettuce cream soup) are served in a dining room with a leopard-patterned carpet. Leopard? This reference to the decor of Parisian townhouses of this type at the end of the 19th century was chosen by Bambi Sloane, who designed this remix of Napoleon III style. The ground floor decor is enhanced by numerous reproductions of artworks. The rooms are unusual, and the black cat, Pilou, has been stretching out on the banquettes for nine years.

SHANGRI-LA HOTEL

10, avenue d'Iéna, 16th
Metro Iéna
Tel 01 53 67 19 98
www.shangri-la.com
101 rooms and suites, €900 to €20,000

ABSOLUTE LUXURY

In 1891, Prince Roland Bonaparte, great-nephew of Napoleon, assembled in this sumptuous mansion on the Chaillot Hill what was then the largest herbarium in Europe, with millions of plants. Today, the huge fern collection has been bequeathed to the Muséum d'Histoire Naturelle in Paris, and the other plants, as well as 1,800 books, to Claude-Bernard University in Lyon. Since nature played such an important role here, it's only logical that the hotel's bar is called **BOTANISTE** and has a wall of plants that goes perfectly with a cocktail list featuring génépi, cocoa beans and absinthe. It's a good spot for an intimate moment and a perfect example of the spirit of the Shangri-La: in this historic setting, the salons and restaurants offer a very high level of luxury – even though the service sometimes loses focus – but without overdoing it or slipping into cliché. At the gourmet restaurant **L'ABEILLE**, chef Christophe Moret also perpetuates the former owner's green traditions with his kitchen garden at the bottom of the park, where he picks his thyme and rosemary. Teatime treats are vegan, and the gluten-free "Be Green" breakfasts are served in **BAUHINIA**. On the lower level, the **SHANG PALACE**, the only starred Chinese restaurant in France, attracts a clientele of regulars who enjoy authentic Cantonese dishes in a setting decorated in jade, lacquer and crystal. The spa uses products from the British label The Organic Pharmacy. The sublime swimming pool (16 x 6 metres, 30°C), located in the prince's former stables on Rue Fresnel, is for hotel guests only. The marble and the planisphere with the signs of the zodiac in the library are original. The Hong Kong group deserves credit for restoring to its

SPOTLIGHT

TOP 10 HOTEL SCENTS

"A house without perfume is a house without memories," says perfumer Rami Mekdachi. Here is a short overview of the olfactory identities of some Paris hotels.

THE MOST POWDERY: white narcissus. Created anonymously by a big-name perfumer, the fragrance of the **NARCISSE BLANC** (7th) comes in the form of candles and a bed fragrance to perfume the sheets. Its notes of almond, orange blossom, rose, vanilla and white musk scent all the rooms.

THE MOST POPULAR: amber is the historical olfactory signature of the **RITZ** (1st), where amber is sold in spray and perfume forms. Ambre du Népal by Maître Parfumeur et Gantier is the room fragrance at the **PAVILLON DE LA REINE** (3rd), the **PAVILLON DES LETTRES** (8th) and many other hotels, no doubt for the spicy notes that make you want to throw caution to the wind.

THE MOST RECOGNIZABLE: a woody, penetrating fragrance by the talented Blaise Mautin, created in 2000 for the **PARK HYATT PARIS-VENDÔME** (2nd).

THE MOST INTOXICATING: the olfactory identity of **MAISON SOUQUET** (9th) wonderfully evokes the world of the Belle Époque with its notes of rose, tobacco, jasmine and leather.

THE MOST SUBTLE: the citrusy, woody, musky notes of the **NOLINSKI** (2nd) fragrance, with base notes of tonka bean, tea and cedar.

THE MOST RELAXING: Pour le Matin by Maison Francis Kurkdjian at the **JULES & JIM** (3rd), a fragrance designed to last long into the night.

THE MOST ROCK-AND-ROLL: the Les Bains Guerbois 1885 scented candle created by Dorothée Piot, whose notes perfume **LES BAINS** (3rd), blending spices, papyrus, Atlas cedar, cardamom, violets and tonka beans.

THE MOST FEMININE: the vanilla and sugary touches that perfume the **BAUME** (6th), sold as a room fragrance, candle and fabric fragrance.

THE MOST DESIRABLE: the mild white tea scent at the **SHANGRI-LA** (16th), the group's worldwide olfactory signature, sold as a spray, candle and diffuser.

THE MOST SPICY: composed by Rami Mekdachi, the creator of fragrances for Jacques Garcia, Bensimon and a slew of hotels – including the Costes, Mama Shelter, La Réserve and Sofitel – this woody, masculine scent with cardamom, patchouli, Atlas cedar, papyrus and more is available as a candle or room fragrance at the **SAINT JAMES PARIS** (16th).

former glory this emblem of the Parisian heritage (now listed), under the supervision of Pierre-Yves Rochon. Historical references are everywhere: the bee, symbol of the Bonaparte family, for example, is found here and there, especially in the salons on the first floor. All the south-facing rooms have a view of the Eiffel Tower. One of the most striking, the Shangri-La Suite, with a 100-square-metre terrace, is positively imperial.

ALSO IN THIS NEIGHBOURHOOD

LE10BIS

10 bis, rue du Débarcadère, 17th
Metro Porte Maillot
Tel 01 55 37 10 10
www.le10bishotel-paris.com
23 rooms and suites, €200 to €500

CHIC BIS

The 10bis, formerly a brothel and swingers' club, was run by Katia La Rouquine for forty years and transformed into a four-star hotel in 2016. The style has nothing to do with that of the house of ill repute, with its shimmering draperies, and the disco is gone from the fifth floor. The only nods to the past can be found in the guest rooms, where lamps and mirrors from the house's glory days have been kept. From the fifth floor and above, the rooms have views of the Louis Vuitton Foundation. Located behind the Palais de Congrès, the hotel uses Rituals toiletries.

MONTMARTRE, LA VILLETTE, BELLEVILLE, MÉNILMONTANT

18TH, 19TH & 20TH ARRONDISSEMENTS

Old Paris & modern nostalgia

HÔTEL PARTICULIER MONTMARTRE

23, avenue Junot, Pavillon D, 18th
Metro Lamarck-Caulaincourt
Tel 01 53 41 81 40
www.hotel-particulier-montmartre.com
5 suites, €390 to €590

CHARMING, UNUSUAL

Located up in Montmartre on a private cobblestone street, the Hôtel Particulier is a dream of a hotel. And it's even better if you enjoy partying in the ground-floor cocktail bar, **LE TRÈS PARTICULIER**, designed by architect Pierre Lacroix, which is popular with millennials. This townhouse surrounded by a majestic tree-filled garden is unique on the Paris hotel scene. A former property of the Guerrand-Hermès family, it was converted into a hotel in 2007. It has only five suites, decorated in dandy, arty or naughty styles. Room no. 4 has wallpaper by Martine Aballéa, and no. 3 boasts artworks by Olivier Saillard. There is also a black-and-white photo tribute to Serge Gainsbourg. All the suites have palatial bathrooms straight out of the film *Fitzcarraldo*. When you reserve your suite (they measure between 35 and 85 square metres), don't forget to book a pétanque court on the neighbouring property, a privilege reserved for the hotel's guests and members of a pétanque club. The hotel no longer has its own honey, however, because the neighbours set fire to the hives. The hotel also houses Paris's best-kept secret: the restaurant **LE MANDRAGORE**, now run by Oscar Comtet. Special events enliven the evenings in this hotel that is indeed very particular.

MAMA SHELTER

109, rue de Bagnolet, 20th
Metro Alexandre Dumas
Tel 01 43 48 48 48, www.mamashelter.com
172 rooms and suites, €79 to €299

HIP

Mama Shelter, the only bohemian refuge on the eastern edge of Paris, created by the Trigano family and the businessman Cyril Aouizerate, was a pioneering hotel in this increasingly gentrified hilltop neighbourhood. Located alongside the Petite Ceinture (a defunct rail line that used to circle the city), which is just begging for help from a landscape designer, the hotel has a restaurant, late-night bar, roof terrace (open when the weather permits) and shop, all designed by Philippe Starck. With graffiti everywhere, the decor also includes waxed concrete, black lacquer, a giant foosball game, luminous buoys and TV screens on the ceiling of the toilets. With its good vibes, it has been busy ever since it opened in 2008. The pizza restaurant serves until 1:30am, and the bartenders choreograph their cocktails to the DJ's sounds. The Mama concept is so successful that it has been duplicated around the world, from Marseille to Rio. Guests are advised to get a room on the highest floor possible if they want to get some rest. Either that or just forget about rest and hang out in the bar. The rooms are equipped with microwave ovens, giant mirrors, Apple TV and Absolution-Mama Shelter toiletries. Chef Guy Savoy created the restaurants' menus. We love the idea of sharing super-sized desserts like the Paris-Brest or baba au rhum.

TERRASS HOTEL

12-14, rue Joseph de Maistre, 18th
Metro Place de Clichy, Blanche
Tel 01 46 06 72 85
www.terrass-hotel.com
92 rooms and suites, €400 to €1,200

ELEGANT, FRIENDLY

This hotel dating from 1910 still has its original facade and period decoration, with contemporary touches. The rooms are decorated in the spirit of the artists of Montmartre or of the Polydor musicians who used to stay here when the headquarters of the record company were located nearby on Rue Cavallotti. The Terrass now seems to have come back to life. It has six (very large) suites, a roof terrace (with a bar, foosball table, lounge chairs, salon) and a restaurant on the seventh floor with a view of the city (open to the public). The artists' studios are furnished with warm-coloured leather, and L'Occitane products can be found in the bathrooms. There is a fitness centre, and the panoramic penthouse has a private terrace and jacuzzi. A small shop sells original souvenirs of Montmartre: honey, organic beauty products and even pétanque balls. An interactive map of the neighbourhood and phone chargers are available in the lobby, and the spa uses Nuxe products. The most original touch can be found in the courtyard, where three hens – Édith, La Goulue and Blanche – provide fresh eggs for breakfast every morning.

ALSO IN THIS NEIGHBOURHOOD

B MONTMARTRE

6, rue Lécluse, 17th, metro Place de Clichy
Tel 01 42 93 35 77
www.b-montmartre.com
36 rooms and suites,€150 to €500

TROPICAL CHIC, QUIET

This former 19th-century family guest house converted into a four-star hotel is located on a quiet street behind the Place de Clichy, offering an alternative way to discover Montmartre. At the back of the courtyard, a second architect-designed building has eight charming rooms facing the palm trees in a pleasant paved courtyard that serves as a terrace. Fragonard bath products, double showers, Japanese toilets and a warm welcome.

CHECKING IN WITH DOMINIQUE PERRAULT

I never stop travelling, so naturally I live in hotels, which are often located in my own buildings, such as the two leaning towers in Milan at the Rho-Pero trade fair, the Meliá in Vienna on the banks of the Danube, and my Barcelona hotel, whose cantilevered overhang dominates the Avinguda Diagonal. Of necessity, whether at the Regent in Berlin or elsewhere, in Saint Petersburg or Tokyo, I spend my days between the lobby and the bar – I practically invented coworking! In Naples, I set up my office on the terrace of the Excelsior, overlooking the sea. In Paris, my favourite hotels are Le Meurice, the doyen of luxury hotels, Le Royal Monceau, with its terrace that's ideal for meetings, and the Mama Shelter, for the Philippe Starck design.

LE MEURICE

228, rue de Rivoli, 1st, metro Tuileries, tel 01 44 58 10 10, www.dorchester.com

LE ROYAL MONCEAU

37, avenue Hoche, 8th, metro George V, Ternes, tel 01 42 99 88 00, www.raffles.com

MAMA SHELTER

109, rue de Bagnolet, 20th, metro Alexandre Dumas, tel 01 43 48 48 48, www.mamashelter.com

RESTAURANTS

CULINARY CLASSICS TO BISTRO FARE: EATING OUT IN THE CITY

In spite of what they say in New York, London, Madrid and Copenhagen, the Parisian restaurant scene is not in such bad shape after all, thank you very much. If "French bashing" occurs regularly in the media, perhaps it is because the general public and most visitors are not yet aware of the major changes that have been revolutionising the geography and sociology of Parisian restaurants over the past ten years. Classic establishments, which are no bad thing but can be pretentious, have given way to a generation of new-wave bistros, whose airs may one day grow tiresome as well.

Basically, Paris is still questioning not its culinary wealth but its culinary identity. Is it associated with those mummified restaurants where you can't have a meal for less than €450 per person or with the bearded, tattooed chefs who put meals together without knowing how to make a sauce? This tension between tradition and modernity resurfaces regularly. In any case, it stimulates a healthy and interesting debate about what defines the city and its table manners. The best thing to do is to continue this debate – and nourish it – at the table: what better place than a restaurant to talk about who we are and what we eat.

LOUVRE, TUILERIES, PALAIS-ROYAL, LES HALLES

1ST & 2ND ARRONDISSEMENTS

Royal residences & top shopping

CAMÉLIA

Hôtel Mandarin Oriental,
251, rue Saint-Honoré, 1st
Metro Concorde
Tel 01 70 98 74 00
www.mandarinoriental.fr
Fixed-price menus €60 to €116,
à la carte €100

REFINED, GASTRONOMIC

It has almost become a game: rather than having their wallets cleaned out at leading gourmet restaurants, guests at grand hotels have learned to opt for the "secondary" restaurant, often run by young talents eager to outdo their masters. At the Mandarin Oriental, why prostrate oneself before the altar of Thierry Marx in his famous restaurant Sur Mesure when you can dine instead on the Camélia's garden terrace? The exquisite service is attentive but never intrusive. Try the crab Rotolino with mango, Tomka broth, and miso and parsley condiment, for example. It is not unusual for diners to leave with big smiles on their faces.

CHEZ GEORGES

1, rue du Mail, 2nd, metro Bourse
Tel 01 42 60 07 11
À la carte €55
Closed Saturday and Sunday

VINTAGE BISTRO

This 1950s bistro changed hands a few years ago, always a dangerous moment, since ghosts from a former life may return and avenge themselves by overturning a gravy boat or encouraging a customer not to return. Chez Georges (the name of one of the former owners), however, remains true to itself. Now owned by Jean-Gabriel de Bueil (Bistrot de Paris, Chez René, Fred, Savy, among others), it still has its white tablecloths and cotton napkins, and continues to serve dishes like *sole meunière* and steak with a calorie-laden sauce. Better still, the vivacious, feisty waitresses with white aprons still work there. Sometimes, when the door opens, you almost expect the past to walk in . . . Customers here have nothing to prove, which makes a nice change.

CLOVER GRILL

6, rue Bailleul, 1st
Metro Louvre-Rivoli
Tel 01 40 41 59 59
www.clover-grill.com
Fixed-price menu €69, à la carte €70
Closed Sunday

MEAT, FASHIONABLE

The advantage of the profusion of restaurants owned by leading chefs (Jean-François Piège, in this case) is that in the secondary restaurants we don't have to stroke their ego – that's what the main restaurant is for. Here we get the great food without the frills. The Clover Grill is a meat-lover's haven, with perfectly grilled cuts from the four corners of the world (Kansas, Bavaria, Australia, etc.). The burger is juicy, the steaks nicely seared and, apart from a grilled split banana that is a bit too conventional, everything works like a charm. The customers know what they are there for, the decor is appealing and the service wonderful.

KEI

5, rue Coq Héron, 1st
Metro Les Halles
Tel 01 42 33 14 74
www.restaurant-kei.fr
Fixed-price menus €56 to €198
Closed all day Sunday and Monday,
and for lunch on Thursday

GASTRONOMIC, LUXURIOUS

Kei Kobayashi was well trained by Jean-François Piège at the Plaza Athénée, part of Alain Ducasse's empire.

À LA CARTE
Average price of a three-course meal, excluding wine.

He assiduously applied the lessons learned while keeping an open mind and then took the risk of opening his own place in the former restaurant of Gérard Besson. This young peroxided chef serves up brilliant, poetic dishes of Japanese inspiration, arranging them like landscapes, with alternating mild and vivacious flavours, counterpoints and arrhythmias. His influences come from all over, including Alsace, Italy and Provence. Try the whole bass with caramelized citrus sauce and Thai basil purée, or the Iberian pork with piperade espuma and almond emulsion. The service is still a bit stiff, unfortunately, and the dining room's pervasive whiteness seems designed to highlight the visual impact of the food.

LOULOU

Musée des Arts Décoratifs,
107, rue de Rivoli, 1st
Metro Palais-Royal–Musée du Louvre
Tel 01 42 60 41 96
www.loulou-paris.com
À la carte €60

FASHIONABLE, TERRACE

This place blessed by the gods – with a huge terrace overlooking the gardens of the Louvre – is run by artificers used to this type of exercise (the crew from Monsieur Bleu: Gilles Malafosse, Laurent de Gourcuff and Benjamin Cassan), where an attractive (read banal) setting appeases a clientele that has seen it all and is still strangely benevolent. The Italian food (the preferred cuisine in fashionable places) sticks to the menu in a rather distracted way, probably so as not to frighten sharp-tongued customers. Luckily, the vitello tonnato and the house tagliatelle with veal stew benefit from this indifference, since the diners are more interested in themselves, their neighbours and the references in the decoration by Joseph Dirand, Jean-Charles de Castelbajac and Alexis Mabille.

SATURNE

17, rue Notre-Dame des Victoires, 2nd
Metro Bourse
Tel 01 42 60 31 90
www.saturne-paris.fr
Fixed-price menus €45 to €140
Closed Saturday and Sunday

NORDIC DECOR, NATURAL WINES

Ewen Le Moigne (who handles the wine and front of house) and starred chef Sven Chartier (formerly of Arpège and Hégia) have been running this place with great composure since 2010, serving natural wines and food that plays with trios of ingredients (oysters-pears-watercress) in a simple setting with a blond-wood decor. The locavore cuisine shows a penchant for northern influences (think Noma). The duo is so taken with this style that it has not only recreated it at the **CLOWN BAR** but also replicates the experience for the happy few who can, by appointment, eat at **MAYARO**. The latter is a private restaurant for aesthetes and artisans that serves up unforgettable bespoke meals for eight people for €4,000. **Other locations:**
CLOWN BAR 114, rue Amelot, 9th, metro Filles du Calvaire, Oberkampf, tel 01 43 55 87 35
MAYARO 20, rue Amélie, 7th, metro La Tour Maubourg, tel 01 80 06 04 41

SPRING

6, rue Bailleur, 1st, metro Louvre-Rivoli
Tel 01 45 96 05 72
www.springparis.fr
Menu €84
Closed for lunch and all day Sunday and Monday

REFINED, FASHIONABLE

We first met chef Daniel Rose off the beaten track, on the slopes of the ninth arrondissement, and now he has several restaurants. In addition to Le Coucou (in New York, with partners), he also officiates with panache at **LA BOURSE ET LA VIE** (leeks in vinaigrette with toasted hazelnuts, fried quails with buckwheat) and at **CHEZ LA VIEILLE**, decorated by the talented Elliott Barnes, where he has revived an institution famous for its pot-au-feu, blanquette and terrine. But it is especially at Spring that all his good humour, boldness and edginess come through in such dishes as "Bernard Bos" *sole meunière* and slow-roasted shoulder of milk-fed lamb with almond purée. Marie-Aude, his teammate and wife, shares his enthusiasm. The clientele of beautiful people is sensitive to this controlled energy. The service is easy-going, but only one tasting menu is offered.

Other locations: LA BOURSE ET LA VIE 12, rue Vivienne, 2nd, tel 01 42 60 08 83
CHEZ LA VIEILLE 1, rue Bailleur, 1st, tel 01 42 60 15 78

YAM'TCHA

121, rue Saint-Honoré, 1st
Metro Louvre-Rivoli, Les Halles
Tel 01 40 26 08 07, www.yamtcha.com
Fixed-price menus €65 to €135
Closed Sunday and Monday, and for lunch Tuesday

CHINESE-FRENCH KITCHEN

Adeline Grattard (formerly of L'Astrance) didn't lose anything when she moved from Rue Sauval to Rue Saint-Honoré. Her husband, Chi Wah Chan, a kind of calm wise man, like Nicolas Bouvier's Buddha – "face shining with mischievousness and radiating compassion" – is still by her side. Her cuisine, immortalized in the documentary series *Chef's Table*, features such dishes as sautéed lobster with salted duck egg yolk, spider crabs and Macvin emulsion, served with roasted Oolong Tie Guanyin tea. The setting is refined and soothing, with nooks and crannies decorated with gold leaf and Oriental frescoes. The attentive service delights a clientele quivering with anticipation. Trying to get a table here may drive you crazy; pray for a cancellation.

ALSO IN THIS NEIGHBOURHOOD

CIBUS

5, rue Molière, 1st
Metro Pyramides, Palais-Royal–Musée du Louvre
Tel 01 42 61 50 19
À la carte €50

TINY TRATTORIA

This little restaurant serving organic Italian food is located in the lobby of an Art Nouveau building, a worldly setting for the well-tempered cuisine of Elio Bombace.

DROUANT

16–18, rue Gaillon, 2nd
Metro Quatre Septembre
Tel 01 42 65 15 16, www.drouant.com
Fixed-price menus €45 to €65, à la carte €80

CHIC, BRASSERIE

The Goncourt and Renaudot literary prizes are awarded here, conferring a special status on Drouant, a cross between a brasserie and a restaurant, where you'll find a bright decor and the soothing cuisine of Antoine Westermann. Weekday specials include roast chicken and vol-au-vent. Known for its brunch (€36).

JIN

6, rue de la Sourdière, 1st
Metro Tuileries
Tel 01 42 61 60 71
Closed Saturday evening, all day Sunday and for lunch Monday and Tuesday
Fixed-price menus €95 to €145
Closed Saturday and Sunday

HIGH-END SUSHI

Owned by Takuya Watanabe, from Hokkaido in northern Japan (famous for having the best fish), this is one of the best sushiyas in Paris. He makes quite an impression with his shaved head and spectacular physique, and delivers top-notch sushi in a refined setting straight out of an Edward Hopper painting.

LE 1 VENDÔME

Hôtel de Vendôme,
1, place Vendôme, 1st
Metro Tuileries
Tel 01 55 04 55 60
www.hoteldevendome.com
Closed Sunday and Monday
Fixed-price menus €45 to €60, à la carte €80
Closed Sunday and Monday

REFINED

With a snack menu in the morning, this boudoir hidden away on the first floor of Le 1 Vendôme offers dishes as refined as its houndstooth armchairs stylishly designed by Michele Bönan. Sometimes it works (Brittany scallops) and sometimes it doesn't.

LE GRAND COLBERT

2, rue Vivienne, 2nd
Metro Bourse
Tel 01 42 86 87 88
www.legrandcolbert.fr
Fixed-price menu €40, à la carte €60

VINTAGE BRASSERIE

There is certainly nothing special about the food here, but the setting is amazing, with a six-metre-high ceiling, frescoes and sculpted columns. And then there is the forced enthusiasm of the waiters, the Parisian ambiance (paradoxical in this milieu) and the comforting dishes – the sole is generous and the tartare, entrecôte, veal stew and pepper steak equally delectable. In short, everything chefs don't like to do but customers love.

LE PETIT CHOISEUL

23, rue Saint-Augustin, 2nd
Metro Quatre Septembre
Tel 01 42 96 02 47
www.petitchoiseul.fr
Fixed-price menu €20, à la carte €25
Closed for dinner Saturday to Tuesday

ORGANIC BISTRO

A solid 1950s-style bar with leopard-skin leatherette, friendly service and a textbook œuf mayo. The rest is of a piece: pâté, steak with shallots, calf's liver purée, stuffed cabbage or rib steak consumed with relish by a lively local clientele. When the downstairs is full, the dining table upstairs takes the overflow.

PASSAGE 53

53, passage des Panoramas, 2nd
Metro Grands Boulevards, Bourse
Tel 01 42 33 04 35
www.passage53.com
Fixed-price menus €60 and €160
Closed Sunday and Monday

FRENCH-JAPANESE FUSION

Shinichi Sato's elegantly minimalist dishes are served as a tasting menu, with high-end service provided by Guillaume Guedj's team.

RESTAURANT DU PALAIS ROYAL

110, galerie de Valois, 1st (from the garden)
or 41, rue de Valois (from the street)
Metro Bourse, Palais-Royal–Musée du Louvre
Tel 01 40 20 00 27
www.restaurantdupalaisroyal.com
Fixed-price menus €48 to €142,
à la carte €100
Closed Sunday and Monday

ELEGANT, GASTRONOMIC

What used to be the Petit Véfour has a princely location with a terrace in the garden, ambitious cuisine and high-level service.

SUSHI B

5, rue Rameau, 2nd
Metro Bourse, Pyramides
Tel 01 40 26 52 87
www.sushi-b-fr.com
Fixed-price menus €58 to €130
Closed Tuesday

SUSHI BAR

The servers wear kimonos in this sushi bar with a blond-wood counter and smiling chef. Masayoshi Hanada (a native of Kyushu) serves his variations on raw and aged fish at an easy pace. The clientele is calm and respectful.

BEAUBOURG, LE MARAIS, PLACE DES VOSGES

3RD & 4TH ARRONDISSEMENTS

Historic landmarks & arty strolls

BOB'S KITCHEN

74, rue des Gravilliers, 3rd
Metro Réaumur-Sébastopol, Rambuteau
Tel 09 52 55 11 66
www.bobsjuicebar.com
À la carte €12

FASHIONABLE, VEGETABLES

Bob's Kitchen is frequented by models hoping to maintain their smooth, flat stomachs. Others – lovers, fools, artists and the damned – go for the veggie stew or carrot juice with ginger. This is one of the most pleasant places to rub elbows in Paris.

BREIZH CAFÉ

109, rue Vieille du Temple, 3rd
Metro Saint-Sébastien Froissart
Tel 01 42 72 13 77
www.breizhcafe.com
À la carte €25
Closed Monday

CRÊPES

The crêpe doesn't always get the respect it deserves. Here, not far from the Musée Picasso, Bertrand Larcher (who also has restaurants in Cancale, Saint-Malo, Tokyo and Kyoto) treats it differently, relying on the excellence of his products (flour, milk, butter, cider, etc.) to make his fried egg, spinach and grated cheese crêpes and other varieties. The result, crispy on the edges and soft in the centre, is served in a timely and friendly fashion. This restaurant is so popular that this native of Brittany has just opened another one at Odéon on the Left Bank in a former pharmacy. These crêpes are just as good for what ails you as the pills once sold there.
Other location: 18, carrefour de l'Odéon, 6th, metro Odéon

CLAUDE COLLIOT

40, rue des Blancs Manteaux, 4th
Metro Rambuteau, Hôtel de Ville
Tel 01 42 71 55 45
www.claudecolliot.com
Fixed-price menus €45 to €79, à la carte €60
Closed Sunday and Monday

ORGANIC, INVENTIVE

This restaurant is an enigma. Claude Colliot has cooked for Sofia Coppola, Quentin Tarantino, Marion Cotillard, Leonardo DiCaprio, Guillaume Canet, and Katia and Marielle Labèque, but his restaurant is often deserted. Yet his precise, inventive cooking produces such surprising knockouts as raw shrimp with shiméji mushrooms, argan oil and nasturtiums, the whole brightened by a touch of acidity. Cod is nicely paired with bok choy (from the house vegetable garden in Saint-Gondon, in the Loiret *département*) and burrata sprinkled with sesame. The dining room has been redecorated by architect Patrick Bouchain for the restaurant's unpredictable clientele.

SPOTLIGHT

PARISIAN LUXURIES: DINING ALONE AND ROOM SERVICE

If you are looking to avoid a tedious one-on-one restaurant dinner, there are alternatives. One is to eat at the counter. Nothing like it for indulging one's solitude or communing with a guest. It also allows you to get to the point quickly: one course, a glass of wine and you're done. Another advantage is that you can avoid the tumult and conversation entirely and enjoy your thoughts in silence. At the hotel, room service is the ultimate dining experience in Paris. Peace and quiet, low lighting, candles, your own vintage champagne and the whole evening in front of you. Nothing can match it. Even if all you have is a club sandwich.

GRANDCŒUR

41, rue du Temple, 4th
Metro Hôtel de Ville
Tel 01 58 28 18 90
www.grandcoeur.paris
Fixed-price menu €30, à la carte €45
Closed Monday

GOURMET BRASSERIE

When summer comes and the windows are open on the dance classes in the courtyard, you might imagine that you are a character in *Les Demoiselles de Rochefort* as you listen to the martial beat of the lessons. This large restaurant is set right in the middle of it all and taps out a pretty rhythm of its own thanks to well-known chef Mauro Colagreco of the Mirazur in Menton, who works his magic for owner Julien Fouin of Glou, Jaja (the mother house), Bonvivant and Pasdeloup, sending out such dishes as marinated fish carpaccio with citrus, razor clams with herb butter, and clam ragout with peas. The terrace is wonderful and the dining room (Le Jardin) is semi-private in the evening.

NOGLU

38, rue de Saintonge, 3rd
Metro Filles du Calvaire, Temple
Tel 01 42 71 15 34
www.noglu.fr
Fixed-price menu €24, à la carte €30
Closed Monday and Tuesday

GLUTEN-FREE

The name alone might frighten you away, but this is one of the most interesting restaurants in the neighbourhood, where high-level gourmet cooking is practised with a light touch for reasonable prices and served casually. Frédérique Jules (from the restaurant Noglu, Passage des Panoramas) and her neighbour from Passage 53, Guillaume Guedj, are behind this project, but credit goes to the chef, Tsuyoshi Miyazaki, who looks like a model but applies himself to producing cuisine that rocks as much as the soundtrack playing in this virgin-white tabernacle: carrots roasted with orange coulis and fromage blanc; potato, haddock and toast soup; cod with spinach and hazelnuts. The only downside was the cheesecake, which was not quite on the same level.
Other locations: 16, passage des Panoramas, 2nd, metro Richelieu-Drouot, Grands Boulevards, tel 01 40 26 41 24; 69, rue de Grenelle, 7th, metro Rue du Bac, tel 01 58 90 18 12

ALSO IN THIS NEIGHBOURHOOD

ANAHI

49, rue Volta, 3rd
Metro République, Arts et Métiers
Tel 01 48 87 88 24
À la carte €90
Closed for lunch

MEAT, FASHIONABLE

Riccardo Giraudi, a specialist in top-of-the line beef, has reopened this former Argentinian fashion world hangout, done up by architects Humbert & Poyet. It will serve "exceptional" meats cooked by none other than former co-owner Carmina Lebrero, backed by Camille (formerly of the Belle Époque).

AU BASCOU

38, rue Réaumur, 3rd
Tel 01 42 72 69 25
www.au-bascou.fr
Closed Saturday and Sunday
Fixed-price menu €30, à la carte €50
Closed Saturday and Sunday

LEGENDARY DISHES

In game season, Bertrand Guéneron (who worked with Alain Senderens at Lucas Carton) brings together lovers of a special dish: *lièvre à la royale*, and when the season changes, a lobster fricassee made according to the recipe of a certain Dr. Parcé.

L'AMBROISIE

9, place des Vosges, 4th
Metro Saint-Paul
Tel 01 42 78 51 45
www.ambroisie-paris.com
À la carte €250
Closed Sunday and Monday

REFINED

A meal here is an impressive secular high mass featuring the cuisine of Bernard Pacaud in a melancholy decor by François-Joseph Graf that is straight out of Lampedusa's novel *The Leopard*. Memorable.

MG ROAD

205, rue Saint-Martin, 3rd
Metro Étienne Marcel
Tel 01 42 76 04 32
www.mgroadrestaurant.com
Fixed-price menu €28, à la carte €30
Closed Monday

INDIAN WITH A TWIST

One of the new generation of Indian restaurants, this Bombay-style coffee shop/canteen offers savoury dishes like tiny grenaille potatoes with crispy skin servedwwith cumin and coriander chutney, or puffed wheat with chickpeas, yoghurt and tamarind chutney. Adorable service, pleasant dining room and a sunny terrace in fine weather.

SAINT-GERMAIN-DES-PRÉS, LUXEMBOURG, QUARTIER LATIN

5TH & 6TH ARRONDISSEMENTS

Literary lights
& chic lifestyle

LA ROTONDE MONTPARNASSE

105, boulevard du Montparnasse, 6th
Metro Vavin
Tel 01 43 26 48 26
Fixed-price menu €44, à la carte €60

HISTORIC BRASSERIE

The menu here was illustrated by Kiraz, famous for his "Parisiennes" drawings. He is just one of the countless artists who have frequented La Rotonde, one of the hotspots of old Montparnasse. Opened by Victor Libion in 1911, it was then just a tavern with a terrace on the boulevard, where it attracted all the starving artists in the neighbourhood. Modigliani paid for a hot meal with a painting, and other foreign and exiled habitués included Foujita, Chaim Soutine, Pablo Picasso, Marc Chagall, Maurice de Vlaminck and their muses (among them Kiki de Montparnasse). Then there were the exiled political leaders like Leon Trotsky and Lenin. Other ghosts of the past include Pierre Mac Orlan, Georges Simenon, Jean Cocteau, Darius Milhaud and Louis Aragon. Renovated in 2013, La Rotonde has retained its cosy decoration, more Belle Époque than Roaring Twenties. The brothers Gérard and Serge Tafanelt have been at the helm for twenty-five years. Originally from the Auvergne region, they inherited the place from their Uncle Georges, who ran it as no one else could. The customers are well-bred tourists, regulars, locals and people from the publishing, newspaper and art worlds, as well as politicians, who are seated discreetly. Former French President François Hollande still has his table behind a thick curtain upstairs, and

President Emmanuel Macron celebrated the first round of the 2017 presidential elections here. On the menu: Salers-beef tartare (the best in Paris) with fat hand-cut chips, eggs mayo, *entrecôte*, *sole meunière* and all the usual Parisian bistro dishes.

LA TOUR D'ARGENT

15, quai de la Tournelle, 5th
Metro Pont Marie
Tel 01 43 54 23 31
www.tourdargent.com
Fixed-price menus €105 to €350, à la carte €250
Closed Sunday and Monday

LEGENDARY, VIEW

One of the finest moments in the world's gastronomic panorama. It starts when you leave the lift on the sixth floor, and the bluish night dramatizes the view of an enthrallingly beautiful Paris. Then the legend comes alive in a world straight out of a Jean Gabin film, with hovering service and duckling expertly carved on a small table by the maîtres d'hôtel, the pride of their profession. The cuisine has been updated, and no one seems to be complaining. The final act, the bill, is exorbitant, but you must go there at least once in your life. This is a place for simple, benevolent souls.

LE 21

21, rue Mazarine, 6th
Metro Odéon
Tel 01 46 33 76 90
À la carte €90
Closed Sunday and Monday

FISH, CHIC

Hidden from the street by an unmarked storefront and continuing the snob appeal inside with a black interior, this chic hideout is run by Didier Granier, one of two owners; his partner is none other than the legendary Paul Minchelli, who opened Le Duc with his late brother, Jean, and launched the fashion for raw fish in 1966. The fish here is often dazzling, just steamed or cooked in court bouillon with seaweed. The same adjective applies to the *mojettes de Vendée* (white beans) with *poutargue* (salted and cured fish roe) and vanilla. The chic clientele is in tune with the dark setting, and the bill is a killer – no surprise there.

LE BON SAINT-POURÇAIN

10 bis, rue Servandoni, 6th
Metro Saint-Sulpice, Saint-Germain-des-Prés
Tel 01 42 01 78 24
À la carte €65
Closed Sunday and Monday

CHIC BISTRO

What is the secret of a good restaurant? The subtle interaction between a clientele making an effort when it comes to conversation and appearance, the freshness of the fish and the quality of the service, supervised here by Dominique Léger, who worked for twenty-five years at the Café de Flore. The cuisine of Mathieu Techer (formerly of Senderens) is impressive without being spectacular, offering such standards as foie gras mi-cuit with pear chutney and rum baba with vanilla-flavoured whipped cream. An exquisite addition to the nonchalant elegance of Rue Servandoni.

LE PETIT LUTÉTIA

107, rue de Sèvres, 6th
Metro Duroc, Sèvres-Babylone
Tel 01 45 48 33 53
À la carte €60

FASHIONABLE BISTRO

Irresistibly Parisian, this Art Nouveau brewery dating from 1912 has been taken over by Jean-Louis Costes and his partner Christophe Ciamos. Both have understood how cool it is to be slightly snobby yet trashy (the entrecôte is described with a naughty word on the menu), with a little whipped cream thrown in to sweeten the mix – not unlike many Parisians themselves, who flock to the place. Pretending to be relaxed and magnificently venting their outrage, they bristle with urban acidity and borrowed smiles, all polished with perfect skin and well-nourished hair. In fine weather, the level of impudence is impressive. The food is an afterthought, and the service overwhelmed, of course.

L'ŒNOSTERIA

40, rue Grégoire de Tours, 6th
Metro Odéon
Tel 01 77 15 94 13
À la carte €35

ITALIAN CUISINE

Located near the original restaurant – the famous and dated Casa Bini (www.casabini.fr) – this little piece of Italy has an appealing, relaxed atmosphere, enhanced by wines that go down easily and such thoughtful touches as little cushions for those who go outside to smoke. Dishes include pasta specials, charcuterie platters, bruschetta and mozzarella with steamed asparagus and shavings of white truffle.

SEMILLA

54, rue de Seine, 6th
Metro Saint-Germain-des-Prés, Mabillon
Tel 01 43 54 34 50, www.semillaparis.com
Fixed-price menu €24, à la carte €50

GASTROPUB

One of the successes in this neighbourhood, Semilla is run by Drew Harre and Juan Sanchez, skilful entrepreneurs who also own Fish la Boissonnerie, Cosi, Freddy's and a wine shop on the same street, as well as La Dernière Goutte on Rue de Bourbon-le-Château, in the same arrondissement. Éric Trochon (holder of the Meilleur Ouvrier de France honour) supervises the kitchen and takes advantage of his professorship at the Ferrandi cooking school to launch fiery young thoroughbred chefs who create dishes full of sensation and flavour without going too far: sea bream ceviche with broccoli and ginger, for example, or guinea fowl with pistachio and creamy polenta. The customers suit the place, some of them celebrities and many of them English speakers, adding to the noise levels.

ALSO IN THIS NEIGHBOURHOOD

CAFÉ TRAMA

83, rue du Cherche-Midi, 6th
Metro Saint-Placide, Vaneau
Tel 01 45 48 33 71
À la carte €40
Closed Sunday and Monday

FRIENDLY BISTRO

A corner cafe with a great terrace for smokers, a bar, ceramic-tile floor and an effusive clientele clamouring for one of the best croque-monsieurs in Paris (made with bread from Poujauran and truffle salt) or the hand-chopped tartare with ginger and basil, served with golden, well-seasoned fried potatoes.

LA SOCIÉTÉ

4, place Saint-Germain-des-Prés, 6th
Metro Saint-Germain-des-Prés
Tel 01 53 63 60 60
www.restaurantlasociete.com
À la carte €80

ELEGANT

This is a hotspot for the dark side of fashion, jetsetters trying hard to remain incognito, with insolently hilarious service: "A bottle of Château-Larose, please," says the customer; "How do you want that cooked?" ripostes the waiter. The fashionable dishes are dull. It has all the ingredients of something eminently detestable yet perfect for developing our desire for what's out of our reach.

LE BAR DES PRÉS

25, rue du Dragon, 6th, metro Saint-Sulpice
Tel 01 43 25 87 67, www.cyrillignac.com
Fixed-price menu €40, à la carte €50

FRANCO-ASIAN

This clever restaurant surfs charmingly on the superficial, offering falsely innocent, playful and provocative dishes. It's a bit like a service station serving cocktails, sushi, lobster rolls, Salers beef tartare, flash-cooked salmon and sashimi to the undecided. Long counter, tables in alcoves.

LENGUÉ

31, rue de la Parcheminerie, 5th
Metro Saint-Michel, Cluny-La Sorbonne
Tel 01 46 33 75 10
Fixed-price menu €19, à la carte €30
Closed Monday and Tuesday
and for lunch Sunday

IZAKAYA

In the area around Rue de la Huchette, dotted with anonymous tourist eateries, this is a peaceful oasis, a lively and lovable *izakaya* (Japanese gastropub) that is simultaneously calm and animated. Not very big, but it's run like a tight ship.

MOISSONNIER

28, rue des Fossés-Saint-Bernard, 5th
Metro Jussieu, Cardinal Lemoine
À la carte €50
Closed Sunday and Monday

TRADITIONAL LYONNAIS

This kitschy, sentimental inn goes back in time and lovingly prepares such vintage dishes as puffy pike quenelles, *tablier de sapeur* (beef tripe), *œufs en meurette* (poached eggs in bourguignon sauce) and *œufs à la neige* (floating island).

TOYO

17, rue Jules Chaplain, 6th
Metro Vavin
Tel 01 43 54 28 03
www.restaurant-toyo.com
Fixed-price menus €39 to €115,
à la carte €60
Closed Sunday and Monday

ELEGANT JAPANESE

It must have taken great vision and talent to be Kenzo's cook for many years. Toyomitsu Nakayama produces some of the finest dishes in town. Mineral and monosyllabic.

MUSÉE D'ORSAY, INVALIDES, TOUR EIFFEL

7TH ARRONDISSEMENT

Fashionable living & ministerial elites

ARPÈGE

84, rue de Varenne, 7th
Metro Varenne
Tel 01 47 05 09 06
www.alain-passard.com
Fixed-price menus €145 to €320,
à la carte €350
Closed Saturday and Sunday

EXQUISITE VEGGIES

Alain Passard certainly wasn't the first chef to focus on vegetables (it was probably Michel Bras), but he was the one who made them glamorous and sexy. In an ill-conceived dining room designed by Lalique, with wavy glass by Bernard Pictet, Passard keeps Parisian gourmets spellbound with the art of boldly raising vegetables to new heights, at sometimes frightening prices. That said, it is all brilliant, ranging from smoking soup with hay to beautiful sushi with geranium flowers and beetroot or Milanese cabbage stuffed with multicoloured Swiss chard in a milky emulsion. Swooning customers are rewarded when the chef comes out to take the plaudits at the end.

DAVID TOUTAIN

29, rue Surcouf, 7th
Metro Invalides, La Tour Maubourg
Tel 01 45 50 11 10
www.davidtoutain.com
Fixed-price menus €55 to €110
Closed Saturday and Sunday

CREATIVE

Here is a striker who has worked in high-stress situations (for chefs Marc Veyrat, Pierre Gagnaire and Alain Passard) and found his own vocabulary. The trends of the moment apply (fixed mealtimes, no-choice tasting menu), but the rewards are there: crispy beetroot with blackberries

OPEN AFTER MIDNIGHT

On the Left Bank, you can eat at **CASTEL**, if you manage to get in, until 12:30am in Le Foyer or the restaurant, with its fashionable dishes. In the same genre, but a few notches below, is **HIBOU** (12:45am), at the Carrefour de l'Odéon. Or cross Boulevard Saint-Germain and go to **IPPUDO** (12:45am on Friday and Saturday, midnight every other day) for ramen or to **ROSEBUD** (2am). **LA COUPOLE** (12:45am) is open, but the food is less than inspiring. On the other side of the river, the Right Bank offers **LE COSTES** (2am), with a chic crowd but uninteresting food. For something more satisfying, the meats at **LA MAISON DE L'AUBRAC** will do the trick, while **LA MAISON DU CAVIAR** lives up to its name. **LE GRAND AMOUR** (like its little brother L'Amour) is open until 12:30am, serving smart dishes, as is **MAMA SHELTER** (1:20am), with its pizzas. **JOE ALLEN** (12:30am) remains faithful to American food and late hours. **DERSOU** (midnight) offers bistronomic cooking and cocktails. Or try **LA CAVE DU PAUL BERT** (midnight). The tireless **LE TAMBOUR** (5 or 6am) and **LA TOUR DE MONTLHÉRY–CHEZ DENISE** (5am) stick to the classics (tartare, chips, meats). Then, of course, there is the inevitable onion soup at **AU PIED DE COCHON** (24/7).

AU PIED DE COCHON 6, rue Coquillère, 1st, metro Les Halles, tel 01 40 13 77 00, www.pieddecochon.com

CASTEL 15, rue Princesse, 6th, metro Mabillon, Saint-Sulpice, tel 01 40 51 52 80, www.castelparis.com

DERSOU 21, rue Saint-Nicolas, 12th, metro Ledru-Rollin, tel 09 81 01 12 73, www.dersouparis.com

GRAND AMOUR HOTEL 18, rue de la Fidélité, 10th, metro Gare de l'Est, tel 01 44 16 03 30. www.hotelamourparis.fr/grandamour

IPPUDO 14, rue Grégoire de Tours, 6th, metro Odéon, Mabillon, tel 01 42 38 21 99, www.ippudo.fr

JOE ALLEN 30, rue Pierre Lescot, 1st, metro Étienne Marcel, tel 01 42 36 70 13, www.joeallenparis.com

LA CAVE DU PAUL BERT 16, rue Paul Bert, 11th, metro Faidherbe-Chaligny, tel 01 58 50 92

LA COUPOLE 102, boulevard du Montparnasse, 14th, metro Montparnasse, Vavin, 14th, tel 01 43 20 14 20, www.lacoupole-paris.com

LA MAISON DE L'AUBRAC 37, rue Marbeuf, 8th, metro Franklin D. Roosevelt, tel 01 43 59 05 14, www.maison-aubrac.com

LA MAISON DU CAVIAR 21, rue Quentin Bauchart, 8th, metro George V, tel 01 47 23 53 43, www.caviar-volga.com

LA TOUR DE MONTLHÉRY – CHEZ DENISE 5, rue des Prouvaires, 1st, metro Les Halles, tel 01 42 36 21 82

LE COSTES 239, rue Saint-Honoré, 1st, metro Palais-Royal–Musée du Louvre, Pyramides, tel 01 42 44 50 25, www.hotelcostes.com

LE HIBOU 16, carrefour de l'Odéon, 6th, metro Odéon, tel 01 43 54 96 91, www.lehibouparis.fr

LE TAMBOUR 41, rue Montmartre, 2nd, metro Sentier, tel 01 42 33 06 90

MAMA SHELTER 109, rue de Bagnolet, 20th, metro Alexandre Dumas, Gambetta, tel 01 43 48 48 48, www.mamashelter.com

ROSEBUD 11bis, rue Delambre, 14th, metro Vavin, tel 01 43 35 38 54

and red onions; slow-cooked eggs with peas and peaches; cod in combava foam with trout roe and cockles; smoked eel with black sesame cream and diced green apple. This is powerful stuff that is also often good. Studious atmosphere and assiduous service.

LE VOLTAIRE

27, quai Voltaire, 7th
Metro Rue du Bac, Solferino
Tel 01 42 61 17 49
À la carte €120
Closed Sunday and Monday

CLASSIC

The perfect place for anyone nostalgic for the France of old, this highly civilized cigar box of a restaurant has an unchanging menu with outrageous prices, with one startling exception: the egg mayonnaise "James" for 90 cents (add truffles in season and the price rises to €79). The *sole meunière* costs €62, the steak tartare €48 and so on. It's a sign of just how chic this place is. It recently changed hands, acquired by the Bullier brasserie. The debonair servers like to discreetly share jokes behind the backs of their customers. The traditional cuisine might be termed grandmother-style, even if none of the customers ever had such a conservative grandmother, so let's call it "bourgeois".

RACINES DES PRÉS

1, rue de Gribeauval, 7th
Metro Rue du Bac
Tel 01 45 48 14 16
Fixed-price menus €29 and €33, à la carte €50
Closed for lunch Saturday and all day Sunday

CHIC BISTRO

When you have a clever restaurant entrepreneur (David Lanher) who knows how to put the proper ingredients together, the recipe is always a success. After Racines, Vivant, the Crèmerie and the Bon Saint Pourçain, here he is again in a forgotten corner of the seventh arrondissement with a restaurant that took off right away. Lanher put a pro in the kitchen – Alexandre Navarro, formerly of the Plaza Athénée, Pré Catelan and Racines 2 – who creates dishes that are simple, slightly sophisticated and a bit insolent. A few examples: roast chicken with a confit thigh, broad-bean stew and peas with marjoram, and line-caught fillet of pollock with spinach and wild garlic. Desserts are just as cheeky, while the service is lively and the setting comfortable.

SYLVESTRE

Hôtel Thoumieux, 1st floor,
79, rue Saint-Dominique, 7th
Metro La Tour Maubourg
Tel 01 47 05 79 79
www.thoumieux.com
Fixed-price menus €85 to €350
Closed Sunday and Monday, and for lunch except on Thursday and Friday

INTIMATE, GASTRONOMIC

Succeeding chef Jean-François Piège is no picnic. It had to be done very well and quickly with the help of the restaurant's owner, Thierry Costes. Sylvestre Wahid, born in Pakistan, has worked for many great shops and restaurants (Alain Ducasse, Thierry Marx, Oustau de Baumanière, Courchevel, etc.). His cuisine resembles him: calm and sharp. In the calm, leafy setting of the restaurant redecorated by India Mahdavi, he offers pastoral cuisine that makes use of the latest techniques, such as wild duckling from Madame Burgaud lacquered with citrus fruits and Sansho pepper, and served with baby endives and radicchio. The attractive, attentive servers contribute to the Parisian club atmosphere. At the brasserie on the ground floor (tel 01 47 05 49 75), the prices are four times lower and the decibels ten times higher.

ALSO IN THIS NEIGHBOURHOOD

DIVELLEC

18, rue Fabert, 7th
Metro Invalides
Tel 01 45 51 91 96
www.divellec-paris.fr
Fixed-price menus €55 to €190

SMART BRASSERIE

This fine restaurant, which was slowly disappearing like an autumn leaf, has benefited from the arrival of Mathieu Pacaud of L'Ambroisie, reportedly with wheelbarrows full of banknotes; the renovation alone is said to have cost €8 million. This electroshock has produced its effect, and the restaurant has come back to life with a solid menu featuring such dishes as tuna pastilla and John Dory with sorrel, judiciously accompanied by Paimpol beans and *mostarda* from Cremona. Showy service.

GAYA RIVE GAUCHE

44, rue du Bac, 7th
Metro Rue du Bac
Tel 01 45 44 73 73
www.pierre-gagnaire.com
Fixed-price menu €65, à la carte €80
Closed Sunday and Monday

CREATIVE, CHIC

The second branch in Paris of Pierre Gagnaire's restaurant offers a sort of jazzy interpretation of his wonderful flagship. Eating here feels like listening to a trio, with the slow, sensual sound of metal brushing cymbals of the John Dory with piquillos and lemon grilled with Espelette pepper and served with white beetroot purée and mustard. A bit stilted, but otherwise perfect.

LA LAITERIE SAINTE CLOTILDE

64, rue de Bellechasse, 7th
Metro Rue du Bac, Varenne
Tel 01 45 51 74 61
Fixed-price menu €25, à la carte €40
Closed Sunday

CASUAL LOCAL EATERY

A peaceful, quiet, classic place for the demanding clientele of the seventh arrondissement, serving such dishes as burrata with figs, mint and nuts; grilled beefsteak with grenaille potatoes; and tasty desserts. The service is friendly and courteous.

L'INCONNU

4, rue Pierre Leroux, 7th
Metro Vaneau, Saint-François-Xavier
Tel 01 53 69 06 03
www.restaurant-linconnu.fr
Fixed-price menus €40 to €80
Closed for dinner on Sunday
and all day Monday

ITALIAN JAPANESE

A Japanese chef (Koji Higaki, formerly of Passage 53) cooking Italian food? Yes, but not Roman or Osaka style, but rather subtle Venetian (or Kyoto) style, with no ostentation. The decor is uninspired, but the meal is a real trip.

FAUBOURG SAINT-HONORÉ, CHAMPS-ÉLYSÉES, MADELEINE, MONCEAU

8TH ARRONDISSEMENT

Gilded neighbourhoods & luxury labels

LA SCÈNE

Hôtel Prince de Galles,
33, avenue George V, 8th
Metro George V
Tel 01 53 23 77 77
www.restaurant-la-scene.fr
Fixed-price menu €65, à la carte €90
Closed for lunch Saturday and all day Sunday

GASTRONOMIC, INVENTIVE

Stéphanie Le Quellec (formerly of the George V and Terre Blanche in the Var) runs a tight ship and offers cuisine that is both classic (pan-roasted veal rib) and risky (pigeon with cucumber – it works!). The handsome marble-decorated dining room was designed by Bruno Borrione, the anonymous clientele knows how to behave, and the attentive servers have a didactic side.

LE CLARENCE

Hôtel Dillon, 31, avenue Franklin D. Roosevelt, 8th
Metro Franklin D. Roosevelt, Champs-Élysées-Clemenceau
Tel 01 82 82 10 10
www.le-clarence.paris
Fixed-price menus €65 to €320, à la carte €400
Closed Sunday and Monday

ELEGANT, GASTRONOMIC

Christophe Pelé's restaurant is located in the magnificent Hôtel Dillon, renovated after four years' work. His cuisine takes purity to a new level of modernity in classical dishes made with great precision: prawns and pig's foot with capers; *sole meunière* and shellfish emulsion; turbot roasted with wild fennel; grilled prime rib of beef and so on. The nimble service, directed by an expert, Antoine Petrus, is as exacting as the cuisine. The prices are predictably scathing.

LE GRAND RESTAURANT

7, rue d'Aguesseau, 8th
Metro Madeleine
Tel 01 53 05 00 00
www.jeanfrancoispiege.com
Fixed-price menus €85 to €560, à la carte €350
Closed Saturday and Sunday

INTIMATE FINE DINING

Jean-François Piège, who now has several restaurants, including Clover and Clover Grill, has understood that one must sometimes assert oneself and leave the support system behind (he previously worked for others at Thoumieux, the Crillon and Alain Ducasse). Now he has boldly (or foolishly) chosen the name "Le Grand Restaurant" (a reference to the famous film with Louis de Funès) for his latest enterprise. Located near the Elysée Palace, it seats only twenty-five. He backs up the name with such dishes as prawns cooked in their shells in fish jus, served with nasturtium leaves and iced turnips. The decor is contemporary, the clientele what you would expect, and, for once, the chef is in the kitchen.

PIERRE GAGNAIRE

6, rue Balzac, 8th, metro George V
Tel 01 58 36 12 50
www.pierre-gagnaire.com
Fixed-price menus €155 to €350, à la carte €400
Closed Saturday and Sunday

GOURMET, ICONIC

Undoubtedly the best restaurant in Paris for its untiring inventiveness inspired by that magical element of gastronomy: doubt. Unlike other great chefs who are attached to their orthodoxy, Pierre Gagnaire takes risks and sometimes slips up, the better to open up new horizons. An example: blanquette of farm-fed calf

SPOTLIGHT

THE TIME IS NOT THE HOUR!

Paris as always, has a complicated relationship with mealtimes. Increasingly, business lunches are scheduled between 12:15pm and 12:30pm, the idea being to finish at 2pm. As a result, it is no longer possible to reserve for those times. The same is true for dinner at 8:30pm. "Ah non, c'est pas possible!" is heard more and more often. In the last decade or so, schedules have changed and, paradoxically, early dinners have become the latest chic, at 7 or 7:30pm, the so-called "German dinner hour", before the "tourists" fill the dining room and the service slows down. Booking in advance requires similar gymnastics. The best tables are taken well ahead of time, sometimes even before the restaurant has opened, infuriating many potential customers. The best technique is to stop by the restaurant yourself or send a friend and ask what's available, which means you must have a very flexible schedule. Or try having a meal at the counter, alone or with a friend, and enjoying the peace and swift service: a dream come true.

veiled with lemon and served with parsnips and nasturtium leaves. The setting is classic, with contemporary touches, and the service imbued with the iconoclastic spirit of the place. Not everything here is understandable, but please persevere; take inspiration from the chef and move forward. The reward will be a memorable experience.

RELAIS PLAZA

Hôtel Plaza Athénée,
21, avenue Montaigne, 8th
Metro Alma-Marceau, Franklin D. Roosevelt
Tel 01 53 67 64 00
www.plaza-athenee-paris.fr
Fixed-price menu €54, à la carte €120

ART DECO, CLASSICAL

This illustrious Paris restaurant has been nicely done up without losing the patinated appeal of its cruise-ship-style Art Deco interior (inspired by the *Normandie*). We owe it all to the restaurant's sporty director, Werner Küchler, who has the manners of a diplomat and occasionally picks up the microphone to belt out Frank Sinatra's greatest hits with real class. The food, strangely, is always slightly disappointing, with a classical repertory (Viennese veal scallop, roast chicken, steak tartare) competently prepared. The clientele remains loyal, with a notable cast of characters. It's livelier at lunch and cosier in the evening, offering the observant some memorable sights. The dining room is also filled with ghosts from the past. Herbert von Karajan, for example, sat at table 20 (on the left) and always dined on vegetable soup, *sole meunière* and a carafe of Burgundy.

ALSO IN THIS NEIGHBOURHOOD

CHEZ ANDRÉ

12, rue Marbeuf, 8th
Metro Alma-Marceau
Tel 01 47 20 59 57
www.chez-andre.com
À la carte €50

CHIC BRASSERIE

Founded in 1936, this brasserie so typical of the eighth arrondissement is full of Jacques Dutronc-style nostalgia. It has a 1930s decor and scrupulous, hovering service. Predictable brasserie dishes such as *sole meunière*, frogs' legs, seafood and tartare.

CHEZ MONSIEUR

11, rue du Chevalier
de Saint-George, 8th
Metro Madeleine
Tel 01 42 60 14 36
www.chezmonsieur.fr
À la carte €50

CLASSIC BRASSERIE

The tablecloths may have disappeared, but this restaurant (formerly the Royal Madeleine) still has the feisty spirit of a Parisian brasserie with all its vivacity. On the menu: veal blanquette, beef cheeks and *sole meunière* prepared in front of you. The authentic atmosphere is regularly disrupted by tables full of Fashion Week participants, drunk on themselves and on Paris.

LAURENT

41, avenue Gabriel, 8th
Metro Champs-Élysées-Clemenceau
Tel 01 42 25 00 39
www.le-laurent.com
Closed for lunch Saturday
and all day Sunday

CLASSIC, ELEGANT

This is where you can take the pulse of Paris's financial health as all the heavyweights in the field feed on spider crab en gelée. Beautiful terrace in fine weather.

LE 114 FAUBOURG

Hôtel Le Bristol, 114, rue du Faubourg
Saint-Honoré, 8th
Metro Miromesnil
Tel 01 53 43 44 44
www.lebristolparis.com
Fixed-price menus €56 and €114,
à la carte €90
Closed for lunch Saturday and Sunday

REFINED, CREATIVE

The main restaurant at the Bristol is, of course, **ÉRIC FRÉCHON'S EPICURE** (tel 01 53 43 43 40), but the brasserie in this grand hotel is one of the pleasant enigmas of the Paris restaurant world, with its improbable decoration featuring multi-coloured dahlias and a monumental staircase decorated with gold leaf. Much of the credit goes to the service directed by Patrice Jeanne, one of the most courteous in Paris (and thus the world), who supervises an eager young team enamoured of their craft. Thanks to them, the food goes down easily, with such dishes as a superb duck pâté; fried frogs' legs with fried onions; 500-gram sole with spinach shoots and virgin olive oil with capers.

LE GRIFFONNIER

8, rue des Saussaies, 8th
Metro Miromesnil
Tel 01 42 65 17 17
Closed for dinner except Thursday
and closed Saturday and Sunday
À la carte €50
Closed Saturday and Sunday
and for dinner except on Thursday

TRADITIONAL BISTRO

A magnificent survivor, saved by its king crab salad and kale and such classics as dishes with sauces, egg mayonnaise, dried sausage, the legendary stuffed cabbage and cheeses. Lively atmosphere.

LE STRESA

7, rue Chambiges, 8th
Metro Alma-Marceau, George V
Tel 01 47 23 51 62
www.lestresa.com
À la carte €80
Closed Saturday and Sunday

LEGENDARY ITALIAN

Time seems to have stopped at Le Stresa, where the clocks give the right time only twice a day. That suits its customers just fine; they are like big children who do not want to hear new stories, only the old familiar ones they have been hearing for the past fifty years. The tide recedes slowly, and so does celebrity and one's hairline. It's time for the Stresa to put a scarf around its neck. Its dishes are nicely dated and very expensive (*pizzetta* with white truffle, rigatoni). Inimitable, fortunately. It's all very Belmondo.

MINI PALAIS

Grand Palais, 3, avenue Winston Churchill,
8th, metro Champs-Élysées-Clemenceau
Tel 01 42 56 42 42
www.minipalais.com
À la carte €50

ATMOSPHERIC

With its imperial columns, immense spaces, south-facing terrace, view of the Napoleon III bridge and menu created by Éric Fréchon of the Bristol, you can count on an aesthetically delicious meal here.

NEVA CUISINE

2, rue de Berne, 8th
Metro Rome
Tel 01 45 22 18 91
www.nevacuisineparis.com
Fixed-price menu €45,
à la carte €55
Closed Saturday and Sunday

REFINED, UNPRETENTIOUS

The current gourmet tumult in the calm 8th arrondissement was initiated by the Mexican chef Beatriz Gonzalez, backed by pastry chef Yannick Tranchant. In a banal setting, she serves on-target dishes like duck foie gras with brioche and maracujà jelly, and a memorable beef tail.

PENATI AL BARETTO

Hôtel de Vigny, 9-11, rue Balzac, 8th
Metro George V
Tel 01 42 99 80 00
www.penatialbaretto.eu
Fixed-price menus €45 and €65
Closed Saturday and Sunday

LUXURIOUS ITALIAN

This is a cosy place, which softens the effects of the bill. Sit down, pick delicately at your food (we can highly recommend the beautifully seasoned and deeply flavoured pappardelle with hare stew). You will leave the restaurant a happy person.

OPÉRA, PIGALLE, FAUBOURGS MONTMARTRE AND POISSONNIÈRE

9TH ARRONDISSEMENT

Saucy streets & bohemian chic

BELLE MAISON

4, rue de Navarin, 9th
Metro Pigalle, Saint-Georges
Tel 01 42 81 11 00
À la carte €50
Closed Sunday and Monday

SEAFOOD

The decor was designed by Émilie Bonaventure, with azulejos on the walls and wooden tables in a tribute to the beach located on the wild coast of the French island Île d'Yeu. The owners of Pantruche and Caillebotte have now added this fish restaurant to their stable of restaurants. On the menu, whelks from Normandy with hay mayonnaise, quality seafood plates and simple dishes carefully made, such as Brittany scallops with purée of parsnips and Brittany turbot with celery, New Zealand spinach and smoked-chestnut broth. Happy (and loud) customers.

Other locations: PANTRUCHE 3, rue Victor Massé, 9th, metro Saint-Georges, Pigalle, tel 01 48 78 55 60 **CAILLEBOTTE** 8, rue Hippolyte Lebas, 9th, metro Notre-Dame-de-Lorette, tel 01 53 20 88 70

LES AFFRANCHIS

5, rue Henry Monnier, 9th
Metro Saint-Georges
Tel 01 45 26 26 30
www.lesaffranchisrestaurant.com
Fixed-price menu €35, à la carte €45
Closed Monday

ELEGANT BISTRO

Set in the heights of the ninth arrondissement, this seemingly ordinary bistro is run by two chefs (Keenan Ballois and Enrico Bertazzo) with highly impressive

SPOTLIGHT

THE DOUBLE NATURE OF RESTAURANTS

Since things are constantly changing and customers are becoming more volatile and contradictory, restaurant owners are now trying to present a united front. While a single imposed menu is losing favour, other types of set menus are multiplying to such an extent that a single restaurant may go from one to another. While they might have a minimal workers' menu at lunchtime, with just one course and a coffee, in the evening they may offer more complex and costlier options. Some dress up with tablecloths and real napkins and bring in better-paid staff to justify prices that double or even triple. Cocktails become available, and eyes are rolled if you don't order one. Some places now close at lunchtime and just serve more profitable dinners.

backgrounds (the Bristol, the Arpège, the Atelier Joël Robuchon, L'Ambroisie). The energy levels here are high and the dishes competitive: slow-cooked egg carbonara, velvety pea soup with smoked herring, John Dory with baby vegetables, lamb with thyme and peas. It's lively and very good. What more do you need to know? Reserve.

PÉTRELLE

34, rue Pétrelle, 9th, metro Anvers
Tel 01 42 82 11 02, www.petrelle.fr
À la carte €80
Closed Sunday and Monday

NOSTALGIC, QUIRKY

A restaurant stuck in the past, all sepia and nostalgia, with its daubes, thyme, lamb and grandma's recipes. Go with an open attitude and a forgiving heart to appreciate the work of a real chef (Jean-Luc André), and don't be shocked when you see the prices. The perfect decor is like a dandy's retreat, with its curtains, chandeliers, stacks of books and fringed lampshades. Appealingly dark.

ALSO IN THIS NEIGHBOURHOOD

ABRI SOBA

10, rue Saulnier, 9th, metro Cadet
No phone
Fixed-price menus €14 and €21, à la carte €30
Closed Sunday and Monday

AUTHENTIC JAPANESE

A branch of the brilliant Abri (where reserving a table is almost impossible). Here, the buckwheat noodles are made fresh in the morning by the graceful cooks labouring in the steamy open kitchen, watched by enchanted customers. Attentive service. **Other location:** **ABRI** 92, rue du Faubourg Poissonnière, 9th, tel 01 83 97 00 00

BOUILLON

47, rue de Rochechouart, 9th
Metro Anvers, Cadet
Tel 09 51 18 66 59
À la carte €40
Closed Sunday and Monday

FASHIONABLE BISTRO

Up-to-date food cooked by Marc Favier, who used to work for Jean-François Piège. All the trends of the moment are put to work with great mastery, notably in the broth of "real" mushrooms of Paris (button mushrooms), duck foie gras, celery and coriander. Lively clientele.

RÉPUBLIQUE, CANAL SAINT-MARTIN, GARE DU NORD

10TH & 11TH ARRONDISSEMENTS

Working-class areas & bobo strongholds

ALBION

80, rue du Faubourg Poissonnière, 10th
Metro Poissonnière
Tel 01 42 46 02 44
www.restaurantalbion.fr
À la carte €45
Closed Sunday and Saturday

BRETON BISTRO, WINE BAR

Matthew Ong and Hayden Clout once worked at Fish Boissonnerie (6th) and now they have their own lively gastropub-style wine shop and restaurant. It's usually packed with customers deep in conversation as they dine on green-bean gazpacho with pan-fried cuttlefish; medallion of cod with mash and olive oil, liquid tapenade, piperade and whole roasted green onion; or octopus from Galicia a la plancha. The relaxed clientele enjoys the wine selection and the very British desserts, which eschew cream.

CARTET

65, rue de Malte, 9th
Metro République
Tel 01 48 05 17 65
À la carte €90
Closed Saturday and Sunday

LYONNAIS

This place is a true enigma. The owner does all the cooking and serving himself, often serving only two tables, with the door locked. You may feel like you are in a David Lynch film in this setting with an almond-green banquette and Art Deco woodwork. Solid terrines, veal kidneys, *bœuf à la ficelle* (poached beef with vegetables) and duck breast with pepper. These plain Lyon-inspired dishes also seem to have been extracted from the past. The rich desserts are made in the afternoon. In fact, this restaurant is almost nonexistent.

LE BISTROT PAUL BERT

18, rue Paul Bert, 11th
Metro Faidherbe-Chaligny
Tel 01 43 72 24 01
Fixed-price menus €20 and €41,
à la carte €50
Closed Sunday and Monday

CLASSIC BISTRO

This is the archetypical bistro, steeped in nostalgia but never lowering its guard thanks to a staunch captain, Bertrand Auboyneau, who watches over everything from the grain of the meat (the *pavé au poivre*, or pepper steak, is spectacular) to the colour of the chips and the depth of the meringue on the floating island. Customers come to relax in a vintage decor, served by staff that keep up the pace. Nice wine list and prices kept within bounds.

SEPTIME

80, rue de Charonne, 11th
Metro Charonne, Ledru-Rollin
Tel 01 43 67 38 29
www.septime-charonne.fr
Fixed-price menus €42 to €80
Closed all day Saturday and Sunday
and for lunch Monday

HIGH FIDELITY BISTRO

Made famous by the foodie craze, Bertrand Grébaut (who used to work with Alain Passard) has realized that there is no need to change. He continues to concentrate on quality producers and seasonal foods, serving such dishes as raw venison with tarragon and Kalamata olives; Saint-Jean whiting with endives and orange butter; quail with carrots and mild spices. The clientele seems to be hypnotized by it all, like deer in headlights.

VIVANT

43, rue des Petites Écuries, 10th
Metro Bonne Nouvelle, Cadet
Tel 01 42 46 43 55
www.vivantparis.com
À la carte €45
Closed Saturday and Sunday

COUNTER CULTURE

A young chef, Pierre Touitou, has arrived at this restaurant, leaving behind the injunctions of his mentors (at Sketch in London, the Plaza Athénée and Kei in Paris, and Mostrador Santa Teresita in Uruguay) for pastoral cuisine featuring dishes like fennel consommé, asparagus, bonito and broccoli, and fresh turbot. The names of the dishes are barely half a line long, perfect for the youthful clientele. In the dining room, Félix Godart (formerly of Saturne) offers a comprehensive list of natural wines. We recommend sitting at the counter.

ALSO IN THIS NEIGHBOURHOOD

BOTANIQUE

71, rue de la Folie-Méricourt, 11th
Metro Oberkampf, République, Parmentier
Tel 01 47 00 27 80
www.botaniquerestaurant.com
Fixed-price menu €55, à la carte €60
Closed Sunday and Monday

APPLIED GASTRONOMY

Sugio Yamaguchi (who has worked with Pierre-Sang Boyer, Nicolas Le Bec and Georges Blanc) has teamed up with a sommelier, Alexandre Philippe, in a two-storey establishment (restaurant upstairs, tapas bistro downstairs). His lively, inventive cuisine includes such dishes as lobster ravioli with spinach and vegetables, subtly flavoured with *dashi* (lobster broth), or simple Angus beef. The ingredients often take precedence over flavours and their tendency to dominate. Very interesting.

BRUTOS

5, rue du Général Renault, 11th
Metro Saint-Ambroise, Voltaire
Tel 01 48 06 98 97
À la carte €45
Closed Monday and Tuesday and for lunch

SOUTH AMERICAN GRILL

In a rough-hewn setting, Lucas Baur de Campos (who trained at Robuchon, then at the Ministry of Foreign Affairs) and his companion, Ninon Camille Lecomte, take inspiration from South America for their grilled meats cooked on a wood fire, natural wines and vegetables. Vibrant.

L'ÉCAILLER DU BISTROT

22, rue Paul Bert, 11th
Metro Faidherbe-Chaligny
Tel 01 43 72 76 77
Fixed-price menu €20, à la carte €60
Closed Sunday and Monday

SEAFOOD

Noblesse oblige, Gwenaëlle Cadoret (from a family of oyster farmers in Brittany) runs her seafood restaurant with the highest standards. No compromise is possible when it comes to the gleaming sole, pearly oysters and other fine dishes, always fresh and sometimes raw. You'd have to go a long way to find better.

LES ARLOTS

136, rue du Faubourg Poissonnière, 10th
Metro Barbès-Rochechouart, Gare du Nord
Tel 01 42 82 92 01
À la carte €35
Closed Sunday and Monday

WINE BAR

Chef Thomas Brachet pampers his customers with wonderful homemade sausages and whipped charlotte potatoes, or roast free-range chicken with Simmental beef tartare. In the dining room, sommelier Tristan Renoux finds the right vintages to pair with them. The clientele is clearly enamoured of the place despite the uncomfortable chairs.

LE SERVAN

32, rue Saint-Maur, 11th
Metro Voltaire, Père Lachaise
Tel 01 55 28 51 82
Closed Saturday and Sunday,
and for lunch Monday
Fixed-price menu €27, à la carte €45

FASHIONABLE BISTRO

Katia and Tatiana Levha enliven this restaurant with their cheerful enthusiasm and spontaneous, wide-ranging cooking. One example: baked turbot presented at the table. Clientele of enthusiastic local foodies.

MOKONUTS

5, rue Saint-Bernard, 11th
Metro Faidherbe-Chaligny
Tel 09 80 81 82 85
À la carte €25
Closed Saturday and Sunday

COSY CANTEEN

Moko Hirayama (former pastry chef at Yam'Tcha) and Omar Koreitem (who used to work at Sergent Recruteur) send out irresistible little dishes like roasted kabocha (Japanese squash) with tahini sauce (crushed sesame seeds) for €7. It's a small place, and the few tables fill up quickly. Private dinners for at least four people can be had for €40 per person.

RETRÒ BOTTEGA

12, rue Saint-Bernard, 11th
Metro Faidherbe-Chaligny
Tel 01 74 64 17 39
À la carte €45
Closed for lunch except on Saturday

INTIMATE ITALIAN

The energetic Pietro Russano, formerly of Rino, offers a cheerful Italian menu featuring, among other things, Italian asparagus with artisanal Parma ham, bread crumbs and citrus vinaigrette; or homemade tagliatelle with courgettes, Carpino broad beans, fresh herbs, organic Piedmont hazelnuts and salted ricotta from Puglia. Watch out for the strong wines.

SOT L'Y LAISSE

70, rue Alexandre Dumas, 11th
Metro Avron, Alexandre Dumas
Tel 01 40 09 79 20
Fixed-price menu €24, à la carte €60
Closed Saturday and Sunday,
and for lunch Monday

REFINED BISTRO

The dining room here couldn't be simpler, but the kitchen is run by Eiji Doihara, who has partnered with Hide Ishizuka of the Petit Verdot and is mad about French cuisine. He cooks sensual, sensational dishes as fricassee of poultry oysters with confit mushrooms and grilled leeks or roasted mallard duck with orange sauce. Akiko, his wife, watches over the dining room, filled with a noisy crowd of fans.

VANTRE

19, rue de la Fontaine-au-Roi, 11th
Metro Goncourt, Parmentier, République
Tel 01 48 06 16 96, www.vantre.fr
Fixed-price menu €24, à la carte €45
Closed Saturday and Sunday

MODERN FRENCH FARE

Iacopo Chomel, a former chef at Passage and Saturne, and Marco Pelletier, once the sommelier at the Bristol and a great guy who knows wine like the back of his hand, take care of the food and wine here. The forthright cuisine offers such dishes as gnocchi with sage and John Dory with Jerusalem artichokes and pomelos, served in a dining room with marble tables and oak parquet.

THE CITY SPECIAL

CHICKEN AND CHIPS

It's easy to make but hard to make well: chicken and chips is one of those traditional dishes that Parisians love, but that chefs hesitate to make because they don't always succeed. Best to go to upscale restaurants like the Relais Plaza, where Werner Küchler officiates and the bird is carved at the table.
Or that fabulous bistro Chez L'Ami Louis, which makes some connoisseurs snort with indignation but enchants those who love lively, high-priced restaurants.
If you opt for a local bistro, watch out for places that reheat a pre-cooked chicken. It is best to find a place that cooks it fresh, even if it takes an hour.
And avoid this dish entirely at the Café du Flore, where it is simply inedible.

ALLARD 41, rue Saint-André-des-Arts, 6th, metro Saint-Michel, tel 01 58 00 23 42, www.restaurant-allard.fr

ATELIER MAÎTRE ALBERT 1, rue Maître Albert, 5th, metro Maubert-Mutualité, tel 01 56 81 30 01, www.ateliermaitrealbert.com

AUBERGE BRESSANE 16, avenue de la Motte-Picquet, 7th, metro La Tour Maubourg, École Militaire, tel 01 47 05 98 37, www.auberge-bressane.com

CHEZ FLOTTES 2, rue Cambon, 1st, metro Concorde, tel 01 42 60 80 89, http://flottes.fr

CHEZ L'AMI LOUIS 32, rue du Bertbois, 3rd, metro Arts et Métiers, République, tel 01 48 87 77 48, www.chez-l-ami-louis.zenchef.com

CLOVER GRILL 6, rue Bailleul, 1st, metro Louvre-Rivoli, tel 01 40 41 59 59, www.clover-grill.com

D'CHEZ EUX 2, avenue Lowendal, 7th, metro École Militaire, tel 01 47 05 52 55, www.chezeux.com

DROUANT 16-18, rue Gaillon, 2nd, metro Opéra, Quatre Septembre, tel 01 42 65 15 16, www.drouant.com

JEANNE A. 42, rue Jean-Pierre Timbaud, 11th, metro Parmentier, tel 01 43 55 09 49, www.jeanne-a-comestibles.com

J'GO 4, rue Drouot, 9th, metro Richelieu-Drouot, tel 01 40 22 09 09, www.lejgo.com

LE COQ RICO 98, rue Lepic, 18th, metro Lamarck-Caulaincourt, Abbesses, tel 01 42 59 82 89, www.lecoqrico.com

LE PÈRE CLAUDE 51, avenue de la Motte-Picquet, 15th, metro La Motte-Picquet-Grenelle, tel 01 47 34 03 05, www.lepereclaude.fr

LE RELAIS PLAZA Hôtel Plaza Athénée, 21, avenue Montaigne, 8th, metro Alma Marceau, tel 01 53 67 64 00, www.alain-ducasse.com

LA RÔTISSERIE D'ARGENT 9, quai de la Tournelle, 5th, metro Pont Marie, tel 01 43 54 17 47

BASTILLE, NATION, BERCY

12TH ARRONDISSEMENT

Outliers & countercurrents

PASSERINI

65, rue Traversière, 12th
Metro Ledru-Rollin
Tel 01 43 42 27 56, www.passerini.paris
Fixed-price menus €30 to €48, à la carte €50
Closed Sunday and Monday,
and for lunch Tuesday

MODERN ITALIAN

In a restaurant decorated by Asma Architects, Giovanni Passerini (former chef at Rino) and his partner, Justine Prot, serve up powerful dishes like the jaw-dropping calf's head *caserecce alla Genovese* with tuna *poutargue* (salted, cured roe) and lemon. The atmosphere is studious, with the gourmet nomenklatura dissecting and analysing each dish with fancy words. On Saturday evening, Passerini, which does not take reservations, becomes an enoteca and offers "good bottles and shared small plates".

TABLE

3, rue de Prague, 12th
Metro Ledru-Rollin
Tel 01 43 43 12 26
www.tablerestaurant.fr
Fixed-price menu €29, à la carte €100
Closed Saturday and Sunday

OPEN KITCHEN

Bruno Verjus, a hedonistic blogger and literate gastronome, has decorated his restaurant with curvy metal furnishings and has thrown himself into the fray. His cooking is elliptical, druidic, mineral: mozzarella served with just a piece of rhubarb and another of smoked eel; line-caught meagre with wild garlic and a carrot that is almost a work of art. He now has a serious following and some critics. Far from stock excellence, this is quiet purity.

VIRTUS

8, rue Crozatier, 12th
Metro Faidherbe-Challigny, Reuilly-Diderot
Tel 09 80 68 08 08, www.virtus-paris.com
Fixed-price menu €59.50, à la carte €50
Closed Sunday and Monday

CREATIVE CUISINE

In this long, narrow restaurant redecorated by the Marcelo Joulia (Unico, Ferme Saint-Simon), Chiho Kanzaki and Marcelo di Giacomo (who both worked at Mirazur in Menton) have scored a huge hit with their intrepid cooking, exemplified by scallops with cauliflower and green apple and the even more precise bonito with salsify and black sesame sauce.

ALSO IN THIS NEIGHBOURHOOD

DO ET RIZ

31, rue de Cotte, 12th, metro Ledru-Rollin
Tel 01 43 45 57 13
À la carte €15
Closed Sunday

VIETNAMESE

Do (the maiden name of chef Thi Thanh Huyen Vu, formerly of Le Jules Verne) means "bean" in Vietnamese, and she makes authentic Vietnamese food, still so hard to find in Paris, where most Vietnamese restaurants serve poor imitations. With its location near the Marché d'Aligre, you can be sure of fresh ingredients in the bo bun, phô and daily specials like noodles with vegetables and prawns. The dining room is small and cramped; the best seating is probably at the counter.

LE TRAIN BLEU

Place Louis-Armand, Gare de Lyon, 1st floor, 12th, metro Gare de Lyon
Tel 01 43 43 09 06, www.le-train-bleu.com
Fixed-price menu €65, à la carte €60

LANDMARK

The thrilling monumental Belle Époque decoration with its frills and frescoes always outshines the food here.

LES GOBELINS, DENFERT-ROCHEREAU, MONTPARNASSE

13TH, 14TH & 15TH ARRONDISSEMENTS

Greenery & family life

L'ASSIETTE

181, rue du Château, 14th
Metro Mouton-Duvernet
Tel 01 43 22 64 86
www.restaurant-lassiette.com
À la carte €60
Closed Monday and Tuesday

TRADITIONAL BISTRO

David Rathgeber, who used to work for Alain Ducasse and undertook the delicate task of following former owner Lucette Rousseau, has succeeded by offering luxury bistro food like calf's head braised with flat parsley, marjoram, chives and savoury, served with a soft- or hard-boiled egg and crayfish and truffles. Then there is the house cassoulet. The decoration is bucolic, with etched-glass windows, veined-marble counters, wooden tables and chairs. It already has a loyal following.

Other location: 168, rue d'Alésia, 14th, tel 01 45 42 64 80

LE CETTE

7, rue Campagne-Première, 14th
Metro Vavin, Raspail, RER Port-Royal
Tel 01 43 21 05 47, www.lecette.fr
À la carte €60
Closed Monday and Tuesday

BISTRONOMIC

This little place with a vintage Left Bank feel opens in the morning and serves cuisine inspired by the hometown of its owner, Xavier Bousquet: Sète (hence the name Cette, as it used to be spelled). On the menu, you'll find such dishes as squid from Sète with semolina and mixed vegetables; and confit lamb shoulder from Lozère with heirloom vegetables. Film buffs might shed a tear or even stagger down the middle of the street in imitation of Jean-Paul Belmondo in *Breathless* (1960), whose character drew his last breath on this street after being gunned down by the police.

LE GRAND PAN

20, rue Rosenwald, 15th
Metro Plaisance
Tel 01 42 50 02 50, www.legrandpan.fr
Fixed-price menu €30, à la carte €50
Closed Saturday and Sunday

MEAT-CENTRIC BISTRO

This seemingly quiet restaurant dedicated to rugby and south-western cuisine could have gotten away with providing minimal service, but just the opposite is true. In the kitchen, Benoit Gauthier cooks up an endearing version of the repertoire, including a memorable lamb shoulder and hare *à la royale* (in season). Cheerful servers take care of a gourmet clientele.

***"If you are lucky enough to have lived in Paris as a young man, then wherever you go for the rest of your life, it stays with you, for Paris is a moveable feast."* Ernest Hemingway, *A Moveable Feast*, 1964**

LE SEVERO

8, rue des Plantes, 14th
Metro Mouton-Duvernet
Tel 01 45 40 40 91, www.lesevero.fr
À la carte €60
Closed Saturday and Sunday

MEAT

Even the two supposed rivals in the butchery business, Hugo Desnoyer and Yves-Marie Le Bourdonnec, agree on one thing: some of the best meat in Paris can be found at Le Severo. Owner William Bernet, a former butcher himself, and his partner, Gaël Marie-Magdeleine, are true meat lovers. The chips are divine, and if you get on the right side of Monsieur William, you might even get seconds. It will be difficult, however, since he's not easy to win over. Lively clientele, impressive wine list.

LES PETITS PLATS

39, rue des Plantes, 16th, metro Alésia
Tel 01 45 42 50 52
Fixed-price menu €45, à la carte €45
Closed Sunday

LIVELY BISTRO

This little gem has a charming location (plan to take a walk in the Villa d'Alésia) and quickly fills up with a clientele delighted to live nearby. Laetitia Casta, among others, enjoys partaking of such dishes as Aubrac beef, veal blanquette, stews and so on. The wine list is the crowning touch on this wonderful bistro, which has a superb wooden bar and lots of nooks and crannies. Cheeky male servers.

AUTEUIL, PASSY, TROCADÉRO, ÉTOILE

16TH & 17TH ARRONDISSEMENTS

Nobility & urban elegance

ASTRANCE

4, rue Beethoven, 16th, metro Passy
Tel 01 40 50 84 40
www.astrancerestaurant.com
Fixed-price menus €70 to €350
Closed Saturday to Monday

GOURMET, CREATIVE

The only restaurant in the canyon-like Rue Beethoven, whose melancholy aura brings to mind a Patrick Modiano novel. Go there for the gentle, intelligent service provided by Christophe Rohat and for the calm, sharp cuisine of Pascal Barbot, who uses acidic flavours to counter bitterness and fat in his lucid compositions: Mozambique shrimp with a full-bodied saté and peanuts; pigeon from the Nièvre with raspberry powder, baby carrots and Brazilian chillies. What's on the menu is a surprise, but rest assured that it will be brilliant.

FRÉDÉRIC SIMONIN

25, rue Bayen, 17th, metro Ternes
Tel 01 45 74 74 74
www.fredericsimonin.com
Fixed-price menus €55 to €155,
à la carte €110
Closed Sunday and Monday

AFFORDABLE GASTRONOMY

Great cuisine by a very good chef who has graced other restaurants with his talents (Arabian, Joël Robuchon) and has a clientele of regulars delighted by the "surprise" menus and other high-flying (sometimes too high) creations.
The service in this plush Art Deco setting is of the same standard.

L'ARCHESTE

79, rue de la Tour, 16th
Metro Rue de la Pompe
Tel 01 40 71 69 68, www.archeste.com
Fixed-price menus €44 to €98
Closed for lunch Saturday and all day Sunday and Monday

REFINED, CREATIVE

This food is not only impressive and precise, but also tastes great. The decor is clean and sleek, the clientele undistinguished and the dishes stunning, among them braised veal cheeks with spinach and pork belly with sliced pink mushrooms and veal jus. You may have to have your clothes refitted after a meal here.

LES TABLETTES

16, avenue Bugeaud, 16th
Metro Victor Hugo
Tel 01 56 28 16 16
www.lestablettesjeanlouisnomicos.com
Fixed-price menus €58 to €150, à la carte €120

GOURMET, SOPHISTICATED

With a very 16th arrondissement (read privileged) clientele, in a decor woven like a shopping basket, Jean-Louis Nomicos manages to create particularly inspired dishes like the pan-fried Roscoff sole with truffles. The servers try to liven up a rather quiet clientele.

LE STELLA

133, avenue Victor Hugo, 16th
Metro Victor Hugo, Rue de la Pompe
Tel 01 56 90 56 00
À la carte €50

CLASSIC BRASSERIE

A lively hangout for the local gentry, with its good and (often) bad manners. Eating is just an excuse for meeting in this colourful, kitschy place. The food is honest, presenting the full repertoire of the genre: terrines, seafood, sole, calf's liver. The upstairs dining room is the quietest, especially the small room in the back.

MONSIEUR BLEU

Palais de Tokyo, 13, avenue du Président Wilson or 20, avenue de New York, 16th
Metro Alma-Marceau
Tel 01 47 20 90 47, www.monsieurbleu.com
À la carte €60

FASHIONABLE, ELEGANT

An impressive setting with monumental spaces. This service is a tad arrogant, and the food is what might be called opportunistic: linguine with lemon and *poutargue* (dried, cured fish roe); caramelized blackened cod with grilled vegetables; "traditional" beef tenderloin; and so on. The grandiose setting is decorated in gold and greens, the work of interior designer Joseph Dirand, who took the opportunity to name the restaurant after his . . . dog, perhaps a sly dig at this upscale world all in velvet, with Lalique bas-reliefs and light fixtures, and Connemara marble.

ALSO IN THIS NEIGHBOURHOOD

CORETTA

151bis, rue Cardinet, 17th
Metro Brochant
Tel 01 42 26 55 55
www.restaurantcoretta.com
Fixed-price menus €30 to €41, à la carte €50

CHIC CANTEEN

Overlooking Martin Luther King Park, Coretta (the name of Martin's wife), run by the team from Neva Cuisine, offers lively, attractive and piquant food like the sea bream with purple cabbage, blackberries and hibiscus broth. Some dishes are as appealing as a bunch of fresh flowers: crisp green asparagus and marinated sardines; fried cod with saté sauce, coconut and lemongrass, broad beans and bok choy.

LA TABLE D'HUGO DESNOYER

28, rue du Docteur Blanche, 16th
Metro Jasmin, Ranelagh
Tel 01 46 47 83 00
www.hugodesnoyer.com
À la carte €45
Closed for dinner and all day
Sunday and Monday

MEAT

A large shared table and a few smaller ones are set up in the middle of the shop of one of the best butchers in Paris. Customers are surrounded by display cases and knives in an atmosphere full of testosterone. The food is tops with, of course, the very best meat for fans of the genre. The place can be hired for private dinners in the evening for €3,600 for eight people, including fine wines and big menus. No bones to pick here.
See website for other addresses

LES MARCHES

5, rue de la Manutention, 16th
Metro Iéna, Alma-Marceau
Tel 01 47 23 52 80
www.lesmarches-restaurant.com
À la carte €30

ROADSIDE CAFÉ

The last thing you expect to see in this neighbourhood is a *routier* (truck stop – there are three in Paris) that keeps its prices low while all around it restaurant bills are rising to three figures. With its checked tablecloths, a good-natured clientele and overwhelmed but friendly service, it's almost too good to be true. On the menu: lentil salad and Lyon sausage, *pâté en croûte, œuf en meurette,* calf's head with gribiche sauce and so on. Old-fashioned dining room with mouldings on the ceiling, mosaics on the floor, a solid bar and an overloaded coat rack. A minor miracle.

NON SOLO CUCINA

135, rue du Ranelagh, 16th
Metro Ranelagh
Tel 01 45 27 99 93
www.non-solo-cucina.fr
À la carte €50
Closed Sunday and Monday

SICILIAN

This fine restaurant plays up the Sicilian connection, sometimes a bit too much for the local gentry. Dishes include Sicilian caponata and pasta with fresh sardines, pine nuts, raisins, wild fennel and crispy breadcrumbs. Also home to the Non Solo Pizze pizzeria. **Other location: NON SOLO PIZZE** 5, rue Mesnil, 16th, tel 01 47 04 69 03

PAGES

4, rue Auguste Vacquerie, 16th
Metro Charles de Gaulle-Étoile, Kléber
Tel 01 47 20 74 94
www.restaurantpages.fr
Fixed-price menus €50 to €90,
à la carte €80
Closed Sunday and Monday

ASIAN FRENCH

Ryuji Teshima and his team in black aprons and white outfits work in an open kitchen. The setting is as refined as the impressive cuisine: hay-smoked bonito; wagyu beef carpaccio; Brittany lobster with wild rice and bisque; line-caught bluefin tuna tartare with brie-egg emulsion.

SAN FRANCISCO

1, rue Mirabeau, 16th
Metro Mirabeau, Église d'Auteuil
Tel 01 46 47 75 44
www.restaurant-sanfrancisco.com
À la carte €65
Closed Sunday

ELEGANT ITALIAN

Father and son Carlo and Lorenzo Bianchi have understood perfectly their neighbourhood customers, who go there (fortunately for them) with eyes closed to dine on easy-to-love food like *spaghetti alla botarga e calamaretti* (€27!). A great place to be seen.

MONTMARTRE, LA VILLETTE, BELLEVILLE, MÉNILMONTANT

18TH, 19TH & 20TH ARRONDISSEMENTS

Old Paris & modern nostalgia

LE BARATIN

3, rue Jouye-Rouve, 20th
Metro Pyrénées, Belleville
Tel 01 43 49 39 70
Fixed-price menu €19, à la carte €50
Closed Sunday and Monday

CLASSIC BISTRO

In a Paris straight out of a Doisneau photograph, this bistro is a magnificent enigma. The wonderful pastoral cuisine is prepared by Raquel Carena, and the occasionally brusque welcome is provided by Philippe Pinoteau (known as "Pinuche"), who sometimes seems to find his customers too demanding, and wants to protect his excellent wine cellar. The clever dishes turn gastronomy upside down with their simplicity: escabeche of quail with hazelnuts and grapes; crispy beef cheeks and sautéed vegetables; tuna steak with squid heads and green olives. Sometimes the whole world is there: other times it's strangely quiet.

LE COQ RICO

98, rue Lepic, 18th, metro Lamarck-Caulaincourt
Tel 01 42 59 82 89, www.lecoqrico.com
À la carte €70

CHICKEN, CHIC

When a multi-starred chef (Antoine Westermann) decides to work on a concept, in this case poultry, one would expect him to start in the centre and avoid all the boring tricks of haute cuisine. In the heart of Montmartre, this efficient restaurant serves beaked and feathered animals with stoicism and ardour. Try the farmhouse guinea fowl from Auvergne; the black free-range chicken from Challans, Maine or Bresse; or the pigeon from Poitou. Eggs come in all the expected forms: soft-boiled, devilled, in salads, fried. And don't forget the desserts, including a vacherin topped with whipped cream.

LE GRAND BAIN

14, rue Dénoyez, 20th
Metro Belleville, Pyrénées
Tel 09 83 02 72 02
www.legrandbainparis.com
À la carte €30
Closed for lunch

GASTRONOMIC TAPAS

A new gourmet local with a preference for natural wines and crowds of customers squeezed together elbow to elbow to sample such dishes as scallops with celeriac; cuttlefish with pumpkin and dashi; asparagus with egg yolk and hazelnuts; and stew with gnocchi. In short, good food.

ALSO IN THIS NEIGHBOURHOOD

AU BŒUF COURONNÉ

188, avenue Jean Jaurès, 19th
Metro Porte de Pantin
Tel 01 42 39 44 44, www.boeuf-couronne.com
Fixed-price menu €34, à la carte €50

BRASSERIE, MEAT

A neo-1930s dining room and a menu that pays tribute to the meat traders of La Villette of yesteryear with a 300-gram steak, a 700-gram chateaubriand and a 1.2-kilogram prime rib of beef. Best to see your cardiologist after eating here.

LE DESNOYEZ

3, rue Dénoyez, 20th
Metro Belleville, Pyrénées
Tel 06 61 19 18 31
À la carte €30
Closed Tuesday and Wednesday

MINI-BISTRO

The chef here is a former lawyer working in a pocket-sized restaurant with only six tables and serving up such carefully judged and sunny dishes as green asparagus with Greek yoghurt, lemon and *poutargue*; and hake with mashed almonds and piquillos. Adorable. Not to be confused with butcher Hugo Desnoyer.

LE GRAND 8

8, rue Lamarck, 18th
Metro Anvers, then funicular up the hill, Chateau Rouge
Tel 01 42 55 04 55
Fixed-price menu €26, à la carte €45
Closed all day Monday and Tuesday, and for lunch Wednesday to Saturday

BISTRO, ORGANIC WINE

At the end of Rue Lamarck, this bistro looks like any other but has a great view of Paris through its narrow windows. It has a spectacular cellar of natural wines and, in the kitchen, Masahide Ikuta (formerly of Rae's, Bal Café and Table) sending out lovely dishes of sea urchins, farmer's pork fried with endives and served with pan juices flavoured with orange juice, and cod with beurre blanc. Excellent.

MENSAE

23, rue Mélingue, 19th
Metro Jourdain, Pyrénées
Tel 01 53 19 80 98
www.mensae-restaurant.com
Fixed-price menu €20, à la carte €40
Closed Sunday and Monday

CONTEMPORARY BISTRO FARE

Thibault Sombardier and Kevin D'Andréa, immortalized in Top Chef, are making a splash in this lively (noisy, some might say) bistro. The menu goes straight to the heart of things with oblique, graphic, Instagram-ready dishes. One example, the grilled octopus, came with a questionable *sauce vierge*, but the baked whiting with French-style peas (cooked with onions and lardons) was a success. The meal ended with a disarming chocolate fondant-mousse. The service was friendly and attentive.

MON CŒUR

1, rue des Envierges, 20th
Metro Pyrénées, Couronne
Tel 01 43 66 38 54
www.moncoeurbelleville.com
Fixed-price menu €16.50, à la carte €30

VIEW, TERRACE

With a great view of Paris and the Parc de Belleville and a sun-bathed terrace, this restaurant could get away with not making much of an effort, but that is not the case. The food is nimble and sincere, with such dishes as mushroom risotto, Iberian beef *picanha*, and mushroom-stuffed *conchiglioni* with Mornay sauce and rocket. The brunch is always crowded.

QUEDUBON

22, rue du Plateau, 19th
Metro Buttes Chaumont
Tel 01 42 38 18 65
www.restaurantquedubon.fr
À la carte €55
Closed all day Sunday and Monday, and for lunch on Saturday

BISTRO, NATURAL WINE

At Gilles Bénard's restaurant, you are guaranteed a range of natural wines served in a bacchic atmosphere, backed up by lively seasonal food, such as farmhouse rabbit thigh, white Ardennes asparagus served warm in vinaigrette and Kalamata watermelon soup.

WEPLER

14, place de Clichy, 18th
Metro Place de Clichy
Tel 01 45 22 53 24, www.wepler.com
Fixed-price menu €32, à la carte €50

BRASSERIE

A wonderful Parisian brasserie that mixes all sorts of people in an unpredictable way. Sometimes it is magnificent with its muses, braggarts and local characters. Other times, it's somnolent, with customers daydreaming over predictable foods (seafood platters, choucroute, sole, etc.).

DINING OUT WITH DOMINIQUE PERRAULT

Every day I eat lunch and dinner in a restaurant – the food has to be good, simple and fast. I never read the set menu or the à la carte. I just order the dish of the day, or one dish to share. In my early days, when I wasn't at the Royal Mondétour, my usual hangout was Joe Allen, where I ate chilli con carne at the counter. Over the five years while the National Library was being built, there was only one place to go in the no-man's-land of the 13th arrondissement, namely Lao Viet, which served – and still serves – the best nems (crispy rolls) in Paris. Today, given the choice, I always opt for fish. I like L'Écailler du Bistrot for its fresh, perfectly shucked oysters, or Commode, a restaurant close to the "tanker". Clamato, on Rue de Charonne offers good, creative menus, and I'm a big fan of Le Square Trousseau. When I feel like Italian, I go to Osteria Ferrara, which is also in the neighbourhood, or else, I'll go to Le Duc, on Boulevard Raspail, for its super-fresh fish. Otherwise, I'll head for Kunitoraya, for its udon, *and its virtuosic Japanese cuisine, or to Isami, on the Île Saint-Louis, for its tasty sushi. My old friend, Alain Passard, might entice me to the 7th arrondissement, and his restaurant Arpège. Or I might visit another friend, Alain Ducasse, in Versailles, where he has opened his restaurant Ore, serving cuisine inspired by history.*

LAO VIET
24, boulevard Masséna, 13th, metro Porte d'Ivry, tel 01 45 84 05 43, www.restaurantlaoviet.com

L'ÉCAILLER DU BISTROT
22, rue Paul Bert, 11th, metro Faidherbe-Chaligny, tel 01 43 72 76 77

CLAMATO
80, rue de Charonne, 11th, metro Charonne, tel 01 43 72 74 53, www.septime-charonne.fr

LE SQUARE TROUSSEAU
1, rue Antoine Vollon, 12th, metro Ledru-Rollin, tel 01 43 43 06 00, www.squaretrousseau.com

OSTERIA FERRARA
7, rue du Dahomey, 11th, metro Faidherbe-Chaligny, tel 01 43 71 67 69

LE DUC
243, boulevard Raspail, 14th, metro Raspail, tel 01 43 20 96 30, www.restaurantleduc.com

KUNITORAYA
1, rue Villedo, 1st, metro Pyramides, tel 01 47 03 33 65, www.kunitoraya.com

ISAMI
4, quai d'Orléans, 4th, metro Pont Marie tel 01 40 46 06 97, www.isami.zenchef.com

ARPÈGE
84, rue de Varenne, 7th, metro Varenne, tel 01 47 05 09 06, www.alain-passard.com

ORE
Château de Versailles, tel 01 30 84 12 96, www.ducasse-chateauversailles.com

GOOD THINGS

GOURMET DELIS TO FARMERS MARKETS: THE TASTE OF THE CITY

Many thirty- and forty-something Parisians who are crazy about food and bored to tears with their careers – think banking, marketing, fashion or computers – are reinventing themselves by entering the restaurant and food business. Often graduates of top business schools, they bravely embrace this new world, daring to launch original concepts (Du Pain et des Idées, Papa Sapiens and Chez Hélène) and prepared to do the washing up or baking themselves. They try to find the best produce and ingredients and explore exciting new realms of flavour.

In a world of changing tastes and sensations, desserts, from the most traditional to the most contemporary, are part of this quest for true flavours and authenticity. The preference is for lighter, more sensual and irresistible desserts that are not as sweet. The Parisian approach to gourmet food is still irreverent and open, elegant and straightforward, faithful to infidelity – because what really counts is falling in love.

ELEV
BERKEL

UR & BOUCHER

À LA MÈRE DE FAMILLE

35, rue du Faubourg Montmartre, 10th
Metro Le Peletier, tel 01 47 70 83 69
www.lameredefamille.com
Open 9am to 8pm, Sunday 10am to 7:30pm

REGRESSIVE PARADISE

À la Mère de Famille has been making chocolate, ice cream and confectionary since 1761. The emblematic green facade with gold lettering at 35, Rue du Faubourg Montmartre is a small piece of Paris's history and heritage. A new chapter in the success story began when it was taken over in 2000 by the Dolfi family: Étienne, the patriarch, a former supplier to the house, and his four grown children: Sophie, Steve, Jane and Jonathan. The family empire now counts ten shops in Paris, with the historic store still the flagship – and the one with the most cachet since it seems to have stayed exactly as it was when it was founded, with its antique tiles and metal chandeliers. The packets and trays are full of colourful candies, candied fruits of all sizes and vintage sweets in bulk (*négus* from Nevers, *calissons* from Aix, *bêtises* from Cambrai). Made in the firm's factory in Chambray-lès-Tours, the chocolates sit quietly in a big wooden display case. Among them are the Palets Montmartre, a house speciality: thin discs filled with fruity ganache or praline. You'll also find *mendiants*, florentines with caramelized almonds, fruit pastes of all kinds and pillowy chocolate-covered marshmallows. A huge choice for creating your own beautiful assortment.

See website for other locations

ALEXANDRE STERN

15, rue Vignon, 8th, metro Madeleine
Tel 09 52 37 04 54
www.alexandrestern.net
Open 9:30am to 7pm, closed Sunday

ROYAL HIVE

Alexandre Stern, who has been selling honey as a luxury product since 2014, has found a niche for himself as a self-proclaimed "creator of honeys". At first, he supplied only professionals and hotels (the George V offers it at breakfast, and it can be found in the Grande Épicerie in Paris and Harrods and Selfridges in London), but then he opened his first shop under his own name in November 2015. The chic boutique in the Madeleine district, decorated with a beeswax fresco by the Canadian artist Penelope Stewart, looks like a rare perfume shop. A lot of this is marketing, of course, but the quality of the nectars sold here is such that it's worth a visit. Stern's speciality is the blending of honeys to create some fifteen varieties. These astute blends might be floral or spicy, liquid or creamy, pale yellow or dark brown like the Black Forest with its woody flavour, made from chestnut, pine, heather and buckwheat honey from France and Spain. The range also includes simpler honeys (among them acacia, linden, lavender and pine) stored in large glass jars and sold by the ladle in jars of various sizes. Some exceptional products include the incredibly fresh Sweet Rose, from the Valley of Roses in Bulgaria, and L'Or du Désert, jujube flower honey from Yemen, one of the rarest – and most expensive – in the world. It is sold here at nearly €700 a kilo (€89 for a 130-gram jar)!

BERTHILLON

29–31, rue Saint-Louis-en-l'Île, 4th
Metro Pont Marie
Tel 01 43 54 31 61
www.berthillon.fr
Open 10am to 8pm, closed Monday and Tuesday

GOURMET ICE CREAM

Generations of children, lovers and visitors, Parisians at heart or by birth, still take pleasure in queuing up to sample the crème de la crème of ice cream. As early as 1954, the artisan Raymond Berthillon (who died in 2014) dared to offer a great product, honestly made with natural flavours, eggs, cream and fresh milk, with no preservatives or sweeteners, paying special attention to vanilla, that most common of flavours. The challenge he successfully met was

SPOTLIGHT

CAVIAR

Although it is now farmed, caviar remains an exceptional delicacy that is savoured by initiates in the cosy salons of chic Parisian restaurants. One of the best, located near the Champ de Mars, is PETROSSIAN (www.petrossian.fr), a legendary house run by Armen Petrossian, son and nephew of its founders. On Place de la Madeleine, at KASPIA (www.caviarkaspia.com), a refined restaurant is hidden above the store. In the heart of the 16th arrondissement, PRUNIER (www.prunier.com) has a sumptuous Art Deco interior befitting a restaurant listed as a historic monument. Stimulated by the competition, other players are on the move, coming up with innovations (a container shaped like a spoon, another like an inkpot) or following the branding trends, as in the "Yves Saint Laurent for Prunier" Valentine's Day promotion. All types of accessories are being introduced, while retailers are changing their practices. Véronique Yoon-Kyung Martin, who launched her ULTREÏA (www.caviar-ultreia.com) brand at the end of 2014, gives tastings of schrenki, baeri and beluga roe in an elegant private lounge, hidden in a courtyard in a dream location: the Place Vendôme. In December 2016, Keyan Eslamdoust of LA MAISON NORDIQUE (www.lamaisonnordique.com), a respected producer of Imperial caviar in the Sologne region of France, opened a large boutique with a stylish, relaxed restaurant on Rue Saint-Honoré, the perfect spot for a working lunch or a break from shopping. At the same time, the Nebots, from KAVIARI (www.kaviari.fr), unveiled their Manufacture, located near the Bassin de l'Arsenal in the house's former workshops (processing laboratory, cold room, etc.) renovated for the occasion. In this polymorphous place with a refined look, the family history is explained in modern displays. All-caviar breakfasts and lunches, chef's dinners and tastings take place in a convivial atmosphere. The sacred aura of caviar may be disappearing, but it is not about to become a mass product. The result of a long, complicated process, caviar still retains its prestige – it is not called "black gold" for nothing.

to ensure that his ice cream – light, milky and velvety – became a benchmark for all ice creams. Muriel, his granddaughter, following in the footsteps of his daughter Marie José, continues the family's passion for frozen desserts. The house has only one shop, in the back of which the ice cream is still made. Berthillon's fame extends beyond the Île Saint-Louis to encompass the world. Some seventy flavours of ice cream and sorbet are offered, depending on the season (twenty to twenty-five flavours available every day), and come in cones, cups and half-litre or litre containers to take away. They can also be eaten in the tearoom next to the shop. And now, miraculously, credit cards are accepted.

CAFFÉ JUNO

58, rue Henri Barbusse, 5th
RER Port-Royal
Tel 01 42 38 92 48, www.caffe-juno.com
Open 9am to 6pm, Saturday 10am to 5pm, closed Sunday and Monday

COFFEE SHOP

The friendly and courteous Bartolomeo Dibenedetto, a native of Puglia, comes from a family that has been roasting coffee for three generations. His little Paris coffee shop, where he serves an exceptional mocha and homemade Italian delicacies in a simple setting, is located near the maternity hospital (unfortunately, coffee is not recommended for future mothers) at Port-Royal, next to the We*Do design showroom. The five or six seasonal coffees from the most exotic and unusual plantations in Rwanda, Nicaragua, Mexico, among others, are all selected by his wife and partner, Catherine Baldo, a veritable coffee sommelier, then roasted by him and ground to your specifications (mocha, filter, etc.) and vacuum-packed in an elegant black packet marked with the provenance and date. The prices are also reasonably filtered, making your morning tasting of a Latimojong Klasik from Indonesia all the more delectable.

COMPAGNIE GÉNÉRALE DE BISCUITERIE

1, rue Constance, 18th, metro Blanche
Tel 06 86 43 40 84
www.ciegeneralebiscuiterie.fr
Open 11am to 6pm, closed Monday

BISCUITS

In the midst of the current creative competition between pastry chefs, there is something wonderful and almost contrarian about yielding to the plainest of sweets: the biscuit. Orchestrating this return to roots is Gilles Marchal, who was already delighting residents of the Butte Montmartre in his shop at 9, Rue Ravignan with revisited – or not – seasonal tarts and classic cakes. In the plain setting of a small artisanal kitchen bathed in a delicate sweet fragrance, his teams bake little gems rich with the taste of butter twice a day. Sold in packets or individually in adorable metal boxes are excellent shortbreads (plain, chocolate or pistachio), rich *financiers* (orange, hazelnut or pecan) and the inimitable Alsatian *kipferls*, crumbly little pastries that are delicious and not too sweet. Another star creation, the Arlette, is a sort of flaky tuile covered in vanilla powder, which is produced only once a day because it is difficult to make. Gilles Marchal also makes an incredible millefeuille, which can be tasted, like all his cookies, in the tearoom of the neighbouring **BISTROT DE LA GALETTE** (102 ter, rue Lepic, 18th, tel 01 46 06 19 65).

ÉPICES ROELLINGER

51 bis, rue Sainte-Anne, 2nd
Metro Quatre Septembre, Pyramides
Tel 01 42 60 46 88
www.epices-roellinger.com
Open 10am to 7pm, closed Sunday and Monday

GOURMET SPICES

Starred French chef Olivier Roellinger is a globetrotter, but he has at last settled down in a dark wooden den where red-labelled jars of spices neatly line the shelves. The pleasant, well-informed Sandrine will tell you about thirty years of research and the invention of "spice powders" with evocative names: daring mixtures of fleurs de sel, rare peppers and oils with herbs, made in the same painstaking way a "nose" would develop a fragrance, with the same level of complexity. Visitors who ask the right questions are offered a private tour of the "vanilla cellar", the only one in the world, where large tin cans contain some twenty "grands crus" of vanilla in a mysterious, dark setting. In particular, Roellinger found the original vanilla of the Mayans in northern Chiapas, pollinated by hummingbirds so discerning that they fertilize only the three most beautiful flowers in the bunch. However, this is a wild vanilla so, nature being what it is, it's not always available in the shop.

FOIE GRAS LUXE

26, rue Montmartre, 1st
Metro Les Halles, Étienne Marcel
Tel 01 42 36 14 73, www.foiegrasluxe.com
Open 10am to noon and 1pm to 7pm, closed Sunday and Monday

FOIE GRAS

For many years, buying one's *mi-cuit* duck foie gras (the best in Paris) at Foie Gras Luxe, a family business since 1948, had a charmingly clandestine edge to it. Customers entered through the front door of no. 26 and ventured into the courtyard to find this rustic Ali Baba's cavern. In late 2016, the company opened a small, modern shop (Foie Gras & Co.), but the bulk of the stock is still displayed in a hangar-like room that looks like a contraband shed. On the simple wooden shelves you'll find the pride of south-western France: prepared dishes (excellent confit duck legs from the Landes, Tarbais beans, Basque piperade), duck rillettes and country pâté, tuna belly and canned sardines. The foie gras from small local producers (whole with sauternes, figs or truffles, *mi-cuit* terrine or *au torchon)* takes up a whole refrigerated display case. Smoked salmon from Scotland, Norway and Ireland, as well as products from Kaviari, round out this wide, high-quality selection.

G. DETOU

58, rue Tiquetonne, 2nd
Metro Étienne Marcel
Tel 01 42 36 54 67
Open 8:30am to 6:30pm, closed Sunday

GROCERY, PASTRY SHOP AND MORE

Detou encompasses almost everything. The great pastry chefs have long been familiar with this mouth-watering shop, but the general public is now discovering it, too, with good reason. The shop is always packed just before the holiday season. This treasure trove offers a wide variety of products: chestnut flour from the Cévennes mountains, thyme honey, pistachios, puff pastry, dried fruit, liqueur, Guénard gourmet oil, Italian rice, foie gras, smoked salmon and top-of-the-line preserves. It's a true delight for puxisardinophiles (sardine-can collectors), who will find the best sardines from La Pointe de Penmarc'h and La Belle Îloise.

HERBORISTERIE DU PALAIS-ROYAL

11, rue des Petits Champs, 1st
Metro Bourse, Palais-Royal–Musée du Louvre
Tel 01 42 97 54 68, www.herboristerie.com
Open 10am to 7pm, closed Sunday

CULT HERBALIST

Michel Pierre's herbalist's shop, the oldest in France, has been busy for more than forty years, but is especially popular now, with the sharp rise in demand for natural herbal products. Alas, in the European country that consumes the most pharmaceuticals, this profession is still fighting to be officially recognized by the health authorities. The Herboristerie du Palais-Royal, one of the last to survive, offers herbal teas (already blended or to blend yourself), essential oils, plant extracts, herbal remedies, floral waters, cosmetics and especially an impressive quantity of bulk herbs (around 300) to help you sleep better, promote lymphatic drainage, manage stress and replenish minerals. The staff offer excellent advice.

HISADA

47, rue de Richelieu, 1st
Metro Pyramides
Tel 01 42 60 78 48
www.hisada.fr
Open 11am to 8pm, tasting room open noon to 6pm, closed Sunday and Monday

CHEESE

This cheese shop has been in Paris since 2004, first in the 16th arrondissement and, since 2010, near the Palais-Royal. Sanae Hisada, who works with her daughter Eri, has redesigned and redecorated the small shop. The once-minimalist space is now warmer and more welcoming. It is a pleasure to hear Eri, as precise as she is friendly, extol the merits of her products. All are of excellent quality and most are made with raw milk. Pressed, soft and blue cheeses rotate on the shelves according to the seasons. In the cellar, Sanae ages a few wonderful fusions found nowhere else: Parmesan with Japanese whisky, goat cheese with wasabi, Brillat-Savarin with hojicha tea or with sesame and filled with quince paste, among others. Upstairs is a little tearoom. In the afternoon, you can sit down for a cheese tasting (everything in the shop is available), accompanied by a glass of wine or sake, and some small plates, made with cheese, of course, such as baked Mont d'Or or raclette.

POINT OF VIEW

A CASE OF MONOMANIA

Paris is sick, Paris is feverish. The doctors are anxious. The symptoms? The capital is awash with shops, cafés and other conceptual places that are all dedicated to just one single product. They are spreading from one bank of the Seine to the other just to be sure that no one is spared. This is not a new epidemic, but it's one that's getting worse every year. Burgers, bagels, cookies, cheesecake, éclairs, choux, croque-monsieur, profiteroles, *boulettes*, madeleines, brioches and hot dogs – there is something for everyone and every (bad) taste. There are crazy concepts galore, all driven by skilful marketing: *saucisserie, lasagneria, omeletterie, mueslerie, gratinerie, bolerie*, cakerie and even a patisserie specializing in baba. Since *baba* also means "flabbergasted" in French, it at least suggests they have a sense of humour.

JEAN-CHARLES ROCHOUX

16, rue d'Assas, 6th, metro Rennes
Tel 01 42 84 29 45
www.jcrochoux.com
Open 10:30am to 7:30pm,
Monday from 2:30pm, closed Sunday

CHOCOLATE CREATIONS

Unlike many of his fellow chocolate makers, Jean-Charles Rochoux has resisted the temptation to open numerous stores. He may open one on the Right Bank someday, and he opened one in Tokyo in late 2017, but he is attached to his original shop on Rue d'Assas (opened in 2004), where he also has his laboratory in the basement. It is like a cabinet of curiosities, inhabited by his signature creations: chocolate sculptures displayed on big wooden shelves. Empire-style busts, languid cherubs and monuments of all kinds sit beside an impressive and improbable bestiary composed of bears, horses, rabbits, elephants and the house star, the crocodile ("which stares at its prey in the same deep, piercing way that a chocoholic looks at a chocolate bar"). The details are so refined and precise that it seems like sacrilege to bite into them. That's not a problem with the fifty or so chocolates sold individually or in assortments, so good that some fans cross the city to buy them. Among them are the Macas (a praline rocher coated with nougatine and grilled almonds), Louise (truffle paste with fresh basil) and Sanshyo (praline with Japanese pepper). Another speciality and an ingenious invention is the "ephemeral" bar with fresh fruit, sold only on Saturday. Lychees, muscat grapes, figs, plums, strawberries and kiwis, depending on the season, are coated with 70% chocolate and explode in the mouth when tasted. Original, as always!

JEUNE HOMME

17, rue de Bourgogne, 7th
Metro Assemblée Nationale, Varenne
Tel 09 67 72 31 75
www.epiceriejeunehomme.fr
Open 10am to 8pm, closed Sunday

GOURMET DELI

In the same way that some new bistros make traditional ones look old-fashioned, this gourmet shop offers a new template for fine groceries. That may explain the name chosen for his first business by Nicolas Fortchantre, grandson of Gaston Lenôtre, who knows a thing or two about gastronomy. After several years in the family business, Fortchantre became a hunter of exceptional products, both sweet and savoury, which he presents in this chic, seemingly disorderly bazaar. The selection is wide, with over 800 products available, including 600 in the shop. This *terroiriste* selection includes remarkable prepared dishes from Argaud (duck stew with ceps, sausages with lentils), *mi-cuit* duck foie gras from Barthouil and Bonnat chocolate bars.

There are also rare spices and salts, exceptional vanilla, a strong selection of organic jams, Japanese teas from Jugetsudo and vintage champagnes. This is the place to go when you need to quickly throw together a drinks party, a dinner or a last-minute gift basket.

LA GRANDE ÉPICERIE DE PARIS

38, rue de Sèvres, 7th
Metro Sèvres-Babylone
Tel 01 44 39 81 00
www.lagrandeepicerie.com
Open 8:30am to 9pm,
Sunday from 10am to 8pm

INTERNATIONAL FINE FOOD

Bon Marché's Grande Épicerie is the only equivalent in France of the food halls that are so popular in London and Los Angeles. Founded in 1852 by Aristide Boucicaut, the Bon Marché is one of the oldest department stores in the world. The Comptoir de l'Alimentation, the predecessor of La Grande Épicerie, opened in 1923 with a selection of the best, freshest produce and thematic displays. In 1978, it became La Grande Épicerie, with twice the space. It underwent a dramatic facelift in 2013, but the shelves continue to display unique, exclusive, French and international grocery items to a very upscale clientele, who are advised by knowledgeable salespeople. There are eighty different kinds of pasta (including those eaten by the Pope); the most expensive mineral water (€60 a bottle); more than forty types of bread, including the Grand Pain made with einkorn wheat; sixty-two-year-old Scotch; 3,500 bottles in the new 550-square-metre wine cellar; and 10,000 grocery products that are rare, exotic and often exclusive. All that makes La Grande Épicerie, now open on Sundays, an extraordinary playground for foodies from around the world. The offerings now include La Grande Épicerie de Paris's own line of 800 savoury, sweet, fresh and luxury products. Launched in January 2016, it combines La Grande Épicerie's expertise in selecting excellent products with the talents of the best artisanal producers of French and international gourmet goods. The artisans' shops are signposted with superb mosaics illustrating their specialities – *poissonnerie, boucherie, boulangerie, fromagerie, pâtisserie* – recreating the atmosphere of a mega-chic market. Tasting counters offer a gourmet break. Topping it all off is **LA TABLE DE LA GRANDE ÉPICERIE**, a brasserie under the splendid glass roof, open for lunch, afternoon tea and, since March 2017, for the aperitif, from 6pm to 8:30pm.

LA MANUFACTURE DE CHOCOLAT ALAIN DUCASSE

40, rue de la Roquette, 11th
Metro Bastille
Tel 01 48 05 82 86
www.lechocolat-alainducasse.com
Open 10:30am to 7pm,
closed Sunday and Monday

URBAN CHOCOLATE FACTORY

Alain Ducasse admits that he has "always been enchanted by chocolate". After working for twelve years with Nicolas Berger, the pastry chef for all his restaurants, he entrusted him with the ambitious project of creating a bean-to-bar chocolate factory in the heart of Paris. Located in a former Renault garage at the back of a courtyard in the Bastille area, it handles everything from roasting the beans to making the finished product, which is sold on-site. Visible behind steel-framed windows is a magical industrial space furnished with second-hand machines, some of them painted a very photogenic orange, which Berger patiently sought out all over Europe. Recycled, adapted, adjusted and reassembled, they now work for the delight of chocolate lovers, who flock there to buy the chocolates created by Alain Ducasse: ganaches, truffles, candies, *dragées* and superb bars – made from beans from Peru, Cuba, Java, Venezuela, São Tomé and Príncipe, and Vietnam – all the fruit of

THE UNMISSABLES

Chopped chicken livers and other Jewish delicacies from Eastern Europe and Russia: **FLORENCE KAHN** 24, rue des Écouffes, corner of rue des Rosiers, 4th metro Saint-Paul, tel 01 48 87 92 85, www.florence-kahn.fr

Alsatian sauerkraut and pretzels: **SCHMID** 76, boulevard de Strasbourg, 10th, metro Gare de l'Est, tel 01 46 07 89 74, www.schmid-traiteur.com

Vol-au-vent Régence: **MAISON POU** 16, avenue des Ternes, 17th, metro Ternes, tel 01 43 80 19 24, www.maisonpou.com

Puits d'amour *(puff pastry shell filled with pastry cream):* **PÂTISSERIE STOHRER** 51, rue Montorgueil, 2nd, metro Étienne Marcel, tel 01 42 33 38 20, www.stohrer.fr

Meringue pavlovas with fresh fruit: **LA MERINGAIE** 21, rue de Lévis, 17th, metro Villiers, tel 01 44 71 94 16, www.lameringaie.com

Artisanal ravioli made by a leading chef: **PASTIFICIO PASSERINI** 65, rue Traversière, 12th, metro Ledru-Rollin, tel 01 44 74 67 84, www.passerini.paris

American pulled-pork sandwich: **FRENCHIE TO GO** 9, rue du Nil, 2nd, metro Sentier, tel 01 40 26 23 43, www.frenchietogo.com

Date makroudhs (North African pastry): **NANI** 102, boulevard de Belleville, 20th, metro Belleville, tel 01 47 97 38 05

Unbeatable egg mayo for €0.90, served with freshly grated and sliced vegetables: **LE VOLTAIRE** 27, quai Voltaire, 7th, metro Rue du Bac, tel 01 42 61 17 49

Caesar salad: **LES COCOTTES DE CHRISTIAN CONSTANT** 135, rue Saint-Dominique, 7th, metro École Militaire, tel 01 45 50 10 28, www.maisonconstant.com

Excellent, not-too-sweet Paris-Brest with sesame: **GÂTEAUX THOUMIEUX** 58, rue Saint-Dominique, 7th, metro La Tour Maubourg, tel 01 45 51 12 12

Artisanal mozzarella and burrata, made on-site: **OTTANTA** 19, rue du Cardinal Lemoine, 5th, metro Jussieu, Cardinal Lemoine, tel 09 52 77 03 62, www.ottanta.fr

Light-as-air cream pie: **LIBERTÉ** 39, rue des Vinaigriers, 10th, metro Jacques Bonsergent, tel 01 42 05 51 76, www.libertepatisserieboulangerie.com

Freshly made dorayakis *(Japanese pancakes filled with red bean paste):* **TOMO** 11, rue Chabanais, 2nd, metro Bourse, Pyramides, tel 09 67 77 96 72, www.patisserietomo.fr

Rustic bread (also found in many Parisian bistros): **LA POINTE DU GROIN** 8, rue de Belzunce, 10th, metro Gare du Nord, Poissonnières, www.lapointedugrouin.com

meticulous work worthy of the best craftsmen. The packaging – cardboard boxes or brown paper bags – is as straightforward and elegant as the place itself. You'll leave with some good advice worth remembering: keep your chocolate in its packaging in a dry place, and never put it in the fridge.
See website for other addresses

LASTRE SANS APOSTROPHE

188, rue de Grenelle, 7th
Metro La Tour Maubourg
Tel 01 40 60 70 27
Open 10am to 2pm and 4pm to 7:30pm, Friday until 8pm, Saturday 10am to 8pm, closed Sunday and Monday

HIGH-END DELI

Yohan Lastre is a star (the meaning of "astre" in French) in the world of *pâté en croûte*, winner of the fourth prestigious *pâté en croûte* world championship in 2012. Four years later, the former sous-chef of La Tour d'Argent opened his own shop, located between the Champ de Mars and the gourmet haven that is the Rue Cler. The shop, with its rustic-chic decor, is a hit in the 7th arrondissement. It's such a success that customers have to get there early to be sure of obtaining a slice of the famous homemade pâté, which changes regularly – farmhouse pork, chicken and pistachios; chicken with morels and asparagus; foie gras, pine-bud alcohol and port jelly – all of them sublime. But don't neglect the other homemade products like black pudding (with pork belly, slow-cooked for eight hours); pot-au-feu in jelly, which just needs to be heated up; *bœuf à la mode*; and cakes that change with the seasons. If there is one thing that must not be missed, it is the Saint-Mamert-du-Gard fougasse: crisp puff pastry with pork scratchings. Yet another star.

LA TÊTE DANS LES OLIVES

2, rue Sainte-Marthe, 10th
Metro Goncourt
Tel 09 51 31 33 34
www.latetedanslesolives.com
Open 2pm to 7pm, Saturday 10am to 1pm and 2pm to 7pm, closed Sunday and Monday

OLIVE OIL

If it wasn't for the sign, this rustic boutique straight out of the past, which looks like an alchemist's lair, could easily be missed. Cédric Casanova calls himself a "taster, selector and creator of extra-virgin olive oil from Sicily". Formerly a tightrope walker in the Cirque du Soleil, he decided at the age of forty to return home and devote himself to making his homeland better known thanks to an exceptional oil, Nocellara del Belice, which has a designation of protected origin, as well as Biancolilla and Cerasuola, all of them very herbaceous. Each oil in the shop bears the name of the olive producer, among them Nunzio, which has only one tree, but that one tree is 1,000 years old and produces 50 litres of Etruscan olives per year, which end up here. The Sicilian farmers decide on the colour and aroma of olives on harvest day in October. The oils wait proudly in their bulging 25 or 50 litre cans and are sold "in bulk", if you bring your own container, at almost half price. In season, you will also find figs, dried tomatoes, capers in salt, oregano, fennel, tuna bottarga, tapenade, honey, anchovies, raw-milk cheese, fresh produce and citrus fruit – all Sicilian. The shop can be "privatized" for a tasting in the evening at a small table that seats six. Book one month in advance. A slightly larger store, which opened in the Alésia neighbourhood in the 15th arrondissement in 2016, can accommodate up to ten people for tasting dinners. And Cédric Casanova has since set out to conquer the world with two new shops, one in London and the other in Tokyo. **Other location:** 54, rue du Couedic, 14th, tel 09 70 93 66 58

LE BEL ORDINAIRE

54, rue de Paradis, 10th
Metro Poissonnière
Tel 01 46 27 46 67
www.lebelordinaire.com
Open 11am to 11pm,
closed Sunday and Monday

GASTRONOMIC HYBRID

It's more than a grocery store or a wine bar but not quite a restaurant. Le Bel Ordinaire, opened in March 2017, is the polymorphic shop of Sébastien Demorand, a former food writer who once wrote for the *City Guides*, and his partner, Cyrille Rossetto, who used to work in the digital world. They thought about the project for months and raised some of the money needed to open it through crowdfunding. Eventually, they plan to have several locations in Paris, but for the moment it is all happening in a stripped-down room of impressive size with a welcoming shared table in the middle. Old and new friends chat over agreeable little dishes like eggs mayonnaise, escargot and pancetta *tartines* or Morteau sausage couscous, prepared by a chef in the open kitchen. While they eat, others drop in to do a little shopping in the grocery, picking up Italian pasta, Corsican lonzo and coppa, smoked Guérande *fleur de sel* and Lucques green olives or choosing from the superb selection of wines. All of the 600 products were chosen with great care. Stop by once and you'll be hooked.

LE BOULANGER DE LA TOUR

2, rue du Cardinal Lemoine, corner of quai de la Tournelle, 5th
Metro Sully-Morland, Maubert-Mutualité
Tel 01 43 54 62 53, www.tourdargent.com
Open daily 7am to 8pm, Sunday from 8am

BREAD AND PASTRY

Located at the foot of the legendary restaurant La Tour d'Argent, enthroned on its panoramic pedestal, is the house bakery, right next to the rotisserie. It's a godsend for lovers of the restaurant's breads, soft and delectable, with crunchy crusts. Honourable mention goes to the bitter-cocoa bread with walnuts, the Punchy bread (made with high-quality wheat flour, raisins, pistachios and hazelnuts) and the buckwheat wreath. Other temptations include the baguettes and fine white bread (the latter makes fantastic French toast when stale). The understated marble and glass interior offers a view of the kitchen, and the service is pleasant and patient – it has to be, since everyone asks so many questions! The longest waits are in the pastry section, whose classics are just as desirable.

LE GARDE MANGER WAGRAM

8, rue Meissonier, 17th, metro Wagram
Tel 09 67 12 81 81
www.legardemangerwagram.com
Open 11am to 2:30pm and 5:30pm to 11pm, closed Saturday and Sunday

PREPARED DISHES

This is a couple story, a clever pas de deux. Laura Portelli has created an annex next to the restaurant Papillon, which belongs to her partner Christophe Saintagne, former lieutenant of Alain Ducasse at the Meurice and the Plaza Athénée. With a pleasant, informal setting, it plays two roles, as a canteen at lunchtime and a deli throughout the day. In addition to sausages, cheeses and well-sourced bottles, the shop offers a changing menu of vegetable, meat and fish dishes, as well as freshly prepared salads and sandwiches. All have a homemade spirit but always with a little twist that makes the difference: braised celery with tapenade; smoked herring, beetroot and pickled onions; house-made dumplings with Sicilian caponata; roast pork belly with cep sauce; and fillet of brill with pesto. The chocolate cake is served with a spoon and has become a permanent fixture on the menu of the restaurant next door. Have a bite there or take something home. Especially fine groceries include Casa del Dolci panettone, Cédric Casanova's olive oils and cured meats from Domaine de Saint-Géry.

LEGRAND FILLES ET FILS

1, rue de la Banque and
7-11, galerie Vivienne, 2nd
Metro Bourse
Tel 01 42 60 07 12
www.caves-legrand.com
Open 10am to 7:30pm, Monday 11am to 7pm, closed Sunday

FINE WINES, CONFECTIONERY

The Nakashima family, the current owners of this institution, is maintaining the traditions of the founders, the Legrands, with the help of such pillars of the company as cellar master Jean-Jacques Moncomble, whose advice is always worth getting. The shop boasts a welcoming tasting room where there is something new to try every week. In the Galerie Vivienne, either at the counter or at tables (offering good classic cuisine at lunchtime), you can taste any wine in the shop, with a corking charge of €15. In addition to prestigious bottles like François Mitjaville's Bordeaux, Alsatian wine from Zind-Humbrecht (Clos Saint-Urbain), not to mention Pétrus and Romanée-Conti and other more reasonably priced bottles, you will find what made the reputation of this shop: Legrand Champagne, made by the Tarlant family in Œuilly, the first ultra-brut before it was fashionable, thanks to Lucien Legrand. Unusually, a selection of superb wines, ranging from €30 to €670 in price, is also available by the glass. The shop also sells books, decanters, glasses and wine accessories. Classes are held on Monday evenings, tastings with wine producers on Tuesdays, and evenings devoted to wine and the arts are held on the last Thursday of the month. But Legrand is also a grocer and confectioner, proud to sell sweet treasures from all over France such as bergamot from Nancy and *bêtises* from Cambrai.

PAPA SAPIENS

24, rue Feydeau, 2nd
Metro Bourse, Grands Boulevards
Tel 01 40 26 16 82, www.papasapiens.fr
Open 10:30am to 9pm, closed Saturday and Sunday

ÉPICERIE ULTRAFINE

This makes three for Alexandra Lepage and her group of gourmets, who opened the third of their food shops in early 2017 (after those at the Marché Poncelet and on Rue de Bourgogne). This one is located next to the Bourse. The whole range of products selected by Lepage can be found here: Emmanuel Chavassieux's salted meat, Rodolphe Paquin's terrines (from the excellent restaurant Le Repaire de Cartouche), Alexandre Polmard's beef, Marc Peyrey's preserved tomatoes, Cédric Casanova's olive oil, the exquisite eaux-de-vie of Laurent Cazottes and other sweet and savoury products. There is one difference about this shop: it is also a restaurant and has a small, welcoming terrace where you can sample a selection of products as well as a few other dishes (tuna salad, Italian-style beef tartare) accompanied by excellent wines sold in the shop (including Saint-Romain from Domaine de Chassorney and a Jura from Jean-François Ganevat) for a corkage fee of €10. Highly professional, ultra-attentive service. **Other locations:** 7, rue Bayen, 17th, tel 01 58 57 82 81; 32, rue de Bourgogne, 7th, tel 01 44 05 97 54

PÂTISSERIE DU PANTHÉON

200, rue Saint-Jacques, 5th
RER Luxembourg
Tel 01 43 07 77 59
www.sebastien-degardin.com
Open 9am to 8pm, closed Monday and Tuesday

PASTRIES

When he started out, Sébastien Dégardin was one of the youngest pastry chefs at a three-star restaurant, the Troisgros. He stayed there eight years before developing his creativity with Pierre

Gagnaire (Gaya in Paris and Sketch in London). In 2006, he opened his first bakery, an instant success, in Paris's 12th arrondissement, on Boulevard Reuilly. Since 2014, when he moved into an old delicatessen near the Panthéon, whose decor is listed as a historic monument, all his former customers, and new ones as well, have been racing across the city to snap up the city's best cakes. At the top of the list are the baba and Paris-Brest, which are simply outstanding, and such creations as the Passiflore (passion fruit, mango and white-chocolate cream on shortbread) and the fabulous Pavé du Panthéon (hazelnut *dacquoise* with praline-and-coffee cream). Otherwise, the puff-pastry brioches and raspberry tarts and pastries are to die for. Savoury treats – a rarity in a shop like this – include a legendary *pâté en croute, bouchées à la reine* with sweetbreads. At lunchtime, locals enjoy his soup, quiche and chocolate mousse.

R.A.P.

4, rue Flechier, 9th
Metro Notre-Dame-de-Lorette
Tel 01 42 80 09 91, www.rapparis.fr
Open 10.30am to 7:30pm, Sunday until 1pm, closed Monday

ITALIAN DELI

Anyone who loves Italian food knows that in Paris they will find their joy at Alessandra Pierini's place. This native of Genoa first opened her shop a few years ago at the top of Rue Rodier, where she also had a restaurant, which she then closed to concentrate on the store. She stayed in the neighbourhood but moved down the hill to a long, narrow shop that makes one wonder how she manages to stock so many products, among them capers in salt from Pantelleria, artisanal panettone, wine jam, wild bluefin tuna belly, virgin olive oil from Puglia and Sicily, the best dried pasta brands (Setaro, Martelli), artisanal rice and organic honey. The selection of fresh products is just as wide: pasta, ravioli, top-notch charcuterie (don't miss the *capocollo* of Martina Franca in Puglia, a kind of coppa with a slightly smoky flavour; dry Neapolitan sausage with fennel; and pork *guanciale* for making authentic carbonara), and cheeses with very special appellations (*piacentinu ennese* with saffron, pecorino with pistachios, spoon gorgonzola). And then there is a corner with such fresh produce as radicchio, bergamots and *cime di rapa,* the broccoli rabe that gives its name to a pasta recipe. The basement is entirely devoted to natural wines from Italy.

TERROIRS D'AVENIR

3, 6, 7 and 8, rue du Nil, 2nd
Metro Sentier
Tel 01 85 09 84 47 (deli), 01 85 09 84 48 (meat), 01 85 09 84 46 (fish), 01 85 09 84 45 (bakery)
www.terroirs-avenir.fr
Open 9:30am to 8pm, Saturday until 7:30pm, Sunday until 1:30pm, closed Monday; the bakery is open from 8am

EXCEPTIONAL REGIONAL PRODUCE

Since 2008, Samuel Nahon and Alexandre Drouard have been seeking out small, quality regional producers who work for the leading chefs in Paris. At the end of 2012, they decided to offer these products to the public and opened their first shop on Rue du Nil (no. 7), selling groceries and produce. They soon followed that with a fishmonger (no. 8), a butcher (no. 6) and, at the end of 2015, a bakery (no. 3). It is always a pleasure to wander down this small gourmet street filling one's bag with the best fruits, vegetables, fish (line-caught hake from Saint-Jean-de-Luz, fera, Arctic char and other freshwater fish) and meats (including rare beef Mirandais from the Gers). Their success is such that the duo opened a grocery store on Rue Jean-Pierre Timbaud in March 2017. We happen to know that some neighbouring premises are being renovated, and we are prepared to predict that they are going to repeat their accomplishment in this part of town.
Other location: 84, rue Jean-Pierre Timbaud, 11th, tel 01 84 25 00 77

COOKING WITH DOMINIQUE PERRAULT

I am always trying to diet, albeit without success. So I decided to eat better quality food. As Alain Ducasse says in his latest book, Manger est un acte citoyen, *eating means being a good citizen. And that means buying Alain's chocolates! Unfortunately – or fortunately – for me, his Manufacture de Chocolat is not far from the "tanker". My favourite is the minimum 70% dark chocolate, in a big tablet you break up with a hammer.*

When I go shopping, I head for the organic grocery POS, and for fish, the fishmonger Paris Pêche at Place d'Aligre market is wonderful. My catch will include sea bream, hake or brill – just gutted and left whole. Another fascinating market is on Avenue du Président Wilson, between the Palais de Tokyo and the Palais Galliera. It's so chic that on each stand (selling foie gras, flowers or heritage vegetables) the stallholders speak at least four languages.

Early Saturday mornings are a pure pleasure for me. For a long time I've been playing tennis in the 12th arrondissement. On my way back, I undo all my good work by treating myself to a chocolate ice cream at Raimo – I'm heading over there today to buy litres of delicious cinnamon and chocolate sorbet and their famous whipped cream.

LA MANUFACTURE DE CHOCOLAT ALAIN DUCASSE
40, rue de la Roquette, 11th, tel 01 48 05 82 86, www.lechocolat-alainducasse.com

MAISON POS
90, rue de Charonne, 11th, tel 09 81 72 37 80

PARIS PÊCHE
17, rue d'Aligre, 12th, tel 01 43 43 12 11, www.paris-peche.com

MARCHÉ PRÉSIDENT WILSON
Avenue du Président Wilson, 16th

RAIMO
59-61, boulevard de Reuilly, 12th, tel 01 43 43 70 17, www.raimo.fr

BARS, CAFÉS AND TEAROOMS

BREAKFAST TO DRINKS ON A TERRACE: TAKING A BREAK IN THE CITY

Cafés, bars and tearooms are an important part of the fabric of life in Paris. Their terraces are permanently packed with people chatting or daydreaming, reading or working on a laptop, engaged in tête-à-têtes or simply enjoying a caffeine hit and a cigarette that can no longer be smoked indoors.

The city boasts establishments of every kind, from the old-fashioned (Au Sauvignon, Brasserie de l'Isle Saint-Louis) to the fashionable (Fondation Café, Café Loustic), hidden away (Salon du Cinéma du Panthéon) and legendary (Les Deux Magots, Café de Flore), all mostly attracting regular customers who meet up in these places as though they were in a new type of library.

Tearooms are mostly frequented by women, young people taking a break from the frantic activity of the city and chic grandmothers taking their grandchildren to Mamie Gâteaux. Tea in a grand hotel is a special, discreet moment usually reserved for an important guest. It is often followed by a visit to a nearby bar or a place more appropriate for the famous apéro (aperitif). This immutable ritual has lost none of its appeal.

ES DEUX MAGOT
MAGOTS

AU SAUVIGNON

80, rue des Saints Pères, 7th
Metro Sèvres-Babylone, Saint-Sulpice
Tel 01 45 48 49 02
www.ausauvignon.com

TRADITIONAL BISTRO

A real Parisian bistro can't be explained – it must be experienced. This little bar with a terrace strategically placed at the corner of Rue de Sèvres and Rue des Saint-Pères is the perfect place for it. It has long attracted intellectuals, local celebrities and the uninitiated, all delighted to be there. It still has its original decor, with woodwork, mini-bar and Bacchic baubles. Purchased by the Auvergnats Henri and Alice Vergne in 1954, it is now run by their granddaughter, Émilie, and her husband, who have the good taste to keep it as it was and continue to serve hearty snacks all day long, among them tartines on Poilâne bread (legend has it that Henri Vergne and his neighbour Lionel Poilâne invented it here) topped with ham from Auvergne or Salers. The rest of the menu offers gourmet delicacies like thin strips of superb beef sausage and other charcuterie from Jurasserie Fine (6th arrondissement), homemade foie gras, Christian Parra black pudding and desserts by pastry chef Christophe Rhedon (Notre Pâtisserie, 7th), holder of the Meilleur Ouvrier de France award. These delicacies can be accompanied by fine wines direct from the producers – not uncommon here – with about thirty available by the glass, ranging from Beaujolais Villages to Condrieu.

CACHETTE

8, rue des Chartreux, 6th
Metro Vavin, RER Port-Royal
Tel 01 43 26 66 34
Closed Sunday

HIDDEN NEIGHBOURHOOD BAR

Once a local shop tucked between the small part of the Luxembourg garden on its south side and the Rue d'Assas, just opposite the Hôpital Tarnier, the Cachette is a genuine hideaway from the overcrowded and over-casual neighbouring Coffee Club. A friendly, quiet and beautifully decorated, vintage-style café with none of the usual excesses, it was taken over in 2013 without much fanfare by Vincent Faivre and Fred Testot – yes, the Fred of the French TV tandem Omar & Fred. And yes, that's Omar Sy, the actor. Which accounts for the comings and goings, between the inside room and the outside terrace, of very familiar faces from the worlds of film and theatre. They all come here strictly incognito – even Catherine Deneuve. Cachette, which means hideaway, opens early in the morning, so it's ideal for a cappuccino and buttered toast, and closes late at night, perfect for a fuss-free drink. It also serves lunch and dinner (in particular, excellent fish from Dôme) on the go, or a *plat du jour*. There is plenty of quality quiet time to be had here, so, even better than a hideaway, it's a godsend on the Left Bank of the Seine.

CAFÉ DE FLORE

172, boulevard Saint-Germain, 6th
Metro Saint-Germain-des-Prés
Tel 01 45 48 55 26, www.cafedeflore.fr

LEGENDARY

This is the most famous café in Paris. Writers, publishers and artists have always felt at home in the Flore. It was frequented by illustrious figures such as Apollinaire, who invented "surrealism" in 1917, before Breton and Aragon came on the scene. Picasso, Giacometti, Sartre, Simone de Beauvoir and Hemingway would hang out here, followed later on by figures from the fashion world, such as Lagerfeld, Saint Laurent and Mugler. Gainsbourg and Francis Bacon also lingered into the wee hours. Parisians still prefer to hole up inside, generally leaving the terrace to the tourists. Celebrities give interviews on the first floor, where politicians tuck into a quiet lunch. Regular customers often order a Welsh rarebit washed down with a glass of house white, but the great morning treat is boiled eggs served with buttered *ficelle* bread sticks and a small pot of coffee on a silver tray. It's pricey as cafés go, but you're paying for a piece of history.

CLAUS

14-15, rue Jean-Jacques Rousseau, 1st
Metro Louvre-Rivoli
Tel 01 42 33 55 10, www.clausparis.com

BREAKFAST

The classic interior of this comfortable tearoom hidden away from the tumult of Les Halles makes a nice change from today's pseudo-hip places with near-identical minimalist decors. Behind the elegant white facade, the interior is discreetly handsome, with black-and-white tiling, a fresh floral decoration and a marble countertop, where the pastries (scones, carrot cake, cookies, financiers, shortbread) are displayed. Take a seat on the ground floor or upstairs in a comfortable armchair in an arcaded room and enjoy a model breakfast, the favourite meal of the German owner, Claus Estermann, who used to work for major fashion houses. In addition to the regular menu, there are five set menus featuring sweet and savoury specialities, including the unbeatable granola served with fresh fruit and organic fromage blanc, cinnamon-nut brioches, matcha-raspberry yoghurt, salmon rösti and eggs cooked in different ways. Mariage Frères teas and fresh fruit juices complement the selection, and salads, sandwiches and soups are available at lunchtime. At the grocery store across the street, you can pick up delectable items like Christine Ferber jams and Alain Milliat fruit juice.

COLOROVA

47, rue de l'Abbé Grégoire, 6th
Metro Rennes, Saint-Placide
Tel 01 45 44 67 56
Closed Monday

MULTI-PURPOSE PÂTISSERIE

Pastry is a hot trend at the moment in Paris, but it is also a serious business. Among those who have impressive references is Guillaume Gil, who worked for several years with Christophe Michalak at the Plaza Athénée. His boutique/tearoom, opened in 2012 with his companion, Charlotte Siles, with whom he studied at the École Ferrandi, is a calm place with nothingeasonal fruit and vegetables, fancy about it. Attention is focused on the pretty blond-wood display case filled with cakes freshly made throughout the day in the semi-open laboratory kitchen. Sample them at any time or have lunch in the cosy, colourful dining room with small tables and mismatched chairs. The shop really comes into its own, however, on Saturday and Sunday, when the wonderful brunch comes out. Families and groups of friends flock there to enjoy the flexible offerings, beginning with a drink, a compote, Viennese pastries or a delicious brioche, jams and sandwiches (all of them homemade, except the excellent bread from the neighbouring Thévenin bakery). That's followed by a starter (*œuf parfait*, grilled bacon and chickpea salad, for example) and then a gourmet main course (beef kefta with mashed potatoes or duck ravioli with parsnips) followed by a pastry of your choice. After all that, customers often choose to prolong the pleasure by requesting a doggy bag.

COMPAGNIE DES VINS SURNATURELS

7, rue Lobineau, 6th, metro Odéon
Tel 09 54 90 20 20
www.compagniedesvinssurnaturels.com
Closed during the day

WINE BAR

Compagnie des Vins Surnaturels is an unusual wine bar. It has the feel of an elegant, cosy apartment, with a slightly English vibe, the kind of place where you might entertain your friends every day. It was designed by the now illustrious Dorothée Meilichzon, who has created a muted atmosphere, with subdued lighting, fireplace, glass roof, velvet curtains and snug armchairs and couches with oddly assorted upholstery prints, making it a perfect place for romantic trysts. It's run by the team from the Experimental Cocktail Club and the Prescription Cocktail Club, which offer 500 different wines to choose from, ranging from the affordable to the highly extravagant (at stratospheric prices), which you can supplement with refined bites such as ham with truffles and *pata negra*, mature cheeses from the Île Saint-Louis cheese factory and pastries by Gérard Mulot. The clientele is very Left Bank, and given the popularity of the place, booking is strongly advised.

FOUCADE

17, rue Duphot, 1st
Tel 01 42 36 11 81
www.foucadeparis.com

GLUTEN-FREE TEAROOM & PÂTISSERIE

Seasonal fruit and vegeatbles, less sugar and less fat, unrefined ingredients, allergens ruthlessly eliminated – Foucade's policy might seem reductive, austere even, but not a bit of it. Here you can look after your body and your health with small fresh dishes served for lunch– truffle risotto, squash soup, canneloni and aubergine stuffed with quinoa, and your mood with pastries as pretty as jewels. For afternoon tea, people treat themselves to plant-based lattes or sophisticated teas, accompanied shamelessly by a pastry with fruit or chocolate. After all, here is nothing wrong with doing yourself some good.

LA CLOSERIE DES LILAS

171, boulevard du Montparnasse, 6th
Metro Vavin
Tel 01 40 51 34 50, www.closeriedeslilas.fr

HISTORIC

"Paris is a moveable feast", wrote Ernest Hemingway, who sat here night after night. Today, the august Closerie – the property, like the Café de Flore, of Miroslav Siljegovic – has taken on a youthful look and has extended its open-roofed (in summer) glass-walled room (seating 100), yet has managed to retain its character. In the restaurant, chef Johann Staskiewicz offers traditional cuisine (pigeon coated in honey and black pepper, French asparagus, sole fillets, sabayon with champagne), while the brasserie offers even simpler fare: egg mayo, homemade pike quenelles with Nantua sauce and, of course, the famous steak tartare with fries prepared in front of the customer. Some of the wait staff can speak Russian. And every night there's the splendid piano bar, with its intellectuals, attractive young women, regulars and cocktails.

LA DÉGUSTATION

93, rue Lepic, 18th
Metro Abbesses, Lamarck-Caulaincourt
Tel 01 46 06 25 20
www.ladegustation.fr
Closed in the morning

CHAMPAGNE BAR, DELI

Right at the top of Rue Lepic, near the Moulin de la Galette, and beyond the reach of many of the tourists who flock to this district, La Dégustation is frequented by Parisians – all, naturally, lovers of champagne, but not only since you can also sip a Petit Chablis or Grignan-Les-Adhémar, a Rhône Valley wine. Cyril Ménard, head sommelier at Drouant, offers sixty top wines. La Dégustation was the brainchild of Michelin-starred chef Antoine Westermann, owner of Le Coq Rico restaurant a few doors down. Here he has created an unpretentious champagne and tapas bar, a far cry from the usual airs and graces. The small portions concocted in the kitchen – such as chicken burgers and the flank steak cooked in pinot noir and served with roast potatoes – are quite filling. Plus you can stock up from the grocery corner on delicacies to enjoy at home or in situ: gravlax, rillettes, mackerel with olive oil, cheese, products from Drouant, Mon Vieil Ami and Le Coq Rico, and wines at wine-merchant prices. Since brunch here is a roaring success, you must book ahead.

L'AVANT-COMPTOIR DU MARCHÉ

14, rue Lobineau, 6th
Metro Saint-Germain-des-Prés, Mabillon
No phone

TAPAS BAR

The Béarnais chef Yves Camdeborde seems to have come down with expansionist fever, which will need treatment some day. Christian Constant's former second from the Hôtel Crillon era has just quintupled his presence in the Saint-Germain and Odéon areas. In addition to his hotel, Le Relais Saint-Germain, and gourmet restaurant, the Comptoir du Relais (tasting menu on weekday evenings and brasserie menu on the weekend), he has opened three Avant-Comptoirs within the space of a few years. The latest addition to these tapas bars, opened at the end of 2016, is in the Marché Saint-Germain. It is also the most spectacular, with a big glass facade under the arcades and gleaming chromed wine cabinets. The motto of the latest addition to the empire is *tout est bon dans le cochon* (every part of the pig is good), and every bit of the animal is used to make crispy ears, cheeks in broth, frankfurters in salad, streaky bacon with rosemary and, of course, a very serious selection of charcuterie (including black pudding made by brother Philippe, coppa from Éric Ospital and homemade *pâté en croûte*). Order anything from the colossal menu, scattered puzzle-like around the restaurant on little hanging signs, and enjoy it with the best natural wines, all served by the glass. Beware of a prolonged cocktail hour!

LE BÉGUIN

2, rue du Cardinal Mercier, 9th
Metro Liège, Place de Clichy
Tel 01 42 81 58 20, www.lebeguin.com
Closed Sunday

PRE- AND POST-THEATRE

You might run into Laetitia Casta and Raphaël Personnaz relaxing in front of a slice of quiche and a plate of charcuterie in this charming café. Nothing could be more normal. It is located next door to the Théâtre de l'Œuvre and over the years has become a canteen for actors, technicians and spectators. When a play's run comes to an end, the cast changes, but not the slightly grotty 1950s decor, with moleskin banquettes, wooden chairs, old photos and vintage lighting, nor the relaxed service. Country-style terrine, Prince of Paris ham and aged Comté are served at any time, and at lunch and dinnertime you can have a more elaborate dish (like pollock ceviche with ginger, Puy lentil soup with fresh herbs or hand-chopped Italian-style beef tartare). Since January 2016, the café has been run by the young Florian Diday and Alexis Coutin, who carry on the family spirit of this eminently appealing place. A real discovery.

LE NEMOURS

2, place Colette, 1st
Metro Palais-Royal–Musée du Louvre
Tel 01 42 61 34 14
www.lenemours.paris

CHIC CAFÉ

This historic café has something of a royal setting: imagine having for neighbours the Comédie-Française, the Ministry of Culture, the Council of State, the Louvre and the Tuileries Garden. This is the perfect setting for the terrace of the Nemours, which was taken over in February 2016 by Olivier Coustou, until then its manager. Tourists and regulars like to linger on its carefully aligned rattan chairs, sheltered by the monumental columns of the Place Colette. Revamped from top to bottom by the architect Michaël Malapert, the Neoclassical-style interior also deserves a glance, with its blond-wood walls, vintage chandeliers and works by the artist Béa Corteel adorning the long, narrow room. The sometimes grumpy waiters run up and down it all day, from 7am (8am on weekends) to midnight. The menu, created by consulting chef Daniel Hudry, suits the setting, mixing classic café dishes (baguette sandwiches, croque monsieurs, quiches)

SPOTLIGHT

RAILWAY TERMINUS CHEFS

While any good player of French Monopoly loves Paris's railway stations, gourmets snub them, usually with good reason. They tend to serve frozen pastries, industrial hamburgers and burning-hot coffee diluted with water. Only a passenger about to miss a train or a lost tourist would eat the horrors sold by a collection of soulless chains. Paris, however, has a very real history of train-station buffets where travellers could order a *jambon-beurre* (baguette sandwich with butter and ham) worthy of the name.

The SNCF (French state-owned railway company), aware that there was a problem and consequently an opportunity, came up with a bright idea and found some great chefs willing to listen – it's good for business and good for the image – and quick to react when it comes to expanding their activities. The latest to arrive on the platform is Thierry Marx. The chef of the Mandarin Oriental created the menu for L'ÉTOILE DU NORD (www.letoiledunord.fr), located in a building with an imposing glass facade designed by architect Patrick Bouchain in the Gare du Nord, from which Thalys trains depart for Brussels and Amsterdam and the Eurostar for London. It has two dining rooms with different atmospheres: a brasserie on the ground floor and a cosier modern bistro upstairs, both with the same perfectly mastered menu with a few nods to the cuisine of the northern countries (endive au gratin with ham, waffles, etc.).

Further to the west, Éric Frechon, chef at the Hotel Bristol, watches over LAZARE (www.lazare-paris.fr), a superb neo-brasserie opened in late 2013 in the newly renovated Saint-Lazare station. The menu is a skilful compilation of dishes, adaptable to each customer's needs: wonderful sausage and mash and other daily specials served all day long at the bar, and more lyrical dishes for those who do not have a train to catch. The only sticking point is that it is always crowded.

At the Gare de Lyon, LE TRAIN BLEU (www.le-train-bleu.com) takes a different tack, exhibiting its polite indifference. Opened at the beginning of the last century, this legendary restaurant and bar was redecorated in 2013 and now has small, comfortable lounges. Beyond the contents of the plate, nicely prepared and scandalously expensive, it is the grandiose setting that justifies the journey: a gigantic Art Nouveau dining room, without doubt one of the most impressive in the city. On the Left Bank, at the Gare du Montparnasse, a sinister train station if there ever was one, a counterattack is being prepared. In 2019, another Grand Poobah of the pots and pans will arrive: Alain Ducasse. This challenge is one the chef (who has just opened a restaurant in the Château de Versailles) is well equipped to meet.

POINT OF VIEW

A TASTE FOR TEA

Tea is a noble product. After having been used for centuries and in so many civilizations, it deserves a little more consideration today than to be stuffed into a sachet and dunked in a cup of hot water. While Paris has suddenly acquired a legitimate passion for tea leaves – with a sharp increase in the number of shops and quality brands – the service offered is not always up to snuff. Aside from a few choice places, the beverage is too often mistreated. The ultimate in bad taste are the big neighbourhood brasseries serving up unbelievable quantities of industrial teabags wrapped in plastic packets and set down next to a cup of lukewarm water. Charming! And it doesn't help to offer teabags in fake antique wooden boxes as if they were cheap cigars. Even more annoying and dismayingly common are chic, cosy tearooms that don't make much of an effort. Yes, they serve respectable brands with better-quality sachets, but the service – unlike the prices – seldom suits the pretensions.
And what about the teapot, plopped down on the table with no information offered on the infusion time or the temperature of the water. And then there are the cups, always cold. As every tea lover knows, the ceremony requires that hot water should be poured over whole leaves in a filter so that they swell up and release their perfume. The brew must then be consumed at the right moment, when properly infused but not too strong. Let's hope that this approach will soon become the rule rather than the exception.

with more contemporary veggie plates or diet-friendly dishes (chicken with confit lemon, coriander, quinoa and cumin-flavoured carrots) and branded treats like Kaviari tarama or pastries from Matthieu & Pauline. Many French politicians, lawyers and actors are regulars at this great spot for a quick lunch or an aperitif before a show.

LE ROUQUET

188, boulevard Saint-Germain, 7th
Metro Saint-Germain-des-Prés
Tel 01 45 48 06 93
Closed Sunday

NEIGHBOURHOOD BISTRO

At a time when most of the capital's cafés and tobacconist-bars are coming down with the Costes virus and trading in their ordinary furnishings for padded sub-Jacques Garcia creations, Le Rouquet is a small outpost of resistance; as a result, it is packed. Who would have thought a frankfurter and fries could be so appealing? Careful, however – service is not non-stop. It's the atmospheric, authentic 1950s decor that is the main claim to fame of the place.

LE SALON DU CINÉMA DU PANTHÉON

13, rue Victor Cousin, 5th
RER Luxembourg
Tel 01 56 24 88 80
www.whynotproductions.fr/pantheon/
Closed Saturday and Sunday

FILM-LOVERS' LOUNGE

The illustrious Cinéma du Panthéon, mentioned by Sartre in Les Mots and by Jacques Prévert, was the first to screen the films of the Nouvelle Vague in the 1960s and since then many twists and turns occurred before it became a place where film lovers could meet and discuss their passion in this café designed by Catherine Deneuve and her friend Christian Sapet. The temporary exhibitions are chosen by the actress and changed approximately every three months. Film books and periodicals are scattered all over. This hidden café, which can be rented for a private event in the evening, is open to the public from 12:30pm (reservation recommended) until 7pm. It's a great place to hang out, with free wifi and lively conversations among film lovers. The blackboard menu lists simple dishes for lunch (seasonal soups, smoked salmon, quiche, dietetic salads, daily specials, with bread from Bread & Roses), afternoon tea (green-tea cheesecake, chocolate cake, crumble) and wines selected by Le Thé des Écrivains.

LES DEUX MAGOTS

6, place Saint-Germain-des-Prés, 6th
Metro Saint-Germain-des-Prés
Tel 01 45 48 55 25, www.lesdeuxmagots.fr

INSTITUTION

Les Deux Magots and the Café de Flore have been polite rivals forever. And so much the better! Apart from visitors to the city, most have an allegiance to one or the other. Les Deux Magots establishment started life in 1813 as a novelty store, only becoming a café in 1884. Much of its popularity is due to its three terraces, one with an excellent view of the picturesque cobblestone square dominated by the bell tower of Saint-Germain-des-Prés church. This terrace was recently converted into a covered terrace garden, filled with boxwood topiaries, and can seat up to seventy people. Or maybe people love it for the creamy-thick, old-fashioned hot chocolate they serve up.

MAISIE CAFÉ

32, rue du Mont Thabor, 1st, metro Concorde
Tel 01 40 39 99 16, www.maisiecafe.com

DETOX CAFÉ

Veggie, healthy and girly – that's Maisie, the café where Isabella Capece and Xavier Barroux cook up healthy eats all day long. Nestled between Place Vendôme and the Tuileries, this coffee shop boasts a pretty pastel-coloured interior (featuring murals with tropical motifs by artist Vincent Scali, and light-coloured wooden chairs by the Bouroullec brothers) created by Californian designer Mallery Roberts Morgan. This Zen canteen serves up light lunches with a focus on dips (alternating chickpeas, avocado, broccoli and sweet pepper to scoop up with vegetable and seed crackers), seasonal soups and various gluten-free focaccias straight from the Chambelland bakery ovens in the 11th arrondissement, topped with creamed cashew nuts (the Mediterraneo version contains courgettes, aubergine caviar, tomatoes, peppers and baby spinach). The detox menu also features cold-pressed organic fruit and vegetable juices, infused waters and vegetarian milkshakes made from cashew or rice milk. At breakfast, bowls of gluten-free granola cooked at low temperature and served with various seeds and vegetable milk take pride of place, while at teatime the pastries take over (cake made with raw chocolate and ground almonds, apple pie with cashews, almonds and dates, and more). If you thought vegetarian food lacked glamour, think again!

MAISON DES TROIS THÉS

1, rue Saint-Médard, 5th, metro Place Monge
Tel 01 43 36 93 84
www.maisondestroisthes.com
Closed Monday

TEA

The Maison des Trois Thés looks like the right place to select the best of the camellia. The world's leading chefs, as well as gourmets and lovers of wine and spirits all pass around the address of Yu Hui Tseng. The daughter of an illustrious Chinese family, she is the only woman to join the exclusive club of the world's top-ten tea experts. In the extraordinary oriental setting of a conservatory of objects and antique furniture that houses the world's largest tea cellar, with more than 1,000 different kinds, she sells and officiates at tastings in a fascinating ceremony of delectably precious and expensive teas. Numerous vintages come from Yu Hui Tseng's tea gardens. Neophytes can use an explanatory map to make their choice, guided by a highly

attentive staff. You need to make an appointment before coming to inhale the fragrance of these rare wonders and then taste them. Handy tip: don't dab on any perfume before a tasting!

MIZNON

22, rue des Écouffes, 4th, metro Saint-Paul
Tel 01 42 74 83 58
Closed Saturday

PITA EXTRAVAGANZA

This is definitely the most vibrant Jewish eatery in the Marais. Rather than stand in a long queue in front of the popular As du Fallafel, try this nearby restaurant, opened by Eyal Shani, a leading Israeli chef, who already has two such establishments in Tel Aviv. Inside, the speakers blare out local music, with staff and regulars joining in to create a joyful cacophony. The focus of this animated little world is the superb pita sandwich, whose various fillings are scribbled by hand on the menu – lamb kebab, beef bourguignon, ratatouille, breaded hake – all garnished with fresh herbs and topped with homemade sauces. We have a weakness for the whole cauliflower, braised in the oven until almost burnt, lashed with olive oil and sprinkled with *fleur de sel*. Street food at its best!

MOKONUTS

5, rue Saint-Bernard, 11th
Metro Faidherbe-Chaligny
Tel 09 80 81 82 85
Closed Saturday and Sunday

DE LUXE COFFEE SHOP

No need to search any further. This is where you will find the best cookies in Paris. The combinations – olives and white chocolate, miso and sesame seeds – are as unusual as the cooking times are perfect. The maker of these sweet little marvels is Japan's Moko Hirayama, former pastry maker at Adeline Grattard's restaurant Yam'Tcha and the soul of this tiny but vibrant coffee shop, which she runs along with her companion, Omar Koreitem (formerly of Le Sergent Recruteur). From early in the morning until late in the afternoon it is filled with fans, computers tucked under their arms, answering emails while nibbling on a piece of pecan and muscovado-sugar cake or a light chiffon cake with crème anglaise, accompanied by a freshly made drink (such as spicy clementine juice or iced tea with hibiscus). At lunchtime, it becomes a small canteen in which the completely unruffled Omar sends out totally disarming seasonal dishes with numerous influences: roasted pumpkin with kale and sesame cream; *labneh* with confit tomatoes and *za'atar* directly from Lebanon; or black mullet with *pommes tapées* (dried apples), Brussels sprouts and bergamot. In the evening, the chef cooks a five-course tasting menu for private dinners of six to ten people (reserve in advance). In other words, this is not your typical coffee shop.

PIERRE GERONIMI

5, rue Férou, 6th, metro Saint-Sulpice
Tel 01 42 38 00 67
www.glacespierregeronimi.com

TEAROOM, ICE CREAM

Corsican ice cream-maker Pierre Geronimi has moved to Paris and found an impressive location. With neighbours like the Hotel Récamier, the restaurant Le Bon Saint-Pourçain and photographer François-Marie Banier's mansion, this ice-cream parlour with a contemporary interior is not the kind of place where you would just have an ordinary dish of ice cream. Famous for his radical, sometimes Corsican-influenced flavours – *brocciu* (a Corsican cheese), seawater, bitter-orange flower, myrtle, grated cocoa, Cervione hazelnuts, whisky – Geronimi has revolutionized ice cream and sorbet, and makes them with the best ingredients. Originally from Sagone, on the west coast of the Isle of Beauty, he is now present in Monaco and elsewhere in the world. At lunchtime in winter, don't miss the *petit-salé* with lentils and grain-mustard ice cream.

SÉBASTIEN GAUDARD – PÂTISSERIE DES TUILERIES

1, rue des Pyramides, 1st
Metro Pyramides, Tuileries
Tel 01 71 18 24 70
www.sebastiengaudard.com
Closed Monday

CHIC PASTRY SHOP AND TEAROOM

Under the arcades of the Rue des Pyramides, Sébastien Gaudard has opened his second pâtisserie (the first is on Rue des Martyrs), coupled with a lovely French-style tearoom on the first floor of what had been an art gallery since 1870. Amid its half-moon windows, embossed wallpaper, old prints and palm trees, Sébastien's fans will enjoy his lemon tarts and "mussipontains" (a speciality of Sébastien's father Daniel based on meringue, vanilla cream and slivers of caramelized almond) in the cosy atmosphere of a very early 20th-century setting. The ultra-classic tearoom hums to the same tune as the pâtisserie. A savoury menu offers soup (e.g. vichyssoise), boiled eggs and market salads, and toasted sandwiches and Lorraine tarts give the place a very French flavour. Fresh seasonal fruit juices and a selection of tea, herbal tea and coffee with a "drop" of Evian complete the superb menu. On the ground floor you'll find a gourmet shop. The production workshop can be found in the vaulted basement under the Rue des Pyramides, which dates back to the same era as the Louvre. **Other location:** 22, rue des Martyrs, 9th, tel 01 71 18 24 70

VERLET

256, rue Saint-Honoré, 1st
Metro Palais-Royal–Musée du Louvre
Tel 01 42 60 67 39, www.cafesverlet.com
Closed Sunday and in August

TEA AND COFFEE

The address is so classic you would almost forget about it. But it would be a mistake. This emporium founded in 1880 by a high-seas adventurer and former Cape Horner was originally a colonial trading post before specializing in coffee and tea. In this wood-panelled decor, Éric Duchossoy and his son Thomas continue the family tradition. The selection varies according to the season and the arrivals, and might include Jamaican, Panamanian, Hawaiian or Burmese. Fans of mocha or excellent freshly roasted and ground coffee, journalists from the satirical weekly *Le Canard enchaîné* and actors from the Théâtre Français mingle here with an often female clientele drawn by the fine tea selection. The menu has the same high standards, with delicious pastries from Carl Marletti, tasty Mediterranean candied fruits, and salads and quiches of the day from Stohrer's.

WILD AND THE MOON

55, rue Charlot, 3rd
Metro Temple, Filles du Calvaire
Tel 09 51 80 22 33
www.wildandthemoon.com

CAFÉ GREEN

It's already a familiar formula – vegetable and fruit juices (cold-pressed to retain the vitamins), gluten-free pastries, and healthy vegan dishes to meet every demand – but its execution here in one of Emma Sawko's two Parisian "green canteens" (she used the same concept in Dubai, where she had followed her banker husband) is a great success. First, because of the attractive New York coffee shop decor (light colours, dozens of hanging plants, glass-enclosed laboratory kitchen). Second, because it all tastes so good. The lavish selection is served from breakfast time through the afternoon: unbeatable avocado toast, excellent house granola (buckwheat, dried fruits, pumpkin and sunflower seeds, dates and seasonal fruits), rotating daily specials (such as Thai curry and coral lentil dahl), mixed bowls, great smoothies and hot drinks with vegetable milk (excellent chai latte with almond milk, cinnamon, maple syrup and coconut milk). Even the vegetable-and-dried-almond crackers for dipping into the hummus are vegan.

A COFFEE WITH DOMINIQUE PERRAULT

I love coffee, although after 3pm I move onto decaffeinated. I like it short and strong and I have a weakness for gingerbread-flavoured coffee. No frills – I drink it standing up at the counter, as they do in Italy. I love it, and it always makes me feel good. At Le Rouquet, I enjoy the Formica ambience like at my mother's. But that doesn't stop me from enjoying a coffee sitting in the bar of a large hotel such as La Galerie in the Plaza Athénée or the garden courtyard of the Costes. At the Café des Beaux-Arts, the student I used to be meets the member of the Institut that I have become, from the school to the cuploa of the Académie.

LE ROUQUET

188, boulevard Saint-Germain, 7th, metro rue du Bac, tel 01 45 48 06 93

LA GALERIE

Hôtel Plaza Athénée, 25, avenue Montaigne, 8th, metro Alma-Marceau, tel 01 53 67 66 65, www.dorchestercollection.com

HÔTEL COSTES

239-241, rue Saint-Honoré, 1st, metro Concorde, tel 01 42 44 50 00, hotelcostes.com

CAFÉ DES BEAUX-ARTS

7 quai de Malaquais, 6th, metro Pont Neuf, tel 01 43 54 08 55

NIGHTLIFE

JAZZ CLUBS TO TECHNO DANCE FLOORS: WINDING DOWN IN THE CITY

Paris's festive nightlife sparkles with creativity and culture, attracting a colourful assortment of merrymakers ready to revel in all its mysteries as soon as the sun melts into the Seine. Arriving by metro, scooter or Uber, night owls start as early as 6pm with a craft beer or sophisticated cocktail before moving on to a jazz concert or hip-hop DJ set. The ongoing after-dark Paris party offers an endless variety of pleasures and places.

You are more likely to find cool cocktail bars with skilled bartenders shaking up their concoctions on the Right Bank than on the Left. The recently arrived world of mixology is dominated by groups of experts like Experimental Cocktail Club (owners of the bar of the same name and Night Flight) and Quixotic Project (La Candelaria, Mary Céleste), as well as independents. They all have carefully designed concepts and cocktails with turntables spinning in the background and are a big hit with a globetrotting clientele eager to satisfy all the senses.

Faced with this tidal wave of cocktails, clubs have changed their approach to win back night crawlers, offering such innovative, appealing new concepts as cocooning at Maison Sage, artistic expression at Salò and drag shows at Divan du Monde (which recently partnered with Madame Arthur). Hemingway called Paris a moveable feast, but it's a special kind of feast for Parisians attached to certain values: conviviality, Epicureanism and freedom.

BADABOUM

2 bis, rue des Taillandiers, 11th
Metro Ledru-Rollin
Tel 01 48 06 50 70
www.badaboum-paris.com
Closed Sunday to Tuesday

COCKTAIL BAR, CONCERTS, CLUB

La Scène Bastille, well-known for electro, funk and hip-hop concerts, was replaced in 2014 by Badaboum. This new club was founded by the team that had previously initiated the Cliché nights at the Concorde Atlantique and opened the Panic Room, a club for twenty-somethings and fashionistas mad about Berlin electro. Featuring emerging pop, rock, house and other great DJ sets (Miss Kittin, Clara 3000) you can also catch gay events and performances in the huge room superbly lit by the French label NYX Visual, specialized in digital settings. The Bastille wildlife is pretty mixed, but the atmosphere represents the chic face of Bastille rather than its wild side, as customers enjoy house cocktails served until 6am at the bar. Dilan Kavak learned the bartending trade in London and serves up such drinks as American whisky with popcorn syrup and Russian vodka infused with rosemary. At 1:30am, Badaboum opens the doors of "MacGuffing & Associés" to clubbers with sensitive palates. This speakeasy, which looks like the office of an old-school English detective agency, discreetly serves refined mixtures and quality spirits. A great way to end the evening.

BARANAAN

7, rue du Faubourg Saint-Martin, 10th
Metro Strasbourg-Saint-Denis
Tel 01 40 38 97 57
www.baranaan.com
Closed Sunday and Monday

INDIAN, RESTAURANT, CONCERTS

First stop: Elaichi (which means "cardamom" in Hindi), an organic, vegan Indian canteen with an atmosphere that calls Mumbai to mind. This snack is essential before continuing your journey through a door adorned with paintings (not kitschy) honouring the Bengal tiger and the sacred elephant. Once inside, the Bollywood adventure continues in this speakeasy decorated like the Orient Express, with leather banquettes, vintage suitcases and luggage racks. The owners, Raphaël and Kristhan, have also had the bright idea of installing TV screens on which railway tracks run through an exotic landscape, with no noisy locomotive to disturb you. The journey does not end there, however. Your cocktail purchases are duly stamped in a passport and may be served in a coconut shell or a metal mug. Heavily perfumed with spices, they are made with Indian spirits and homemade mixtures. You can also sample a naan cooked on a tandoor. A festive atmosphere is guaranteed on weekends by DJs playing pop, electro and "Hindi music".

BLUEBIRD

12, rue Saint-Bernard, 11th
Metro Charonne

INTIMATE COCKTAIL BAR

After hiding out at the Moonshiner, a speakeasy for whisky buffs, this trio with a Mediterranean accent – Pasa Omerasevic, Danilo Grenci and Pedro Martinez – is back in the spotlight with a neighbourhood bar for gin junkies. Leaving behind the Roaring Twenties style, this cosy, stylish cocktail bar conjures up California in the 1950s. You might expect to run into the dapper Don Draper and his acolytes here. These Italian and Spanish cocktail geeks have boned up on the history of the Dutch gin genever and other spirits and offer a "Gin Cocktail Experience". You'll find well-known and unknown gins, along with mezcal, rum and Italian bitters. They start to shake up amazing mixtures to the sounds of jazz beginning at 6pm, accompanied by the irresistible smiles of the staff. Even non-smokers must take a trip to the *fumoir* (smoking room) for the hypnotic effect of the goldfish in an aquarium that provides the backdrop.

CABARET MICHOU

80, rue des Martyrs, 18th
Metro Pigalle
Tel 01 46 06 16 04
www.michou.com

LEGENDARY

Michou is a legend in Montmartre. One Mardi Gras sixty years ago he transformed his bar, Madame Untel, into a fun, cheeky cabaret, presenting a number of stunning drag artists with delightful names like Lady Paic, Miss Glassex and La Grande Eugène. Each evening, from behind the curtain by Jean-Marie Fonteneau – who also designed some famous theatre posters, such as for *La Cage aux Folles* – Michou presents his actors and drag artists (some now showing their age a bit). They celebrate legendary figures like Édith Piaf and Dalida, and gently poke fun at others like Céline Dion, Cher and Whitney Houston. On the tiny stage, glittery gowns, bejewelled beehives and specially made costumes bring laughter and song to the world. The dinner, with good food and champagne on every table, is served by the artistes themselves until 10pm sharp, when it's showtime!

CANDELARIA

52, rue de Saintonge, 3rd
Metro Filles du Calvaire
Tel 01 42 74 41 28

COCKTAIL BAR

Candelaria is like a cosy speakeasy. Out front is a *taquería* jam-packed every evening and serving tacos, guacamole and frijoles from a tiny counter. A crowd of thirty-something Hispanics, Parisians and New Yorkers eventually relocate to the bar at the back, beyond the taco counter. There, in a decor of Mexican religious knick-knacks lit by candlelight, the hip barmen shake up spicy cocktails. Try the buzzy Guêpe Verte (green wasp) cocktail here, made with tequila, chilli and cucumber, or the fashionable beers and "flights" of agave-based spirits for a tasteful journey to the homeland of the Aztecs.

CASTOR CLUB

14, rue Hautefeuille, 6th
Metro Odéon
Tel 09 50 64 99 38
Closed Sunday and Monday

COCKTAIL BAR, CLUB

Wood panelling and candlelight give this place an American West feel. Great folk and country music, from honky-tonk to bluegrass, is served up with creative cocktails. A veritable hole-in-the-wall, albeit without cowboy boots or fringed shirts, it's a favourite with Le Montana regulars, Saint-Germain locals and Americans passing through Paris. The bartender, Thomas Codsi, who also owns the **REFLET** in the Latin Quarter (6, rue Champollion, 6th, tel 01 43 29 97 27), includes all the classics on his menu (with the tiresome mojito consigned to oblivion), and has fun with his own little treasures – cumin liqueur, hop-flavoured vodka, quail's eggs – to make fantastic cocktails. His Chirac 95, made with calvados, Génépi des Pères Chartreux, apple shrub and egg white, is one of the best. Happily ignoring fashion, the regulars let down their hair at weekends, dancing in its vaulted cellars.

DANICO

6, rue Vivienne, 2nd
Metro Bourse
Tel 01 42 21 93 71

COCKTAIL BAR, NIBBLES

Danico is hidden behind Darocco, the chic trattoria/pizzeria owned by Alexandre Giesbert and Julien Ross Its mission is not to provide the thirsty with the omnipresent spritz and other drinks imported from the Veneto and Lombardy. Nico de Soto, a leading French bartender on the international scene and founder of the bar Mace in New York City's East Village, is in charge of the libations in this cocktail bar with an Art Deco decor jazzed up by tattoo artist SupaKitch. The team of bartenders, who look like sailors from a Pierre and Gilles painting (a nod to the Jean Paul Gaultier store that used to be located here), know how to please the chic clientele, who do a little trading between cocktails with names like "Prends l'Oseille et Tire-Toi" ("Take the Money and Run") or "Un Petit Pois dans l'Ascenseur" ("A Pea in a Lift"). They are made with the most sophisticated liquid techniques, including clarification, vacuum-infusion and fat-washing. They are so good that the cosy chairs are already full as of 6pm. An addictive bar.

DUC DES LOMBARDS

42, rue des Lombards, 1st
Metro Châtelet
Tel 01 42 33 22 88
www.ducdeslombards.com

JAZZ CLUB

Rue des Lombards is home to several legendary jazz clubs, including the **SUNSET** (www.sunset-sunside.com) and **LE BAISER SALÉ** (www.lebaisersale.com). The Duc des Lombards, which opened in 1984, has hosted concerts by some of the biggest names in jazz, including trumpeter Wynton Marsalis and pianist Martial Solal, while also showcasing the talents of up-and-coming musicians. Its programme is eclectic and stimulating.

GOLDEN PROMISE

11, rue Tiquetonne, 2nd
Metro Étienne Marcel
Tel 01 42 65 03 16
www.goldenpromise.fr
Closed Sunday and Monday

COCKTAIL BAR, WHISKIES

This is the favourite bar of vintage malt lovers, which is not surprising considering its high-flying origins as a collaboration between Youlin Ly, founder of the award-winning Sola, and the Maison du Whisky, an institution. Hidden under the Maison du Saké, Golden Promise fulfils all its pledges. At the entrance is a bar with a neatly aligned display of 200 whiskies, surrounded by exposed stone, and an impressive list of mixed drinks, highballs, whisky on the rocks and chasers. But the real golden promise lies hidden behind a metal door. Ring the bell to gain access to the two fantastic tasting rooms, where more than 800 whiskies await their fate. François Piriou serves as your guide, choosing libations to suit your taste and desires. The salon offers collector's whiskies from around the world, some aged up to 80 years, while the Japanese room offers only rare Japanese whisky. The prices are made to measure.

GRAVITY BAR

44, rue des Vinaigriers, 10th
Metro Jacques Bonsergent
Tel 06 98 54 92 49
Closed Sunday and Monday

HIP COCKTAIL BAR

With cocktails called "Disorientation", "Zero Gravity", "Vertigo" and "Exaltation", the Gravity Bar knows how to grab your attention. The bar has a striking contemporary decor, with wavy wood structures and sky-blue banquettes. Sit at the curved concrete bar and give into such heady concoctions as Fruit du Passé, made with Strega liqueur, Dolin *génépi*, house-made celery syrup, lemon juice, liquorice powder and fennel seeds. It's sure to spin you into orbit. You can also dine on small plates of black pudding or squid a la plancha. Once the kitchen closes, the cocktail shakers set the pace. The place has been packed ever since it opened. Patience is a must here.

HIPPO PUB – HIPPODROME DE VINCENNES

2, route de la Ferme, 13th
Metro Château de Vincennes
Tel 01 49 77 17 17
www.vincennes-hippodrome.com
Open Friday evenings only,
closed in July and August

BEER, RACECOURSE

Every Friday evening at 7pm, this bar at the "trotter's temple" that is the Vincennes racecourse fills up with bettors attracted by the aroma of good malt and hops.

SPOTLIGHT

TIME FOR A DRINK!

Paris has long been a capital of gastronomy; now it is also a great place to drink, whether it's a late-afternoon refreshment, a sophisticated pre-dinner cocktail, an after-dinner drink for a touch of sweetness or an exotic concoction for a night rich in surprises. Here are some of the best places to savour the right drink at the right time.

6PM Have a refreshing beer, artisanal or not, in a cabin at the PERCHOIR MK2 before trying out the MK2 VR virtual reality experience, 162, avenue de France, 13th, metro Bibliothèque François Mitterrand, www.leperchoir.tv

7PM Try the legendary spritz from the Veneto in a new version with cucumber vermouth, fresh mint, elderflower soda and Prosecco at the most authentic and popular Italian restaurant in Paris, POPOLARE 111, rue Réaumur, 2nd, metro Étienne Marcel, tel 01 42 21 30 91, www.bigmammagroup.com

7:30PM How about a Thai cocktail called Curry Colada, with rum, pandan syrup, coconut milk, green curry and lime juice? Just spicy enough to excite the senses while curled up on a couch in the smoking room like a character in *In the Mood for Love,* in the basement of the trendy canteen BAMBOU 23, rue des Jeûneurs, 2nd, metro Grands Boulevards, Bourse, tel 01 40 28 98 30, www.bambouparis.fr

8PM Time for a gourmet drink: the Spicy Sea, made with oyster leaves, white rum, a bitter Italian liqueur, grapefruit juice, lime and Tabasco. Drink it while looking at the divine view at the bar of the prodigious APICIUS, located in a townhouse, 20, rue d'Artois, 8th, metro Saint Philippe du Roule, tel 01 43 80 19 66, www.restaurant-apicius.com

10PM For an after-dinner drink, try a classic "dry & strong" Manhattan made the old-fashioned way at DUKE'S BAR in the Westminster Hotel, 13, rue de la Paix, 2nd, metro Opéra, tel 01 42 61 55 11, www.leceladon.com

11PM Before midnight strikes, share a gin punch made with a recipe from New York City, Audrey's Gin Gin Mule, containing gin, lime, sugar, mint and ginger beer, in the chicest cocktail bar on the Left Bank, the PRESCRIPTION COCKTAIL CLUB 23, rue Mazarine, 6th, metro Odéon, Mabillon, tel 09 50 35 72 87, www.prescriptioncocktailclub.com

1AM Recharge your batteries with a *rhum arrangé* with a thousand and one flavours from Cape Verde at EMBUSCADE 47, rue de la Rochefoucauld, 9th, metro Pigalle, Saint-Georges, tel 01 42 80 19 50, www.rhumerie-du-cap-vert.com

2AM Time for another energy boost with a Tiki, a fruity Polynesian cocktail shaken by bartenders in Hawaiian shirts at the DIRTY DICK 10, rue Frochot, 9th, metro Pigalle, tel 01 48 78 74 58

3AM Sip a classic gin and tonic jazzed up with an infusion of toasted maté on the dance floor of CAFÉ CARMEN 34, rue Duperré, 9th, metro Blanche, tel 01 45 26 50 00, www.le-carmen.fr

5:30AM By now, you may need a coffee urgently (you'll have to wait until 6am for the croissant). Have a strong one in an interior designed by Jacques Garcia at the GRAND CAFÉ CAPUCINES 4, boulevard des Capucines, 9th, metro Opéra, tel 01 43 12 19 00, www.legrandcafe.com

This minimalist setting with a lounge decor, high-tech equipment and an amazing 360-degree view of the track is a great place to calm an overdose of adrenaline between three-minute races with something from the eclectic list of beers. All the big names are there, but aficionados will appreciate the French organic craft beers before paying a visit to the stables. This is what a pub should be!

JOSÉPHINE – CAVES PARISIENNES

25, rue Moret, 11th
Metro Couronne, Parmentier
Tel 01 48 07 16 70
www.cafejosephine.fr
Closed Sunday to Tuesday

COCKTAIL BAR, CLUB, RESTAURANT

Located near the frenetic Oberkampf and Belleville areas, this bar has quietly made a place for itself with no help from media hype, techno stars or famous cocktail makers. The team from the Cannibale – a popular bistro – had the right idea when they opened this spot for an epicurean clientele tired of places where people go to be seen. One can keep a low profile here, with little lamps lightly illuminating rows of stylish wines and whiskies but also an array of cocktail ingredients in shimmering colours in a decor that pays homage to Josephine Baker. Food is available at the bar or in the lounge all night from a limited menu created by a guest chef or featuring food pairings ranging from smoked albacore accompanied by an organic Bergerac to burrata with a French Negroni shaken up by Thomas Frenay, a bartender worth watching. The bar also gets the sounds right. From Wednesday to Saturday, the turntables spin out electro, soul and funk rhythms selected by excellent DJs.

KIEZ

24, rue Vauvenargues, 18th
Metro Guy Môquet
Tel 01 46 27 78 46
www.kiez.fr

BIERGARTEN, RESTAURANT

This is the only *Biergarten* in Paris. Owned by a native of Hamburg and a young Germanophile, it offers an opportunity to discover – if you are not already familiar with it – the beer-drinking culture of Germany, from Munich to Berlin, with no Tyrolean music. Decorated like a German brasserie in wood and stone, it has weathered advertising posters, a projector for football matches and a foosball game. You will want to shout "wunderbar" when you see, behind the black, red and yellow flag, a verdant courtyard with long tables like those at an authentic beer festival. The list of beers will have the same effect on aficionados: five draught beers, including the best of Munich and Angela Merkel's favourite. The food is of the same calibre, with currywürst, Kreuzberg kebab, spätzle of the month and pretzels with cheese on the menu. *Ein Prosit!*

LA COMMUNE

80, boulevard de Belleville, 20th
Metro Couronnes, Belleville
www.syndicatcocktailclub.com
Closed Sunday and Monday

SPECIALIST COCKTAIL BAR

The Belleville area, which until now has had no cocktail bars, has become the new playground of Sullivan Doh and Romain Le Mouellic, fervent defenders of French spirits. The two founders of Le Syndicat – a stronghold of French beverages – have moved into this working-class neighbourhood with another revolutionary concept. In this bar decorated in industrial/ flea market style, the only drink served is punch, the granddaddy of the cocktail. Head bartender Sullivan Doh offers several recipes using French spirits like rum, calvados and cognac. Customers share authentic punch bowls among two, four or six friends, toasting their 18th-century ancestors while enjoying fresh fruits and blended flavours without the risk of hangovers. The mix of hip-hop, funk and rap in this magical place is as carefully considered as the drinks.

LA MANO

10, rue Papillon, 9th
Metro Poissonnière
Tel 09 67 50 50 37
Closed Sunday to Tuesday

RESTAURANT, CLUB

Opened in 2015 by the former owner of the now-defunct Le Baron, La Mano is a pocket-sized club that looks like a Mexican hut, a very hot Mexican hut! Just about all the Parisians who count can be found crowded onto the dance floor gyrating, with a glass of Raiz (mezcal, ginger) in hand, under a huge ball with golden facets. Salsa, Afro-Cuban jazz and reggae music follow each other in incessant waves all night long. It's a dance marathon worthy of *They Shoot Horses, Don't They?* in a caramba version. When customers leave, they are breathless and exalted. Before midnight when the excitement begins, the club offers organic ceviche served on a few wooden tables near the bar, but La Mano is primarily a new temple of dance. BootyShake and Afro-dancing courses are offered every Saturday at 5pm.

LA ROBE ET LA MOUSSE

3, rue Monsieur le Prince, 5th
Metro Odéon
Tel 09 81 29 29 89
www.lafinemousse.fr
Closed Sunday to Tuesday

FRENCH CRAFT BEERS

The mission of Fine Mousse – the name of a bar, restaurant and distributor, a pioneer in craft beer in Paris – is to promote French microbreweries as well as the country's wines and spirits in its new bar near Odéon. It combines the elegance of a cocktail bar with the simplicity of a beer bar and offers sixteen draft beers and two casks – like in the good old days – including the best pale ales, triple beers, white beers and stout brewed in France, from the Rhône-Alpes to the Paris region, an approach that charms the melting-pot clientele curious about French savoir-faire. About time! The staff knows everything about the malts and hops of each vintage and can suggest pairings of a certain beer with a vegan tart, for example, or a meat dish, depending on appetite and convictions.

LE BAR BOTANISTE DU SHANGRI-LA

Shangri-La Hotel,
10, avenue d'Iéna, 16th
Metro Iéna
Tel 01 53 67 19 93
www.shangri-la.com

COCKTAIL BAR, LUXURY HOTEL

Ever since it opened, this grand hotel has always had a *je ne sais quoi* that distinguishes it from other five-star luxury establishments. Maybe it's because of its location away from the Golden Triangle, its haute-couture elegance and its discreet bar tucked away at the back of the lobby. The winter garden pays tribute to Prince Roland Bonaparte, the building's former owner, and his hobby, a giant private herbarium with millions of specimens. Today, the decor consists of rows of apothecary bottles arranged around flourishing greenery. The voluptuous cocktails invented by Clément Emery echo this green universe. This intellectual bartender takes inspiration from the culinary arts and culture to thrill all the senses. Herbal infusions, old-fashioned herbal liqueurs and exotic citrus fruits are stirred or shaken and served in extravagant containers – a sandstone flower pot, a cocoa pod or a piece of wood – for a new taste sensation that is positively rejuvenating.

LE BLACK DOG

26, rue des Lombards, 4th
Metro Châtelet
Tel 01 42 71 16 47
www.blackdog-bar.com

CONCERTS, BAR

For more than a decade, the most celebrated rock bar in Paris has played host to metalheads from the world over, plus mystic Goths, Highlander lookalikes and ageing leather-clad rockers. The sombre decor, its gallery of death's heads topped with skullcaps, bowler hats and wedding veils, the grotto below straight out of *Pirates of the Caribbean* and the free-flowing beer might all seem a bit much, but don't be put off. It's much friendlier than you'd think, with rock ballads punctuating the heavy stuff, and an open and friendly clientele. At the back, the blood-red restaurant, complete with mural that might have come out of the catacombs, serves a good Argentine steak until midnight. Very rare, of course.

LE FORVM

29, rue du Louvre, 2nd, metro Sentier
Tel 01 42 65 37 86
www.bar-le-forum.com
Closed Sunday

COCKTAIL LOUNGE

After eighty-five years on Boulevard Malesherbes near the Place de la Madeleine, this historic Parisian cocktail bar, owned as always by the Biolatto family, has moved to Rue du Louvre, near the pedestrian streets of Rue Montorgueil and Rue Montmartre. The new location is opposite the former Bourse du Commerce, the future Paris headquarters for the Pinault Foundation. Savvy travellers, locals and businesspeople flock there, loyal to this establishment that serves distilled spirits and the best whisky from Scotland and Japan. Some eighty are on the menu, along with thirty cocktails, including the Forvm Cocktail, the house version of the Dry Martini, revisited in 1929 by Antoine Biolatto. The address may have changed, but the decor and furniture have not. Regulars will recognize the old bar and the two 1970s jukeboxes, framed by old wood panelling to create a gentlemen's-club ambiance.

LES BAINS PARIS

7, rue du Bourg L'Abbé, 3rd
Metro Étienne Marcel
Tel 01 42 77 07 07
www.lesbains-paris.com

CLUB, CELEBS

Since March 2015, this legendary club of the 1980s has been awakened from the long sleep that followed a tumultuous period. It has a new decor and new functions, and offers new pleasures. It is now a five-star hotel with a design and services that are up to the standards of the grand hotels of the Golden Triangle, and its club/cocktail bar is now more festive than worldly.
A legend for a whole generation, the club, still in the basement, has been redesigned by the decorator Tristan Auer. It is smaller, but the crackled white tiles and checkerboard dance floor by Philippe Starck are still there. Clubbers can no longer have a midnight swim, however, since the pool is now part of the hotel's spa. While the unmovable bouncer Marie-Line is gone, the music is still eclectic and electrified, with concerts and trendy events. The cocktail bar, located next to the gourmet restaurant, has gradually become the new nerve centre of this institution. Its U-shaped bar, red-lacquered decor and glass case full of beautiful bottles attract a tasteful clientele in the evening. Julien Lebas, an old hand in the nightlife world, has surrounded himself with a youthful team of experts. Using "beachy" or "cowboy" flavours, this head mixologist comes up with innovative creations mixed with purée of peas or cold brew syrup, some of which come in pitchers to be shared. Lovers of strange potions go for preparations aged in sherry or bourbon casks. The turntables are spinning in the bar as well, with special soirées vibrating

POINT OF VIEW

HOTEL COCKTAILS: REFRESHMENT REQUIRED

The startenders and promising young recruits at the cosy bars of the grand hotels have created quite a stir, the first result of which was to disorient a clientele not accustomed to so much excitement. The Plaza Athénée, Bristol, George V, Prince de Galles and Shangri-La bars, usually bathed in a soft golden haze of tranquillity, are shaking up cocktails to help customers forget that all that luxury is billed at exorbitant prices. The competition inspired by a new wave of mixologists has changed the situation. For the past ten years or so, a string of quality cocktail bars have succeeded in attracting neophytes and connoisseurs by popularizing the Manhattan and the Ramos gin fizz, offering affordable prices and great know-how. London's grand hotels quickly figured out how to deal with this crisis situation. The mixologists of places like the Savoy racked their brains to come up with innovations that create buzz and attract a highly loyal local clientele. Paris, which still capitalizes on Hemingway to justify its celebrations, has woken up but is still slow to rally a new customer base, frightened away by the prices in the bars of multi-starred hotels, especially when the tiniest bite to eat served with the beverages is also expensive. Even though things have improved dramatically, we eagerly look forward to a sublime experience with fantastic service and a less intimidating bill. It's a challenge, yes, but it will be worth it.

the bottles, including "Les 7 Salopards", where you'll meet a whole gang of influencers and mixers like FFF, Gunther Love and Solo. Don't miss it.

LE TIGRE

5, rue Molière, 1st, metro Pyramides
Tel 06 81 09 58 72
www.tigrebylalternative.fr
Closed Sunday

NIGHTCLUB

Taken over by the charming Roxane de Courtois – whose grandfather once owned the place – Le Tigre has established itself as one of the top music venues in Paris. It has hosted a number of famous after-show parties (Franz Ferdinand, Temples, The Horrors), a seemingly endless roster of great gigs and every A-list music celeb in attendance – Jamie Hince of The Kills, Pete Doherty, Justice. This Tigre still roars, and now opens at 6pm with rock and rockabilly karaoke. Great atmosphere and decor – indeed, the owner has been asked to export it to the Boom Boom Room in New York, and to Rome, London and Istanbul.

LE TRÈS PARTICULIER

23, avenue Junot, 18th
Metro Lamarck-Caulaincourt
Tel 01 53 41 81 40
www.hotel-particulier-montmartre.com
Closed Monday

COCKTAILS, BARBECUE

The Très Particulier, the private bar at the Hôtel Particulier in Montmartre, is a delightful place, especially in summer, when night starts in the daytime and you can enjoy a drink and a smoke in the garden, like a 19th-century artist. Pressing on the intercom, it's almost as Gainsbourg described it in his song *L'Hôtel particulier*: "First one knock, then three more and you can go in. Alone or possibly accompanied." Say that you have come for a drink. Then walk down a cobblestoned path before crunching across the gravel in the garden, where you'll find the house's new salon-bar. The brainchild of architect Pierre Lacroix, of the India Mahdavi school, and Oscar Comette, son of decorator Morgane Rousseau, the place is covered in velvet, with the feel of a gold-carpeted, lost paradise or a Cluedo setting. It also features a garden that's perfect after midnight, and that produces the fruit and vegetables that appear on the menu, and even Oscar's honey. You leave like Michael Jackson in *Thriller* via the private passage and its "Witch's Rock" leading to Rue Lepic. DJ sets at the weekend for people who like a clubbing ambiance.

MABEL

58, rue d'Aboukir, 2nd
Metro Sentier
Tel 01 42 33 24 33
www.mabelparis.com
Closed Sunday

RUM AND COCKTAILS

Mabel, a Paris rum bar, is an ironic tribute to Mabel Walker, the famous US assistant attorney general under Prohibition. A dark, bare cinderblock bar is hidden behind a small restaurant serving grilled Cheddar-cheese sandwiches. Fronting the bottles arranged in a pyramid and illuminated by neon is neither a pirate nor a privateer, but Joseph Akhavan, former bartender at Mama Shelter and the Conserverie. Here you will find fine cocktails made with the latest techniques, among them "Nutty By Nature": white Embargo rum with grilled peanut oil, white Clément rum, organic coconut water, clarified hazelnut milk, organic banana, organic maple syrup with spices, *genmaicha* tea, vanilla and *togarashi*. This complex mixture is served in a small milk bottle. The bar offers 160 rums, ranging from dry to very dry.

MADAME ARTHUR – DIVAN DU MONDE

75, rue des Martyrs, 18th
Metro Place Pigalle
Tel 01 40 05 08 10
www.divandumonde.com
Closed Sunday to Tuesday

HISTORIC CABARET, COCKTAILS

For a very French evening, first hit the drag show at the cabaret Madame Arthur – the first of its kind in Paris – now run by the team from its neighbour, the Divan du Monde. It reopened in 2015 with the same no-frills Art Deco decor, and with a new show featuring wild young troubadours like Charly Voodoo the sexy pianist and the seductive Miss Morian, who has the voice of a goddess. A hypnotic repertoire of French songs can be accompanied by a cocktail and snack from a limited menu that is not bad. As soon as the show ends, an armada of DJs takes over these two festive places and makes the old parquet floors vibrate all night long with French sounds, from Jacques Brel to Alain Chamfort and C2C. So Pigalle!

MAISON SAGE

15, boulevard Saint-Martin, 3rd
Metro République
www.maison-sage.com
Closed Monday and Tuesday

LIVE MUSIC, COCKTAILS, STREETFOOD

Far from the follies of Pigalle, this hybrid nightspot offers something different. Have a cocktail with no fuss and bother, sample the street food of a great chef, and dance to good music – just as you would at home. Once you have gotten past the bouncer and the staircase with red neon lights, the atmosphere becomes cooler on the first floor of this stylish loft: a Scandinavian-style lounge surrounded by a cocktail bar, and a corner with foosball and pinball. You will also find a small room and kitchenette for chilling with a group of friends. Before the sun has even set, the library is transformed into a concert hall with a surprise programme. Well-known musicians and emerging indie pop and rock groups disturb private conversations before the DJs take over with soul, funk and hip-hop sounds. On the top floor is the smoking room, a bachelor pad where customers place their bar orders using a telephone from another century. What could be better?

MAISON SOUQUET BAR

10, rue de Bruxelles, 9th
Metro Blanche
Tel 01 48 78 55 55
www.maisonsouquet.com

VALET PARKING

The Maison Souquet, a mansion that became the brothel of Madame Souquet in 1905, was transformed into a five-star hotel in 2015. Decorator Jacques Garcia cleverly retained the bordello spirit, with a touch of Belle Époque added to his famous Empire style. The huge boudoir-like public spaces include three plush rooms with whimsical, evocative names: the Moorish-style "salon des Mille et une Nuits" ("Arabian Nights Room"); the "presentation room", where the courtesans awaited their customers; and the "recovery room", now discreetly renamed the "winter garden".
The intoxicating cocktails, which may be conducive to intimacy among urban voyagers, have names that awaken the ghosts of the past: "Rita", "Mimi", "Douchka" and so on. This is probably one of the best-kept secrets in Paris.

MANKO CABARET

15, avenue Montaigne, 8th
Metro Alma-Marceau
Tel 01 82 28 00 15
www.manko-paris.com
Closed Sunday to Thursday

CABARET, CLUB

Josephine Baker herself performed in this historic place before it became part of the Drouot auction house. Since February 2016, it has once again been transformed, this time into a temple of Peruvian gastronomy and cocktails. On Friday and Saturday, the show starts in the cabaret at 10:30pm, when black dresses and white shirts take their place at tables and sip champagne while watching the phantasmagorical circus-style spectacle. It was created by Manon Savary, daughter of the great Jérôme, with artistic direction by Marc Zaffuto and Emmanuel d'Orazio, who are behind the wild "Club Sandwich" evenings. As soon as Allanah Starr, the high priestess of the show, and Jean-Biche, a performer in full body paint, arrive onstage, a magical connection is formed between the public and performers. Dancers, drag acts, trapeze artists and other extravagant muses follow one another. You won't be bored. This picturesque cabaret is subtly creating a new kind of club.

M'SIEURS DAMES

30, avenue Parmentier, 11th
Metro Saint-Ambroise, Voltaire
Tel 01 48 05 08 20
Closed Sunday and Monday

GAY-FRIENDLY BAR

This bar seamlessly combines the atmosphere of a friendly neighbourhood watering hole with that of a sophisticated cocktail bar. Owned by Frédéric Nicod, who proclaims it "hetero-friendly", it is located in the prime setting of the Square Gardette, already home to the recommendable restaurants Brutos and Salt, and the cocktail bar Monsieur Antoine. Smart and welcoming, this bar with a tattooed decor also holds exhibitions of graphic artists and works from the personal collection of M'sieur Fred, a man of proven taste(s). From the bar to the small terrace, he has reinvented the concept of the local bar where people go to converse. There are drinks, of course, including a well-made spritz, and, to accompany (or soak up?) the alcohol, plates of Aubrac charcuterie and cheese, and the chocolates of his friend Vivien, whose home bakery **CHEZ VIVIEN** (www.chezvivien.fr) is a big

"It's midnight. One half of Paris is making love to the other half."
Ernst Lubitsch, *Ninotchka*, 1939

success. It's a cheerful place where the regulars know they will run into friends. The barmaid who rides a motorcycle like Yoko Tsuno is a doll.

NEW MORNING

7-9, rue des Petites Écuries, 10th
Metro Château d'Eau
Tel 01 45 23 51 41, www.newmorning.com

LEGENDARY JAZZ CLUB

Hidden behind the heavy wrought-iron gate of an ugly building, next to the bustling Faubourg Saint-Denis, lies this temple to jazz. Art Blakey and his Messengers inaugurated the place in 1981, shaking up the Paris jazz scene that had been rather listless up until then. The jazz stars that have played here since, keeping its legendary name as intoxicating as ever, include Terence Blanchard, Gil Scott-Heron, Betty Carter, Dizzy Gillespie, Dexter Gordon, Stan Getz, Michel Petrucciani. A must.

NIGHT FLIGHT HÔTEL BACHAUMONT

18, rue Bachaumont, 2nd
Metro Sentier, Les Halles
Tel 01 81 66 47 55
www.nightflightbar.com

INTIMATE COCKTAIL BAR

The Experimental Cocktail Club's bar in the Hotel Bachaumont attracts an adventurous crowd every evening for a trip to cocktail heaven. The interior, by designer Dorothée Meilichzon, is not surprising but is pleasant and cosy, with a velvet sofa, wood panelling, warm colours, 1930s-style lamps and details that refer to Antoine de Saint-Exupéry's legendary work *Night Flight*. The bar manager, Karim Hamadouche, worked for a short time at the Grand Pigalle hotel. Today, he continues to concoct cocktails for adventurous but sometimes novice drinkers. Examples: the Aviateur (pisco infused with cinnamon) and Vol de Nuit (vodka infused with hibiscus). You'll be flying high by the end of the evening.

OUTLAND BAR

6, rue Émile Lepeu, 11th
Metro Charonne
Tel 01 46 59 04 28
www.outland-beer.com
Closed Sunday and Monday

BEER, BREWERY, NIBBLES

Owners Julien and Philippe, who also own Trois 8, are well on their way to changing Paris's beer scene. The decor borrows a few ideas from the Scandinavians, and there is a restaurant in the basement decorated in stylish black-and-white marble with faience tiles and rough wood. But this fine-dining spot is first and foremost a showroom for an artisanal brewery, and not just any one: Outland, with its sexy brewer from Fontenay-sous-Bois, titillates the taste buds of beer geeks with eight house beers in the style of American artisanal beers – American pale ale, for example, or coffee American wheat ale – and others pulled from the chrome taps. The menu offers a tempting selection of mixed plates of artisanal products, including pickles, AOC cheese and cured meats. Those who don't want beer will find their joy in a good choice of natural wines and spirits.

RITZ BAR

15, place Vendôme, 1st
Metro Tuileries, Madeleine
Tel 01 43 16 33 74
www.ritzparis.com

LUXURY HOTEL BAR

We had to wait four long years to experience a divine moment in the bar of one of the most luxurious hotels in Paris. The renovation begun in 2012 was completed in June 2016, and the new Ritz finally emerged in all its splendour. The neighbours – yes, people live in this area – are once again in the habit of dropping by for a bubbly aperitif or cocktail in one of the hotel's three bars. Beginning at 6pm, aficionados and curious crowds start queuing up at the Hemingway Bar, anxious to get in to fight for a stool and have a chat with Colin Field, the illustrious bartender of the 1990s, still faithful to his post. Hotel guests take refuge across the hall, at the Ritz Bar – the hotel's first bar, opened in 1921 – now totally remodelled, unlike the Hemingway Bar. It is more intimate, more bling-bling, more fashionable and more creative. There are some nice surprises on the menu – no boring list of ingredients, but a charming story for each of these delicious cocktails made by up-and-coming 21st-century bartenders.

ROSEBUD

11 bis, rue Delambre, 14th
Metro Vavin
Tel 01 43 35 38 54

HISTORIC COCKTAIL BAR

A living remnant of the Vavin strand of the Montparnasse legend and an American bar of the type that was popular before and after World War II, the Rosebud is, of course, a reference to Orson Welles's *Citizen Kane*. Legend has it that Hemingway came here, but in fact the place opened in the 1960s (Ernest's haunt was La Closerie des Lilas, a bit farther along the boulevard). Closer to the truth is that Sartre (with a flock of disciples) was a regular when he wanted a change from the Café de Flore. At the Rosebud, the waiters, wearing impeccable white jackets, serve a more contemporary bunch of celebrities. With the trace of a knowing grin, behind the bar or delivering a perfect steak tartare, double fried eggs and ham, or chili con carne (even after 11pm), they feign to recognize no one. Anonymity is the house rule. So terribly Parisian.

SAINT JAMES CLUB

43, avenue Bugeaud, 16th
Metro Porte Dauphine
Tel 01 44 05 81 81
www.saintjamesclub.com

COCKTAIL BAR

Entering the bar at the Saint James Hotel, with its exuberant interiors by Franco-American designer Bambi Sloan, is like stepping back into the 19th century. The place is reminiscent of a British gentleman's club, conjuring up a world of hot-air balloons, safaris, polar expeditions and croquet. The leather armchairs in this vast room would be perfect for making crazy bets as you smoke a cigar (except it's prohibited, so a game of cards will have to do). *Harry Potter*? *Dead Poets Society*? *Out of Africa*? At Versailles? In Visconti's palace, at Ascot, at home with Joséphine de Beauharnais or Keith Richards? Yes, yes, yes, the Saint James, a one-of-a-kind place in Paris, is all this at once. Night owls can even come here to refuel until 1am, when they might stumble across some Victor Hugo enthusiasts in the library.

SALÒ

142, rue Montmartre, 2nd
Metro Grands Boulevards
www.salo-club.com
Closed Sunday to Wednesday

ART CLUB, CONCERTS, EXHIBITIONS

This is the third concept bar at 142 Rue Montmartre, along with Triptyque and Social Club. Salò, owned by the Manifesto group (which also owns Silencio and Wanderlust), has undergone a total about-face. When it opened in 2008 it was frequented by a smart, young crowd, but today it is popular with those in search of Berlin-style experimental evenings. Run by Coralie Gauthier and Dactylo, responsible for the exciting Flash Cocotte and Possession soirées, Salò is now considered an "artistic" club, fittingly considering that it is named after Pier Paolo Pasolini's steamy cult film. Every week, an artist has carte blanche to decorate the bare walls and surprise Parisians thirsty for alternative culture. Abel Ferrara, Michel Gondry and Larry Clark have already left their mark. The evening ends with resident or guest DJs spinning platters for a clientele unaccustomed to the dance floor.

SOLERA

283, rue Saint-Jacques, 5th
Metro Saint-Jacques, RER Port-Royal
Tel 06 24 69 69 49
Closed Sunday and Monday

COCKTAIL BAR, CLUB

Christopher Gaglione, who used to run the bar at the Hôtel Prince de Galles, has opened his first cocktail bar near the Val-de-Grâce Church. The sign on the discreet facade says it all: "FOODRINK EXPERIENCE", a five-star tasting experience. This Left Bank refuge has a refined decoration with "palm-tree" wallpaper, "sun" mirrors, a black rattan armchair ("Emmanuelle"), onyx tables and a bar covered in black faience. The show begins when he arms himself with his tools and dances with his bottles of rare spirits. Each cocktail is carefully designed and measured and served in unexpected containers, from a multi-coloured watering can to Aladdin's lamp, using tongs as in a luxury hotel. On weekends, beginning on Thursday, the shakers move to the beat of club music: hip-hop, rap and jazz. An electrifying experience.

SUNSET SUNSIDE JAZZ CLUB

60, rue des Lombards, 1st
Metro Châtelet
Tel 01 40 26 46 60
www.sunset-sunside.com

JAZZ LEGENDS PAST AND PRESENT

Opened in the Les Halles quarter in 1983 and establishing the Rue des Lombards as a jazz enclave, the Sunset Jazz Club invited only the very best jazzmen of the day to play, such as Jaco Pastorius, Didier Lockwood, Sixun, Barney Wilen; and legends including Miles Davis, Herbie Hancock, Lee Konitz and Benny Golson followed. With the launch of Sunside a few years later, the two clubs, opened seven days a week, offered a feast of the greatest jazz sounds. And this bonanza continues today with such names as Brad Mehldau, Kenny Barron, Malia and Kyle Eastwood.

YEEELS

24, avenue George V, 8th
Metro George V
Tel 01 42 88 75 75
www.yeeels.com

SMART COCKTAIL BAR, CLUB

Benjamin Artis, a prominent nightlife figure in Paris, has chosen Avenue George V for this chic lifestyle bar. To get in, you'll have to follow certain rules of the Golden Triangle: no trainers, flashy outfits or baseball caps. At the entrance, yellow neon lights and a black marble staircase give you an idea of what to expect in the basement: a bar, restaurant and club where festive souls, nostalgic for Studio 54, dance to DJ sets from the 1980s to the present. There is no point in going to the restaurant; just head for the imposing, luminous onyx bar. Cocktail aficionados revel in Aurélien Fleury's balanced, sophisticated concoctions. This excellent self-taught bartender makes his own champagne syrup and hot wines; gin infused with dates and grapes; and tequila with red tea. Customers come back for more – and pay well for the privilege.

A NIGHT OUT WITH DOMINIQUE PERRAULT

For an architect, night-time is often synonymous with a charrette, *an expression created in the 19th century by the students of the École des Beaux-Arts, which means working at night to make up lost time and finish your project on schedule. At the moment, for us, the Poste du Louvre project and that of the new Longchamp racecourse is a* charrette. *When I'm not working hard, I like Minato, a Japanese cocktail bar where, after dinner, a small bottle of Japanese whisky can work magic. My other evening venue is Silencio, where David Lynch's fantastic interiors are very popular in the neighbourhood.*

MINATO

5, rue de Louvois, 2nd, metro Quatre Septembre, tel 01 42 96 94 50

SILENCIO

142, rue Montmartre, 2nd, metro Bourse, tel 01 40 13 12 33, www.club-silencio.com

A SENSE OF STYLE

HIGH FASHION TO EMERGING DESIGNERS: SHOPPING IN THE CITY

It seems that some naysayers have been bemoaning Paris's fate. Are vibrant New York or elegant Milan about to deprive Paris of its status as the "capital of fashion"? Not at all. Haughty and hardworking, Paris keeps its chin up, fights to maintain its preeminent position, and flirts its way through its ignoble abandonment.

But both customers and designers, whether locals or from abroad, know what's what, and they all put in an appearance, if only for the duration of Paris Fashion Week. So is Paris the go-to destination for fashion victims? Yes, but not just them. Where else can you find such an abundance of clothes shops, flagship stores and fashion studios tucked away in little courtyards, or jewellers in upstairs apartments and hairdressing salons that offer every home comfort? Where better than Paris to help you navigate the extremes, from the latest hip trainers to traditional handheld fans, from the haute couture feather-worker to the up-and-coming conceptual creative, while treating you to its myriad stories and legends, in which local seamstresses rub shoulders with the designer – sorry, artistic director – of genius?

Such is the world of Paris fashion. Multifaceted, excitable, with a passion for the outlandish and for bouquets of old-fashioned flowers such as gladioli, Paris is essentially unfaithful to trends and fickle in style. Paris is the Don Juan of clothes and hairstyles, the Casanova of shoes, the Grayson Perry of the unisex accessory. This is the source of the city's charm and the foundation of its uniqueness.

Google

PEP'S
Réparation et vente
De parapluies, ombrelles
et cannes.
www.peps-paris.com

FASHION AND ACCESSORIES

AGNELLE

19, rue Duphot, 1st, metro Madeleine
Tel 01 42 33 31 40, www.agnelle.com
Open 10am to 2pm and 3pm to 6pm, closed Sunday

GLOVES

Agnelle was founded in 1937 in the town of Saint-Junien, in the Limousin, the French glove-making centre, and for years supplied gloves to the great Parisian houses (Lanvin, Saint Laurent, Mugler, Dior, Alaïa, Givenchy). Today, the firm, led by Sophie Grégoire, granddaughter of the founder, is still a manufacturer and supplier for the best houses, but also designs its own gloves and has opened its first store in Paris, preferring a site near Madeleine over the Palais-Royal, where most luxury glove-makers are located. The firm sells its collections of gloves for men, women and children, which it personalizes with unusual stitching or linings. The gloves come in forty-eight shades of leather, full-grain or braided. Agnelle, a poster child for all things "made in France", has also forged notable partnerships – with Guerlain for perfumed gloves, for example – and has just started making wedding gloves.

À LA VILLE, À LA MONTAGNE

3, boulevard Richard Lenoir, 11th
Metro Bastille
Tel 01 43 57 20 89
www.cordonnerie-deuso.com
Open 9am to 7:30pm, Monday and Saturday until 7pm, Wednesday until 9pm, closed Sunday

SHOEMAKER, OUTERWEAR

This mountain chalet in the heart of Paris was the crazy idea of the son of the original Deuso, whose shoe-repair shop first opened here in 1960. Thierry Hoo has brought in tons of blond wood from Chamonix and Mont Blanc (he's climbed them both twice), along with a deer's head, his collection of climbing boots – the oldest dates from 1900 – a rustic farmhouse door and plenty of kitsch details from the mountains. In the ground-floor workshop, redolent of polish and fresh glue, the full range of traditional shoemaking services is provided by a team of apprentices, part of the "Compagnons" scheme, an old French tradition and also part of UNESCO's Intangible Cultural Heritage of Humanity. The young people trained by Thierry Hoo can easily switch from repairing a pair of Louboutin heels to making bespoke sports footwear (ski boots, hiking boots, etc.), the shop's speciality. Its skills have earned it the after-sales contract for Au Vieux Campeur and Paraboot shoes. Upstairs, you'll find a range of outdoor wear for sale: it's the only shop in Paris to stock Fjällräven, the Swedish brand known for its warm, durable clothes and multi-coloured backpacks – the ones you see being bundled on and off the tourist buses.

ALEXANDRA SOJFER

218, boulevard Saint-Germain, 7th
Metro Rue du Bac
Tel 01 42 22 17 02
www.alexandrasojfer.com
Open 10am to 7pm, closed Sunday

UMBRELLAS

Hidden behind a delightful sculpted facade is one of the last vestiges of the Saint-Germain-des-Prés of yesteryear. The store's magnificent umbrellas shelter most of the French political establishment – from the rain, at least – with discreet elegance. The place also offers large rainproof wraps that protect ladies' fur coats. Expanded and renovated in 2007–08 by the owner, Alexandra Sojfer, a worthy successor to Madeleine Gély (who ran the boutique for nearly fifty years), this store makes rainy days in Paris almost welcome.

ANNA RUOHONEN – PETITE MAISON DE COUTURE

227, boulevard Raspail, 14th
Metro Raspail
Tel 01 43 27 08 89
www.annaruohonen.com
Open noon to 8pm, Saturday until 6pm and by appointment, closed Sunday and Monday

CUSTOM-MADE, TIMELESS

More than fifteen years after coming to Paris and creating her own label, Finnish designer Anna Ruohonen has built up a clientele of men and women in the creative sectors – architecture, design, graphics, art – for whom, from one season to the next, she creates what she herself calls "addictive" clothing. After opening her first shop in Helsinki in 2009, she took over an entire store on several floors, stacking up boutique, salon and workshop, in April 2013, just steps from the Cartier Foundation and the École Camondo. Her architect friend Pekka Littow decorated the interior. Here, somewhere between semi-couture and custom design, Ruohonen has put together a timeless, delightful wardrobe.

ANTOINE

10, avenue de l'Opéra, 1st
Metro Palais-Royal–Musée du Louvre, Pyramides
Tel 01 42 96 01 80
www.antoine1745.com
Open 10:30am to 1pm and 2pm to 6:30pm, closed Sunday

UMBRELLAS AND CANES

Antoine was founded in 1745 on the Pont Neuf, where, rain or shine, Monsieur and Madame Antoine rented umbrellas to people crossing from one bank of the river to the other. In 1760, it moved to the Palais-Royal, where it remained until 1885, then to Avenue de l'Opéra, at the time the chicest address in the new Paris of Haussmann. Today, Antoine is the last remnant of the frivolities of what used to be a triumphal avenue, before it became an outdoor shopping mall. For years, people rushed past the umbrella-filled shop windows, thinking Antoine was a tourist trap. Wrong! Inside is a delightfully unique world with its original decor of mouldings still intact. Antoine, which used to supply the Comédie-Française and the Grand Hôtel du Louvre, was purchased in 1964 by Maurice Purorge, the manufacturer of ONM umbrellas. His wonderful daughter and granddaughter now run the shop. The product offer – umbrellas, parasols, fans, whips, hats, caps, panama hats and antique canes – may seem old-fashioned, but it is miraculous in demonstrating that these trades are still alive and that elegance still exists. The men's umbrella with a sheep's-horn handle and the English Fox umbrellas are insanely chic. Then there are the deliberately kitschy women's umbrellas with gilded handles and 1950s-style frills – very ooh-là-là Paris! All that's missing is a standard poodle on a leash. The blue braided-paper hats for summer are perfect, as are the peccary gloves. If you've been the victim of a strong gust of wind and/or your brolly's frame has been bent out of shape, take it along to **PEP'S**, the last umbrella repair shop in Paris (passage de l'Ancre, 223, rue Saint-Martin, 3rd, tel 01 42 78 11 67).

ATELIER RENARD

3, place Bourbon, 7th
Metro Assemblée Nationale
Tel 01 45 51 77 87, www.atelierrenard.com
Open 8:30am to 6pm, closed Saturday and Sunday

LEATHERWARE ARTISAN

Nestling among the camellias in a paved courtyard where it's been since 1930, Atelier Renard is surely one of Paris's most jealously guarded secrets. The business was founded by Joseph Renard, saddler and Compagnon du Tour de France, before it was revived by the delightful Brigitte Montaut, who breathes life into the craziest of ideas, whether in the choice of leather (taurillon, calfskin, croc and ostrich), the colour of the zip or the stitching. For example, there's a leather case for transporting a tart tin(!), a giant handbag created for Dior, and unique items made for the Hun collection by designer Rick Owens, who's set up shop next door. The workshop also supplies films, recruiting Fanny Ardant and Marina Hands as the brand's ambassadors in the film *Chic*. Renard makes a gorgeous collection of lambskin-lined handbags, briefcases and suitcases. If you order one, be prepared to wait up to three months before it's ready.

AUBERCY

34, rue Vivienne, 2nd, metro Bourse
Tel 01 42 33 93 61, www.aubercy.com
Open 11am to 7pm and by appointment, closed Sunday

SHOEMAKER

Xavier Aubercy might as well have been born in a shoebox. A member of the third generation of a dynasty of Parisian shoemakers, he is the worthy heir of the savoir faire passed on from his grandfather, André Aubercy, who founded the house in 1935, to his father, Philippe. With six thousand customers, among them the nation's leaders, the firm perpetuates fine craftsmanship and takes pride in a job well done. Whether bespoke, partially bespoke or ready to wear, the offering is classic, of course, but with embellishments: Aubercy avocado green, "Reverso" stitching, "castagna" patina, shagreen (difficult to work with, but the result can have a marbled effect), sharkskin (now rare but finally stripped of its "Prince of the Night" image), stunning crocodile, asymmetrical derbies, Lupin ankle boots, Étretat loafers. The rare talent and remarkable elegance of this shoemaker is enhanced by hidden attention to detail. Aubercy recently turned its second shop in the 7th arrondissement into its Haute Cordonnerie Workshop.
Other location: 9, rue de Luynes, 7th, tel 01 45 44 30 80

AZZEDINE ALAÏA

7, rue de Moussy, 4th
Metro Hôtel de Ville
Tel 01 42 72 30 69, www.alaia.fr
Open 10am to 7pm, closed Sunday

INNOVATIVE COUTURE

Alaïa's decision to sell his designs in a different district from the top names in international fashion is further evidence of this designer's independent spirit and the confidence he has in his clientele of models and celebrities. His boutique, which adjoins his studio, is located in a loft-like space in a former warehouse.
Other location: 5, rue de Marignan, 8th, tel 01 76 72 91 11

BALENCIAGA

10, avenue George V, 8th
Metro Alma-Marceau
Tel 01 47 20 21 11, www.balenciaga.com
Open 10am to 7pm, closed Sunday

LUXURIOUS

This is where Cristóbal Balenciaga opened his couture house in 1937 and where he invented the "semi-fitted look" and the "sack dress", creating what could almost be called "abstract couture". The fashion house, based in Madrid, Barcelona and Paris, where André Courrèges worked for ten years, closed in 1968. Acquired in 1986 by Jacques Bogart, it regained its allure with a refit by interior designer Andrée Putman. Following designers Michel Goma and Josephus Melchior Thimister, Nicolas Ghesquière took over in 1997 and revived the company, which soon became part of the Kering group. Artist Dominique Gonzalez-Foerster, winner of the 2002 Marcel Duchamp Prize, redesigned the space as a landscape to be explored, with black stone furniture, a light-filled cave, a crater where bags are displayed and an artificial sky on a ceiling that changes with the seasons. The exercise has been repeated but not duplicated in the other Balenciaga stores, including on Rue Saint-Honoré. After fifteen years with Ghesquière as house designer, a period

characterized by scholarly research and powerful, sculptural creations, art direction was briefly turned over to Alexander Wang, before being entrusted to Demna Gvasalia, who founded the Vetements label with his brother Guram. Through his sensational catwalk shows, XXL puffer jackets and sock boots, the Georgian-born designer has turned the company into today's most fashionable brand, riffing brilliantly on the legacy of its Spanish founder to create contemporary iconic looks for both men and women. The small store at 5, rue de Varenne, 7th, is reserved for menswear.
See website for other locations

BERLUTI

14, rue de Sèvres, 7th
Metro Sèvres-Babylone
Tel 01 53 93 97 97, www.berluti.com
Open 1am to 7pm, closed Sunday

MEN'S SHOES, READY-TO-WEAR

A love of shoes has been handed down for over a century through four generations of Berlutis. Over the decades, the knowledge and talents of Alessandro, Torello, Talbinio and Olga Berluti, four very different personalities, have helped to perpetuate the tradition of made-to-measure footwear. Their half-scientific, half-intuitive method of grouping classic shapes on a chart allows customers to find the shoes to fit both their feet and their temperament. In July 2011, Berluti took up the challenge of dressing "the contemporary man from head to toe" and added shoes, leather goods, accessories and ready-to-wear collections – now entrusted to the designer Haider Ackermann. They are displayed in the former home of that bastion of masculine elegance Arnys, a historic location if ever there was one, acquired to provide an elegant setting for the new men's clothing line. On the ground floor, you'll find small leather goods, weekend ready-to-wear, shoes and even a shoe-polishing workshop. Upstairs, you can still browse the fabrics from the Arnys range, and the tailoring shop still makes traditional suits for its customers, while the new patina bar offers a polish of your Berluti shoes. On the shop floor, the Arnys Forestière jacket, designed for Le Corbusier in 1947, is still available alongside fisherman's jerseys and Berluti suits. Customer service is impeccable.
Other location: 26, rue Marbeuf, 8th, tel 01 53 93 97 97

BERNARD ZINS

11, rue de Luynes, 7th
Metro Rue du Bac
Tel 09 82 54 70 66, www.zins.com
Open 10:30am to 2pm and 3pm to 7:30pm, Monday by appointment, closed Sunday

CHIC TROUSERS

This shop, specializing in men's trousers, styles itself as a "trouser engineer since 1967". Known to insiders, the company owned by Bernard Zins has subcontracted for the big names – Arnys, Hermès, Old England, Lanvin and others – while opening spaces in its own name in department stores, accumulating fantastic archives. This family affair is now run by Frank Zins, aided by his partner Jacqueline and now his nephew Augustin Durand. Together, they decided to reposition the brand, eliminating the department store spaces and opening (in between two shoemakers, Aubercy and Matthew Cookson) this store designed by the Be-Pôles studio to look like an intimate workshop. The company carries on the traditions of a misunderstood profession, producing trousers in many shapes, sizes and styles (chinos, slim-fit, lounge, French pleats, etc.) up to size sixty, identified as BZ V2, BZ V3, BZ CA, William, etc. A wide range of materials, both sturdy and refined (linen and silk, cashmere, Donegal tweed, houndstooth, seersucker, cotton, velvet, etc.), is available in bold, exciting colours. Every detail – waistbands, cuffs, lapels, buckle prongs, buttonholes, pockets, draping and so on – has been honed to achieve great practicality and elegance, close to perfection. In addition Jérôme Polny, formerly of Girbaud, makes sure you receive a friendly welcome and ultra-professional service. The fitting rooms are roomy, and alterations are done quickly. The attention to detail extends to the packaging: each pair of trousers is rolled in pattern paper and tied up in black and white. And don't miss the travel line. The address in the 6th arrondissement is a bit more casual (20, rue du Vieux Colombier, 6th).

BERTEIL

3, place Saint-Augustin, 8th
Metro Saint-Augustin
Tel 01 42 65 28 52, www.berteil.com
Open 10am to 6:45pm, closed Sunday

MEN'S WARDROBE

Founded by Alfred Berteil in 1840, this venerable bastion of a certain type of classic Parisian elegance tends to be overlooked, but nevertheless remains a reassuring presence opposite the Cercle National des Armées. Berteil specializes in hats – for everyone, every day, every moment and every occasion. It is said that a certain Giuseppe Borsalino learnt his trade here. Gloves, frock coats, capes and tricorn hats soon made an appearance, and were then sold in shops along Rue du Quatre Septembre and Boulevard Saint-Germain. The company has been a purveyor of headgear for town, for hunting and for sporting occasions, for horsemen and horsewomen, and its success has led to more branches being opened in locations as far flung as Scandinavia and Argentina. Workshops in Rue du Temple were responsible for the crowning glories sported by marshals Joffre and Foch, as well as presidents Doumer, Poincaré and Lebrun. Berteil's creations have been worn by financial kingpins, surgeons, ship's captains, racing stud owners, John Wayne, Michel de Brunhoff (former editor of French *Vogue*) and celebrity artist Jean-Gabriel Domergue, among others. Much later on, in the 1970s, a ready-to-wear line was launched, and the heirs of the founding family took charge. It was they who sold their wonderful brand to Vianney Houette, a man of taste from the world of insurance, who is passionate about beautiful things. Since June 2016 he has been aiming to relaunch the brand to better suit the modern era by pursuing a philosophy of change within continuity. For example, the brand's signature green has been swapped for chilli red, the decor has been gradually redesigned, and in terms of style Berteil now seeks to attract a clientele of thirty-five- to fifty-five-year-olds hoping to spice up their urban uniform with snazzier fabrics and colours. In the shop, look out for the blazers, velvet, cotton or linen trousers (all in sizes and cuts), knitted ties, printed scarves, shoes (by Alden and Alfred Sargent), panama hats, caps, Paris-cut or bespoke suits with a private fitting room, large sizes (up to sixty-two), dinner jackets on request, among much more. As purveyor to members of the Automobile Club and the Jockey Club, Berteil stocks cotton socks and "special" boxer shorts with a supporting, interior brief, and provides a complementary refitting service for old Berteil garments that have become too large due to weight loss, for example. Alongside handkerchiefs, swimwear, colognes, bow ties, clothes for the country and for the hunt, shaving accoutrements, watches and polishes, Berteil provides a range of weekend luggage made from the same canvas used in the sails of the replica of the 18th-century French frigate *Hermione* – the rediscovery of a classic in every sense. **Other location:** 7, rue de Solférino, 7th, tel 01 45 51 00 53

CAMPS DE LUCA / STARK & SONS

16, rue de la Paix, 2nd
Metro Opéra
Tel 01 42 65 42 15, 01 42 61 68 61
www.campsdeluca.com
www.starkandsons.com
Open by appointment, closed Sunday

BESPOKE TAILORING

The workshops of high-society tailor Camps de Luca were originally located on Place de la Madeleine, while Stark & Sons, tailors by appointment to General de Gaulle and members of the Académie Française, had occupied upstairs premises on Rue de la Paix ever since 1910. This was before the latter was bought out by the former, who set up salons and workshops behind these beautiful historic walls, where designer Frédéric de Luca (co-founder of the gallery En Attendant les Barbares and brother of Marc de Luca, head of Camps de Luca) achieved some notable decorative successes. Stark's ready-to-wear line was discarded and only the bespoke business has been preserved, at more affordable prices, while the company continues to "assemble" the ceremonial outfits of academicians and the traditional ones of prefects, and to "spin" ties and socks. Completely bespoke, Camps de Luca suits demand much more time and many more fittings. They are distinguished by a particularly subtle cut, whose particular telltale signs are the signature crescent shoulder known as "la cigarette" and the famous hidden inside "drop" pocket. Supplied with two pairs of trousers for every jacket – a tradition that has increasingly been abandoned – these suits bear the customer's initials on the bottom of the left sleeve and jackets can be lined with old Hermès squares or other scarves provided by the customer. Working alongside his two sons, Julien and Charles, Marc de Luca himself also operates in Hong Kong and Moscow, and all three of them know how to welcome clients here, even those who turn up unexpectedly, proposing a visit to the workshops where more than thirty experienced artisans cut, pin and sew. As a bonus, they also supply beautiful shoes made by fellow designer Aubercy.

CARVIL

67, rue Pierre Charron, 8th
Metro George V
Tel 01 42 25 54 38, www.carvil.com
Open 11am to 7pm, closed Sunday

MEN'S SHOES

In 1966, the playboys in Jacques Dutronc's song of the same name were "suited by Cardin and booted by Carvil", a brand which was then at the height of its popularity. Established in 1952 by Henri Ledermann, the store created the famous tasselled Triumph loafer, a favourite of Lino Ventura, as well as the horsebit loafer, exemplified by the Carvil model worn by Alain Delon in *Purple Noon*. Carvil also launched the Dylan patent white ankle boot, which became a cult fashion item when worn by Claude François and Joe Dassin. This branch in Rue Pierre Charron played host for twenty years to stars, crowned heads and politicians before launching a women's collection and welcoming Brigitte Bardot and Jeanne Moreau as regular customers. After a long period in the doldrums, Carvil shoes have polished up their image. Nostalgic neo-dandies who hanker after a good shoe can still find model numbers 26909 and 26907, new-look loafers, ankle boots, the most elegant of evening heels and summer slippers. Throw in a patina and shoeshine bar, brilliant customer service and the entertaining anecdotes of Jan Deheer, a long-serving shop director, and this shop could become an addiction.

CÉLINE

53, avenue Montaigne, 8th
Metro Alma-Marceau, Franklin D. Roosevelt
Tel 01 40 70 07 03, www.celine.com
Open 10am to 7pm, closed Sunday

LUXURIOUS, MINIMALIST

Céline was founded in 1945 by Céline Vipiana, a visionary woman who designed children's shoes. The brand really took off in 1963 with its famous Inca loafers, which became a must for bourgeois Parisians. Shoes were then joined by accessories, and later clothes. Part of the LVMH group since 1996, this label has had a succession of talented design directors, including Michael Kors and Ivana Omazić. Today, it is making a comeback under the stewardship of British designer Phoebe Philo (who revived Chloé), appointed artistic director in 2010. Thanks to her determination and flair, she has completely reinterpreted the brand. Céline's designs – minimalist, urban, structured – appeal to everyone. The materials are high-tech yet feminine. The designer shoes and bags are musts. See website for other locations

CHANEL

27-31, rue Cambon, 1st
Metro Madeleine, Concorde
Tel 01 44 50 66 00, www.chanel.com
Open 10am to 7pm, closed Sunday

HAUTE COUTURE

Gabrielle Chanel set up her atelier at 21, Rue Cambon in 1910, initially working as a milliner for high society (she later went on to merge the spaces at nos. 27, 29 and 31 in the same street). This visionary opened her first store three years later in Deauville, where she sold simple designs made of jersey, a "poor" material used for men's underwear. After the iconic little black dress (called the "Ford" by Americans) and daring costume jewellery, the house's first, subsequently legendary No. 5 fragrance was launched in 1921. In 1954, she introduced her braid-trimmed tweed suits, made to measure and accessorized with a quilted lambskin shoulder bag (the 2.55), two-tone sandals and strings of pearls. In 1983, the indefatigable Karl Lagerfeld became the company's artistic director and began to design the couture, ready-to-wear, Métiers d'Art, Croisière and accessory lines. He also oversees the house's image and the media coverage of the famed supermodels. By breathing modernity into the house, he has brought it new fame and fortune. After 51, Avenue Montaigne and its 600 square metres, brilliantly transformed by Peter Marino in the spirit of a private apartment, 19, Rue Cambon has been acquired by the house, which will enable the iconic shop to expand.
See website for other locations

CHARVET

28, place Vendôme, 1st
Metro Opéra
Tel 01 42 60 30 70
Open 10am to 7pm, closed Sunday (and Monday in August)

SHIRTS, TIES

Of the various famous shirt-makers – such as Poirier, Seelio and Bouvin – that made Paris a mecca for men's shirts, only this one remains. It was founded in 1838 by Joseph Christophe Charvet, inventor of the shirt with the removable collar and cuffs, supplier to princes, kings, financial barons and gentlemen travellers. Long accused of being unadventurous and conservative due to its narrow range, Charvet was saved from disaster in the early 1960s by Charles de Gaulle, a loyal customer who took it upon himself to find a trustworthy soul to take over the business and keep it from falling into the wrong hands. De Gaulle's hand-picked white knight was Denis Colban, and the company is currently run by his descendants. It now produces both off-the-peg and bespoke shirts in Charvet's French workshops, where each shirt is still made by a single employee. Count at least thirty days for a bespoke shirt and three weeks for the semi-bespoke variety. Charvet also sells excellent ties, lapel flowers, pocket squares and bow ties, as well as silk undershirts and underpants, wonderful pyjamas and eaux de toilette.

CHLOÉ

253, rue Saint-Honoré, 1st
Metro Tuileries
Tel 01 55 04 03 30, www.chloe.com
Open 11am to 7:30pm, closed Sunday

INTIMATE, PARISIAN CHIC

Chloé was founded in 1952, during the great couture era, by Gaby Aghion. The remarkable shop on Faubourg Saint-Honoré has the atmosphere of an inviting Parisian home, the feel of an elegant *hôtel particulier* that is seductive and surprising. There is not one false note in architect Joseph Dirand's design, in perfect harmony with the brand's ethos: luxury without bling, an infusion of freshness and elegance in a play of powdery beige and ivory dotted with gold. The racks are reminiscent of the coat trolleys in a chic hotel, the glass boxes seem suspended in the air, the display cases, also designed by Dirand, were inspired by Gabriella Crespi and Maria Pergay and are totally at home alongside an Oscar Niemeyer armchair, Louis Weisdorf chandeliers and Gio Ponti wall lamps. Added delights are spacious dressing rooms, a perfume bar, a tree-shaded patio and the assistance of stylists of all nationalities. The appointment of Natacha Ramsay-Levi – a Parisian with an impeccably Parisian pedigree – as artistic director marked the beginning of a new chapter in the story of the "Chloé girls". Don't miss the **MAISON CHLOÉ** (28, rue de La Baume, 8th), located next door to the brand's ultra-chic headquarters in the 8th arrondissement, where you can view archives from sixty-five years of the company's heritage, and enjoy exhibitions that pay homage to Guy Bourdin, Karl Lagerfeld and Stella McCartney. **Other location:** 44, avenue Montaigne, 8th, tel 01 47 23 00 08

CHRISTIAN LOUBOUTIN

19, rue Jean-Jacques Rousseau, 1st
Metro Palais-Royal–Musée du Louvre
Tel 0800 945 804
www.christianlouboutin.com
Open 10:30am to 7pm, closed Sunday

ICONIC WOMEN'S SHOES

Nicknamed the "man with red soles" by novelist and Académie Française member Érik Orsenna, Louboutin apprenticed with Charles Jourdan and then the great Roger Vivier before striking out on his own in 1992. Since then, this amazing talent has created famous, eminently recognizable shoes with red soles that flirt openly with fetishism. Fervent fans include Arielle Dombasle, Caroline de Monaco, Sofia Coppola, Dita Von Teese, the Crazy Horse girls, and Dana Delany in the series *Body of Proof*. They can now shop in the Galerie Véro-Dodat, where the designer has opened a beauty space that sells only nail polish in more than thirty shades, including Rouge Louboutin, of course. Adjoining the store, the new cobblers shop, **MINUIT MOINS SEPT** (10, passage Véro-Dodat, 1st, tel 01 42 21 15 47), specialist in high-end shoe repairs, is also the only establishment authorized to repair Louboutins using the famous red rubber sole. See website for other locations

COLETTE

213, rue Saint-Honoré, 1st
Metro Tuileries
Tel 01 55 35 33 90, www.colette.fr
Open 11am to 7pm, closed Sunday

CONCEPT STORE

This three-level monument to the new mode of mixing and matching is reflected in sections dedicated to fashion, cosmetics, jewellery, electronics, design and art, juxtaposing brands and labels, young designers and fashion icons, and constantly changing the items that make it famous. Trainers, T-shirts, watches, headphones, magazines, music, souvenir postcards of the store and children's goody bags – all this and more are spread over the ground floor.

On the first floor, you'll find the creations of both established designers (Garçons, Alaïa, Jourden, Off-White and Paskal) and up-and-coming talents. While you're there, grab a pair of iconic shoes by Charlotte Olympia, or hit the Beauty Box area, which stocks products by Byredo, Edward Bess, Gosha Rubchinskiy and Marc-Antoine Barrois. Don't miss the art gallery, the iPad listening wall, the restaurant and the water bar, which is open from noon to 6:30pm. Eagerly awaited, creative new displays appear every week. There's never a "best" time to visit this store as it's always crowded and has been since 1997, the date when Colette first opened its doors – an anniversary which is being celebrated in great splendour at the Musée des Arts Décoratifs with the installation of a huge ball-pit. It was announced in July 2017 that after twenty years Colette would be closing at the end of the year.

COMMUNE DE PARIS 1871

19, rue Commines, 3rd
Metro Filles du Calvaire
Tel 09 81 90 13 37
www.communedeparis1871.fr
Open 11am to 7:30pm, Sunday and Monday 2pm to 7pm

INSURRECTONAL STYLE

From a purely historical viewpoint, the Paris Commune in 1871 was a time of anti-government insurgency that lasted seventy-two days in a city rendered helpless by the Prussian siege and French defeat in 1870. The insurgents, of modest backgrounds, raised the red flag over the French capital, pulled down the Vendôme Column and set fire to the Hôtel de Ville, the Tuileries Palace and a few ministries and other symbolic buildings. It all ended in one bloody week, with the last battles taking place on Rue de la Fontaine-au-Roi (11th arrondissement). The Paris Commune has remained in the memory of the French thanks in part to literature (Zola and Hugo spring to mind), music (the song "Le Temps des Cerises") and the cinema. Now the fashion world is mounting the barricades: since 2009, Commune de Paris 1871 has been gently revolutionizing Parisian style with clothing, maps, objects and accessories that can now be considered true made-in-Paris artefacts and souvenirs. The leaders of these modern insurgents with the best of intentions are Maïsetti and Sébastien Lyky, backed up by an army of artists, illustrators, graphic designers, stylists and fashion designers, who are invited to put their mark on clothes, shoes, watches, sunglasses and purses through exclusive, ephemeral or occasional collaborative projects. Try Astier de Villatte for a range of scented candles, or Lip, Pairs in Paris, Pierre Jeanneau, Helmo or Macon & Lesquoy embroidery services, which are also featured at **L'EXCEPTION** (24, rue Berger, 1st, tel 01 40 39 92 34), the self-proclaimed "select store for French designers", not to be missed under the bronze roof of the Forum des Halles.

DIDIER LUDOT

Jardins du Palais-Royal, 20 and 24, galerie de Montpensier, 1st
Metro Palais-Royal - Musée du Louvre
Tel 01 42 96 06 56, www.didierludot.fr
Open 10:30am to 7pm, closed Sunday

VINTAGE

Collectors of fashion the world over know this address, which after every season is rumoured to be about to close. But the boutiques of Didier Ludot, known as the "pope of vintage", are still there, with near museum-quality collections of 20th-century fashion. The first boutique is devoted to clothes and spans the entire history of French, Italian and Spanish haute couture, from Balenciaga to Yves Saint Laurent by way of Chanel, Courrèges, Dior, Piguet and Patou. The second, where wedding receptions used to be held, is devoted to vintage accessories, including Chanel jewellery and sandals, Pucci belts and Hermès bags.

DIOR

30, avenue Montaigne, 8th
Metro Franklin D. Roosevelt
Tel 01 40 73 73 73, www.dior.fr
Open 10am to 7pm, closed Sunday

COUTURE AND READY-TO-WEAR

Christian Dior installed his salons at this legendary address in 1946, and a year later came out with his daring collection then known as the "New Look". After he died in 1957, he was succeeded by such talents as Yves Saint Laurent, Marc Bohan, Gianfranco Ferré and John Galliano. Lavishly renovated by the American architect Peter Marino, the boutique reflects the spirit and magnificence of an 18th-century townhouse, celebrating the symbols and furnishings that were dear to the couturier. Following the sudden and unexpected departure of Raf Simons, artistic direction was entrusted to the Italian designer Maria Grazia Chiuri in July 2016, who until that time was at Valentino in Rome alongside Pierpaolo Piccioli. With women's haute couture, ready-to-wear and accessories, Chiuri's vision of a rapidly changing feminist and feminine world has been creating a splash since autumn 2016, when her first collections for the prestigious grey house were revealed. Belgian Kris Van Assche, who arrived in 2007 and who has closed down his own brand, is the artistic director of the Dior Homme collection, sold at 24, rue François Ier (8th) and 25, Rue Royale (8th), as well as at Le Printemps de l'Homme (9th), Lafayette Homme (9th) and Le Bon Marché (7th). The poetic, dreamlike collections of jeweller Victoire de Castellane are presented in the adjoining boutique on Avenue Montaigne (no. 28) and at 8, Place Vendôme (1st). The Baby Dior range can be found in the separate store next door at 26–28, Avenue Montaigne (8th), and the first Dior beauty shop has taken up permanent residence at 368, Rue Saint-Honoré (1st), featuring the brand's iconic fragrances alongside Christian Dior Collection Privée, which offers totally bespoke products. Skincare consultations and catwalk makeovers are also available. The same goes for the new Right Bank and Left Bank stores.

THE DUKE

Marché Vernaison – Allée 1,
stand 37 99, rue des Rosiers, Saint-Ouen
Tel 06 32 37 17 11
Open Saturday and Sunday 10am to 6pm,
Monday by appointment only

VINTAGE

For authentic American vintage clothing, go to the Saint-Ouen flea market. Elie Zaffran, the expert everyone calls the Duke, brings out pieces from the collection he has been building up for the last thirty years, like a genuine letter jacket, wrongly known as a Teddy these days, made of boiled wool and with its original 1940s badges, awarded to the best students at US high schools and universities. Another cult buy is his B3 sheepskin bomber jackets worn by Second World War pilots. Get into the into gangster spirit, Scarface-style, with a fur-trimmed fitted overcoat or into a 1950s feel with rare Three Palms Hawaiian shirts, as worn by Montgomery Clift in the film *From Here to Eternity*. Besides his huge selection of original items, the Duke also stocks ultra-faithful reproductions, like the first flying jacket issued to pilots in the US Air Force, the A-1 (recently these fetched more than 20,000 dollars), the military jacket worn by Robert de Niro in *Taxi Driver*, and the eternal, but rare, Levi's 501 jeans. For real connoisseurs, the Duke will display his set of Buddy Lee dolls, the Lee jeans mascot from the 1920s, a cheeky little boy that comes in different versions – dressed as a fireman, railman, gas station attendant and others. Originals fetch more than 750 euros.

DUVELLEROY

17, rue Amélie, 7th
Metro La Tour Maubourg
Tel 01 42 84 07 52
www.eventail-duvelleroy.fr
Open 10am to 6pm,
closed Saturday and Sunday

COUTURE FANS

The brand's tagline roughly translates as "Majestic Accessories Since 1827", and indeed if sceptres and crowns make a queen, it is surely fans that bring a touch of glamour to any blue-blooded icon. Queen Victoria and Empress Eugénie both carried fans made by Duvelleroy, which in the 19th century owned shops on both Rue de la Paix in Paris and Bond Street in London. Launched at the famous costume ball given by the Duchesse de Berry at the Tuileries in 1829, the fashion for carrying this accessory stirred up a creative tsunami which has carried the company along in its wake ever since. Artists Ingres and Delacroix were soon brought on board in an early kind of creative collaboration, quickly followed by the stars of the Art Nouveau movement. Meanwhile, fan-carrying came to express a special language that further complicated the minefield of social interactions, involving coded gestures that might mean "follow me", or "I love you". With fans made of mother-of-pearl, ostrich feathers, precious woods or stuffed birds' heads, nothing was too beautiful for the socialites, who gobbled up Duvelleroy's creations until the Roaring Twenties. Then the wave crashed. Miraculously preserved ever since, the pleating moulds and its expertise have allowed Duvelleroy to regain its spark, thanks to two Parisian enthusiasts and the talent of Frederick Gay, who has created dozens of classics, from the Pop art-style "Oui" fan to the tad more expensive "Palmettes" model in monochrome leather, via the spectacular "Peacock", on which you can lavish more than 3,000 euros. Fans are a great way to turbocharge your powers of seduction, as Cab Calloway sang: "She's the lady with the fan, When she comes by, hold your man, She made Smokey Joe so ginny, He forgot about his Minnie."

FAURÉ LE PAGE

21, rue Cambon, 1st
Metro Madeleine, Concorde
Tel 01 49 27 99 36, www.faurelepage.com
Open 10:30am to 7pm, closed Sunday

LEATHER GOODS

Fauré Le Page was at one time an arquebus manufacturer for kings and princes, and proud winner of innumerable prizes and medals at universal exhibitions. Founded in 1717 in Paris, it focuses today on more urban needs, including bags that, in war as in the hunt, were essential companions. It knows the world of cartridge belts and pouches, shoulder bags, haversacks and hunting bags. This is the place to get a Gun pouch with strap, Parade handbag, Calibre pouch, boot bag, hip flask or the bag in the emblematic scalloped canvas with its graphic pseudo-Japanese motif, coated and impermeable, waxed and grained.

FRED MARZO

11, rue de Thorigny, 3rd
Metro Saint-Sébastien-Froissart
Tel 01 42 78 37 24, www.fredmarzo.com
Open 2pm to 7pm, by appointment
Tuesday and Wednesday,
closed Sunday and Monday

GLAMOROUS HEELS

Elegantly curvy, slightly skimpy, the Titine stiletto in snakeskin, glossy calf leather, leopard print or fishnet, with slits or transparent, is a sexy, creative shoe. Frédérick Foubet Marzorati draws inspiration from the women around him and those who are icons – from Audrey Hepburn to Cinderella, by way of Moulin Rouge dancers and Frida Kahlo. This young designer displays his creations in an old storeroom at the Musée Picasso, which has attracted huge crowds since its reopening in November 2014. Working with the finest materials made in France, this designer is quite fearless. From his Cocorico stiletto in jazzy red, white and blue to a glamorous 1950s look, each shoe carries his signature red line running from the back of the shoe right down the heel. At the same time, the designer is nurturing partnerships with artists, notably Bernard Bousquet, seen at the Galerie Nec in Rue Vieille du Temple, whose brushwork features on a fabulous limited-edition shoe.

GIVENCHY

36, avenue Montaigne, 8th
Metro Franklin D. Roosevelt
Tel 01 44 43 99 90, www.givenchy.fr
Open 10am to 7pm, closed Sunday

HAUTE COUTURE, BAGS, JEWELLERY

Swapping Avenue George V for Avenue Montaigne, the Givenchy store has seized the opportunity for a makeover, overseen brilliantly by Riccardo Tisci, artistic director until winter 2016, and architect Joseph Dirand, the man behind the Monsieur Bleu restaurant. This new space, selling womenswear only, is a paragon of elegance, its stripped ceiling retaining elements of its former incarnation as a 19th-century bakery. The decor all fits together, just like Givenchy's unique dresses, in a sublime play of materials, including Breccia Verde marble, anthracite-coloured felt, raw steel and lava stone. The ground floor showcases accessories in the form of scarves, leather goods, jewellery, watches and handbags. A spiral staircase leads upstairs to the ready-to-wear collections, classic trench coats, evening gowns and furs, where the hand of Clare Waight Keller, the house's new artistic director, can be felt. Garments can be tried on in enormous changing rooms. It's all quite fabulous. Male customers must go to the Rue des Archives in the Marais, where Givenchy's menswear has joined Fendi, Moncler, Valentino and Gucci, another sign of the controversial transformation of that neighbourhood.
See website for other locations

GRATIANNE BASCANS

38, avenue Matignon, 8th
Metro Miromesnil
Tel 01 53 75 39 35
www.gratiannebascans.com
Open 11am to 7pm, closed Sunday

BAGS

The family business dates back to 1830, but it was not until 1895 that Alexis Bascans, the second to bear the name, founded a sandal-making factory in Oloron-Sainte-Marie in the Pyrenees. The factory also made espadrilles by attaching Tissages Lartigue canvas to Bascans soles to produce models with evocative names like L'Indécousable, La Basquaise Extra and La Bordelaise Claquée. Gratianne Bascans, a professional horse rider and thoroughbred trainer, inherited the family business and, with her daughter Amandine, started using linen and cotton printed with Bascanaise or Bayadère symbols to create a collection of women's and men's bags, accessories and small leather goods made of bull leather or nubuck. The first store opened in Biarritz, and there is now one in Paris, not far from the Hôtel Bristol, bringing a touch of Basque colour to the streets of the capital.

GUIBERT

22, avenue Victor Hugo, 16th
Metro Kléber, Charles de Gaulle-Étoile
Tel 01 53 64 74 74, www.guibert.fr
Open 10:30am to 7:30pm, closed Sunday

EQUESTRIAN DESIGNS

The son and grandson of horse riders and himself a keen rider at the Club de l'Étrier, in the Bois de Boulogne, the congenial Pierre Guibert specializes in high-quality saddles, tack and equestrian clothing. The tone is set as soon as you walk through the door, with a wall of saddles custom-made in Saumur by Frédéric Butet, the Rolls-Royce of saddlers. Next come bridles, halters in tanned leather lined with Barénia calfskin, boots, and a range of breeches, jodhpurs and jackets (the belted show jackets with three buttons and a velvet collar easily convert to city wear), not to mention delightful cashmere pullovers. The silk ties, like the new collection of jacquard bags, carry the Quarter Marker motif, the pattern formerly created on a horse's rump using a stencil and now the company's emblem, also found on a small selection of dog accessories.

HERMÈS

24, rue du Faubourg Saint-Honoré, 8th
Metro Madeleine
Tel 01 40 17 46 00, www.hermes.com
Open 10:30am to 6:30pm, closed Sunday

FASHION, ACCESSORIES, SADDLERY

Hermès was founded in 1837, supplying saddles and harnesses to Parisian aristocrats, and subsequently to royal courts around Europe. From the silk square to the Kelly bag (designed in the 1930s, adopted by Grace Kelly and renamed after her in 1956), and the dog-collar bracelet to the anchor chain, Hermès has constantly succeeded in creating timeless objects of stylish luxury. Following on from Martin Margiela, Jean Paul Gaultier and Christophe Lemaire, who left to launch his own Lemaire label, designer Nadège Vanhee-Cybulski (formerly of Martin Margiela, Céline, The Row) is now designing the ever chic, terribly luxurious womenswear collection. Men's ready-to-wear, brilliantly designed by Véronique Nichanian for more than twenty years, places the emphasis on comfort, ultra-luxurious materials and great simplicity. Jewellery, shoes and tableware all display the commitment to excellence spearheaded in the 1980s by Jean-Louis Dumas, who managed to expand this Parisian family affair into an international group rooted in the values of craftsmanship. After his departure, his son Pierre-Alexis Dumas was named artistic director. In November 2010, Hermès set up shop in the legendary Lutetia hotel swimming-pool building, an Art Deco monument designed by Lucien Béguet in 1935. The lion's share of the space is devoted to home decoration, including Pippa nomadic furnishings designed by Rena Dumas, new editions of furniture by Jean-Michel Frank and contemporary items by Enzo Mari, Antonio Citterio, Eric Benqué, Denis Montel, Michele De Lucchi and Philippe Nigro, together with wallpaper, fabrics, carpets and of course fragrances by Christine Nagel, the company's new perfumer, who succeeded the legendary Jean-Claude Ellena.
See website for other locations

HILDITCH & KEY

252, rue de Rivoli, 1st
Metro Concorde
Tel 01 42 60 36 09
www.hilditchandkey.co.uk
Open 10am to 6:30pm, closed Sunday

HIGH-END SHIRTMAKER

Rich Argentineans visiting Paris in the 1930s feature prominently in the history of this shirt-maker, which was launched during the Belle Époque by two English brothers. Since then the shop – which closed briefly during the Second World War – has supplied the top tier of the political, finance and business worlds, all of whom are fans of Egyptian cotton, fitted (but never slim-fit) tailoring and timeless British chic. Moreover, the company proudly employs French workers in the Indre *département*. Karl Lagerfeld has his bespoke collars made by Hilditch & Key, and the store also stocks trilbies and fedoras by the milliner Bates. Upstairs, don't miss the wonderful view from the windows across Rue de Rivoli – and enjoy the added benefit of a bit of leg exercise, as the vintage pneumatic elevator is out of order.

JEAN ROUSSEAU

9, rue Duphot, 1st
Metro Madeleine
Tel 01 47 03 05 32
www.jean-rousseau.com
Open 10am to 7pm, closed Sunday

SMALL LEATHER ITEMS

Based for the last sixty years in Besançon and now listed as an *entreprise du patrimoine vivant* (living heritage company), Jean Rousseau continues to deploy its unique expertise (including the *coupé sellier* technique) with finely crafted animal skins, most of which have gone through its tanning and finishing workshops. It is perhaps best known for its watch straps in calf, python, alligator, lizard, ostrich, shark and shagreen, but it also makes bags for men and women (the Anaïs bag, notably) and diamond-dust evening clutches, simple but beautifully finished coin purses, card holders and cases for iPhones, iPads and laptops. The company offers a personalized service, ranging from hand stitching in gold or platinum thread to a lining in a contrasting colour. The prices are far from silly.

KARL LAGERFELD

194, boulevard Saint-Germain, 7th
Metro Saint-Germain-des-Prés
Tel 01 42 22 74 99
www.karl.com
Open 10:30am to 7pm, closed Sunday

ICONIC CONCEPT STORE

Karl Lagerfeld's concept store is a showcase for technology, an experience in itself. The iconic fashion designer – open to all innovations and truly in sync with the times – surprises us yet again. The store covers 200 square metres on two levels, mixing matte and shiny materials in a predominance of black and white, with mirrored walls reflecting the men's and women's ready-to-wear lines and accessories. Not forgetting his countless collaborations with artists such as Steven Wilson (in 2017) and prestigious brands, such as Faber-Castell for the superb KarlBox, as well as an original jewellery collection that the pony-tailed maestro has designed in conjunction with Swarovski. But the most surprising thing of all, apart from Choupette, Lagerfeld's star-studded cat appearing on everything from books to ballerina pumps, is the store's use of new media: Karl's Booth, in the dressing rooms, lets customers immortalize their "look of the day" and share it over the internet; Karl's Book and his iPads present the brand and give customers freedom to photograph and share favourite items; iPad Minis in the racks allow you to explore the entire collection. And last but not least, there is not a cash register in sight – you pay using a mobile terminal. Just steps away is Karl's bookstore, **7L** (7, rue de Lille, 7th, tel 01 42 92 03 58), specializing in the decorative arts, fashion, design, architecture and curiosities.

LA FABRIQUE GÉNÉRALE

2 bis, rue Léon Cosnard, 17th
Metro Malesherbes
Tel 01 86 95 81 73
www.lafabriquegenerale.com
Open 11am to 7pm,
closed Sunday to Tuesday

HATS AND MOTORBIKE WEAR

Whether panama hat, taupe-coloured or waterproof fedora – each and every customer can make their own choice, as in this shop hats are only available made-to-measure. Madame Cerise launched her business in the heart of the 6th arrondissement, fully equipped with blocking machines and grosgrain hatbands, before opening another shop on Paris's Right Bank in La Fabrique Générale, a strange mixture of a place that is the brainchild of her biker husband. While people come here for the hats, which can be customized to fit every occasion, it's also the place for all kinds of motorbike equipment, including the correct gear you'll need to make an impression on two wheels. In this former mirror factory tucked behind the Rue de Lévis you'll find helmets, jackets, Helstons leathers and courier bags, as well as reissued design classics and vehicle workshops. It's also the starting location for full-throttle bike rides through the capital on Sundays.

LANVIN

15 and 22, rue du Faubourg Saint-Honoré, 8th, metro Madeleine
Tel 01 44 71 33 33, www.lanvin.com
Open 10:30am to 7pm, closed Sunday

PARISIAN CHIC, LUXURIOUS

Facing each other on the corner of Rue Boissy d'Anglas, the Lanvin men's and women's boutiques form a huge space covering over 1,000 square metres. The interiors were designed by Armand-Albert Rateau in the days when Jeanne Lanvin was at the helm. Lanvin was bought in 2001 by a holding company. A few weeks later, the talented Alber Elbaz, fresh from stints at Guy Laroche and Yves Saint Laurent, was appointed design director and entrusted with safeguarding the subtle femininity of the women's collections, close to couture. In 2014 the company celebrated its 125th anniversary. On its website and through various social media networks Lanvin revealed secrets of its history, photos and videos taken from the archives, as well as vintage gouache drawings by Jeanne Lanvin. Continuing the celebrations, 2015 saw a major Lanvin exhibition at the Palais Galliera. In October of the same year, a dramatic turn of events occurred: Elbaz was requested to pack his bags. Bouchra Jarrar was tasked with reinvigorating Lanvin. Born in Cannes, she has already demonstrated her mastery of form, by turns sharp and delightfully fluid. The Lanvin Femme collections (ready- to-wear, accessories and perfume) are housed at no. 22, while Lanvin Homme, in the hands of Lucas Ossendrijver since 2006, fills four floors at no. 15, offering ready-to-wear and formal collections, accessories, homeware and fragrances.

LAULHÈRE

14-16, rue du Faubourg Saint-Honoré, 8th
Metro Madeleine
Tel 01 42 65 90 59
www.laulhere-france.com
Open 11am to 7:30pm, closed Sunday

AUTHENTIC BERETS

Alongside the French stick and Camembert, it's the third member of the most famous French trio in the world. No wonder, then, that the Basque beret is a regular feature on fashion runways, where it can be relied upon to add a touch of French glamour, as well as popping up on tourist souvenir stalls in somewhat cheaper form. To be sure of obtaining the genuine article, go to Laulhère, the last manufacturer in France, which has been in operation since 1840 and has recently set up shop in the Madeleine district. Officially certified as a company that creates a "living heritage", the brand can certainly provide the authentic French peasant look, but that doesn't prevent it from taking liberties with this iconic product – decorating it with sequins or a chic little veil, vinyl effects or embroidery. The Laulhère beret is completely waterproof and can be folded to tuck into your pocket – but we're sure you'll want to keep wearing this little French topknot come rain or shine.

LAURENCE BOSSION

10, rue Saint-Roch, 1st
Metro Tuileries
Tel 01 42 96 80 50
www.laurencebossion.com
Open 11am to 7pm,
closed Sunday and Monday

BESPOKE HATS

Designer Laurence Bossion, a graduate of the École de la Chambre Syndicale de la Couture Parisienne and the Institut de Beauté Français de la Mode, opened her shop with the intention of defending "hat chic". It's true that she often outfits celebrities on their way to the Prix de Diane horse race and similar events, but she is

LOUIS VUITTON

To contact the customer relations service covering all Louis Vuitton stores in Paris, telephone: 09 77 40 40 77. For news on all Louis Vuitton activities, go to: www.louisvuitton.com

CHAMPS-ÉLYSÉES 101, avenue des Champs-Élysées, 8th, metro George V, open 10am to 8pm, Sunday 11am to 7pm
Luggage, leather goods, accessories, ready-to-wear, shoes, watches, jewellery, fragrance

MONTAIGNE 22, avenue Montaigne, 8th, metro Alma-Marceau, open 10am to 7:30pm, Sunday noon to 7pm
Luggage, leather goods, accessories, ready-to-wear, shoes, watches, jewellery, fragrance

SAINT-GERMAIN-DES-PRÉS 170, boulevard Saint-Germain, 6th, metro Saint-Germain-des-Prés, open 10:30am to 7:30pm, Sunday 11am to 7pm
Luggage, leather goods, accessories, women's ready-to-wear, shoes, watches, jewellery, writing, fragrance

PLACE VENDÔME 4, place Vendôme, 1st, metro Tuileries, open 10am to 7pm, Sunday from 1pm
Luggage, leather goods, accessories, ready-to-wear, shoes, watches, jewellery, fragrance

LE BON MARCHÉ 24, rue de Sèvres, 7th, metro Sèvres-Babylone, open 10am to 8pm, Thursday until 9pm, Sunday from 11am
Luggage, leather goods, accessories, women's ready-to-wear and shoes, fragrance

GALERIES LAFAYETTE 40, boulevard Haussmann, 9th, metro Chaussée d'Antin-La Fayette, open 9:30am to 8:30pm, Sunday 11am to 7pm
Luggage, leather goods, accessories, women's ready-to-wear and shoes, watches, jewellery, fragrance

PRINTEMPS HAUSSMANN 64, boulevard Haussmann, 9th, metro Havre-Caumartin, open 9:35am to 8pm, Thursday 10:30am to 7:30pm, Sunday 11am to 7pm
Luggage, leather goods, accessories, women's ready-to-wear and shoes, watches, fragrance

also there for the woman in the street. Her warmly inviting atelier-cum-shop, with its intentional air of a bazaar, is filled with drawers overflowing with grosgrain, feathers, ribbons and flowers, destined to adorn fascinators and cloches, as well as berets dressed up with stylish bows. She can make classic men's hats, including fedoras, bowler hats and trilbies. Her speciality, however, is one-off pieces and bespoke designs for women, for which you should be prepared to wait from two to six weeks.

LE BON MARCHÉ RIVE GAUCHE

24, rue de Sèvres, 7th
Metro Sèvres-Babylone
Tel 01 44 39 80 00, www.lebonmarche.com
Open 10am to 8pm, Thursday and Friday until 9pm, closed Sunday

DEPARTMENT STORE

Le Bon Marché, the only department store on the Left Bank, was bought in 1984 by Bernard Arnault, who commissioned Andrée Putman to redesign the interiors. The store has become both more luxurious and more stylish, with exclusive areas resembling private lounges, and it continues to spur stylistic, creative, innovative and cultural revolutions. Now at the cutting edge of fashion, Le Bon Marché remains a small universe of charming Parisian sophistication. Revamped in 2014 with the addition of an extra floor, store number 2, located at the corner of Rue du Bac and Rue de Sèvres, it has gone back to its roots. Built in 1923 by Louis-Hippolyte Boileau, the architect who designed both Prunier restaurant and the entrance to the Parc des Expositions at Porte de Versailles, this store has become once again the focus of homeware, interior decoration, tableware and design. It also houses the restaurant **LA TABLE** beneath a striking new glass roof. The food section, the Grande Épicerie, has been completely redesigned, but can still be found on the ground floor and in the basement. Now that the fashion department is back in the main store, there are clothes on every level. Ready-to-wear designers can be found on the second floor with footwear displayed under a beautifully restored 19th-century glass ceiling. Make-up, perfume, creams and lotions from the Florentine pharmacy Santa Maria Novella, watches, jewellery, accessories and luxury goods call out to customers on the ground floor, while menswear takes up the entire basement. Formerly just a pop-up, its concept gift area, La Galerie Imaginaire, is now a permanent fixture offering an exceptional selection of unusual must-haves. Particularly welcome are the valet parking service, shoe shine, barber, wine bar and cellar and, on the first floor, "by appointment" lounges for astute fashion advice, and for women, the Marisol hairdresser.

LOUIS VUITTON

101, avenue des Champs-Elysées, 8th
Metro George V
Tel 09 77 40 40 77, www.louisvuitton.com
Open 10am to 8pm, Sunday 11am to 7pm

LUXURY HOUSE

Over 100 years ago, in 1914, Louis Vuitton set up shop on the Champs-Élysées, at no. 70, opening what was then the city's largest store devoted to travel. This remained the famous trunk manufacturer's Parisian address until 1954. The company later returned to its roots and now has an immense flagship store on the corner of Avenue George V and what the French proudly call the "most beautiful avenue in the world". The store, which covers 1,800 square metres, displays a consummate use of light, which adds to an impression of uncluttered space, unostentatious luxury and intimacy, all of which was masterminded and extended in 2005 by architects Eric Carlson and Peter Marino. The entire interior eschews the idea of floors, inviting visitors to embark on a promenade from terrace to terrace that inexorably leads to a spectacular 20-metre-high atrium from which some

1,900 polished steel tubes are suspended, reflecting the light like an inverted waterfall. This invitation to travel continues with more areas to discover, more artworks and more unique sensory experiences that dovetail with the ready-to-wear collections, bags, luggage, leather goods, shoes, watches, jewellery and fragrance. The bookshop is as delightful as ever and is naturally well stocked with the popular City Guide series, the eagerly awaited new titles in Louis Vuitton's Travel Book series, and the already iconic Fashion Eye collection of photography books.

MAISON BONNET

Passage des Deux Pavillons,
5, rue des Petits Champs, 1st
Metro Bourse, Pyramides
Tel 01 42 96 46 35, www.maisonbonnet.com
Open by appointment 11am to 7pm,
closed Sunday

ARTISAN EYEWEAR

Opticians, optometrists and manufacturers of high-quality spectacles, the Maison Bonnet company is currently in the safe, efficient hands of Franck and Steven Bonnet, cool-eyed members of the fourth generation of the family. A giant turtle in the lobby sets the tone. Here, noble tortoiseshell is king, together with water buffalo and ram's horn. The company's eyewear has adorned the faces of the likes of Jackie Onassis, Audrey Hepburn, Yves Saint Laurent, François Mitterrand and Jacques Chirac, to name some of the most famous. There is much to admire on the different floors, where you can revel in the cosy yet contemporary decor, a listed glass showcase and a veritable library of styles, collections, materials and colours. Upstairs there is an extraordinary collection of vintage glasses. Below street level, a 17th-century vaulted cellar contains the workshop and laboratory. Opposite, a tiny workshop provides a glimpse of the savoir faire of this establishment that is rightly classified as a "living heritage business".

MAISON CAILLAU

124, rue du Faubourg Saint-Honoré, 8th
Metro Saint-Philippe-du-Roule
Tel 01 43 59 06 86
www.maisoncaillau.fr
Open 10am to 7pm, closed Sunday

HAIR ACCESSORIES AND MORE

Formerly a men's hairdressing salon now converted into a perfumery, this venerable family firm founded in 1924 has avoided being gobbled up by the big cosmetic conglomerates by focusing on hair accessories. Now Maison Caillau is the first outlet to sell designs by the hairdresser Alexandre, and these combs, barrettes, scrunchies and other accessories continue to attract customers who drop in for a flowery bath cap or a Peggy Sage nail polish – the oldest brand in France. Alongside the hairpins and real umbrellas of Cherbourg, owner Sophie also stocks German-made cashmere brushes. But undoubtedly the ultimate treasure is still the scrubbing brush: available for less than ten euros, this is the most successful and on-trend gift in the neighbourhood.

MAISON CLAIRVOY

18, rue Pierre Fontaine, 9th
Metro Pigalle, Blanche
Tel 01 48 74 44 03, www.clairvoy.fr
Open 9am to noon and 2pm to 7pm,
closed Saturday and Sunday

MADE-TO-MEASURE SHOES

Maison Clairvoy has been instrumental in the continuing success of the French cancan. Édouard Clairvoy, a bootmaker from Montmartre as well as a notable painter, became the go-to man for the Paris art world in the late 1940s. In the 1960s Maison Clairvoy made shoes and boots for the dancers at the Moulin Rouge, then at the Paradis Latin and the Crazy Horse. The business was acquired, astutely, by the Société du Moulin Rouge (along with the *plumassier* Maison Février), which appointed bootmaker Nicolas Maistriaux to take charge. The company made the cowboy boots worn by Jean Dujardin in the film version of *Lucky Luke*, as well as the shoes worn by award-winning Guillaume Gallienne in his dual role as mother and son in *Me, Myself and Mum*. Since 2006 Clairvoy has also been serving the general public with a collection of eight styles, hand-stitched and crafted in the workshop over the road, a centre of bespoke shoes and fine Parisian craftsmanship, whose collection of lasts contains some real treasures. The shop still prioritizes commissions from the world of entertainment, so the ordinary customer may have to wait up to eight months for a pair of their legendary shoes. Also worth a visit, and reachable on foot of course, is the **MAISON ERNEST** (75, boulevard de Clichy, 9th, tel 01 45 26 97 20) store. Founded in 1904, from its base on the formerly X-rated Boulevard de Clichy, the brand's trademark indecently vertiginous killer heels embody the spirit of Pigalle.

MAISON RABIH KAYROUZ

38, boulevard Raspail, 7th
Metro Sèvres-Babylone
Tel 01 45 48 21 00
www.maisonrabihkayrouz.com
Open by appointment only

FRENCH-LEBANESE DESIGNS

Rabih Kayrouz has set up shop in the former Théâtre de Babylone, where *Waiting for Godot* was premiered in 1953. Decades later the curtain has gone up on a new creative scene – luxurious ready-to-wear collections celebrating a thrilling femininity of split skirts, drapery and stripped-down silhouettes that forges an elegant link between the French and Lebanese cultures. For the winter 2017–18 collection the workshops, located here as well as in Mayenne, have launched a collection inspired by floral hues, including pale rose, cream and iris blue in tandem with modern, striped kaftans, conjuring up a luxurious stroll in an oriental garden of your dreams.

MES CHAUSSETTES ROUGES

9, rue César Franck, 15th, metro Ségur
Tel 01 76 53 96 20
www.meschaussettesrouges.com
Open 10am to 6pm, Saturday from 11am, closed Sunday

SOCKS

Pity the poor sock. Boutiques and department stores are not interested in selling a wide range of sizes, colours and types, and hipsters are not interested in wearing them with their late-model Church's (real or knock-offs). Luckily, Jacques Tiberghien and Vincent Metzgerthis have founded Mes Chaussettes Rouges, devoted exclusively to humble hosiery. They are the only retailers to import to Paris the legendary purple cardinal's and white papal socks made by the ecclesiastical tailor Gammarelli. And they are the only ones selling the green socks worn by members of the Académie Française, made by Mazarin, a sign of sartorial coquetry. Other socks in stock include the colourful fantasies of Gallo and the linen and silk pairs by Bresciani. They come in every imaginable style and material: plain, striped, moss stitched, caviar, cashmere, merino, lisle, Tyrolean, Norwegian, Scottish or yak wool (overlocked by hand). This complete range has it all, right up to super-luxurious, extremely expensive vicuña models, and sizes up to fifty. In addition to socks, the store sells Simonnot-Godard handkerchiefs and pocket squares, monogrammed Pasotti umbrellas, and Saphir shoe polish, all of which can be examined while sipping coffee served on a tray. Mes Chaussettes Rouges also has an excellent online shop – each purchase comes with advice and a travel bag. The store is located within walking distance of the Racing Club de France de Natation and its pool. While there is no connection – swimming in socks would be more than eccentric – it is mentioned as a way of situating the address on the border of the 7th arrondissement.

MOLLI

252, boulevard Saint-Germain, 7th
Metro Solférino
Tel 01 43 25 87 91, www.molli.com
Open 10:30am to 2pm and
2:30pm to 7pm, closed Sunday

KNITWEAR

Made in Switzerland since 1886 by the Rüegger family, Molli is the elite, the Rolls-Royce of knitwear, the ultimate in garter-stitched cardigans with mother-of-pearl button. The products of this pillar of Swiss textile know-how have been sold and recognized around the world for over a century. Bought in 2015 by the young French entrepreneur Charlotte de Fayet, Molli has carried on without losing its touch. The colourist Amandine Gallienne contributed some hues, while Fayet designed the knitwear lines for women and newborns – it was impossible to stop making the layettes that had made the house's reputation. Its collections, made of pure cotton or virgin wool, seem to be perfumed with water, soap and lavender. They are sold in two pristine stores in Paris, one on the Left Bank and the other on the Right. A new era, a new air.

Other location: 71, avenue Paul Doumer, 16th, tel 09 81 92 48 24

MOYNAT PARIS

348, rue Saint-Honoré, 1st
Metro Tuileries
Tel 01 47 03 83 90, www.moynat.com
Open 10am to 7:30pm, closed Sunday

LEATHER GOODS, LUGGAGE

The sober facade of the Moynat store designed by Gwenaël Nicolas, founder of the Tokyo-based agency Curiosity, conceals curving walls and serene, majestic volumes inside. The curves recall the form of the legendary Malle Limousine, designed to fit snugly on the curved roof of a car. Moynat, one of the oldest and most prestigious French luggage-makers, founded in 1849, grew rapidly under the direction of Pauline Moynat, a pioneer in this field, who also made bags for women. The house closed in the 1970s, but was later revived by Bernard Arnault, who is keeping it very low profile, with no advertising, famous face or "It" bag. Previously at Hermès, Ramesh Nair is rewriting the history of the Pauline, the Holdall, the Quattro (tote bag) and the equally desirable Paradis, as well as the Limousine briefcase, whose concave shape echoes the curved boot of a limousine. He's also launching some special projects that showcase exceptional craftsmanship, ranging from the breakfast trunk, a masterpiece designed for chef Yannick Alléno, to champagne cases and a collection of train-shaped bags designed by Pharrell Williams. Such creations are like works of art and travel the world, in particular London, Hong Kong and Seoul, as well as Paris's Bon Marché and the Galeries Lafayette, which also stock the brand.

OLYMPIA LE-TAN

Passage des Deux Pavillons,
5, rue des Petits Champs, 1st
Metro Palais-Royal–Musée du Louvre
Tel 01 42 36 42 92
www.olympialetan.com
Open 11am to 7pm, closed Sunday

EXTRAVAGANT DESIGNS

Olympia Le-Tan has just opened her first boutique in a former antiques shop, which she first spotted in 2009. Daughter of the illustrator Pierre Le-Tan, who created the shocking pink decor, the extravagant designer, known in particular for her book-cover clutch bags, presented a series of Hitchcockian heroines for her recent autumn-winter collection. In another example of her signature sense of humour look out for Le-Tan's Psycho collection of acid yellow sweatshirts and malabar pink gloves, among other things. Cinematic references go hand in hand with a very Le-Tan-style kind of femininity, making her fun range look picture-perfect against the backdrop of her tiny store.

PERRIN

3, rue d'Alger, 1st
Metro Tuileries
Tel 01 42 36 53 54
www.perrinparis.com
Open 10am to 7pm, closed Sunday

LUXURY LEATHER GOODS

A family-owned French house founded in 1893 in Saint-Junien, Perrin began as a tanner and went into the glove-making business in 1920, opening stores in Paris, London, New York, San Francisco and even Sydney. After decades of slumber, the house has been relaunched in the United States by Michel Perrin, who used to work for Microsoft and has lived in Los Angeles since the 1980s. He and his wife Sally have positioned the brand in a creative luxury niche and opened a store in Beverly Hills, their first and only in town. In Paris, after opening a showroom, they now have a real store, patronized by nearby designers (AMI, Vanessa Seward, etc.), where the collections of bags, small leather goods, pouches, saddlebags, wallets, boxes and travel kits are made of precious, exotic leathers, including shagreen, and have a surrealistic look. Superb!

PRINTEMPS DE L'HOMME

64, boulevard Haussmann, 9th
Metro Havre-Caumartin
Tel 01 42 82 50 00
www.printemps.com
Open 9:35am to 8pm, Thursday until 20:45pm, closed Sunday

MEN'S DEPARTMENT STORE

The latest venture at Printemps, the venerable department store opened by Jules Jaluzot in 1865, is a man's world showcased over five floors and 11,000 square metres. Back in the day, a gentleman's clothing department took some thirteen years to emerge, and the Brummell department at Printemps always seemed stuck in the 1960s, so today an astonishing transformation awaits the crowd of elegant young men drifting about in these five worlds of fashion. It is carefully curated, but with an incredibly global range. Look out for the accessories showcased on white marble and metal mesh stands, luxury ready-to-wear and designers, 300 square metres devoted to Printemps's favourite buys, a totally hip denim department, plus everything you could dream of in the way of sneakers and shoes. There's also a café and a shoe repair counter. It's all connected by a spectacular 26-metre-high screen that brings together the work of the three architectural firms (Wilmotte & Associés, Universal Design Studio and Ciguë), who have left their mark on this project costing over 100 million euros. VIPs head to Rue de Provence, where they are treated to discreet private lounge access.

RIVIERAS

127, rue de Turenne, 3rd
Metro Filles du Calvaire
Tel 09 50 60 00 96
www.rivieras-shoes.com
Open 11am to 7pm, closed Sunday and Monday

LEISURE FOOTWEAR

When it comes to evoking the vintage fashions of a bygone France, Dan Amzallag and Fabrizio Corveddu have played a blinder with their summery, cotton-mesh shoes (think old French guys playing boules under the plane trees). These pumps have become the iconic footwear for young urban tribes who travel the world in search of the sun. Rivieras has enjoyed great success since it was launched, collaborating with André, Lord Jacket and Surface to Air, opening stores in Ibiza, Saint-Barthélemy and Beirut, and setting up a new and expanded Parisian store. The latter boasts a beautiful, clean decor, great shoebox graphics echoed in the interiors, and a range that makes you want to buy multiple pairs. Whether it's monochrome Classics (as worn by old French guys), or two-tone or tricolour models, whether woven leather or the superb Montecristi in woven raffia, the range doesn't just cater for summer: the Vinyl Rain high-tops adore the wet, while the low-cut Vinyl Smoking make regular appearances on the red carpet. Rivieras' almost boundless selection conjures up all things French – accordion music, picnicking on checked tablecloths, pétanque, pastis and a dash of olive oil – in short the *joie de vivre* of Saint-Tropez.

ROBERT CLERGERIE

8, rue de Grenelle, 6th
Metro Saint-Sulpice
Tel 01 42 22 15 97
www.robertclergerie.com
Open 10:30am to 7pm, closed Sunday

MEN'S SHOES

Energized by its takeover by Fung Brands and by creative director Roland Mouret, in 2012 the brand treated itself to a new store in Rue de Grenelle, designed by art director Thierry Dreyfus. In a beautiful, timeless space, the interplay of mirrors and white wood creates the perfect setting for men's footwear, with the women's footwear taking centre stage in Rue du Cherche-Midi. Inspired by the brand's earliest origins, a menswear collection in 1895, the designer adds a colourful, creative rock touch to his Oxfords and brogues.
He focuses on the best materials, puts latex soles on a few comfortable sandals and keeps classic styles, notably the best formal boots for men in Paris, worn by celebs from Bruce Springsteen to former president François Hollande. Continuing its androgynous tradition with Communal, the range offers the same styles for women, in the interests of equality. All the footwear proudly claims it is made in France – the factory is at Romans-sur-Isère – and its slight air of insolence has earned it some successful collaborative projects, not to mention the favours of Selena Gomez and Kristen Stewart. **Other location:** 5, rue du Cherche-Midi, 6th, tel 01 45 48 75 47

ROGER VIVIER

29, rue du Faubourg Saint-Honoré, 8th
Metro Madeleine
Tel 01 53 43 00 85
www.rogervivier.com
Open 11am to 7pm, closed Sunday

SHOES, LUXURIOUS LEATHER GOODS

Roger Vivier, the greatest 20th-century French shoe designer, who died in 1998, was intimately linked to the Parisian avant-garde scene. He designed not only the shoes worn by Queen Elizabeth during her coronation but also Brigitte Bardot's thigh boots and the iconic ballet slippers with square chrome buckles worn by Catherine Deneuve in *Belle de Jour*, a model now known as Belle Vivier. His constant cutting-edge innovations (stilettos, the Choc heel, Virgule) still seem visionary. Now part of the portfolio of the Italian company Diego Della Valle (Tod's, Hogan, Fay), the brand was relaunched in 2002 under the artistic direction of Bruno Frisoni. His distinguished, daring, lively designs include the ready-to-wear and Rendez-Vous collections, the latter a rare limited-edition line that is the embodiment of luxury. New stores have been opening around the world since the relaunch. Located in the former Pierre Cardin store, the Parisian Vivier shop was designed by architect Philippe Maillols and Inès de La Fressange, the brand's perfect ambassador.

SAINT LAURENT PARIS

6, place Saint-Sulpice, 6th
Metro Saint-Sulpice
Tel 01 43 29 43 00, www.ysl.com
Open 10:30am to 7pm,
Monday from 11am, closed Sunday

LEGENDARY, ULTRA-SLIM SILHOUETTE

Yves Saint Laurent, the visionary who created the modern woman, took his "aesthetic phantoms" with him when he died on 1 June 2008. Two biopics, released in 2014, reached a non-couture audience. Part of the Kering group since 1999, Saint Laurent hired designer Tom Ford, then Stefano Pilati, to take over ready-to-wear

SPOTLIGHT

BESPOKE SHOES

Shoes have never been so important – perhaps even crucial. And the Parisians are totally up to speed, as they happily combine fast-fashion jeans with designer jackets, cheap trinkets with branded accessories – from the shoes up. Whether your manor is pavement or penthouse, bespoke is the real deal, and for more than a century the craft has been nurtured by two institutions.

From the Duchess of Windsor to Lady Gaga, **MASSARO** conducts its business according to established rituals: the feet of each lucky customer are measured and then sculptured in elm wood, to create a mould which is the *fons et origo* of almost anything – crocodile moccasins for him, feathered pumps for her, wedges with sculpted soles, boots made of exotic skins, among many more. One little-known fact is that in the early 1950s this very discreet upmarket brand designed Chanel's iconic two-tone sandal with its flirty, six-centimetre heel. 2, rue de la Paix, 2nd, metro Opéra, tel 01 42 61 00 29, www.massaro.fr

Another great Parisian icon, which is now a player in the world of ready-to-wear and bespoke, **BERLUTI** has not forgotten its beginnings as a shoemaker, and continues to produce heel counters, chamfers and welts with the surgical precision adored by Marcel Proust and Andy Warhol back in the day. Berluti's craftsmen are always happy to argue the toss over close-seat or extended sewn-seat heels, sewn or Norwegian welts. 26, rue Marbeuf, 8th, metro Franklin D. Roosevelt, tel 01 53 93 97 97, www.berluti.com

In this new universe of modern shoemaking, Olivier Guyot opened his own workshop under the **GEORGE & GEORGES** brand, offering, in addition to variations on classic Oxfords and derbies, a refurbishment service for old Stan Smiths. It's the ultimate footwear experience: the choice of colours, shades and shine is everything upper-class feet adore. 41, rue de Verneuil, 7th, metro Rue du Bac, tel 06 72 56 86 19, www.george-georges.fr

Head for the elegant west of the city, where **LE CALCÉLOPHILE**, manufacturer and designers of smart pumps, has chosen to set up shop. 85, rue de Courcelles, 17th, metro Ternes, tel 09 84 03 10 78, www.lecalceophile.com

DEVOIR DE COURT (under the slogan "Salon d'excellence") has raised the bar even higher, offering a shoe-glazing service that combines wax with an interesting spirit concoction. 6, rue de Monceau, 8th, metro Saint-Philippe-du-Roule, tel 01 77 12 66 69, www.devoirdecourt.com

from 2004 to 2012, the year Hedi Slimane was appointed creative director in charge of brand image and collections. This was a notable comeback for the man who left Yves Saint Laurent menswear in 2000: between 2001 and 2007, Slimane, this "quiet man who made a lot of noise", a photographer in his spare time and for a while a furniture designer, took over the design of the Dior Homme line, completely changing the male aesthetic. This radical visionary imposed an ultra-slim look that was adopted by women. While the company was still basking in the glow of the phenomenal publicity whipped up by Hedi Slimane and his triumphant farewell runway show, Slimane himself nevertheless stepped aside in favour of thirty-something Anthony Vaccarello. The new boy brings with him a new muse in the form of an ultra-sexy woman, placing as much emphasis on YSL's legendary Sahara suits and dinner jackets as on frilly dresses in dark brown leather, long rhinestone-encrusted thigh boots, Mongolian lambskin-lined hoodies and high heels etched with logos.

SONIA RYKIEL

175, boulevard Saint-Germain, 6th
Metro Saint-Germain-des-Prés
Tel 01 49 54 60 60
www.soniarykiel.com
Open 10:30am to 7pm, closed Sunday

PARISIAN FASHION

The spirit of Saint-Germain is not just about frittering the days away in the Café Flore. Happily, on the other side of the boulevard, on the corner of Rue des Saints-Pères, Sonia Rykiel still keeps the flame of the founder's joyous approach to fashion alight – a deconstructed kind of fashion, or *démode*, as the redheaded Rykiel herself called it. Rykiel started out playing shop in the 1960s on the unglamorous side of the Porte d'Orléans. By May 1968 the future designer had arrived in the heart of Saint-Germain-des-Prés – and she never left. With seams on the outside, reinvented sizes, acid-colour stripes or head-to-toe-black for dazzling young women, Rykiel's fashion threw a hand grenade into the dreary acres of poplin that characterized French post-war taste. And the same went for her collections over the next forty years, as Rykiel's famous knitwear turned into one of the most amazing adventures in luxury French ready-to-wear. Rykiel's daughter and long-time assistant, Nathalie, who occasionally strayed into erotic accessories, took over the brand's artistic direction when, in 2016, at the age of eighty-six, Sonia Rykiel finally took a back seat. Meanwhile, the house was sold to the Fung Brands group, and it is now the divine Julie de Libran, originally from Aix-en-Provence but brought up in California, who runs the studio, cleaving to Left Bank traditions while infusing it with new life. She is responsible, among other things, for the impressive shop interiors: 50,000 books scattered throughout the ground floor, first floor and the fitting rooms, in a decor of light wood and vermilion lacquer – the iconic red, proving, if proof were needed, that Saint-Germain fashion is still a force to be reckoned with. A hundred metres down the road, **RYKIEL ENFANT** (4, rue de Grenelle) provides a child-sized version of the same spirit in a lively and amusing setting.
See website for other locations

STOULS

36, rue du Mont Thabor, 1st
Metro Concorde
Tel 01 42 60 29 97, www.stouls.paris
Open 10:30am to 7:30pm, closed Sunday

LUXURY LEATHERWEAR

At one time a shoe designer, fashion expert Aurélia Stouls (Esmod, Studio Berçot, Fashion Institute of New York) set up her own business with a very precise idea: to design leather clothes that feel like a second skin and are machine washable. Avoiding the pitfalls of gimmickry, the biker community or the Goth dominatrix brigade, Aurélia has built up an impressively loyal customer base, including many Rue Saint-Honoré designers, who are thrilled to be able to chuck their pencil skirt or beige shirt into the washing machine as if it were an ordinary pair of jeans. But it is for the extremely precise cut and the exceptional texture of this lambskin that customers crowd into the Arab-style changing rooms of this shop designed by interior designer India Mahdavi. Boys are welcome, too, with their own range of trousers, sweatshirts and jackets. Also look out for Aurélia Stouls' amazing collaborative work – she's dressed Barbie dolls and the kitchen staff who work at Ma Cocotte, the fashionable restaurant in Clignancourt's flea market.

TEINTURERIE GERMAINE

11 bis, rue de Surène, 8th
Metro Madeleine
Tel 01 42 65 12 28
www.teinturerie-germaine.fr
Open 9am to 6pm, Saturday until 5:30pm

LUXURY DRY-CLEANER

Located behind the Rue du Faubourg Saint-Honoré since 1938, this luxury dry-cleaner that boasted as many as thirty employees in the 1960s is still run by Madame Lesèche, now in her nineties. With thirty years of experience, Véronique manages this business that occupies two floors, providing miracle cleaning for your stained blouses, faded bags and ruined wedding dresses or furs. In the expert hands of a mini-team working in-house (a rare occurrence these days) and using completely artisan methods (even more unusual) dirt and damage just fade away. It can be expensive but work starts only once a price has been quoted and agreed. The cleaners specialize in leather, suede and exotic skins, and their rejuvenation work has become a legend from Parisian mansions to the palaces of Monaco, where Véronique regularly sends back Kelly bags, Birkins and Keepalls once they've had a facelift. The only other similar service in Paris is provided by big sister **PARFAIT ÉLÈVE DE POUYANNE** (57, boulevard Haussmann, 8th, tel 01 42 65 34 23), which has specialized in the cleaning of academic ceremonial dress and gowns, among other items, since 1903. A useful address for those expecting a call from the palace.

U.N.X

Galeries Lafayette,
40, boulevard Haussmann, 9th
Metro Opéra, Chaussée d'Antin-La Fayette
www.unx-paris.com
Open 9:30am to 8:30pm,
Sunday 11am to 7pm

YOUNG DESIGNER

A product of one of the best schools – which incidentally was Azzedine Alaïa's alma mater too – Hedi El Chikh has signed up to one of Paris's latest fashion adventures, the result of Marie and Olivier Dall'Arche's passion for combat sports. Put as bluntly as that, it sounds astonishing, but under the baton of this young artistic director, this martial arts-inspired brand, with two seasons already under its belt, is an attractive proposition. Successfully splicing sportswear and couture, judo suits and power dressing, obi-belted coats, striped blouses, structured trousers and eye-catching tops made using "technical materials", the brand is perfectly in sync with Parisians' unhealthy fitness obsession. But more than that, it's chic: the cuts are perfect, the knitwear drapes beautifully and the consciously limited colourways express a philosophy of "less is more" that chimes wholeheartedly with the spirit of the times.

VANESSA SEWARD

10, rue d'Alger, 1st, metro Tuileries
Tel 01 85 65 88 89
www.vanessaseward.com
Open 11am to 7:30pm, closed Sunday

READY-TO-WEAR DESIGNER

When she left Azzaro in 2012 to work for A.P.C., this Argentinean-born French designer hit a sweet spot with everything from her evening dresses to minimalist jeans, seen on red carpets and Parisian streets. Vanessa Seward brought high fashion and 1970s-chic inspirations to the basics of the house of Jean Touitou. Three years and as many capsule collections later, A.P.C. encouraged her to launch her own brand. After unveiling her first collection in March 2015, she opened her shop in September of the same year at 10, rue d'Alger. Close to her adopted home, it is a reflection of her warm, refined style, aimed at globetrotting Parisian women. Decorated in elm and South American veined stone, the store is as welcoming as the designer, who shows up regularly to present her feminine, Parisian, intellectual – but never strict – designs. **Other locations:** 7, boulevard des Filles du Calvaire, 3rd, tel 01 70 36 06 11; 171, boulevard Saint-Germain, 6th, tel 01 70 36 06 12

WATCHES AND JEWELLERY

AGRY

14, rue de Castiglione, 1st
Metro Tuileries
Tel 01 42 60 65 10, www.agry.fr
Open 10am to 7pm, Saturday 11:15am to 6pm, closed Sunday and Monday

ENGRAVED SIGNET RINGS

Dating back to 1825, this was one of the first shops to open under the arcades of the Rue de Castiglione, newly laid out and divided into lots on the site of the Feuillants monastery. Since that time, Agry has barely changed. An engraver of coats of arms and purveyor to the aristocratic elite of Paris for as many as seven generations, this is the place where you can order your insignia and buy hunting jewellery and blazer buttons bearing a family crest. They also engrave cufflinks, key chains and signet rings with monograms or coats of arms. Everything is made to order in their workshops, where knowledge of heraldry is elevated to a science, yet contemporary creation is not frowned upon.

ANTOINE DE MACEDO

28, rue Madame, 6th
Metro Rennes, Saint-Sulpice
Tel 01 45 49 14 91
www.adm-horloger.com
Open 11am to 7pm,
closed Sunday and Monday

COLLECTOR TIMEPIECES

Now an undisputed master in his field, the charming Antoine de Macedo entered the world of watchmaking at the age of nineteen. For many years, his shop was a little farther up in the same street, but he now occupies the more spacious premises of Hilton McConnico's old gallery. The elegant, chic interior consists of several large rooms punctuated with huge windows and gilt porticos. Modern furniture by Knoll and Kagan is dotted around the white-wood parquet floor. Four

SPOTLIGHT

THE SCHOOL OF JEWELRY ARTS – SUPPORTED BY VAN CLEEF & ARPELS

Established in 2012 and supported by the prestigious company located on the Place Vendôme, this school, which is open to all, offers introductory courses in the art of jewellery making. These enjoyable and highly professional classes are taught by experts in superb 18th-century premises. In three- or four-hour sessions, and in groups of between six and a maximum of twelve students, the topics (twenty to date) range from the history of jewellery to gemology, via the different techniques used in the creation of the most beautiful jewellery: sketching, drawing, gouache painting, then 3D modelling, adaptation, enamelling, stone-setting techniques (using claw settings or closed settings) and polishing. Each stage of creation is explored, and each student gets to create their own design. Organizational flexibility makes it possible to tailor your courses to suit your own schedule. All courses are also available in English, and the history of jewellery includes a visit to the jewellery history gallery of the nearby Musée des Arts Décoratifs, of which the School of Jewelry Arts is a patron. This offers the opportunity of discovering 1,200 exceptional pieces from the Middle Ages to today. Alongside all these practical and hands-on courses are monthly thematic talks in the evening, plus a library and creative workshops for children. These introductory courses make it possible to understand the complexity of the art of high jewellery, and become an enlightened amateur with a great degree of knowledge.

22, place Vendôme, 1st, students' entrance at 31, rue Danielle Casanova, 1st, tel 01 70 70 36 00, www.lecolevancleefarpels.com

watchmakers are hunched over their work repairing and restoring, while a female colleague custom-makes leather bracelets (allow one week for any order). In the display cases are the prestigious brands that made history from 1920 to 2000, from Patek Philippe and Rolex to IWC, Jaeger-LeCoultre, Hermès, Piaget, Longines, Vacheron Constantin and a few forgotten labels like Universal. There are also interesting anonymous models and Lip! watches designed by Roger Tallon. All have been checked and are in working order, with a two-year guarantee. There is also a "new" range of Breguet, Omega, Laurent Ferrier, Ressence and Tudor. Before leaving, take a look at the beautiful little Lawson "streamline" clocks. A few doors away is Antoine de Macedo's recently opened **L'HORLOGERIE POUR DAMES** (46, rue Madame, 6th, tel 01 53 71 98 03), with styles in the same spirit but just for women. An excellent watch and clock repairman, **FRANÇOIS HUBERT** (no. 43, tel 01 45 44 22 00), can be found just across the street. If you can't find exactly what you want, head up the street to the Boulevard Saint-Germain and browse the 250 square metres of Antoine de Macedo's elegant shop, which is devoted to fine watchmaking, new and vintage. **Other location:** 201, boulevard Saint-Germain, 7th, tel 01 45 48 36 52

AU VASE DE DELFT

2, rue du Marché Saint-Honoré, 1st
Metro Tuileries, Pyramides
Tel 01 42 60 92 49, www.vddparis.com
Open 10:30am to 6:30pm, Saturday from 11:30am, closed Sunday

ANTIQUE JEWELLERY

Obliged to move from Rue Cambon when Chanel took back the lease, the affable Brigitte Gy closed the chapter on a century of history. This shop has been a celebrity favourite over the years, with Coco Chanel herself setting the trend. Mick Jagger came here for his cushion-cut stud earrings and Lauren Bacall, Salvador Dalí and Romy Schneider were all customers. Its carefully guarded guest book is full of signatures and drawings. Two years of research and building work went into the new place. Katherine Souillac, the elder of the founder's granddaughters, has another shop, also selling vintage jewellery, **DARY'S** (362, rue Saint-Honoré, 1st), while Brigitte Gy is responsible for the new store. In an elegant blue velvet decor, Art Deco display cases offer a superb collection of unique antique pieces. There is no silver or base metal here, just gold and precious stones. A yellow gold and diamond dog's-head brooch, Napoleon III enamel, rings worthy of Joan Collins in *Dynasty*, a selection of vintage pieces from Cartier, Patek, Jaeger-LeCoultre, cameos, solitaire and multi-stone rings, and forgotten objects like the 18th-century vinaigrettes, which once concealed a flask of liquid to revive elegant ladies suffering from the vapours. Men have their own selection of fine objects, from sapphire and diamond tiepins to fob watches and cigarette cases, each piece described for you by the owner with relaxed and unhurried enthusiasm.

BURMA

16, rue de la Paix, 2nd, metro Opéra
Tel 01 42 61 60 64
www.bijouxburma.com
Open 10:30am to 6:30pm, closed Sunday

FAKE HIGH JEWELLERY

It is said that the elegant Parisiennes of the Roaring Twenties, anxious to leave their diamonds in the safe, were on the lookout for perfect reproduction sparklers they could wear in the evening without the fear of being robbed. True or not, since 1927 this anecdote has been integral to the history of Burma, which is still a family-owned company. Thanks to Burmalite, a synthetic stone made of the best-quality zirconium oxide, they are past masters in the creation of precious fakes. All the showgirls of the time, Mistinguett and Josephine Baker most of all, adored these highly realistic-looking jewels. Burma caused a sensation with its replicas of Marie Antoinette's and Tutankhamun's jewellery, and since 2015 the company has also worked with precious stones (amethysts, sapphires, topazes, etc.), using the traditional techniques of high jewellery, thereby making the task of telling real from fake even harder. Burma's customers are thrilled with their long necklaces or miles of super-perfect pearls. See website for other locations

CARTIER

13, rue de la Paix, 2nd
Metro Opéra
Tel 01 58 18 23 00, www.cartier.com
Open 11am to 7pm, closed Sunday

HISTORIC, LUXURIOUS

This store, which dates back to 1847 and is Cartier's historic home, is a must for jewellery lovers. There have been more than a few milestones along the way, including the creation in 1914 of the iconic "panther" decor, and in 1924 the emblematic three-ring bracelet commissioned from Louis Cartier by Jean Cocteau. Among the eye-catching innovations is a bold line of bracelets aptly named "Juste un Clou" (Just a Nail). In a daring move, the Nail bracelet, originally designed for Cartier New York during the free, festive 1970s, has been reinvented for men and women in pink, yellow or white gold or diamond-studded versions. Among the watches, the Tank has been reincarnated in three versions: English, American and French, with the English Tank being rounder, larger and more contemporary. The Tank Folle, inspired by the 1960s Crash model, brings to mind Dalí and delights with its wavy, diamond-studded lines. The ultra-thin Tank Louis Cartier XL (5.1 millimetres thick) crystallizes vibrant, harmonious, timeless elegance into one timepiece. In 2014, to coincide with the release of the biopic *Grace of Monaco*, directed by Olivier Dahan and starring Nicole Kidman as Grace Kelly, Cartier recreated the jewellery worn by the princess. In the movie, Kidman wears a replica of the 10.47-carat emerald-cut Cartier engagement ring given by Prince Rainier to his fiancée, as well as a three-strand diamond necklace and a diamond poodle brooch, both by Cartier. See website for other locations

CHAUMET

12, place Vendôme, 1st
Metro Tuileries, Opéra
Tel 01 44 77 26 26, www.chaumet.com
Open 10:30am to 7pm, closed Sunday

HISTORIC, PRECIOUS GEMS

In 1780, jeweller and watchmaker Marie-Étienne Nitot set up shop on Place Dauphine at 1, Quai des Orfèvres, opposite the Pont Neuf. The house, which moved to 12, Place Vendôme in 1907, when Joseph Chaumet was in charge, enjoyed a period of unprecedented creativity during the Belle Époque. Tiaras, emblems of social status and fashion accessories, were in fashion, along with aigrettes and headbands. At the turn of the 21st century, the bee, the powerful emblem of empire chosen by Napoleon, became a major theme. On backlit wall panels, the Bourbon-Parma tiara made by Joseph Chaumet is on display, etched into the glass like an echo. On the mezzanine, a new space has been opened for engagement rings. The historic Chaumet salons on the first floor of the mansion, all elegance and refinement, are testimony to 230 years of Parisian taste: the Grand Salon (designed by Béranger in 1777 for Louis XVI's general treasurer of the Navy), the Salon of Tiaras, the Salon of Pearls, the Salon of Jewellery and the Petit Salon Bleu are as mesmerizing as the jewels themselves. **Other location:** 56, rue François Ier, 8th, tel 01 56 88 50 20

CIE BRACELET MONTRE

23, rue du Dragon, 6th
Metro Saint-Germain-des-Prés
Tel 01 45 44 99 37
www.cie-bracelet-montre.com
Open 11am to 7pm, closed Sunday

WATCHBANDS

Opened in January 2014, this elegant little shop designed by Thierry Michault of the Lieu-Dit agency is a treasure trove for watch aficionados tired of always wearing the same band. A lover of and expert in antique watches, Hady Ouaiss makes a great effort so that each customer finds the right one among the ten thousand bands in 2,700 styles in stock. Your choice is quickly found and attached to the watch so you can judge the effect. The selection is so extensive – everything from NATO straps to crocodile – that you will wish you had more watches so you could try them all. The store is a huge success, and has expanded to a second address on the Right Bank. **Other location:** 11, rue des Rosiers, 4th, tel 01 48 87 22 13

CONTRE TEMPS

93, rue du Bac, 7th
Metro Rue du Bac, Sèvres-Babylone
Tel 01 45 48 61 24
www.contretempsparis.com
Open 11am to 6:45pm,
closed Sunday and Monday

VINTAGE WATCHES, REPAIRS

Although the chapel of Notre-Dame-de-la-Médaille-Miraculeuse still attracts the crowds a mere stone's throw from the Bon Marché, there's still a lot more to this district than just religion. Food stores might be getting thin on the ground, but the local shops – starting with the engraver Olser (96, Rue du Bac) – are still in their pomp. Just opposite, Contre Temps's windows feature vintage timepieces (Rolex, Omega, Cartier, Jaeger-LeCoultre, etc.) selected by the attentive Jean-Yves Vergara, an enthusiast who was brought up in the world of cogs and complications. As a distant descendant of the watchmaker

Lepaute, Vergara will also be able to find your dream watch, whether for men or women – but always vintage. As a bonus, his wife presents a selection of jewellery that delights the locals, as well as accessories, starting with leather jewellery rolls for collectors on the move, and multicoloured nylon bracelets designed by NATO. **Other location: GALERIE VIVIENNE** 4, rue des Petits Champs, galerie 43, 2nd, tel 01 42 96 04 49

DARY'S

362, rue Saint-Honoré, 1st
Metro Tuileries
Tel 01 42 60 95 23
www.darys-bijouterie-paris.fr
Open 10am to 6pm, Saturday from noon, closed Sunday

VINTAGE

It's a little-known fact that the grandmother, named Mary, wanted to name this shop of antique jewellery and curios "Mary's". Since the name was already taken, she chose Dary's instead. At first, Mary sold bags and hats. Colette Jacob, her daughter-in-law, studied gemology and took the store in a new direction. She now runs it, together with her own daughter Katherine Souillac and her nieces Vanessa and Lisa. This female tribe offers a selection of jewellery pieces dating from the 18th century to the present, displayed on vibrant violet velvet. Cufflinks from the 19th century and jewellery in various styles – Art Nouveau, Art Deco, minimalist, 1960s geometric – share the limelight with pyrites, silver cups, thimbles, medallions and dance cards in old-fashioned ivory, full of emotional resonance.

GALERIE MINIMASTERPIECE

16, rue des Saints-Pères, 7th
Metro Saint-Germain-des-Prés
Tel 06 62 01 63 06
www.galerieminimasterpiece.com
Open 10am to 6pm, Thursday and Saturday from 2pm, Monday by appointment, closed Sunday

JEWELLERY BY CONTEMPORARY ARTISTS

In 2012, the charming Esther de Beaucé opened the first Paris gallery devoted solely to the production and sale of jewellery by contemporary artists and designers. The entrance may be hidden in a courtyard, but the shop still attracts collectors entranced by pieces with powerful, daring and radical designs created by such great artists as Claude Lévêque, Vera Molnar, Bernar Venet, Andres Serrano, Pablo Reinoso, François Morellet (who died in May 2016) and Zhou Yiyan (who makes porcelain jewellery). MiniMasterpiece also produces jewellery by designers François Azambourg, Constance Guisset, Christian Ghion, Nestor Perkal, the late Cédric Ragot and the architect Odile Decq. Some pieces are one of a kind, while others are produced in editions of three to thirty. An exhibition is held each time a new piece comes out. This is a unique store.

GALERIE NAÏLA DE MONBRISON

6, rue de Bourgogne, 7th
Metro Assemblée Nationale
Tel 01 47 05 11 15
www.naila-de-monbrison.com
Open 11am to 1:30pm and 2:30pm to 7pm, closed Sunday and Monday

ARTIST DESIGNS, EXCLUSIVE

In December 1987, Naïla de Monbrison, displaying a special flair, started seeking out, exhibiting and selling jewellery by major contemporary artists in different styles, made out of precious or non-precious materials. The pieces by the likes of Taher Chemirik, Giorgio Vigna, Violaine Febvret,

Paloma Canivet, Dominique Biard, Gilles Jonemann, Giampaolo Babetto and Juliette Polac are fascinating as well as beautiful.

GRIPOIX

14, place des Victoires, 2nd
Metro Bourse
Tel 09 51 58 49 53
www.gripoixparis.com
Open 11am to 7pm,
closed Sunday and Monday

COSTUME JEWELLERY

Coco Chanel swore by it. So did Sarah Bernhardt before her, and later Christian Dior and Hubert de Givenchy. The house of Gripoix, which has been around since 1869, spent a century and a half making its creations out of sight of the public, supplying retailers. For the first store in its long history, the house chose Place des Victoires, which has been more or less forgotten since the fashion designers moved out. The store has its design workshops in the back, and though the elegant contemporary decor is a bit intimidating, the jewellery dazzles with its great novelty. The house is now part of the Chanel galaxy of artisanal gems. A wonderful (re)discovery.

MAISON AUCLERT

10, rue de Castiglione, 1st
Metro Tuileries
Tel 01 42 61 81 81
www.maisonauclert.com
Open 10:30am to 1pm and 2pm
to 6:30pm, closed Sunday

EXTREMELY RARE

Grandson of an antiques dealer and art collector, Marc Auclert trawls the auction houses of Paris, London and New York in search of antique treasures, which he reworks to create beautiful contemporary jewellery. Between the pearls older than the pyramids of Egypt, a bear's-head brooch from Mesopotamia set with diamonds and a ring that opens to reveal a curious coral and gold phallus dating from the 3rd century BCE, you'll find unique pieces transformed into extravagant new creations. An interesting collection of antique cameos made into earrings set with sapphires and opals and of rock crystal beautifully reworked into necklaces and Art Deco rings completes this little cabinet of curiosities.

MAISON ELIE TOP

217, rue Saint-Honoré, 1st
Metro Tuileries
Tel 01 42 21 40 97, www.elietop.com
Open by appointment only

BOLD STATEMENT JEWELLERY

Paragon of the authentic Parisian dandy (nothing to do with the vulgar hipster), whose tie is always as faultless as his temperament, Elie Top won his spurs working with Loulou de la Falaise in the Yves Saint Laurent jewellery department. Spotted by Baccarat, for which he redesigned the carafe stopper, he then went to Lanvin, where his spectacular creations, half-glam, half-industrial, thrilled fashion lovers season after season. They almost fainted when the elegant Top, satisfying his desire for precious materials, unveiled his first collection of luxury costume jewellery under his own brand. Taking inspiration straight from a Jules Verne novel (or perhaps a Méliès film) the rings, chokers, pendants and earrings adorned with spheres articulated in hard stones unleashed as many magazine features as AmEx Black credit cards. Top's second collection, inspired by medieval themes (coats of arms in gold and rock crystal, mysterious knights of the zodiac), attracted similar plaudits. And it won him even more visitors to his neo-Art Deco lounge, styled from floor to ceiling by interior designer Vincent Darré, where the modern dandy receives visitors on a carpet woven with his initials.

MARC DELOCHE

36, rue Jacob, 6th
Metro Saint-Germain-des-Prés
Tel 01 49 27 03 79
www.marc-deloche.com
Open 10:30am to 1:30pm and 2:30pm to 7pm, closed Sunday and Monday

SILVER, CONTEMPORARY

An architect by training and a native of Toulouse, Marc Deloche has achieved great success with his shop in Saint-Germain-des-Prés. Some of the most popular pieces are his medal rings and his solid silver jewellery, which he combines with leather and semiprecious stones. His stunning animal and figurative themes feature in his debut collection of fine jewellery, launched in 2015. But alongside these models, created according to the theme of the four elements, including a surprise ring which conceals a dragon with scales made of yellow and white diamonds, the designer also caters for gifts to celebrate a birth or for the man desperately searching for a silver tie clip or a pair of cufflinks.

MARIE-HÉLÈNE DE TAILLAC

8, rue de Tournon, 6th, metro Odéon
Tel 01 44 27 07 07
www.mariehelenedetaillac.com
Open 11am to 7pm, closed Sunday

SIMPLE, PRECIOUS DESIGNS

In addition to this Left Bank boutique, Marie-Hélène de Taillac has a branch in Tokyo. Her jewellery is simple yet precious. She loves the transparency, intriguing imperfections and pure lines of fine and semiprecious stones, and she has reintroduced the briolette cut. The boutique's decor, by Tom Dixon, is anything but boudoir style; it's more like a colourful, contemporary private salon, with a gracious, tranquil atmosphere. Marie-Hélène de Taillac is only too happy to talk about stones; she is well versed in their virtues and sees them as living organisms. On show are pendants with iridescent moonstones, "toi et moi" rings in pink spinel with pivoting settings, "Pantone" necklaces with gradations of multicoloured stones, and gold and gems from the Gem Palace in Jaipur. Her talent has led to some distinguished collaborations, one of which resulted in a limited series of cashmere gloves, bonnets and scarves with E+J that were decorated with some of de Taillac's jewellery motifs embroidered by the famous house Lesage. In 2014, her work entered the collections of the Musée des Arts Décoratifs.

MARTIN DU DAFFOY

16, place Vendôme, 1st
Metro Tuileries, Opéra
Tel 01 42 61 55 61
www.martin-du-daffoy-achat-vente-bijoux.fr
Open by appointment only

EXCEPTIONAL AND HISTORIC JEWELLERY

This astonishing mezzanine on the Place Vendôme, with a view overlooking the Ritz, and populated by Moorish statues wearing feathery loincloths against a backdrop of 18th-century paintings, is not something you'd stumble upon easily. For twenty years Martin du Daffoy has been located in what used to be the bachelor pad of jeweller Pascal Morabito (father of the designer Ora Ito). Here he entertains clients whose identities remain a secret but who know that this is where they will find exceptional jewels, all of them unique pieces, essentially French, and ranging from the mid-19th century to the mid-20th century. An expert connoisseur and doctor of law who worked at the former Louvre des Antiquaires, having owned up to four boutiques in Paris, and who cultivates a lofty disdain for anything related to mechanical or industrial production, Martin du Daffoy specializes in high-class treasures, such as jewels belonging to countesses straight out of Stefan's Zweig's *The World of Yesterday*, or Proust's *In Search of Lost Time*. These are small wonders made by anonymous craftsmen and worn at the historic courts of Italy. Dealer, expert, storyteller and historian, with a look as impeccable as his deliciously acid sense of humour, Martin du Daffoy clearly deals only in the best for his carefully chosen collectors. But he's still happy to offer a few "charming" engagement rings that in no way take the shine off the necklace of Eugène Bonaparte or the corsage decoration of the Duchess of Newcastle, a recent acquisition. Amid the current fashion for political correctness, du Daffoy is a breath of fresh air. His collection for the general public is also showcased in the Ritz itself.

MELLERIO DITS MELLER

9, rue de la Paix, 2nd
Metro Opéra
Tel 01 42 61 57 53, www.mellerio.fr
Open 10:30am to 7pm, closed Sunday

CUSTOM-MADE PIECES

The display windows may be small, but the savoir faire is great. In the 21st century, this house – which sees itself as "French, Parisian and of the neighbourhood" – is proud of its fourteen generations and 400 years of loyal service to a parade of queens, from Marie-Antoinette to Empress Eugénie and Queen Marie-Amélie. The archives, kept in the basement and shown to certain lucky people and to the public on Heritage Days in September, include fascinating account books, which have that special scent of parchment, listing elite customers. The only entirely family-owned French jeweller, Mellerio dits Meller was the first jeweller to have the foresight to move to Rue de la Paix 200 years ago. The company makes unique and custom-made pieces that are often inspired by nature. There is nothing stuffy about the calm Art Deco store; you will receive a friendly welcome from this rather secretive house. Together with engagement rings, they make the characteristic oval watches, inspired by the oval Mellerio cut for gems, as well as swords for the Académie Française and the Musketeers Trophy for the French Open.

HEALTH AND BEAUTY

ALAIN, MAÎTRE BARBIER

8, rue Saint-Claude, 3rd
Metro Saint-Sébastien-Froissart
Tel 01 42 77 55 80
www.maitrebarbier.com
Open 9:15am to 7pm, Saturday until 6pm, closed Sunday and Monday

BARBER

You can get a close shave in Paris, but it will cost you. The trend for barbers, a pale imitation of the American version, leaves its fans on the razor's edge. Most of the amateurish barbershops beloved of hipsters should be avoided, while the grand hotels are desperately seeking barbers who will not be sent away by a furious Italian customer or an Arab prince. Alain Backman is one of the few master barbers around. His salon-cum-museum is a temple untouched by trends, featuring a collection of manual clippers, earthenware shaving bowls and razors – that of the Baron de Redé, for example, and those used by actors and celebrities who never really struck one as being that well groomed. Aided by his skilled assistants, Alain practices his craft on his loyal clientele, and also on film sets where "historical beards and hairpieces" are needed, and he always uses a straight razor. An old-fashioned shave takes no more than twenty minutes before the dampened alum stone is applied. Proraso moisturizer is massaged in and the face is wrapped in a warm towel. Final touch: a pat of unscented Venetian talc and a spritz of cologne. Bliss. You'll never feel lighter than after such a shave.

AROMA ZONE

25, rue de l'École de Médecine, 6th
Metro Odéon
Tel 01 43 26 08 93
www.aroma-zone.com
Open 10am to 8:30pm,
closed Sunday and Monday

ORGANIC COSMETICS

It's certainly not the soulless expanse of this store that is the main attraction here – rather, it's the beautifying effects of its products. Located a stone's throw from Odéon, this 250-square-metre space sells over 1,600 top organic brands with which you can assemble an entire beauty kit. Products include a neutral nail polish base (to which you can add a dye made from radish or pink sweet potato extracts), concentrated micellar water to concoct your own lotions and miraculous potions, and silica microspheres to make a bespoke blusher. These products are also featured in workshops where you can learn how to make your own BB cream or a bespoke hair mask. Prices are unbeatable, and of course there's also a substantial range of ready-made creams, shampoos and essential oils.

BIOLOGIQUE RECHERCHE

32, avenue des Champs-Élysées, 8th
Metro Franklin D. Roosevelt
Tel 01 42 25 02 92
www.biologique-recherche.com
Open 9:30am to 8pm, closed Sunday

HIGH-END SKINCARE

For more than thirty years Biologique Recherche products that brim with botanical extracts have been revolutionizing the already crowded world of cosmetics. Now distributed in fifty countries (as well as in the air, as it supplies Air France's first class lounges), Dr Allouche's brand has headquarters located on the Champs-Élysées. In a townhouse that was once home to actors Marie Bell and Miou-Miou (though not at the same time), you can find all the brand's iconic, outstanding treatments in one place. Structured in three acts like a play (assessment, initialization, treatment), sessions also make use of world-class technology, starting with the Skin Instant Lab to guarantee an absolutely bespoke experience that boosts the skin's potential for self-healing. Locals have rushed to sign up for the programmes that last between one and six months, while visitors adore the facials ranging from thirty minutes to two hours. The Haute Couture programme takes place in an idyllic 120-square-metre suite, which can be booked and is apparently a particular favourite of Sofia Coppola.

CREED

38, avenue Pierre Ier de Serbie, 8th
Metro George V, Alma-Marceau
Tel 01 47 20 58 02, www.creed.eu
Open 10:30am to 6:30pm,
Monday from 2:30pm, closed Sunday

CLASSIC COLOGNE

When we are always seeking the latest thing, we end up forgetting about the classics. One of them is the perfumer Creed, whose superb bottles have not changed a bit. Founded in London in 1760 by James Henry Creed, the house crossed the English Channel to Paris in 1854, heralding the advent of the Anglomania that overtook the capital a few years later. During the next century, Creed also became a skilled tailor, but this activity was abandoned in the 1980s. All that remains are the ties, cufflinks and shirts. The company is run by Olivier Creed, of the sixth generation of the family, who was recently joined by his children, Olivia and Erwin. It remains fiercely traditional, with fragrances made by infusion from fine essences, leaning towards the masculine, that are mixed, macerated and filtered. It has 200 references, many of them still in production, including Pure White Cologne, Bois de Cédrat, Green Irish Tweed and Bois du Portugal. They are sold in the famous emblazoned crystal glass bottles in matte silver, white or black. The fragrances can also be found in the brand's

soap, shower gel and shaving cream, sold in the world's smartest concept stores. This centuries-old citadel of perfume now has stores in New York and Dubai and has finally crossed the Seine in Paris to open another shop.
Other location: 74, rue des Saints Pères, 7th, tel 01 42 84 06 44

DETAILLE

10, rue Saint-Lazare, 9th
Metro Notre-Dame-de-Lorette
Tel 01 48 78 68 50, www.detaille.com
Open 11am to 2pm and 3pm to 7pm, closed Sunday, Monday and in August

FACE CREAM

As one of the first women to obtain a driving licence at the beginning of the 20th century, the Countess de Presle was amazed at how much the traffic dried out her skin – cars of the time had no windscreen and the capital was at least as polluted as it is today. Invented especially for this colourful Parisienne, today the Baume Automobile is still Detaille's top product. Since the 1950s the company has been located on the edge of La Nouvelle Athènes district. The Countess's portrait watches benignly over the shop, which still boasts its period woodwork, and looks on as customers come to stock up on Citrovinaigre de Beauté, Manudouce lotion and rice powders, which are named for actresses of the Belle Époque such as Rachel, Aida and Aurore, who often lived in the neighbourhood. Whether locals or out-of-towners, well-informed customers also know that Detaille has launched a range of essential oils, with varieties for the face, hair and legs, as well as perfume, packaged in a vintage-style bottle and available in women's, men's and even unisex versions, proving that this company, which has been around for over a century, can certainly sniff out a new trend.

ÉDITIONS DE PARFUMS FRÉDÉRIC MALLE

37, rue de Grenelle, 7th
Metro Rue du Bac
Tel 01 42 22 76 40
www.fredericmalle.com
Open 11am to 7pm, Monday from noon, closed Sunday

EXCLUSIVE SCENTS

Part of the Estée Lauder group since late 2014, Éditions de Parfums Frédéric Malle has climbed in less than fifteen years to the top ranks in the very closed world of perfume thanks to exclusive fragrances created for the house by twelve major perfumers, including Édouard Fléchier, Sophia Grojsman, Ralf Schwieger, Bruno Jovanovic and Dominique Ropion (who created, among other scents, Vétiver Extraordinaire). Another fine perfume is Dans Tes Bras by Maurice Roucel, a former Chanel chemist, who also created Musc Ravageur. Men will fall for French Lover and Géranium pour Monsieur, rare contemporary fragrances with a heady trail. Frédéric Malle, grandson of the founder of Parfums Christian Dior and nephew of filmmaker Louis Malle, remains managing director and creative director, guaranteeing new, exclusive fragrances inspiring emotion, beginning with the Superstitious range created by Alber Elbaz.
See website for other locations

GELLÉ FRÈRES

19, avenue de l'Opéra, 1st
Metro Pyramides
Tel 01 40 26 06 25, www.gelle-freres.fr
Open 10:30am to 7:30pm, closed Sunday

ROYAL PERFUMES

Very few companies can boast a royal genealogy, but Gellé Frères certainly can. Founded in 1826 by Augustin and Jean-Baptiste, who had themselves taken over the company belonging to Marie-Antoinette's perfumer, the business not only became the queen of luxury soap, tooth powders with flowery names (Caboquina Rose), nostalgic perfumes

(Trianon, Noblesse Oblige or Pour Être Aimée) and other more robust-smelling products (such as Le Motophile, a perfumed soap for drivers), it is also a competition-winner. As inventor of one of the first toothpastes, Gellé Frères scooped up prizes at the World's Fairs, and also became icons of contemporary beauty by using fashionable Parisian actresses in its advertisements. This pungent history has now been resurrected on the Avenue de l'Opéra, where you can discover new essences as refined as their name – Fleur d'Or Enjouée, Rose Galante, Lys Audacieux. They have been inspired by the idea of the "queen next door" (in essence, the client). Young Marseille designer Margaux Keller has managed to successfully modernize this new boudoir, enriching its history without descending into cliché.

GENTLEMEN 1919

11, rue Jean Mermoz, 8th
Metro Franklin D. Roosevelt, Saint-Philippe-du-Roule
Tel 01 42 89 42 59
www.gentlemen1919.com
Open 11am to 11pm, closed Sunday and Monday

BARBERSHOP, SMOKING ROOM

A disciple of Alain Backman, the likable Sébastien Paucod had his first shop at the bottom of Rue Caulaincourt, then moved his Atelier Gentlemen to the top of the same street, where, assisted by an excellent team, he shaved cheeks, sculpted beards and cut hair while offering treatments, advice, products and conversation. Paucod has nothing in common with the fake old-fashioned barbers in Paris who charge a fortune. He has left Montmartre and moved to this chic quarter, where he has a new salon-club with a retro-chic decor and a bar-smoking room-speakeasy perfumed with Havana cigars. With its walls in shades of tobacco, velvety chairs like those in a Citroën SM and well-thought-out lighting, the salon has a soothing, reassuring atmosphere. Razor and scissors in hand, Paucod plies his trade with great skill. Meticulous and attentive, he uses the excellent Milanese liquorice-scented Bullfrog shaving products and stays open until 10pm. To get to the bar and smoking area, customers must go through an airlock of obscure design to enter the elegant club run by the good-natured Frédéric Lafleur. The Prohibition- and aviation-inspired decor features chesterfields, industrial lighting and plans for biplanes on the walls; the tone is masculine, but women love it. The usual drinks and excellent cocktails are on offer, with special mention for the whisky (notably Mac Malden), the platters of charcuterie and cheese, and the relaxed atmosphere. You will have to call to get in after the barbershop closes. Paucod's Montmartre shop, with a top-notch staff, is still there.

INSTITUT DARPHIN VENDÔME

350, rue Saint-Honoré, 1st
Metro Tuileries
Tel 01 47 03 17 70, www.darphin.fr
Open 10am to 7pm, Monday and Saturday until 6pm, Wednesday and Thursday until 9pm, closed Sunday

FACIALS, BODY CARE, PARISIAN

In 1958, the physiotherapist Pierre Darphin created his own line of sensual, enveloping skincare in Paris. He was both demanding and obstinate: he loved inventing creams and other beauty elixirs, but they had to be nothing less than perfect. This old company, now owned by Estée Lauder, still adheres to these same proven quality standards almost sixty years after first opening. The focus is on the details – pure essential oils, noble botanical ingredients and ultra-soft textures. Institut Darphin provides excellent facials and body care in a cosy, quiet setting inside a pretty courtyard, also decorated, where you feel very at ease, far from the urban bustle.

JANE DE BUSSET

30, rue Pasquier, 8th
Metro Madeleine, Saint-Augustin
Tel 01 42 65 53 55
www.janedebusset.com
Open by appointment 8:30am to 5:30pm, closed Saturday and Sunday

SKINCARE SPECIALIST

This is an odd place to come across a good skincare specialist. Tucked between Saint-Lazare station and La Madeleine, Rue Pasquier is far from being a centre of luxury goods, but during Fashion Week it nevertheless attracts gaggles of long-legged girls, all heading towards no. thirty. It was here in 1958 that Jane de Busset opened her institute, and where Sylvie Puig continues to provide outstanding treatments in a pearl-grey ambience that's more Chabrol than Proust. The plate on the wall on the way in immediately conveys a sense of the slightly outdated character of the place. But after an hour and a half of beautifully executed facial treatment, including blackhead removal, you'll be convinced that the old ways are often the best – in beauty matters as in everything else.

JAR PARFUMS

14, rue de Castiglione, 1st
Metro Tuileries
Tel 01 40 20 47 20
Open 10:30am to 6:30pm, closed Sunday

JEWELLER'S FRAGRANCES

This cabinet of fragrance curiosities, owned by the mysterious American jeweller Joel Arthur Rosenthal, is decorated like a boudoir. A velvety crypt suffused with an amethyst light, it is glamorous and cabalistic, adding to the enigmatic dimension of this unclassifiable artist who stubbornly avoids media exposure. Located near the Place Vendôme and open by appointment only, his shop, which opened in 1977, is surrounded by legends created in secrecy and adorned with elitism and exclusivity. Each strictly unique piece is unusual, extravagant and poetic. They have been worn by the likes of Marella Agnelli and Liz Taylor, and are enthusiastically collected by Uma Thurman, Ellen Barkin and Maryvonne Pinault. The Metropolitan Museum in New York even held a retrospective of JAR's work a few years ago. Long ago, Rosenthal himself wrote a book that is as coveted as his jewellery and sells for stratospheric prices. This "perfume shop" is his only concession to the public, the only door open to his world. There are just eight extracts of perfume, all sensual and heady. Golconda, the first, was composed in 1987 and was followed by Jardenia, Jarling, Ferme tes Yeux. Sold in 30-millilitre bottles, they can be test their scent on chamois-covered balls that are kept under glass, like truffles, but it's difficult to choose among them. They are fabulous, enchanting.

JEAN PATOU

9, rue Saint-Florentin, 8th
Metro Concorde
Tel 01 42 92 07 22, www.jeanpatou.com
Open 11am to 4pm and 3pm to 7pm, closed Sunday and Monday morning

LEGENDARY PERFUMER

Jean Patou opened his fashion house on Rue Saint-Florentin in Paris in 1914. At the time, he was considered the most elegant man in Europe, a kind of woman-adoring Gatsby – he dressed Louise Brooks – who invented the swimming costume, the first

"Ah! Paris . . . what a beautiful city. Look at it. Just beautiful." "So what." says Zazie, "All I wanted was to ride the metro."
Raymond Queneau, *Zazie in the Metro*, 1959

suntan oil, the first sportswear and the first fashion monogram, and who was Chanel's great rival. He was also the first fashion designer to import American models from the US to create a leaner and sportier look. Over 100 years on, the brand is now part of the British group Designer Parfums, and it has gone back to its roots by opening this beautiful white-and-gold shop. Here, in-house perfume designer Thomas Fontaine has created an eau de toilette called Joy Forever, a powdery floral fragrance inspired by Patou's legendary Joy, "the most expensive perfume in the world", created by Henri Alméras in 1929 as an antidote to the economic crisis. It took 10,000 jasmine flowers and 288 May roses to make 30 millilitres of Joy – and it made Jean Patou one of the greatest perfumers of all time. For the company's centenary, three perfumes were reissued as part of the prestigious Collection Héritage: Chaldée, Eau de Patou and Patou pour Homme, alongside traditional fragrances Joy, 1000 and Sublime. When the legendary perfume Huile de Chaldée was launched in 1927 its scent enchanted holiday makers as it intensified under the heat of the sun. Created in 1976, Eau de Patou is one of the first unisex perfumes. In turn, Patou pour Homme is a men's fragrance inspired by the free spirit of the great designer himself, and created with a sophistication that had up until then been the preserve of the great feminine perfumes. A major fashion house has rising like a phoenix from the ashes.

JOVOY

4, rue de Castiglione, 1st
Metro Tuileries
Tel 01 40 20 06 19, www.jovoyparis.com
Open 11am to 7pm, closed Sunday

RARE PERFUME

Designed by Géraldine Prieur, the Jovoy shop is a genuine curiosity cabinet of fragrances. The shelves here contain rare, exclusive, original essences evincing a commitment to quality, all of which give true meaning to the art of fragrances. You can also check out the vials of an old perfume organ holding scents with such names as Roja Dove, Andy Tauer, Aedes and Venustas. If you're lucky, your head will spin with the extreme luxuriousness of Clive Christian. This is where Olivier Madeline chose to relaunch Volnay fragrances, which had fallen into olfactory oblivion during the Second World War after having been founded, in fact, in the 1920s by his great-grandfather René Duval, a perfumer for Coty.

MAISON FRANCIS KURKDJIAN

5, rue d'Alger, 1st, metro Tuileries
Tel 01 42 60 07 07
www.franciskurkdjian.com
Open 11am to 1:30pm and 2:30pm to 7pm, closed Sunday

BESPOKE FRAGRANCE

A star nose famous for having composed Jean Paul Gaultier's Le Mâle, For Him by Narciso Rodriguez and Christian Dior's Cologne Blanche, Francis Kurkdjian is now experimenting with more personal compositions under his own name and is bringing a new feel to the world of great fragrances with perfumes such as Lumière Noire for men and women, Cologne pour le Matin Cologne pour le Soir, Petit Matin and Grand Matin. But it is in the highly sophisticated register of bespoke perfumes (allow at least €12,000 for yours) and special-order fragrances that the man excels. Anniversaries also inspire him: for the tenth anniversary of his own debut in the profession, he created the Edition Cristal, bottled in three Saint Louis crystal flacons in an edition of only twenty. The more recent eau de parfum Baccarat Rouge 540 is a less expensive version of the fantastic perfume created for the 250th anniversary of Baccarat. Maison Kurkdjian, which also has a corner at Printemps Haussmann (64, boulevard Haussmann, 9th, tel 01 42 82 50 00) and has opened several outlets in Asia, opened a new perfume shop in the Marais in 2015.

This success attracted the attention of LVMH, global leader in luxury, which acquired it in 2017. **Other location:** 7, rue des Blancs Manteaux, 4th, tel 01 42 71 76 76

MAISON GUERLAIN

68, avenue des Champs-Élysées, 8th
Metro Franklin D. Roosevelt
Tel 01 45 62 52 57, www.guerlain.com
Open 10:30am to 8pm, Sunday noon to 8pm, until 9pm in summer

EXCEPTIONAL PERFUMES

France's oldest perfume house changed scale in 2014, 185 years after opening, by inviting Peter Marino, the architect behind many French style luxury brands, to design a new boutique. There is marble galore and ubiquitous repeats of the brand's distinctive elements, especially the bees and gilding, that hark back to the original shop. The building itself, now listed, dates back to the 1910s and was designed by Charles Mewès, architect of the Ritz. Works by artists and craftsmen also dot the incredibly luxurious interior. The men's corner is in onyx, and some of the ceilings undulate like wafts of eau de parfum; the walls of the customizing salons are covered in sublime straw marquetry, while other rooms feature frosted glass. The gloves and fans are all perfumed to offer total sensual pleasure, which can also be found in the Institut Guerlain beauty salon, founded in 1939 and completely reinvented. Guerlain invites the young and not so young to learn the art of fragrances in thematic workshops with evocative names such as Bouquet de Senteurs, Contes Parfumés and Bois et Merveilles. You'll learn about the production secrets and history of the house's mythical fragrances. The workshops last either a whole day or two-and-a-half hours, which will leave time to discover the menu of the restaurant helmed by chef Guy Martin. The perfume shop on Rue Saint-Honoré carries 111 fragrances. It has also returned to the house's original business of creating the fragrance profile of each customer, now a digitized operation. The house perfumer has the perfect name: Thierry Wasser (German for "water", as in Eau de Cologne). **Other location:** 392, rue Saint-Honoré, 1st, tel 01 42 60 68 61

MONT KAILASH

19, rue Pierre Leroux, 7th
Metro Vaneau
Tel 01 53 86 94 73
www.montkailash-bien-etre.fr
Open 10am to 8pm, Sunday by appointment

TIBETAN MASSAGES

In the current wave of Thai and Chinese massage parlours of sometimes dubious expertise, this Tibetan salon stands out. And the launch of a second location is indication of its popularity. Fashion editors and other girls-about-town scamper in to attain the nirvana of relaxation (Mount Kailash in the Himalayas stands over 6,000 metres high). Inspired by traditional medicine, the range of treatments tackle water retention, nervous tension and stimulation of the facial meridians to achieve a kind of facelift that makes you look as if you've actually just been up a mountain. Try the Ayurvedic hot oil and massage peel to emerge on cloud nine, or sample their traditional acupressure technique for a burst of energy.
Other location: 16, rue Saint-Marc, 2nd, tel 01 42 36 03 30

NOSE

20, rue Bachaumont, 2nd
Metro Sentier
Tel 01 40 26 46 03, www.nose.fr
Open 10:30am to 7:30pm, closed Sunday

NEO-PERFUMERY

Seven partners founded this unusual project, in which participants share their olfactory sensations over a cocktail during a workshop led by one of the seven in question, among them Nicolas Cloutier, Mark Buxton and Romano Ricci. Ricci is known for having created the brand Juliette Has a Gun. All have worked in the fragrance business in one capacity or another and have a desire to share their experience. The idea goes beyond just selling fragrances. Around forty brands are on offer – including Memo, Lorenzo Villoresi, Atelier Cologne, Diptyque, État Libre d'Orange, and hundreds of products on the shelves. They are adding new collaborative projects, notably with the florist Baptiste. Located on a quiet pedestrian street in the Montorgueil area, their store has a clinical look: the fragrances, skincare products (including the magical brand Retrouvé), creams and cosmetics on the shelves are all testers.

PALAIS ROYAL – SERGE LUTENS

Jardins du Palais-Royal,
142, galerie de Valois, 1st
Metro Palais-Royal–Musée du Louvre
Tel 01 49 27 09 09, www.sergelutens.com
Open 10am to 7pm, closed Sunday

PERFUMER

The purple salons intoxicate customers even before they fall in love with one or another of the rich, heady oriental fragrances composed by Serge Lutens. The names alone start the process: Bas de Soie, Ambre Sultan, Miel de Bois, Bornéo 1834, Fourreau Noir and so on. As for Vitriol d'Œillet, Fumerie Turque and Tubéreuse Criminelle, they will whisk you off into a phantasmagorical world. The latest creations include La Religieuse, with a white jasmine note in purple eau; and the more devilish, intensely luxurious fragrance line called Section d'Or, of which the first scent, Incendiaire, was released in September 2014. Other elixirs, whose names are every bit as bewitching, would follow: L'Haleine des Dieux, Cannibale, Cracheuse de Flamme. A spiral staircase leads to an equally baroque upstairs room, where you will find beautiful make-up boxes that transport the eye (and prices) to a new dimension.

PHARMACIE SWANN

6, rue de Castiglione, 1st
Metro Tuileries
Tel 01 42 60 72 96
Open 9am to 8pm, closed Sunday

APOTHECARY

As the inscription emblazoned on the shop front announces, Pharmacie Swann was founded in 1850. And the name Swann itself also appears in blue mosaic lettering on a white background on the flooring of the elegant Rue de Castiglione arcades. It's almost a walk of fame, which underlines Swann's status as an authentically historic company. As a chemist, Monsieur Swann concocted clever remedies that he sold here, such as a diuretic balsam syrup with extract of buchu leaf, or those devised by his colleagues, which he was just as happy to sell, such as Dr Churchill's Hypophosphites. Today, Swann is a small pharmaceutical wonder where you might drop by for aspirin or toothpaste and emerge having bought a brush, a shaving brush, Savonnerie de Nyons soaps, a magnifying mirror or an Eloi manicure set, or any of the higgledy-piggledy piles that fill the shop windows. But the real treasures here are the flowery, ruffled German-made bathing caps that make Doris Day's and Esther Williams's bathing caps look like those sported by the East German Olympic team.

PLANÈTE RASOIR

58, rue de Clichy, 9th, metro Liège
Tel 01 42 85 16 08
www.planeterasoir.com
Open 10am to 7pm, closed Sunday

SHAVING ACCESSORIES, BARBER

Looking to discover French shaving culture? Look no further than this shop-cum-barber's where 1,500 iconic brands are deployed in the age-old war of man against his bristles. Mechanical shavers, folding razors with rosewood, carbon or pistachio-wood handles and shavettes of all kinds are showcased in this temple to Plisson shaving-brushes, Martin de Candre soaps and Thiers-Issard blades, which one has to learn to strop on leather, rather than sharpen. Beardies too are catered for: thanks to the Fournival Altesse range, the last French brush-maker still in business, you can discover which oval beard brush to use dependent on the state of your keratin, and can primp in front of a Brot mirror, a distant relative of those adorning Versailles's Hall of Mirrors. Don't miss the aftershave called Caresse d'Âne, made of rich asses' milk – it's enough to make Cleopatra sorry she wasn't Antony – as well as the boxes of blades for mechanical razors, which are as collectable as cigarette cards.

ROSE DESGRANGES

70, rue du Faubourg Saint-Honoré, 8th
Metro Champs-Élysées-Clemenceau
Tel 01 42 65 40 47
www.rosedesgranges.com
Open 1pm to 7pm, Monday from 2pm, closed Sunday

FRAGRANCE FAMILY

The story of Rose Desgranges makes her sound like the Cinderella of the perfume world. When she arrived in Paris in 1940, this pretty, sensible girl from the provinces was obliged to find a job. Despite dreams of becoming a pianist, she was hired by Albert Meyer, hairdresser and wigmaker to the upper crust of the Elysée district. The inevitable happened and the boss fell madly in love with his employee. A marriage ensued, but so did a fragrance, created by Meyer for his lady. In 1961, Rose decided to sell it in a corner of the shop – a canny saleswoman, she always poured a drop onto the handkerchiefs of her customers. Her granddaughter had the idea of reviving this fragrance, in a floral and sensual formula close to the original, filled with essence of Turkish rose and citrus top notes. The same original bottle design is now on sale in the same corner of Rose and Albert's shop, a tiny doll's house of a store, decorated, of course, in rose pink. It's a story worthy of a fairy tale.

SALON CHRISTOPHE ROBIN

16, rue Bachaumont, 2nd
Metro Sentier
Tel 01 40 20 02 83
www.christophe-robin.com
Open by appointment 10am to 7pm

COLOURIST

As colourist to the stars, Christophe Robin knows all there is to know about redheads and blondes, not to mention the auburn- and raven-haired. All Paris's top models, actresses, politicians and pop stars passing through turn up at his place. Now he's left his salon in the Meurice, where he worked upstairs, in favour of a rococo lounge in the middle of Rue Bachaumont. The shop floor, with its Botticelli-esque conch fountain, fresh flowers and star-covered false ceiling, looks like the set of an American musical, and makes good use of archival fabrics by interior designer Tony Duquette. Here you'll find Christophe Robin's range of treatments, including his cult favourite cleansing and purifying scrub with sea salt and cleansing mask with lemon, or the brilliant intense regenerating balm with prickly pear oil, alongside a whole new range of anti-oxidant infusions. Hidden behind a door, the hair salon resembles a first-class aeroplane cabin, with powder-pink armchairs, kitsch bibelots, illustrated books and an utterly charming staff. Booking is a must if you're determined to have your roots touched up next to Catherine Deneuve, or get the inside gossip from Kylie Minogue.

WARDROBE TALK WITH DOMINIQUE PERRAULT

Like everyone else, I read the book Why Do Architects Wear Black? *by German journalist Cordula Rau. Some of the responses are very amusing. One of my colleagues said: "Because I thought I was the only one doing it." Honestly, there is no more chic and elegant way of dressing, so I dress in black and blue from head to toe, even my scarves and squares, which I get from Issey Miyake. I wear Heschung shoes – or, more precisely, boots with ridged soles that can cope with building sites. My suits are made by Samson – I buy them in packets of six in the sale. Round the back of the Place de la République I recently discovered a jeans manufacturer whose fit is perfect for me, namely Cub Jeans. As for knitwear, I really like the zippered striped sweaters by Comptoir de la Mer. I can only handle one colour – navy blue. Recently I got addicted to the designs by Jean-Charles de Castelbajac (whom I know well) for Le Coq Sportif, and especially for the Tricolore collections in the French colours. As for fragrance, I am amazed at the Liquides perfume bar launched by designer Philippe Di Méo with essences created in Grasse by Givaudan. One of my mischievous gifts is Sympathy for the Sun, an exclusive Dear Rose perfume, created by my friend Alexandra Roos. They are on sale only at Le Bon Marché.*

ISSEY MIYAKE

11, rue Royale, 8th, metro Madeleine, Concorde, tel 01 48 87 01 86, www.isseymiyakeparis.com

HESCHUNG

18, rue du Vieux-Colombier, 6th, metro Saint-Sulpice, tel 01 44 39 17 30, www.heschung.com

SAMSON

15, rue de Tournon, 6th, metro Odéon, tel 01 43 25 13 60, www.samson-costume-sur-mesure.com

CUB JEANS

34, rue de Malte, 11th, metro Oberkampf, tel 06 50 87 98 50, www.cubjeans.com

LE COQ SPORTIF

121, boulevard Saint-Germain, 6th, metro Odéon, tel 09 80 51 50 25, www.lecoqsportif.com

LIQUIDES

9, rue de Normandie, 3rd, metro Filles du Calvaire, tel 09 66 94 77 00, www.liquides-parfums.com

DEAR ROSE

Le Bon Marché, 24, rue de Sèvres, 7th, metro Sèvres-Babylone, www.dear-rose.fr

INTERIOR CACHET

QUIRKY ANTIQUES SHOPS TO CONTEMPORARY DESIGN GALLERIES: LIVING IN THE CITY

In Paris, as in most large cities, the handmade is coming back into fashion. It's as if originals are now a remedy for over-consumption and poor quality, or just rampant standardization. That's fortunate, because Paris has managed to retain its artisanal skills base. The famous upholsterers in Rue Saint-Antoine may be gradually disappearing, but new ones are popping up again everywhere, often in workshops open to the public where the delicacy of pottery work, precision woodworking and the poetry of glassmaking deliver genuine added value.

Although they are mostly trained in industrial manufacturing techniques, designers in Paris are revelling in this return to artisanal skills, and they continue to enjoy an outstanding reputation thanks to astute galleries and stores, which help to boost the value of their designs on the art market. Supported by enthusiastic collectors, these free spirits have now quit the mass market and are busy at work in thoroughly 21st-century styles, functions and materials.

This means there's a hotbed of talent for whom design has always been bound up with ideas, a sense of commitment and of course beauty. Just look back at Paulin's organic style, Perriand's Modernism and Prouvé's Art Deco, as well as Art Nouveau, Napoleonic Neoclassicism and more. This heritage has been carefully preserved by antique dealers and in the old notebooks that have inspired decorators making history in Paris today.

DEDON

1 TO 7

11, rue des Grands Augustins, 6th
Metro Saint-Michel
www.1to7.fr
Open 1:30pm to 7pm, Saturday from 11am, closed Sunday and Monday

JAPANESE CERAMICS AND OBJECTS

Helped by a soundtrack of loud Chopin melodies, Ikumi Inoue showcases jewellery, glasses and ceramics made by a handful of Japanese craftsmen whose work can be found in Tokyo's major galleries. A small selection of books on the shelves explain how to use the variously shaped, unique containers in fascinating colours – earthen, porcelain blue and dark Japanese lacquer – arranged on mats and hemp fabrics covering dusty looms that evoke the workshops of the 19th-century Latin Quarter. Culture clash? In fact, this selection comes from the personal collection of well-known manga publisher Takeaki Tajimi, who regularly shuttles between Japan and Paris to share his discoveries. Unusual and compelling.

ASTIER DE VILLATTE

173, rue Saint-Honoré, 1st
Metro Tuileries
Tel 01 42 60 74 13
www.astierdevillatte.com
Open 11am to 7:30pm, closed Sunday

PORCELAIN

Benoît Astier de Villatte and Ivan Pericoli founded this old-style porcelain studio in 1996. Their plates and cups are hand-moulded and adorned with decorative motifs in relief. Their creations have been described as dream objects, whose charm lies in their un-matching uniqueness, and they are presented here in one of the city's most curious and charming shops. A former paint store, it had been empty for thirty years and was once the home of the Singe Violet, the showcase for Biennais, Napoleon I's great goldsmith. It has been kept in its original state, rustic and slightly rickety, but absolutely enchanting. It's like wandering through the attic of an ancestor blessed with good taste, or like flipping through a humorous diary while inhaling the heady scent by a master candle maker from the South of France: it's a whole world. To give an artistic touch to the Grand Chalet collection, the duo asked Balthus's widow Setsuko Klossowska de Rola to design what turned out to be fantastical pieces in white glazed ceramic, including a cat teapot whose front paw functions as the spout. A tribute to the artist who loved cats.
Other location: 16, rue de Tournon, 6th, tel 01 42 03 43 90

ATELIERS GUILLAUME MARTEL ET MANUELA PAUL-CAVALLIER

2, rue du Regard, 6th
Metro Sèvres-Babylone
Tel 01 45 49 02 07, 06 60 68 10 13
Open by appointment only

FRAMES

Guillaume Martel and Manuela Paul-Cavallier, whose respective workshops are located in the same courtyard, have combined their talents to "invent" the frames of tomorrow. He designs streamlined frames, and she decorates them with gold leaf and pigments, creating a subtle play of light and shadow. The frame lets the work shine through while enhancing it.

BAZARTHERAPY

15, rue Beaurepaire, 10th
Metro République
Tel 01 42 40 10 11
www.bazartherapy.com
Open 11am to 7:30pm, Sunday 2pm to 7pm, closed Monday

GIFTS, ALL AGES

Pascal Bildstein and Emmanuel Attali's concept store, located in an old paint shop near the Canal Saint-Martin, is filled with objects (about 1,200) that a crazy Surrealist with a mania for stocktaking would have loved. The place, filled with poetic, playful, practical bric-a-brac, mixes childish fantasy with adult reverie and reinvents the idea of the gift, ranging from old-fashioned baubles to contemporary furniture issued by furniture makers themselves. Which means you can always find that special something you weren't looking for. Craft items include Schweitzer crystal glassware, Tournerie du Plat d'Or wooden baubles and Ciegerie des Prémontrés candles. In the high-tech section, you might come across a customized USB key and 1950s-style robots, as well as wonderful super-kitsch Artefacto Madrid plates, illustrated in a Venetian *Mars Attacks* style. Plus there's a nod to the treasures that delighted the duo as children: lollipops, goodie bags, balloons, toy box statuettes and a French funfair "tirette" slot machine filled with cheap treasures. As well as remembering things past, the owners enjoy unearthing young talents with fanciful imaginations. Examples are the zany creations of Lili Scratchy and the marine-influenced silicone necklaces by Mary Ross, with subtle luminous effects.

CARPENTERS WORKSHOP GALLERY

54, rue de la Verrerie, 4th
Metro Hôtel de Ville
Tel 01 42 78 80 92
www.carpentersworkshopgallery.com
Open 10am to 7pm, closed Sunday

DESIGN ART

Already present in London, the company owned by Loïc Le Gaillard and Julien Lombrail is solidifying its leadership in the field with a new space in New York and an immense 8,000-square-metre workshop in France, near Charles de Gaulle Airport, where fifteen master craftspeople handle production. The gallery offers collectors one-of-a-kind or limited-edition design pieces, going beyond the "art and design" debate by offering "functional sculptures or sculptural furniture" by top international designers, often with extraordinary projects. Among them are Atelier Van Lieshout, Ingrid Donat, Robert Stadler, Studio Job, Johanna Grawunder, Andrea Branzi, Fernando and Humberto Campana and Rick Owens. They have recently been joined by Vincenzo de Cotiis from Milan and the Korean designer Wonmin Park.

CECCALDI

15, rue Racine, 6th, metro Odéon
Tel 01 46 33 87 20
www.couteaux-ceccaldi.com
Open 10:30am to 1:30pm and 2:30pm to 7pm, closed Sunday

MASTER CUTLER

When Jean-Pierre Ceccaldi began fashioning horn-handled shepherd's knives in Porticcio, south of Ajaccio, in 1978, he was reviving an almost forgotten Corsican craft. He subsequently travelled to Paris, where he set himself up in the heart of the Latin Quarter, opening the small no-nonsense shop where Sylvestre and Simon Ceccaldi now greet customers. They offer a unique range of traditional knives that includes the famous Vendetta, as well as carbon-steel blades for the table and the kitchen.

CLARA SCREMINI

99, rue Quincampoix, 3rd
Metro Rambuteau
Tel 01 48 04 32 42
www.clarascreminigallery.com
Open 2pm to 7pm or by appointment, closed Sunday to Tuesday

GLASS ARTISTS

Clara Scremini, who was born in South America but has long been based in Paris, is a true luminary in the world of contemporary glass and ceramics. With great discrimination, she runs one of the few Parisian galleries devoted to art glass from around the world. It was she who revealed to Parisian glass lovers and collectors the talent of Brian Hirst; Mattei Negreanu, who sculpts pâte de verre, Massimo Micheluzzi, a Venetian antiques dealer who became a glass artist; Barbara Nanning, a ceramist who also converted to working with glass; Perrin & Perrin, a couple who specialize in pâte de verre sculptures and who were recently approached by the Saint-Louis glass company; and Tessa Clegg, an artist also known for her pâte de verre sculptures. In spring 2017, Scremini, who was exhibiting at the PAD art fair, was awarded one of the top prizes for a work by Czech artist Oldrich Pliva – a huge solid-glass ring – while the Hungarian György Gáspár attracted attention with his fascinating monoliths pierced with colourful layers. Other names worth looking out for are Maria Koshenkova, Julius Weiland and Pavel Trnka, representing the gallery's focus on Eastern Europe, historic home of powerful, radical glass art.

DEYROLLE

46, rue du Bac, 7th
Metro Rue du Bac
Tel 01 42 22 30 07, www.deyrolle.com
Open 10am to 7pm, Monday 10am to 1pm and 2pm to 7pm, closed Sunday

NATURAL SCIENCES

Deyrolle was founded in 1831 by Jean-Baptiste Deyrolles. Taken over in 1866 by his grandson, the taxidermist Émile Deyrolle, who was infamous for stuffed animals and insects from the five continents and internationally renowned for his botanical and butterfly displays, the shop has regained its original lustre following careful restoration work that has splendidly revived the historical panelling and gilding. The first floor, a shop of animal curiosities that one could visit and admire in a state of wonder, caught fire in February 2008, and almost all of the treasures were destroyed. A new era has since begun. Louis Albert de Broglie, Deyrolle's current boss, is overseeing the launch of a new taxidermy and entomology project that includes the odd chimera such as Taurus, a (real) fighting bull containing a butterfly box created along with architect Bruno Moinard, and even a unicorn. On the ground floor, "The Gardener Prince" has installed his tools and outdated outdoor furniture modelled on that of the Palais-Royal garden (www.princejardinier.fr).

EN ATTENDANT LES BARBARES

35, rue de Grenelle, 7th, metro Rue du Bac
Tel 01 42 22 65 25, www.barbares.com
Open 2:30pm to 6:30pm, closed Sunday and Monday

CONTEMPORARY DESIGN

Agnès Standish-Kentish has been producing designer furniture for more than thirty years and now ranks as a pioneer in the field. As elegant and energetic as ever, the founder of this famous design gallery in 1983 is now looking ahead to the 50th anniversary of the place and dreaming of becoming the Denise René of design. Known for her work with Garouste et Bonetti, she today mixes styles with designers such as Eric Schmitt, Christian Ghion, Éric Robin, Matt Sindall, Olivier Gagnère, Arik Levy, Éric Jourdan and newbie Margaux Keller, who was noticed at Sam Baron's Fabrica, as well as Nika Zupanc and the gilder Célia Bertrand. All the work here is produced with the greatest of care. The queen of the barbarians has been working since the beginning with the same craftsmen, including Pierre Basse, who was Diego Giacometti's blacksmith. Collectors love the place. Some pieces (including the most expensive) are sold even before they are exhibited.

FCK

10, rue du Faubourg Saint-Martin, 10th
Metro Strasbourg-Saint-Denis
Tel 06 10 13 81 71
fck-frederickgautier.com
Open by appointment only

POST-INDUSTRIAL CERAMICS

When he was an artistic director in films, Frédérick Gautier worked with Martin Scorsese and David Lynch among others before resuming his landscape studies at the Versailles school in 2009. The author of a film of himself swimming up Venice's Grand Canal, this multi-talented character has opted for the medium of pottery in which to express himself and experiment. Housed since 2016 in a workshop called

Le Studio on the Rue du Faubourg Saint-Martin, FCK (an acronymic nod to the compressive strength of concrete) personally welcomes passers-by fascinated by his architecturally inspired pieces. His T teapot shaped like a grain silo was crafted during a ninety-day residency on the barge *Louise Catherine*, renovated by Le Corbusier in 1929 and now moored along the Quai d'Austerlitz in Paris.

GALERIE ALB ANTIQUITÉS

3, rue de Lille, 7th
Metro Saint-Germain-des-Prés
Tel 01 47 03 45 58
www.albantiquites.com
Open 11am to 1pm and 2pm to 7pm,
closed Sunday and Monday

20TH-CENTURY DECORATIVE ARTS

Antoine Broccardo's very personal selection of pieces owes nothing to passing fads. Admittedly, Broccardo seems to be more interested in the history and curiosity value of things than in their function. His favourite period is the century stretching from 1870 to 1970, and it comes as no surprise to learn that he's often called upon to supply antiques to national museums, including the Musée d'Orsay. He's particularly interested in those artistic movements that rebelled against the official art of the 19th century, such as the Vienna Secession, the Wiener Werkstätte and the artists' workshops at Talashkino in Russia. His collection leads you off the beaten track to discover work unknown to all except insiders and the erudite, by figures such as the Russian Sergei Malyutin, the Hungarian modernist Lajos Kozma and Odile Mir, who produces graphic sculptural work.

GALERIE ALEXANDRE BIAGGI

14, rue de Seine, 6th
Metro Saint-Germain-des-Prés
Tel 01 44 07 34 73
www.alexandrebiaggi.com
Open 11am to 1pm and 2pm to 7pm,
closed Sunday and Monday

DECORATIVE ARTS

Pride of place here goes to past masters, including Frank, Poillerat, Adnet, Roche, Arbus and Royère, but Alexandre Biaggi has a talent for digging up rare pieces by famous artists like Diego Giacometti or striking, charming creations by anonymous designers. He's also interested in American furniture from the 1930s to the 1980s, and in particular how it was influenced by French design, evident in the work of architect and designer T.H. Robsjohn-Gibbings, among others. He sells bold furniture pieces by Hervé Van der Straeten, lamp sculptures made out of parchment and iron by Mauro Fabbro, bronze furniture and fixtures by the caster Patrice Dangel, marble and bronze tables by Patrick Naggar, plaster chandeliers by Alexander Logé and the bronze and rock crystal Terraemotus lamps by Mattia Bonetti.

GALERIE ARMEL SOYER

19-21, rue Chapon, 3rd
Metro Arts et Métiers
Tel 01 42 55 49 72
www.armelsoyer.com
Open 2pm to 7pm,
closed Sunday to Tuesday

21ST-CENTURY DECORATIVE ARTS

This gallery showcases work that is innovative, visually striking and poetic. Many items are veritable sculptures. It has showcased the work of Julian Mayor, with his "organic geometry", Mathias Kiss and his legendary Froissé Mirror, and Pierre Gonalons and his Palais table, inspired by the marble floors at Versailles. For its opening in 2012, the gallery presented the extraordinary Dandelion wallpaper with its inventive plant motifs in relief, designed and hand-crafted by Emmanuel Bossuet. The gallerist opened a second address in 2016, in the Alps, where, in addition to the usual selection, she offers oak furniture carved with a chainsaw by the Russian artist Denis Milovanov.

GALERIE BRUNO MOINARD ÉDITIONS

31, rue Jacob, 6th
Metro Saint-Germain-des-Prés
Tel 01 77 15 67 06
www.brunomoinardeditions.com
Open 11am to 7pm,
closed Sunday and Monday

FURNITURE DESIGNER

Formerly Andrée Putman's right-hand man, Bruno Moinard is a very active interior designer who has worked on Cartier stores, museums, Bordeaux wine estates and private homes. He's now opened a gallery whose interior can be altered to suit the exhibition on display. Currently, the theme is minimalist, with white walls and zinc floors, the perfect space for exhibiting Moinard's collection of furniture inspired by Art Deco, Modernism and Russian Constructivism. On view are around fifty pieces of furniture and objects, whose perfect finish expresses a dialogue between design and craft. Moinard's favourite materials include marquetry, hand-knotted silk, waxed linen, silk velvet, sycamore, lacquer and blown glass. As a young man he loved watercolour, and now he never goes abroad without his sketchbook and pastels. This explains the chromatic subtlety of his work, which is appreciated everywhere from Shanghai to New York and Rome, where his creations – along with those of Christian Liaigre, Philippe Hurel and Christophe Delcourt – were presented in the "Design@Farnese" exhibition at the French Embassy in 2016. The book *Du trait à la lumière* (From Line to Light) by journalist Serge Gleizes, with a foreword by photographer Jean-Paul Goude, retraces this unique and admirable career.

GALERIE BSL

23, rue Charlot, 3rd, metro Filles du Calvaire
Tel 01 44 78 94 14, www.galeriebsl.com
Open 11am to 6pm and by appointment,
closed Sunday and Monday

DESIGN ART AND JEWELLERY

An atypical figure in the small world that commissions design works, Béatrice Saint-Laurent supports artists and designers with a penchant for sensually shaped furniture that thrills collectors around the world. She exhibits at art fairs like PAD and Design Miami/Basel, and in London and China, focusing on extraordinary, avant-garde technologies like carbon fibre and aluminium honeycomb. She looks for both technical and aesthetic expertise such creative, visionary talents as Noé Duchaufour-Lawrance, Djim Berger (who makes fascinating stools of lightweight porcelain or coral), Charles Kalpakian, Nacho Carbonell and Taher Chemirik (his extraordinary, imposing "Interior Treasures" are made of brass, stone, copper and bronze). In a futuristic setting in the Marais designed by one of her protégés, the gallery owner also exhibits the pink jade furniture of the French-Chinese VWD studio based in Shanghai. Refined furniture that can also be found at the other gallery on the Left Bank. **Other location:** 10, rue Bonaparte, 6th, tel 01 56 81 61 52

GALERIE DOWNTOWN – FRANÇOIS LAFFANOUR

18, rue de Seine, 6th, metro Mabillon
Tel 01 46 33 82 41
www.galeriedowntown.com
Open 10:30am to 1pm and 2pm to 7pm
closed Sunday and Monday

ARCHITECTS' FURNITURE

François Laffanour specializes in architects' designs, selling outstanding pieces by Jean Prouvé (such as the Compas table), Charlotte Perriand, Le Corbusier, Pierre Jeanneret and Oscar Niemeyer. The gallery also encompasses an eclectic range of decorative objects, including lamps by Serge Mouille, ceramics by Georges Jouve,

FIVE OBJECTS TO TAKE HOME

SEPT FAMILLES PICASSO GAME **This game arranges Picasso's works into seven families – Labohême, Cubésfère, Sadécoupe, Detraviole, etc. – by colour, design and type. It also contains a booklet with complete reproductions, captions and amusing texts for children.** **LIBRAIRIE BOUTIQUE DU MUSÉE NATIONAL PICASSO** 4, rue de Thorigny, 3rd, metro Saint-Sébastien-Froissart, tel 01 58 65 15 50, open 10am to 6pm, closed Monday

AN UMBRELLA WITH A GOLDEN HANDLE **The umbrellas with frilly ruffled edges here come in candy colours and leopard prints. The only thing missing is a standard poodle on a leash – luckily, the said dog is back in fashion. The prettiest umbrellas are found at the venerable Antoine store.** **ANTOINE** 10, avenue de l'Opéra, 1st, metro Palais-Royal, tel 01 42 96 01 80, www.antoine1745.com, open 10:30am to 1pm and 2pm to 6:30 pm, closed Sunday

SEVEN PAIRS OF MAZARIN SOCKS **Owning a different pair of Academician-green socks for every day of the week doesn't mean you'll be walking in the shoes of French novelist Jean d'Ormesson, but at least you will have the same socks, to be found at this elegant hosiery shop.** **MES CHAUSSETTES ROUGES** 9, rue César Franck, 15th, metro Duroc, tel 01 76 53 96 20, www.meschaussettesrouges.com, open 10am to 6pm, Saturday from 11am, closed Sunday

A STOCK OF THANK YOU CARDS **that couldn't look more proper, on which the word *merde!* (shit) is printed. That's as Parisian as you can get. Send them only to your worst friends or the actors you know (in France, *merde* means "break a leg").** **LE TYPOGRAPHE** 33, rue Mazarine, 6th, metro Odeon, tel 09 83 01 74 02, www.letypographe.be

A HAIR FETISH **or the reinvention by "hair textile finisher" Antonin Mongin of the lost art of creating a relic, picture, accessory or fetish from a lock of the beloved's hair. His Relic'Hair study programme at the École des Arts Décoratifs was awarded the Prize for Young Creative Artists. By appointment** (antonin.mongin@gmail.com) **and in his studio for orders.** **ANTONIN MONGIN, ÉCOLES DES ARTS DÉCORATIFS** 31, rue d'Ulm, 5th, metro Place Monge

furniture by George Nakashima and pieces by Ettore Sottsass and Ron Arad. You'll also find contemporary rarities such as Tokujin Yoshioka's Pane Chair, resembling a big loaf of bread.

GALERIE DU PASSAGE

22-26 galerie Vérot-Dodat, 1st
Metro Palais-Royal–Musée du Louvre
Tel 01 42 36 01 13
www.galeriedupassage.com
Open 11am to 7pm, closed Sunday and Monday

ECLECTIC DESIGN

A prominent personality in the world of 20th-century applied arts, Pierre Passebon's exhibitions do not favour one particular kind of art, preferring to roam freely across stylistic boundaries and hierarchies.
They are eclectic, featuring original and rare pieces, letting visitors enjoy the excitement of making their own discoveries.
Furniture, paintings, sculpture, jewellery and photographs all feature on Passebon's roll-call of good taste. He also loves recreating landmark exhibitions, such as those featuring interior designer Madeleine Castaing, photographs by David Lynch or paintings and ceramics by Gérard Drouillet. Upstairs, Pierre Passebon's interest in the decorative arts and the history of design is showcased in his collection of beautiful

pieces by Royère, Rougemont, Gio Ponti, Franco Albini and Alexandre Noll. The gallery itself is a little gem, tucked away in one of Paris's prettiest arcades – you'll be charmed before you even enter.

GALERIE FAYET

34, passage Jouffroy, entrance
at 10-12, boulevard Montmartre, 9th
Metro Grands Boulevards
Tel 01 47 70 89 65
www.galerie-fayet.com
Open 10:30am to 12:30pm and 1pm to 7pm, closed Sunday and Monday

COLLECTIBLE WALKING STICKS

We are in the Passage Jouffroy with the Chopin Hotel at the back and the Grévin wax museum to our right. Galerie Fayet, on the same side, previously known as Galerie 34, is home to one of the strangest businesses imaginable. Yet it also feels somehow familiar, as if selling canes were the most logical of all activities in this inimitably 19th-century setting. In those days, Paris boasted some 300 cane makers. And Gilbert Segas's showcase of curiosities has drawn collectors from the four corners of the world. Not one to rest on his laurels, Segas owned a collection, recently acquired by Fayet, of over a 1,000 models, each unique, and he flirted with every style, every epoch. Handles are of ivory, horn or pewter, and the canes sometimes hide surprising mechanisms, such as a sword, an easel or a water pistol. Some have belonged to illustrious Parisian figures. Be prepared for several hours of conversation, history and anecdotes when you enter. Even men who are as straight as a stick will strut out of the store like Beau Brummell. Fayet, a century-old company possessing the label Entreprise du Patrimoine Vivant (Living Heritage Business), also sells its artisanal products here: models in silver or exotic wood, luxury umbrellas and parasols.

GALERIE GOSSEREZ

3, rue Debelleyme, 3rd
Metro Filles du Calvaire
Tel 06 12 29 90 40
www.galeriegosserez.com
Open 2pm to 7pm and by appointment, closed Sunday to Tuesday

CONTEMPORARY DESIGN

Marie-Bérangère Gosserez has a hammer, the sort you find in auction rooms. Although she's an auctioneer, she also spent five years in the Saint-Ouen flea market, then opened her own gallery in the Marais. Beneath the stone arches, you get a good overview of young international designers here, including the German Valentin Loellmann, Sacha Walckhoff, Grégoire de Lafforest and Élise Gabriel. Also eye-catching are the works of Éric Jourdan and Valentin Loellmann, a young German craftsman who makes cabinets, benches and cheval mirrors with torch-flamed metal and wood in his Maastricht workshop. Piergil Fourquié's Mursi tables and Damien Gernay's Black Sea pieces transform the traditional appearance of leather, while Anne Büscher's blown-glass mobiles add an extra dash of poetry to this bold enterprise.

GALERIE JACQUES LACOSTE

12, rue de Seine, 6th, metro Mabillon
Tel 01 40 20 41 82
www.jacqueslacoste.com
Open 11am to 1pm and 2pm to 7pm, closed Sunday

1930S-1960S FURNITURE

Grandson of the French tennis champ who created the polo shirt with the crocodile motif, Jacques Lacoste is making a name for himself on the rather different playing field of 20th-century antiques. He started out at the Serpette market in the Paris *puces* in Saint-Ouen, got interested in 1950s furniture and decided to focus exclusively on this period. In 1996, he opened his first gallery in the centre of Paris. At an exhibition, he was attracted to the work of Jean Royère (1902–1981),

A DAY AT THE FLEA MARKET

THE SAINT-OUEN PUCES

Created in the 1870s and now covering nine hectares at the northern edge of Paris, the Saint-Ouen flea market has never been more popular. Gathered mainly around Rue des Rosiers, its fifteen markets have something of Notting Hill's offbeat chic, mixed with the phlegmatic charm of the French provinces. Like the oldest market MARCHÉ VERNAISON (www.marchevernaison.com), a maze dedicated to "anti-design", i.e. old toys, used clothes, Art Deco furniture as shiny as granny's and super-specialist stalls selling a specific product such as pepper mills, pinball machines and geographical globes. You meet improbable characters such as the artist Yuksel Sahin with his portraits of animals dressed as humans, and the accordionists at Chez Louisette's tavern. Opposite, the MARCHÉ DAUPHINE (www.marche-dauphine.com) has an upper floor where you can hunt for books, vintage stereo, records, postcards and antique prints. Under a glass roof, you'll find the Maison Futuro – avant-garde housing designed by the Finnish architect Matti Suuronen in 1968. Still on Rue des Rosiers, the MARCHÉ PAUL BERT - SERPETTE (www.paulbert-serpette.com) provides a sanctuary for all things vintage that attracts fans ranging from American designers to French reality TV stars. It all began with a handful of diehards who have been reviving anything from Pierre Paulin's organic furniture to Louis XV commodes here for ages and have now embraced townhouses and covered stalls rented by famous antique dealers from central Paris, such as Matthieu Monluc (Galerie Steinitz), packed with luxurious bric-a-brac that sets trends in contemporary ceramics (Galerie Gendras Regnier) and Scandinavian furniture (Déjà Vu Design). Behind there's a garden that leads to Marché Jules Vallès, with its informal mix of industrial styles, vintage and 18th century. From there, the Passage Lécuyer-Vallès with its windows packed with retro and style accessories leads to Rue Lécuyer, where the LIBRAIRIE DE L'AVENUE (libraire-avenue.fr) is barely visible at the weekend, hidden by a constant ballet of curbsiders. Saint-Ouen is a shambles at the gates of the capital that has recently been gentrified to the point of welcoming a new ecological family-hotel concept from Cyril Aouizerate, co-founder of Mama Shelter. The hundred rooms of the MOB (www.mobhotel.com) have been furnished by some fellow called Philippe Starck, who had already decorated the restaurant MA COCOTTE in Paul Bert (www.macocotte-lespuces.com). At the first rays of sun, the golden youth of the flea markets line up to enjoy a green juice outside on the terrace and share a pizza cooked on the spot (you wonder how). Fashionable. Elegant. Astonishing.

MARCHÉ AUX PUCES DE SAINT-OUEN Metro Porte de Clignancourt, tel 01 40 11 77 36, www.marcheauxpuces-saintouen.com, Saturday 9am to 6pm, Sunday 10am to 6pm, Monday 10am to 5pm

in particular its extraordinarily decorative look, vibrant colours and wide range of materials. He then began to search the world for other works by this designer, unearthing, preserving and classifying everything he could, and even buying Royère's entire archives (5,000 documents) from a foreign dealer. This proved to be a unique asset when it came to finding the original owners of the various pieces, or their descendants. He then began to showcase these extravagantly beautiful objects, such as a lemon-yellow chair decorated with faux white fur. With Jean Royère as the focus, Jacques Lacoste has also brought together a group of designers who were equally demanding, including Pierre Chareau, Jacques-Émile Ruhlmann, Max Ingrand and André Arbus. "There was and still is in France a combination of taste, daring and money that fuelled the emergence and influence of great interior designers," says this connoisseur of decorative art.

GALERIE KREO

31, rue Dauphine, 6th, metro Odéon
Tel 01 53 10 23 00, www.galeriekreo.com
Open 11am to 7pm,
closed Sunday and Monday

CUTTING EDGE

Design and contemporary art experts Clémence and Didier Krzentowski enthusiastically support a stable of distinguished designers that includes the Bouroullec brothers, Jasper Morrison, Hella Jongerius, François Bauchet, Jaime Hayón, Marc Newson and Konstantin Grcic. They take a sort of laboratory approach, meeting up here to mix and match ideas and research. Eight examples of each design are produced, in addition to four prototypes. Alongside this fertile partnership, the gallery offers a selection of exceptional lamps from the 1950s to today by Gino Sarfatti, Achille Castiglioni and Pierre Guariche. Kreo also publishes books, like the one on the late designer Maarten van Severen, and it opened a second shop in London in 2014.

GALERIE LUMIÈRES

2, rue de Miromesnil, 8th
Metro Miromesnil
Tel 01 81 70 92 80
www.galerielumieres.com
Open 10am to 1pm to 7pm, Monday from 11am, closed Saturday and Sunday

HISTORIC CHANDELIERS

Known for curating mordantly original exhibitions, Philippe Renaud is also the artistic director of the Régis Mathieu chandeliers workshop, highly reputed for its technical expertise. Among other things, the company has been involved in restoring the Hall of Mirrors at Versailles. For twenty years now, these two light freaks, who know more about the subject than a shelf of ten encyclopaedias, have put together a dazzling collection of chandeliers from the 1500s to now. They have even managed to get hold of a twin of the chandelier in *The Arnolfini Portrait* by Flemish primitive painter Jan van Eyck, painted in 1434. In their Paris gallery – a vast white minimalist space – these masterpieces of the genre are all on view at ground level. You can see a 1900 Viennese chandelier alongside a 1940s Jansen pear-drop chandelier or an 1870 Cornelius & Baker number next to a Joseph Hoffmann palm-tree version. Making the most of his genuine taste for creative contrasts, Philip Renaud has scattered around a few pieces of furniture and exemplary objects such as coffee tables with a 1970s Jansen chair, a Vasarely chess set and a Marc Newson chair.

GALERIE MARIA WETTERGREN

18, rue Guénégaud, 6th, metro Odéon
Tel 01 43 29 19 60
www.mariawettergren.com
Open 11am to 7pm,
closed Sunday and Monday

CONTEMPORARY SCANDINAVIAN DESIGN

The gallery opened by the Danish-born Maria Wettergren in 2010, near the École des Beaux-Arts, quickly attracted leading interior designers, such as Peter Jovanovich, eager to discover the latest developments in Scandinavian design from this headhunter of talent and original forms. Thus you can see work by Niels Hvass, Astrid Krogh, Grethe Sørensen, Tora Urup, Cecilie Manz, Mathias Bengtsson and Rasmus Fenhann, among the many artists and designers represented here, along with work by photographers. She is very demanding with regard to quality, and there are plenty of revelations.

GALERIE OSCAR GRAF

15, rue de Seine, 6th
Metro Mabillon
Tel 06 71 43 19 90
www.oscar-graf.com
Open 10am to 1pm and 2:30pm to 7pm, by appointment Sunday and Monday

19TH- AND 20TH-CENTURY ANTIQUES

Antiques dealing runs in Oscar Graf's family. His grandmother was a notable antiques dealer, and his father was the distinguished interior designer François-Joseph Graf, whose excellent eye and cultural knowledge he inherited. After a few months on the Quai Voltaire, he has moved here to Rue de Seine, with Biaggi, Jousse and Kreo for neighbours, but not competitors. Graf the Younger continues to explore French, English and American decorative arts from 1870 to 1910, a narrow but popular niche period for connoisseurs, which he further enhances by introducing exceptional period pieces with Japanese influences.

GALLERY S. BENSIMON

111, rue de Turenne, 3rd
Metro Filles du Calvaire
Tel 01 42 74 50 77
www.gallerybensimon.com
Open 11am to 1pm and 2:30pm to 7pm, closed Sunday and Monday

OBJECTS

In 1992, Serge Bensimon opened the first Home – Autour du Monde concept store, a buzzing, colourful bazaar inspired by a cutting-edge, ethnic, around-the-world attitude and a vitally cosmopolitan identity. In 2009, he opened his own gallery of objects mixing the vernacular with the contemporary, the curious with the crude, the unusual with the stylish. Masterminded by François Leblanc, it thrives on creative young talent from all over the world. The policy, when possible, is to produce environmentally responsible work, where sustainable methods and gorgeous natural materials are key. Among other things, this means small functional objects by the French duo Pool, mirrors by Dutch designers Brit Van Nerven and Sabine Marcelis, bubble suspensions from the Anglo-Italian couple Giopato & Coombes, graceful, lightweight desks by the Czech Lucie Koldova, woodwork by Brent Comber and glass vases blown by Jeremy Maxwell Wintrebert. All these have enabled the gallery to affirm its difference, openness and ethical stance.

GALERIE YVES GASTOU

12, rue Bonaparte, 6th
Metro Saint-Germain-des-Prés
Tel 01 53 73 00 10
www.galerieyvesgastou.com
Open 11am to 1pm and 2pm to 7pm, closed Sunday and Monday

FUTURE ANTIQUES

Sporting a terrazzo front by Ettore Sottsass, this gallery has become a major Parisian destination for art furniture lovers. It's a simple success story: since 1985, the gallery has exhibited limited editions by the greatest living designers, starting with the iconic Memphis group and now including Emmanuel Babled's organic objects in marble and blown glass. Since 2008, Yves Gastou's son Victor has been helping with the epoch-making programming that harks back over thirty years. Tom Dixon, Shiro Kuramata, Zaha Hadid and more have been exhibited by this Toulouse native, who also specializes in Belgian designer Ado Chale's bijou coffee tables, light totems by César and Jean-Claude Farhi, and André Arbus's Art Deco furniture.

HERVET MANUFACTURIER

8, rue Volney, 2nd, metro Opéra
Tel 01 42 86 03 65
www.hervet-manufacturier.fr
Open by appointment only

RETRO-FUTURISTIC CRAFTS

Nicolas and Cedric Hervet come from a family of cabinetmakers and have created a furniture brand specializing in handmade limited editions. Nicolas operates from a workshop in Normandy while Cedric designs in his studio in Los Angeles, where he also moonlights as artistic director for Daft Punk. Inspired by sci-fi and movies, from *James Bond* to Stanley Kubrick, their futuristic creations are decorated with contemporary woodwork by Nicolas Hervet. Strength through contrast. Since 2016, their work is almost all exhibited in a "maker"-style gallery near the Place Vendôme. Presented around a neo-rustic workbench scattered with tools brought in from Normandy, these chairs, desks and coffee tables delight devotees of fine craftsmanship. And also electro music fans, as pieces such as the Satellite range of furniture and the game-arcade consoles are fitted with Bose sound speakers.

JASPER MAISON

203 bis, rue Saint-Martin, 3rd
Metro Rambuteau, Réaumur-Sébastopol
Tel 06 30 61 03 29, www.jaspermaison.com
Open by appointment only

1930S–1960S FURNITURE

A thirty-something antiques dealer from Lille, Steve Proisy recently moved from his gallery in Rue Chapon to a new 200-square-metre, two-level space on the corner of Rue Saint Martin and Rue du Bourg l'Abbe. Between Klein-blue walls, he exhibits a selection of must-haves, including ABCD sofas and Big Tulip armchairs by Pierre Paulin, Danish dining rooms and storage spaces by the Danes Hans Wegner and Børge Mogensen, some Italian lighting and contemporary pottery. Just what you need to tastefully furnish a Paris pad.

LE CUBE ROUGE

270, boulevard Raspail, 14th
Metro Denfert-Rochereau
Tel 06 11 60 30 03
www.lecuberouge.com
Open 1pm to 7:30pm, Saturday from 10:30am, Sunday 10:30am to 1:30pm, closed Monday and Wednesday

VINTAGE DESIGN

From a very young age, Jérôme Godin would accompany his parents to antiques fairs and vintage sales, and ever since then antiques have been his passion. At the age of twenty-two he toured the length and breadth of France in a van on a quest for furniture from the 1950s and 1960s. Today, he attempts to give meaning to the much overused word vintage by presenting good-quality French, Scandinavian, American and Italian items, which he sells at extremely reasonable prices. Here you're just as likely to find a George Nelson desk as little-known chairs by Arne Jacobsen. Passionate about innovative, simple post-war furniture, he explores the forgotten, neglected work of Jacques Hitier, a French designer of those prosperous post-war years that the French call "Les Trentes Glorieuses", the "Glorious Thirties".

MAISON NUMÉRO 20

20, rue de l'Université, 7th
Metro Saint-Germain-des-Prés
Tel 01 77 19 23 03
www.maisonnumero20.fr
Open by appointment only

INTERIOR DESIGN

Housed in the former stables of a private mansion in Saint-Germain-des-Prés, the studio and showroom of designer Oscar Lucien (formerly a designer for the Oscar Ono brand) offer an insider's address that looks like an elegant flat. He designs furniture here for a clientele that appreciates his warm, sophisticated style, using luxurious materials such as brass, bronze and walnut to revisit 1950s pieces with his inimical taste. You can also explore the selection of pieces distributed or picked up for a song by the owner – artists mirrors, Greco-Roman busts, custom furniture and rugs made by brands that have set up shop in the neighbourhood.

MAISON SARAH LAVOINE

6, place des Victoires, 2nd
Metro Bourse
Tel 01 40 13 75 75
www.sarahlavoine.com
Open 10am to 7pm, closed Sunday

PARISIAN LIFESTYLE

Sarah Lavoine, born Poniatowski, and the wife of singer and actor Marc Lavoine, is a successful decorator who hardly needs an introduction. In these 400 square metres on two floors she offers a selection of products expertly designed or picked up, making the place look like a real home. Everything here is attractive, inspiring and desirable, from her pastel-tone dishes created for the Gers brand and her striped-cotton house linen, to the pretty Scandinavian-inspired benches and light fixtures. Equally enticing are the heeled shoes she conjured up for the Sézane brand and her felt hats and soft cashmere sweaters. As the current epitome of the Parisian woman for a whole generation of decorators, she has even set up a grocery counter here and a café run by the famous caterer Da Rosa. Lifestyle *oblige*. Note the lovely Place des Petits Pères through the big windows.

MAISON VINCENT DARRÉ

13, rue Royale, 8th, metro Concorde
Tel 01 40 07 95 62
www.maisonvincentdarre.com
Open by appointment only

SURREAL DECORATIVE ARTS

A former artistic director at Ungaro, Vincent Darré switched to home decoration in 2009 by amusingly creating the very baroque Maison Darré, a gallery and curio cabinet housing his own surreal creations of "skeletons" and "shellfish" furniture. The decorator of the Le Baron nightclub in New York for André and his gang, as well as the Hotel Montana, this happy dandy closed his Rue du Mont Thabor outfit and opened this new venue in Rue Royale. This is a genuine apartment open to the public by appointment, where Darré has installed his office, along with a bedroom, bathroom, kitchen and dining room for private dinners in small groups. He has created a beautifully decorated setting, "in a baroque, surreal spirit, but with less Dadaism", for his antiques and contemporary furniture collection, designed with other Parisian designers such as Mathias Kiss, Emmanuel Bossuet and Eric Schmitt. The Lison de Caunes workshops provide the straw marquetry, while Aubusson tapestries and gilding by Manuela Paul-Cavallier have both joined the party. Visit immoderately.

MAYARO

20, rue Amélie, 7th
Metro La Tour Maubourg
Tel 01 80 06 04 41, www.mayaro.fr
Open 10am to 6pm, Saturday 11am to 7pm, closed Sunday

DESIGN AND CRAFTS

Dedicated to the male of the species, this store presents a selection of accessories handcrafted by the shoemaker Corthay and optician Lucas de Stael for admirers. Fashion, and then some. At Mayaro, run by Éloïse Gilles and Raphaelle de Panafieu – who gave a second life to Duvelleroy fans (just opposite) – gentlemen customers can also furnish their bachelor pad with baskets made on demand by professionals, providing a desk by day and a bar by night, with a hi-fi in carved wood, as well as digital mirrors that broadcast video works by artist Stéphane Couturier – in other words, original pieces manufactured exclusively by carefully selected craftsmen. Upstairs, chef Sven Chartier masterminds the kitchen on major occasions, supported once again by Nicolas Floquet, a gourmet, aesthete and hedonist known as a "muse" by his followers at Mayaro, a new wave concept store.

UNDER THE HAMMER

In Paris, the tradition of public auctions dates back to 1524, and anything and everything can come under the hammer. Here's a glimpse of several Paris auction houses for fans of the sport.

DROUOT-RICHELIEU While Christie's and Sotheby's naturally have branches in the city, Drouot is the most famous auction house, with over 100 auctioneers, 74 sales companies, 2,000 sales a year and 600,000 objects scattered to the four winds. There are sixteen rooms on Rue Richelieu devoted to paintings, furniture and objets d'art. In practice, the lots are exhibited on the eve of the sale. Rummaging in one room after another, there's a picturesque herd of dealers and collectors who meet in the hallways and give each other conspiratorial looks, so it's easy enough to spot the newbies and foreign visitors. The setting is nothing special, and the whole interest of the place lies in the objects on sale in this incredible museum of other people's memories, be it a Hermès bag, a Kriki painting, a case of 1947 Château Cheval Blanc wine, furs, an Olmec mask or a section of the Eiffel Tower staircase. The trick is to spot that one magnificent object hidden in the jumble of a themed auction – an antique toy amid a clutch of etchings that will ensure the price will start low. You are usually expected to attend the sale, but the number of purchase orders phoned in or messaged online is often higher than bids from the floor. Drouot also tries to be informative, with its special announcements and its 12 Drouot exhibition space, which displays the flagship items in large upcoming auctions, as well as its comprehensive website with auction instructions, its famous Gazette read worldwide, and also its smart educational project called **DROUOT KIDS** (tel 01 48 00 22 54), launched by Christophe Delavault with the aim of educating children about sales and the auction game. 9 rue Drouot, 9th, metro Richelieu-Drouot, tel 01 48 00 20 20, www.drouot.com

ARTCURIAL Housed in the Hôtel Dassault, Artcurial is an art auctioneer organizing over 100 sales a year (here and elsewhere), including some of the most highly publicized events on the auction calendar, due in part to the wide range of artworks and items handled: paintings, sculpture, photographs, comic-book art, jewellery, and also vintage cars and wines, as was the case with the sale of the Hôtel Crillon's entire wine cellar. The building also houses a very up-to-date art library and a café, redecorated by Charles Zana. 7, rond-point des Champs-Élysées, 8th, metro Franklin D. Roosevelt, tel 01 42 99 20 20, www.artcurial.com

PIASA Newly arrived on the Parisian scene, the Piasa auction house is gaining ground: having moved from the Left to the Right Bank in September 2014, it is now part of the hallowed auction-house circuit, which made room for a young and ambitious competitor. Piasa has made its mark with some unusual sales – many based on design, and others featuring Soviet photography, Scandinavian ceramics and garden furniture, part of the Art du Jardin event at the Grand Palais. 118, rue du Faubourg Saint-Honoré, 8th, metro Miromesnil, tel 01 53 34 10 10, www.piasa.fr

PASSÉ-PRÉSENT-FUTUR

82, rue du Faubourg Saint-Honoré, 8th
Metro Miromesnil
Tel 01 42 65 99 14
www.pierrecardin.com
Open 11am to 6pm, Saturday and Sunday from 1pm, closed Monday and Tuesday

FURNITURE

For the record, the fashion designer Pierre Cardin dreamed of becoming a cabinetmaker. In the 1970s, he achieved his ambition in his own way by crafting what he called "utilitarian sculptures". At the time, this meant two-tone coffee tables, dressers and lamps inspired by the themes of his clothing or perfume bottles (Yin and Yang, Enigma, Lightning). This furniture is now making a comeback in a space just opposite the Elysée Palace dedicated exclusively to the design of the 1960s icon. It has been opened by one of his nephews, with a focus on Pop colours and organic shapes. Pierre Cardin, who acquired the Palais Bulles by Antti Lovag in Théoule-sur-Mer in 1992, is once again expressing here his love of organic forms. With its scorpion cabinet, starfish bar andboa dining room, the place offers a functional, lacquered wood bestiary, the ultimate fantasy of a gentleman with an iron handshake and an artistic temperament.

PHILIPPE MODEL

65, rue Condorcet, 9th
Metro Pigalle
Tel 06 63 67 57 03
Open 11am to 7:30pm, closed Sunday and Monday

DESIGNER AND VINTAGE OBJECTS

A designer adept at absorbing various influences, the jovial Philippe Model now has a festive bazaar that confirms how cool the once tranquil Rue Condorcet has become. Having reluctantly left his gallery-apartment on the Place du Marché Saint-Honoré, Model has moved to the SoPi (South of Pigalle) area and opened two boutiques, one for objects and another for shoes a few steps away. The former sells ceramics, glassware, lighting, mirrors, textiles and chairs, a mix of designer, customized or vintage objects in rare colours and a variety of forms: ethnic, exotic or surreal. You'll find lots of chrome and many big names as well as artisanal talents, sought out in the four corners of France and the world and displayed, stacked and contrasted in a forty-square-metre space. Extending his reach into interior decoration, Model recently designed the decor of the restaurants Maison Gradelle, Le Mélécasse and Au Fourreur, located on the Butte-aux-Cailles. Definitely a man of the world.

POUENAT FERRONNIER

22 bis, passage Dauphine, 6th
Metro Odéon
Tel 01 43 26 71 49
www.pouenat.com
Open by appointment only

IRONWORKS, PRESTIGIOUS

Heir to the family ironworks founded in Moulins in 1880, Henri Pouenat, a former disciple of the great Gilbert Poillerat, forged his own reputation by working for the prestigious house of Jansen and building the first-class suites of the famous ocean liner *France*. Now labelled a French "Living Heritage Enterprise", Pouenat is owned by Jacques Rayet, and for the first time in its rich history it has opened a special area to showcase collections of vintage and classic lines of objects and lighting, and also furniture and decorative pieces issued and designed by Gilles & Boissier, Tristan Auer, India Mahdavi, Thomas Boog, Nicolas Aubagnac and Damien Langlois-Meurinne, maker of several Objets Nomades for Louis Vuitton.

PUIFORCAT

48, avenue Gabriel, 8th
Metro Franklin D. Roosevelt
Tel 01 45 63 10 10
www.puiforcat.com
Open 10:30am to 7pm,
closed Sunday and Monday

SILVERWARE

Jean Puiforcat was to tableware what Le Corbusier was to architecture, Charlotte Perriand to furniture and Pierre Chareau to lighting. An early 20th-century designer and master goldsmith, he reinvented the expertise of the Puiforcat cutlery enterprise handed down to him by his grandfather, and geared it to the functionalist ideas of the time. Now located in a shop renovated by architect Tristan Auer at the corner of Avenues Matignon and Gabriel, Puiforcat entrusts its contemporary collections to international designers such as Patrick Jouin, whose Zermatt line was launched in 2010, or, more recently, Londoner Michael Anastassiades with his tasting glasses. The sculptural Fluidité tableware by Dutchman Aldo Bakker recalls Jean Puiforcat's style, often associated with Art Deco. This influence can be found in the new collection of objects for architect Joseph Dirand's office.

STANISLAS DRABER

19, rue Racine, 6th, metro Odéon
Tel 06 75 71 86 02
www.stanislas-draber.com
Open 6:30am to 7pm, closed Sunday

SEASONAL FLOWERS

This shop nestles in a beautiful corner building with a romantic courtyard, home to the first studios of Parisian artists in the mid-19th century. Among the famous denizens of this little-known hive of activity were Gustave Doré, Arthur Rimbaud, James McNeill Whistler and Robert Doisneau. On the north side, at 19, Rue Racine, a frieze of the Parthenon metopes – the shop sign of a former moulding business – can be seen above the entrance to a flower shop with an early edition of Charles Baudelaire's *Fleurs du Mal* in the window. For Stanislas Draber has two passions: Baudelaire and flowers. In his refined, poetic world, flowers are associated with literature, but also with antique Anduze vases and delicate botanical prints by Pierre-Joseph Redouté. Ignoring all the current fashions, he sells only seasonal flowers, rarely more than three at a time, sourced from small growers. In winter, you'll find the delicate buttercup, from the smallest to the most voluptuous; the tulip, a living cut flower that opens in the daytime and closes at night; and his favourite, the anemone, with its brightly coloured petals and black centre. In the spring, he has sweet peas, peonies, garden roses and camellia branches. There is nothing pretentious or fussy about his arrangements, which have no more than two colours or two flowers per vase and no foliage: a beautiful bouquet is made up of one type of flower – that's all there is to it.

STÉPHANE CHAPELLE

29, rue de Richelieu, 1st
Metro Pyramides
Tel 01 40 20 97 63
www.stephane-chapelle.fr
Open 10am to 8pm, Saturday and Monday
until 6pm, closed Sunday

NOTHING BUT FLOWERS

Roses, tulips, anemones and buttercups – simple nature. People adore florist Stéphane Chapelle's shop right next to the Palais-Royal. In twenty years, this discreet yet approachable personality has become a fixture in his field, attracting both the passing trade and discerning locals. In 2016, the upscale Pavilion of Arts and Design (PAD) in the Tuileries asked him to fashion the lobby of this popular rendezvous for design lovers.

STÉPHANE OLIVIER

3, rue de l'Université, 7th
Metro Saint-Germain-des-Prés
Tel 01 42 96 10 00
www.stephaneolivier.fr
Open 10:30am to 1pm and 2pm to 5pm, closed Sunday

HOME AND GARDEN

The spirit of the Saint-Ouen flea market has migrated towards the Seine, ending up in a duplex with a window filled with flowers and nostalgic garden decorations – a Stéphane Olivier speciality. If you only visit the ground floor, the shop boils down to romantic vases, sculpted fountains and Neoclassical columns, which this antique dealer cuts up and grafts onto other objects to give them a second life, for example as light fixtures. But venture upstairs for designs by contemporary artists, like Bénédicte Vallet's porcelain objects, Ludovic Minet's vanities and Brigitte Sauvignac's still lifes – all comfortably displayed amid the profusion of old weathered chests of drawers and 20th-century Italian and Scandinavian pieces.

STUDIO ERIC SCHMITT

24, rue de la Cerisaie, 4th
Metro Bastille
Tel 01 73 77 35 90
www.ericschmitt.com
Open by appointment

CONTEMPORARY CREATIONS

Having owned a foundry at Saint-Denis and today a workshop near Fontainebleau, Eric Schmitt, who comes from Toulouse, has opened a shop in Paris to sell designs not offered by En Attendant les Barbares, Galerie Dukto or IBU Gallery, the three galleries that produce his work. Noticed when very young alongside Christian Liaigre, Schmitt is known for working closely with artisans, whose techniques guide and inspire him. All the objects here are produced in limited editions and are the result of much reflection on materials and assembly, whether they are made with simple or precious materials, used in new ways and in subtle combinations. Schmitt's delicate vases of white and pink Bohemian opal milk glass are virtuoso creations. His ceramics are made in the traditional red, yellow and green of Bisbal in Catalonia, while his Bulb table combines aluminium with fragile crystal legs. Lamps and sconces carved in alabaster or plaster occupy a prominent place in his production.

STUDIO WILLY RIZZO

12, rue de Verneuil, 7th
Metro Rue du Bac, Saint-Germain-des-Prés
Tel 01 42 86 07 31
www.willyrizzo.com
Open 11am to 7pm, closed Sunday

20TH-CENTURY DESIGN AND PHOTOGRAPHY

His "Funny Faces" series is famous worldwide, as are his many photos dating as far back as the 1950s of personalities like Marilyn Monroe, Judi Dench, Jean-Paul Belmondo, Hussein of Jordan and Mohamed V taken for *Point de vue – Images du monde* and *Paris Match* magazines. A brilliant portrait photographer and photojournalist, Willy Rizzo was married to Italian star Elsa Martinelli and covered both the war in Indochina and Dior fashion shows. Based in Rome at the peak of his career in the 1980s, he also designed furniture, first for himself, and then for an affluent clientele including Brigitte Bardot and Salvador Dalí. Displayed in Paris in his

***"In Paris everybody wants to be an actor; nobody is content to be a spectator. People are jostling each other on stage while the hall remains empty."* Jean Cocteau, *Le Coq et l'arlequin*, 1918**

last studio, these sensual, masculine pieces now bear the hallmarks of the "Rizzo period". All of these geometrically shaped bright steel lights, leather and velvet sofas, black marble tables and items of musical furniture are signed by Rizzo, who died in 2013 aged eighty-four after a half-century of post-war creativity.

SWAMI

6, rue Victor Schoelcher, 14th
Metro Denfert-Rochereau
www.swami.fr
Open 10:30am to 1pm
and 2:30pm to 7pm, Sunday 11am
to 2:30pm, closed Monday

CONTEMPORARY CERAMICS

Located opposite the Fondation Cartier and near the École Camondo, Rue Schoelcher is an urban and architectural curiosity. There are not many shops along it, but one immediately draws the eye. Inside is a large table, a potter's wheel, ceramics with simple, pure lines and an artist at work: Karen Swami. You might come across her elsewhere in Paris, in the world of film production, her other life and day job but under another name, Karen Monluc, which she has decided to put a lid on. Now a potter, Karen Swami settles down to her wheel, playing with materials and glazes, taking her skills to the limit. This studio work involves varying and testing different products as she glides happily from one technique to another. She has managed to give white kaolin a greater aura, and to grapple brilliantly with stoneware and earthenware by simplifying their shapes and enhancing colours. From the earth she uses in her Carantec workshop in Brittany, she can summon up old mysteries and beautiful new shadow plays. Whether decorative or utilitarian, her work is already very popular with designers, including Christian Liaigre.

ULTRA MODERNE

8, rue du Bourg l'Abbé, 3rd
Metro Réaumur-Sébastopol, Rambuteau
www.ultramoderne.fr
Open 2pm to 5pm, Saturday from 11am,
closed Sunday and Monday

1970S AND 1980S DESIGN

She goes for modest materials with vibrant colours, like those used in Italy in the 1980s by the Memphis group. He prefers the shiny metal of 1970s French furniture. Respectively a designer for fashion magazines and an expert in modern painting, Lucillia Chenel and Ken Israel have agreed to promote their views on design jointly in a psychedelic setting inspired by Verner Panton's Living Sculptures. The multi-coloured melamine chairs designed for Ikea in 1993 stand alongside the highly cult Carlton shelf by Ettore Sottsass (1981) and François Monnet's aluminium furniture (1970). In this former photo studio near the Pompidou Centre, the conversation about art of all kinds is friendly but impassioned.

VILAC

Jardins du Palais-Royal,
9, rue de Beaujolais, 1st
Metro Palais-Royal–Musée du Louvre, Bourse
Tel 01 42 60 08 22, www.vilac.com
Open 10:30am to 7pm, closed Sunday

TOYS

There have been a number of commercially successful designer toys over the years, including the crafted toys on wheels made by Caran d'Ache (real name Emmanuel Poiré), and, in 1916, designs by Benjamin Rabier with animals taken from his own stories, such as the world-famous duck Gédéon and Briffaut the dog, stars of the exhibition "Vilac – 100 Years of Wooden Toys" organized by the Arts Décoratifs in 2012. Winner of a Wood Industries Design Grand Prix, the venerable French company Vilac has been lacquering wood since 1911 while cultivating an extensive collection of toys by artists such as Keith Haring, Di Rosa, Nathalie Lété and Castelbajac.

This Vosges company was based for many years in the Palais-Royal, where you can easily imagine multitudes of Vilac toys scattered over the gravel in the garden. Its first shop is a regular toy box where adults rather than children babble away at the painted wooden figurines as they would at Petitcollin dolls (www.petitcollin.com).

YVELINE ANTIQUES

4, rue de Furstemberg, 6th
Metro Saint-Germain-des-Prés, Mabillon
Tel 01 43 26 56 91
www.yveline-antiques.com
Open 11am to 7pm, Monday from 2:30pm, closed Sunday

POETIC ANTIQUES

There's no shortage of antique shops and flea markets in Paris. This one emanates something rare, deep and cultured – a sort of sublime presence. The painter Balthus had his studio here, and Yveline Lecerf installed her jewel of an antique shop here between the green bronze walls that have remained almost intact since the 1950s. Today her granddaughter Agathe Derieux keeps watch over the premises.
She collects portraits of philosophers, screens covered with flowers, Flemish painting and oxidized mirrors, as well as models of religious processions, or *capipotas*, which when she was little she imagined waking up at night while she slept. Only objects "with soul" will make their way here, as she puts it. Agathe knows the story of each item by heart, so just ask.

AT HOME WITH DOMINIQUE PERRAULT

Architect Dominique Perrault himself has rarely worked as a product designer, but he collaborates with Gaëlle Lauriot-Prévost, designer and artistic director of the DPA agency. Their range includes the limited edition modular coffee set in solid silver and white porcelain for Alessi, the Tricot armchair for Poltrona Frau, which looks like Ben-Hur trapped in a leather net, the No Design table for Alias, a kitchen and a fridge for Fagor, the ZigZag carpet for Chevalier Édition, Z lights for Fontanaarte, and lots of seating for the Milanese furniture producer Sawaya & Moroni. Not forgetting the BnF chair, designed in 1996 and revived in 2015, for the reading rooms of the National Library of France, of which 4,000 were made. This model was originally produced in Germany by Martin Stoll and revived by Paul Silvera. Then there's the fantastic In The Tube light fittings produced by DCW, a Parisian company founded by Frédéric Winkler and Philippe Cazer, and sold at Merci. And lastly we're still awaiting the work commissioned by the Manufacture de Sèvres.

POLTRONA FRAU

29, rue du Bac, 7th, metro Rue du Bac, tel 01 42 22 74 49, www.poltronafrau.com

CHEVALIER ÉDITION

20, rue Saint-Claude, 3rd, metro Filles du Calvaire, tel 01 43 07 87 44, www.chevalier-edition.com

SILVERA

264, rue du Faubourg Saint-Honoré, 8th, metro Ternes, tel 01 56 68 76 00, www.silvera.fr

MERCI

111, boulevard Beaumarchais, 3rd, metro Saint-Sébastien-Froissart, tel 01 42 77 00 33, www.merci-merci.com

ARTS AND CULTURE

MAJOR MUSEUMS TO RADICAL THEATRES: EXPLORING THE CITY'S CULTURAL RICHES

Cultural life in Paris is no longer restricted to the city centre. It has spread to working-class areas, and even to the outskirts, to Pantin and Le Bourget, where two celebrated galleries have set up shop. The Belleville neighbourhood and surrounding areas have become a creative hub. The French art scene remains vibrant, attracting large numbers of international artists and dealers, as reflected in the recent opening in Paris of the gallery of influential Berlin gallerist Max Hetzler.

The city's museums are drawing increasing numbers of visitors (the Louvre remains the world's most visited museum) thanks to new initiatives designed to make them more in tune with urban habits. Late-night openings of blockbuster exhibitions are a popular new trend. Parisians are also more inclined to venture off the beaten track, flocking in numbers to explore Art Brut, for example, when it was showcased at the first Outsider Art Fair organized in parallel with the FIAC.

Some still say Paris is a "sleeping beauty", simply resting on its impressive laurels. The Centre Pompidou, the Philharmonie de Paris, the Louvre's new Department of Islamic Arts and the Musée du Quai Branly all say otherwise. As for the new Fondation Louis Vuitton, a dramatic steel-and-glass structure designed by Frank Gehry on the edge of the Bois de Boulogne, it is already an architectural icon, a symbol of the art and culture of the 21st century.

AUTUNNO

WORDS, FILM AND MUSIC

7L

7, rue de Lille, 7th, metro Rue du Bac
Tel 01 42 92 03 58, www.librairie7l.com
Open 10:30am to 7pm, closed Sunday and Monday

FASHION, ART

Opened in 1999 by Karl Lagerfeld, this bookstore specializes in art, fashion, design, ceramics, cooking, architecture and gardens, subjects that have seen a growing number of published books and a larger readership. While it carries fewer photography books than it used to, 7L is following the craze for ceramics by stocking beautiful specialist books. This shop with nearly 2,000 titles is a real treasure trove, especially near the end of the year for those looking for erudite, unusual gifts.

ARTAZART

83, quai de Valmy, 10th
Metro Jacques Bonsergent
Tel 01 40 40 24 03, www.artazart.com
Open 10:30am to 7:30pm, Saturday from 11am, Sunday from 1pm

GRAPHICS

In 1999, Jérôme Fournel and Carl Huguenin opened an e-bookshop devoted to graphic design. A year later, they opened a bricks-and-mortar store with a red facade on the banks of the Canal Saint-Martin, which was not yet a stronghold of fun-loving Parisian bobos (the shop itself played a role in the area's gentrification). Since then, they have expanded their stock to include photography, design and street art. Many book signings are held in this friendly store, which attracts both locals and creative types from all over.

BETINO'S RECORD SHOP

32, rue Saint-Sébastien, 11th
Metro Richard Lenoir, Saint-Sébastien-Froissart
Tel 01 43 14 61 34, www.betinos.com
Open 1pm to 8pm, closed Sunday and Monday

NEW AND SECOND-HAND VINYL

Just about every type of current music – experimental, electronic, funk, nu-disco, afro, jazz, soul, Brazilian – can be found in this cult record shop, which carries both new and vintage vinyl. You'll find everything from Flabaire to Parker Madicine, Orlando Julius and Serge Gamesbourg, as well as the original soundtracks of the most wonderful Italian films, from series B to Z. Another recommended shop in the area, **TECHNO IMPORT**, not surprisingly specializes in techno and house. Then there is **KITOKO RECORDS**, specialists in boogie-woogie, funk, soul and "Afro-Caribbean musical delights". Its founder, Séverin, does not have a shop but offers a listening service adapted to your tastes in the comfort of your home (call 06 51 41 36 80 for an appointment or write to kitokorecords@gmail.com). A clever idea. **Other location:** **TECHNO IMPORT** 16, rue des Taillandiers, 11th, tel 01 48 05 71 56

BILIPO

48-50, rue du Cardinal Lemoine, 5th
Tel 01 42 34 93 00
Open 2pm to 6pm, Saturday 10am to 5pm and by appointment, closed Sunday and Monday

CRIME NOVEL LIBRARY

With a collection of more than 50,000 works of fiction, BiLiPo is the only French – and European – institution devoted to the preservation of crime novels. Most contemporary works can be found here, as well as old titles like Edgar Allan Poe's *The Gold-Bug* and the classic collections like Grands Détectives and Série Noire, along with many graphic novels and more than one hundred periodicals, all of which can be consulted on site. Crime fiction fans will also find reference books on espionage, law, real-life crime stories and forensics. They can't be borrowed (what a pity), but you can console yourself by raiding **L'AMOUR DU NOIR**, a crime fiction bookstore located nearby. **Other location: L'AMOUR DU NOIR** 11, rue du Cardinal Lemoine, 5th, tel 01 43 29 25 66

BUFFET CRAMPON

203 bis, boulevard Saint-Germain, 7th
Metro Rue du Bac
Tel 01 45 48 56 13
www.buffet-crampon.com
Open 10am to 6pm, closed Sunday

BRASS AND WIND INSTRUMENTS

The huge Steinway & Sons showroom had barely opened at the corner of Boulevard Saint-Germain and Rue Saint Thomas d'Aquin when the musical profile of the area was enhanced by Buffet Crampon, a maker of wind instruments opened in 1825 in Passage du Grand Cerf (2nd) under the name Denis Buffet-Auger; it became Buffet Crampon in 1836. This world-renowned company makes clarinets, oboes, saxophones, bass clarinets, English horns and bassoons, which are used by top musicians and orchestras. After being acquired in 1981 by Boosey & Hawkes of London, which itself became an independent group in 2005, Buffet Crampon has acquired a number of instrument makers, including Antoine Courtois (tubas, trombones, trumpets) and Besson (euphoniums). The decor of the evocative showroom oscillates between the atmosphere of *Piccolo Saxo* and a Vincente Minnelli musical.

CHARVIN MANUFACTURE DE COULEURS

57, quai des Grands Augustins, 5th
Metro Pont Neuf, Saint-Michel
Tel 01 43 54 98 97, www.charvin-arts.com
Open 10:30am to 1pm and 2pm to 7pm, closed Sunday morning and Monday morning

ARTISTS' COLOURS AND MATERIALS

Based in Nice, Bruno Charvin's colour factory opened a Parisian branch a few years ago, furnished with pieces from the defunct Palette d'Or in Marseille (founded in 1830), acquired when it closed, adding to the store's unique charm. Specializing in fine oils, pure pigments and watercolours, Charvin also carries ink, gold leaf, gouache and, of course, all the tools needed to use them: brushes, knives, pencils, charcoal, canvas, paper and easels. They also sell fine-linen painter's smocks in the original 19th-century design. Sunday painters will be delighted to know that the shop is open on Sunday afternoon.

FLORENCE LOEWY – BOOKS BY ARTISTS

9, rue de Thorigny, 3rd
Metro Saint-Sébastien-Froissart
Tel 01 44 78 98 45
www.florenceloewy.com
Open 2pm to 7pm, closed Sunday and Monday

ARTISTS' BOOKS

Florence Loewy has been promoting artists' books since 1989 and has been located in the Marais since 2001. Now she has reorganized the space originally designed by architects Jakob + MacFarlane. Artists' books, monographs, and rare and atypical works are still available, but in a smaller area next to a gallery section showing the work of artists who use stories and narration in their work. The archives can be consulted on the internet or by appointment.

GALERIE FRÉDÉRIC CASTAING

30, rue Jacob, 6th
Metro Saint-Germain-des-Prés
Tel 01 43 54 91 71
www.galeriefredericcastaing.com
Open 11am to 1pm and 2pm to 7pm, closed Sunday and Monday

ARTISTS' AUTOGRAPHS

Grandson of the great interior designer Madeleine Castaing, Frédéric Castaing modestly calls himself an autograph-seller. He plays host to collectors in his elegant mint-green drawing room – the height of Parisian chic. His list of manuscripts and letters by celebrities, actors, artists, writers and musicians is a veritable who's who (or rather, who *was* who?) of famous people, and is full of surprises. Castaing has written a novel that revolves around manuscripts entitled *Rouge cendres*.

GALIGNANI

224, rue de Rivoli, 1st, metro Tuileries
Tel 01 42 60 76 07, www.galignani.com
Open 10am to 7pm, closed Sunday

INTERNATIONAL BOOKSTORE

Opened in 1801 on the Rue Vivienne, this was the first English-language bookstore "on the continent". Frequented by Thomas Moore and Stendhal, an Anglophile bastion against the embargo imposed by Napoleon, the bookstore-salon published a daily gazette, *Galignani's Messenger*, which counted General Lafayette among its subscribers. The store, which also published books in English, moved in 1856 and was closer to the grand hotels like Le Meurice on the Rue de Rivoli, where it was frequented over the years by such loyal customers as Hemingway, Julien Green, the Duke and Duchess of Windsor, Paul Morand and André Malraux. Today, Galignani's bookcases are lined with some 50,000 British and American novels, general works, non-fiction works and coffee-table books on the arts and fashion.

LE BALZAC

1, rue Balzac, 8th, metro George V
Tel 01 45 61 10 60
www.cinemabalzac.com

ARTHOUSE CINEMA

The Balzac, one of the last independent cinemas on the Right Bank, is run by Jean-Jacques Schpoliansky, grandson of the man who founded it in 1935. Aside from films, it hosts a number of activities, among them a Saturday night film-concert that takes the audience back to the 1920s, when piano music accompanied silent films. And then there is the Festival Jazz & Images, which continues throughout the year.

LE LOUXOR

170, boulevard Magenta, 10th
Metro Barbès-Rochechouart
Tel 01 44 63 96 96, www.cinemalouxor.fr

ARTHOUSE CINEMA

Legendary cinema in the Barbès district, the Louxor was closed for decades but reopened in 2013. Its listed Art Deco facade saved it from demolition. Purchased in extremis by the City of Paris, its original 1921 neo-Egyptian decor was carefully restored before the place reopened as a cinema. The Louxor now welcomes hordes of film buffs from eastern Paris.

LE TYPOGRAPHE

33, rue Mazarine, 6th, metro Odéon
Tel 09 83 01 74 02, www.typographe.be
Open 2pm to 7pm, closed Sunday

STATIONERY, OFFICE SUPPLIES

Cédric Chauvelot, who is passionate about printing, salvaged 800 boxes of used and forgotten lead and wood type from a former typesetter. He then set up a boutique/workshop in Brussels that was an immediate success. In its chic Parisian annex, he offers business cards, writing paper and announcement cards made with lead type printed on Heidelberg presses. Traditional skills are also used on paper that is glued, folded by hand and dyed in dazzling colours. You'll want to touch everything before giving in and buying something from the stock of copybooks, stationery or notebooks with subtle textures (fine or granular) that inspire an urge to travel, as do the speckled sheets made with recycled Japanese origami paper. You will also be charmed by the rubbers, Japanese leather travel kits, writing accessories and pads printed with insects, like the small beetle that has become the emblem of the house. You may also get a kick out of the cards displaying typical irreverent Belgian humour or the birthday cards printed with insults Captain Haddock might have used if he had Tourette syndrome. Le Typographe has been selected by the bookshop at the Fondation Louis Vuitton and can also be found at Bon Marché.

LIBRAIRIE DU CINÉMA DU PANTHÉON – CINÉLITTÉRATURE

15, rue Victor Cousin, 5th
Metro Cluny-La Sorbonne
RER Luxembourg
Tel 01 42 38 08 26, www.cinelitterature.fr
Open 11am to 8pm, closed Sunday

FILM MECCA

The 5th arrondissement is the bastion of art house cinemas in Paris, including the legendary Champo and the Desperado (formerly the Action Écoles), which has been acquired by libertarian filmmaker Jean-Pierre Mocky. Opened in 1907, the Cinéma du Panthéon is one of the oldest still-operating cinemas in the city. Owned by Pathé, it originally showed silent films. Its moment of cinematic glory began in 1930 with the arrival of the great producer Pierre Braunberger, who was in charge for sixty years, until his death in 1990. Modernized with a new sound system, the cinema was also the first to show movies in their original language. Mentioned by Sartre in his autobiography *Les Mots,* this stronghold of the New Wave became the Europa Panthéon, then changed hands six years later. In April 2001, producer Pascal Caucheteux, founder of Why Not Productions, acquired it. Known for producing the films of Philippe Garrel, Bruno Podalydès, Arnaud Desplechin, Jacques Audiard and Claire Denis, he has turned the Cinéma du Panthéon into a meeting place for discussions about film. Following the opening on the first floor of the **SALON DU CINÉMA DU PANTHÉON** (tel 01 56 24 88 80), it now has a film bookshop, one of the last in the city, run by the enthusiastic Marc Benda and Georges-Emmanuel Morali, founder of Thé des Écrivains, in collaboration with the legendary bookstore Ciné Reflet. Together, the two of them know everything about anything published on cinema, from the most avant-garde revues and the memoirs of Jean-Paul Belmondo to the latest news, limited and rare editions, collector's items, posters, DVDs, screenplays and fantastic 1960s magazines like *Cinémonde* or *Ciné Revue.* One could easily spend hours here – or just drop in for one of the book signings.

MICHAEL WOOLWORTH PUBLICATIONS

2, rue de la Roquette, 11th, metro Bastille
Tel 01 40 21 03 41
www.michaelwoolworth.com
Open 9:30am to 6:30pm,
Saturday and Sunday by appointment

ENGRAVINGS AND ARTISTS' BOOKS

The American Michael Woolworth, a great book lover with a special interest in first editions, came to Paris on holiday and never left. He has also devoted himself to the printing and engraving of artists' books. An expert on the subject and the technology, he has been applying his unique talent and attention to detail to the job since 1988 and is sought out by artists, who are fascinated to see their works made by the hand on mechanical machines, with the incessant quest for perfection only traditional printing techniques can provide. These books are then sold to aficionados and collectors, who will also find rare editions going back to the 1980s. The huge space also makes a wonderful setting for exhibitions, poetry readings and concerts. To get there, pass through the portal of Passage du Cheval Blanc and then turn left into the Cour de Février. It's a world apart.

ODÉONS PHOTOS

73, boulevard Beaumarchais, 3rd
Metro Chemin Vert
Tel 01 48 87 74 54
Open 10:30am to 1pm and 2pm to 6pm, closed Sunday and Monday

VINTAGE CAMERA EQUIPMENT

Originally located in the Latin Quarter, this store used to be frequented by students, professors and artists. Since 2006, it has been situated on Boulevard Beaumarchais, known as "Photography Boulevard", but it is still a great place to find used equipment and spare parts, among them early bellows cameras and the legendary Leica, Kodak, Agfa, Nikon and Japanese models so popular in the 1970s. The shop is still highly appreciated by collectors and silver halide aficionados, but professionals and young photographers also visit similar stores on the same boulevard.

RETROFUTUR

55, quai de Valmy, 10th, metro République
Tel 01 48 87 88 04, www.retrofutur.fr
Open 10:30am to 8pm, Sunday noon to 7pm

HI-FI, MULTIMEDIA ACCESSORIES

RetroFutur, originally a specialist blog founded in 2008, became a bricks-and-mortar shop in 2013 with a design by the German-Danish Gesa Hansen, owner of the furniture firm The Hansen Family. The shop's four owners – Matthieu Luong Van Thi, Guillaume Bloch, Vincent Abraham and Timothée Cagniard – took over a former video showroom alongside the Canal Saint-Martin and present their products with contagious enthusiasm. Cagniard is the co-inventor of "Boite Concept" acoustic speakers. In addition to Astell & Kern portable music players, Audio-Technica headphones and British Rega turntables, aficionados will find glass Bluetooth speakers from the Swedish company People People, ceramic speakers by American designer Joey Roth, the best from French firm Elipson and some curious hi-fi revivals, such as 1980s ghetto-blasters, fabulously hacked by the French company Blaster Lab to work wirelessly. The place is a huge success, to the point that Le Bon Marché is thinking of creating a RetroFutur corner.

ROLAND BURET

6, passage Verdeau, access from rue de la Grange Batelière, 9th
Metro Grands Boulevards
Tel 01 47 70 62 99
Open 11:30am to 7pm, closed Sunday and Monday

COLLECTORS' COMICS

The shop of self-proclaimed "comics cultivator" Roland Buret, which opened in 1977, is one of the pillars of this passage, an extension of the Passage Jouffroy. Buret is the leading expert on the ninth art, a.k.a. comics, particularly those of the 20th century, less a few exceptions, with a special preference for Hergé and his Tintin. Albums in all styles and with all kinds of characters are arranged by category, of course, but there are also original drawings. Every quarter, Buret holds a sale at neighbouring auction house Drouot. Also nearby is **LE PETIT ROI** (39, passage Jouffroy, 9th, tel 01 40 22 94 60), a new bookstore selling new, used and collectible comic books, as well as a nostalgia-inspiring selection of old children's books.

RUPTURE

3, rue de la Fidélité, 10th
Metro Gare de l'Est
No phone, www.rupture.tv
Open daily 11am to 8:30pm

VINYL, CAFÉ

The retail outlet of the young label Rupture Records, founded by Alexandre Sap (formerly of Recall) and distributed by Sony Music, this shop and café was opened in collaboration with the Grand Amour Hotel, located just opposite. The sky-blue

GREAT LIBRARIES

As long ago as the Middle Ages, the Sorbonne was already keeping a record of the books it lent out. Clearly, Paris libraries are rooted in a long tradition.

BIBLIOTHÈQUE NATIONALE DE FRANCE (BNF) **François I, who threw his library open to humanists and scholars, decreed the registration of a "legal deposit" for books in 1537, thereby creating the foundations for the future royal, and later national, library. In 1720, it was moved to Rue de Richelieu. In 1996, a large part of its collections were transferred to the banks of the Seine (the Tolbiac site), to the futuristic building designed by Dominique Perrault. As with all new Paris buildings, its architecture was controversial.** Quai François Mauriac, 13th, metro Bibliothèque François Mitterrand, tel 01 53 79 59 59, www.bnf.fr, open 10am to 8pm, Sunday 1pm and 7pm, closed Monday

BIBLIOTHÈQUE FORNEY **In the late 19th century, the capital's libraries became increasingly specialized. In 1886, a Paris merchant, Samuel Aimé Forney, donated to the city his collection of works devoted to the artistic trades (ceramics, metalwork, cabinet-making, bookbinding, etc.). The municipal authorities sought a beautiful setting to house it, settling on the Hôtel des Archevêques de Sens, a jewel of 16th-century architecture right in the heart of the Marais.
In honour of the donor of the original collection, the new library was named Forney. The collection grew substantially over time and now embraces the fields of fashion, design and the graphic arts.** Hôtel de Sens, 1, rue du Figuier, 4th, metro Pont Marie, tel 01 42 78 14 60, open 1pm to 7:30pm, Wednesday and Thursday from 10am, closed Sunday and Monday

BIBLIOTHÈQUE DES ARTS DÉCORATIFS **In 1905, the Louvre began to house furniture collections in its Marsan wing, forming what would become the Musée des Arts Décoratifs. The ground floor is home to the Bibliothèque des Arts Décoratifs. The nucleus of the original collection had been gathered together a few decades earlier (in 1864) on the initiative of the Union Centrale des Beaux-Arts Appliqués. The collection now spans design, architecture, the garden arts, costume history and advertising posters, among other areas.**
111, rue de Rivoli, 1st, metro Palais-Royal–Musée du Louvre, tel 01 44 55 59 36, www.lesartsdecoratifs.fr, open 10am to 6pm, Monday and Thursday from 1pm, closed Saturday, Sunday and in August

BIBLIOTHÈQUE DE LA CITÉ DE L'ARCHITECTURE ET DU PATRIMOINE **This library occupies immaculate premises in the Palais de Chaillot. Its shelves are filled with books devoted to 20th-century architecture, with sections on town planning, landscape and design. A large number of architecture magazines from around the world can be consulted freely.** 1, place du Trocadéro, 16th, metro Trocadéro, tel 01 58 51 59 38, www.citechaillot.fr, open 11am to 7pm, Thursday until 9pm, Saturday and Sunday from 1pm, closed Monday and Tuesday, and in July and August

BIBLIOTHÈQUE ROMÉO MARTINEZ **This library at the Maison Européenne de la Photographie is named after the collector who assembled the bulk of the collection and is the library for photography lovers. This world-renowned library includes illustrated volumes and monographs published all over the world.**
Maison Européenne de la Photographie, 5-7, rue de Fourcy, 4th, metro Saint-Paul, tel 01 44 78 75 00, www.mep-fr.org. The library is currently closed for construction work but can be consulted by appointment. Write to bibliotheque@mep-fr.org

Care Bear decoration is by the artist André, and the bins contain some 1,500 vinyl records, focusing on the current musical trends. The atmosphere reminds us a bit of the record department of Le Bon Marché in 1977, except that everything there was orange. It's all generational. Before or after imbibing a coffee, juice and the obligatory gluten-free carrot cake, peruse this selection of American, Japanese and English imports, and curiosities made at a time when they dared to do anything. A few oddities have slipped in, which is a good thing. Launches of albums by Rupture artists are also held here, among them Chris Stills, Alex Pinanas, Donald Cummings (formerly of The Virgins), Mounir Troudi, Lawrence Rudd (singer of Grand National) and Canadian folksinger Alejandra Ribera.

SHAKESPEARE AND COMPANY

37, rue de la Bûcherie, 5th
Metro Cluny-La Sorbonne, Saint-Michel-Notre-Dame
Tel 01 43 25 40 90
https://shakespeareandcompany.com
Open daily 10am to 11pm

LEGENDARY ENGLISH-LANGUAGE BOOSKHOP

A single book would not be enough to tell the story of this legendary bookstore and its founder, George Whitman, who was also its soul. In fact, a book has already been written, and we are waiting for the sequel. This brilliant trove of English and American literature in Paris is a sanctuary located opposite Notre Dame; it's a phenomenal and fascinating labyrinth, a world unto itself. Once you enter, you will not want to leave. Or you will be transfigured. It has been taken over by George's daughter, Sylvia Beach Whitman, and since 2015 also has a literary café. This inspiring place, which has figured in many films and novels, and has attracted a parade of leading English-language writers and the best-known beatniks, is, paradoxically, a living Parisian monument.

SOUNDS GOOD

Puces de Saint-Ouen, Marché Dauphine, stand 28, 132, rue des Rosiers, Saint-Ouen
Metro Porte de Clignancourt
Tel 06 80 10 82 81
www.marche-dauphine.com
Open from 10am, closed Tuesday to Thursday

VINTAGE HI-FI

In 2006, Hugues Cornière was the first to specialize in vintage hi-fi in the Saint-Ouen flea market, with a stand in the Marché Dauphine. Since then, he has expanded, moving from the first floor to the ground floor. Passionate and inspiring, he is also the man behind the Carré des Disquaires and the promoter in 2011 of the first Salon du Disque de Dauphine, an event that is now held every May. He remembers having sold speakers that belonged to Jean-Luc Godard, renting the ReVox tape recorders needed for Joann Sfar's film on Serge Gainsbourg, and borrowing a huge turntable from the studios of Radio France for the film *Cloclo*. In the store, you'll find historic Elipson Chambord speakers, Teppaz record players, McIntosh amps and more. A columnist for *Rock & Folk* and author of *Objets Cultes du Rock*, Cornière was called in as an expert by the auction house Artcurial for a sale called "It's Only Rock'n'Roll", the first of its kind, held in Paris in November 2013. It all sounds good!

STUDIO HARCOURT

6, rue de Lota, 16th, metro Victor Hugo
Tel 01 42 56 67 67
www.studio-harcourt.eu
Open 9:30am to 7:30pm and by appointment, closed Saturday and Sunday

LEGENDARY PHOTO STUDIO

Since 1934, Harcourt portraits have been the passport to celebrity and even posterity for French actors. Long before the semiologist Roland Barthes declared that in France one was not an actor until photographed at Harcourt, leading film actors passed through the legendary studio, whose signed portraits were then displayed in the lobbies of major cinemas, the offices of great agents and the pages of film magazines like *Cinémonde* and *Mon Film.* From the Champs-Élysées to the studios in Boulogne and Joinville, divas, stars, idolized singers, character actors and starlets considered that a signed Harcourt portrait was just as valuable as footprints in a sidewalk in Hollywood. Even the stars of the Nouvelle Vague adhered to the tradition, both to improve their image and to be part of a pantheon that included Brigitte Bardot, Jean Gabin, Michèle Morgan, Ingrid Bergman and Danielle Darrieux. And then, just as all films must end, the curtain almost dropped on the studio. Revived in 2003, the house profited from the desire for glamour of the time and, after retouching images of Carole Bouquet, Jean Paul Gaultier, Laetitia Casta and Fanny Ardant, allowed all those who are not actors, politicians or literary or media personalities to be subjected to the magical Harcourt treatment. The studio moved from Rue Jean Goujon to the depths of the 16th arrondissement, where anyone can make an appointment for a portrait. All you have to do is let yourself be made up (Harcourt cosmetics are on sale) and pose. Some thirty images will be taken, but only one selected from a contact sheet and then retouched the Harcourt way, still a secret of the gods.

THEATRES AND CONCERT HALLS

LA COLLINE – THÉÂTRE NATIONAL

15, rue Malte-Brun, 20th
Metro Gambetta
Tel 01 44 62 52 52, www.colline.fr

CONTEMPORARY THEATRE

La Colline opened on the heights of Ménilmontant in 1988 and, while it is part of the national theatre network, the members of its troupe are independent actors. This one of the most avant-garde theatres in Paris, where one can see the performances of plays by Bertolt Brecht and Thomas Bernhard, and discover very young authors and directors. The current artistic director is author, director and actor Wajdi Mouawad.

LA COMÉDIE-FRANÇAISE

1, place Colette, 1st
Metro Palais-Royal–Musée du Louvre
Tel 01 44 58 15 15
www.comedie-francaise.fr

CLASSIC AND CONTEMPORARY THEATRE

"Le Français", as this institution is known, has been around since the end of the 17th century, descended from the very troupe directed by Molière for the pleasure of Louis XIV. The troupe moved into this theatre in 1799 and helped create the international reputation of French theatre. With over three thousand plays in its repertoire, the company, now directed by Éric Ruf, performs the great classics by Racine, Molière, Marivaux, Musset, Hugo, Shakespeare, Chekhov and Brecht, staged and acted by leading actors, who often act in films as well; examples are Denis Podalydès, Guillaume Gallienne, Didier Sandre, Dominique Blanc, Clotilde de Bayser, Danièle Lebrun and Laurent Lafitte, all *pensionnaires* or *sociétaires* of the theatre. Outside the main theatre, La Comédie-Française puts on plays at the Théâtre du Vieux Colombier

on the Left Bank, and the Studio-Théâtre in the Louvre's Galerie du Carrousel.
Other locations: THÉÂTRE DU VIEUX-COLOMBIER 21, rue du Vieux Colombier, 6th, tel 01 44 39 87 00
STUDIO-THÉÂTRE Galerie du Carrousel du Louvre, place de la Pyramide inversée, 99, rue de Rivoli, 1st, tel 01 44 58 98 58

LA SEINE MUSICALE

Île Seguin, Boulogne-Billancourt
Metro Pont de Sèvres
Tel 01 74 34 53 00
www.laseinemusicale.com

MUSIC CENTRE

This is the former site of Renault's factories, a car worker's stronghold and a symbol of union struggles from the time the company was nationalized until the dismantling of its asbestos-laden assembly lines in 1992. Luxury magnate François Pinault dreamed of building his foundation on this huge industrial wasteland, but, frustrated by bureaucratic delays, he set it up in Venice instead. The Seine Musicale opened in April 2017 with a concert by Bob Dylan. Part of architect Jean Nouvel's urbanization plan for the Île Seguin, the structure took three years to build. It was designed by Japanese architect Shigeru Ban, who has created a gigantic nest with an egg-shaped auditorium of the same size housing the concert hall, whose capacity ranges from 4,000 seated to 6,000 standing. Jean-Luc Choplin, who catapulted the Théâtre du Châtelet (currently closed for renovation) into the world of musicals, hitherto unknown in Paris, is in charge of programming. Under a huge planted roof with panoramic views, the structure is equipped with the latest technologies, including a gigantic 45-metre-high veil covered with 800 square metres of green photovoltaic panels. Whether one sees the Seine Musicale as resembling a cruise ship, a nest or an egg, one thing is sure: it is the counterpoint in the west of Paris to Jean Nouvel's Philharmonie in the north. The other cardinal points still need to be filled.

LE BAL BLOMET

33, rue Blomet, 15th, metro Volontaires
Tel 01 45 66 95 49, www.balblomet.fr

LIVE MUSIC

Far from the big brasseries of Montparnasse, closer to the Necker Hospital and the old Citroën factories, the Bal Blomet was one of the liveliest halls during the Roaring Twenties, attracting both workers and artists. Josephine Baker danced and Sidney Bechet played his clarinet on its stage. The Caribbean community filled the dance floor. Nicknamed the Bal Nègre by the poet Robert Desnos, who lived in Rue Blomet, it remained open until the late 1950s, and counted Juliette Gréco and Albert Camus among its regulars. Afterwards, it went through many permutations – café, billiard hall, Latino cabaret, jazz club – and finally closed in 2006. It reopened in March 2017 to great fanfare with its original, more politically correct name, resurrected by Guillaume Cornut, ex-trader and pianist, and redesigned by Samuel Zagury in Broadway backstage style.
On the programme, music, music and more music: jazz, classical, tango, musicals, in the form of festivals, recitals, concerts, jam sessions and talks, with special evening, late-night and morning events.
A new addition is the **HÔTEL BLOMET,** designed and decorated by Vincent Bastie and Bruno Borrione in an Art Deco building dating from 1931, a place to sleep after a concert or late-night partying.
Other location: HÔTEL EIFFEL BLOMET
78, rue Blomet, 15th, tel 01 53 68 70 00

LE GRAND REX

1, boulevard Poissonnière, 2nd
Metro Bonne Nouvelle
Tel 01 45 08 93 89
www.legrandrex.com

CINEMA, PERFORMANCES

Listed as a historic monument, the Grand Rex can hold 2,650 people at a sitting and is still the biggest cinema in Europe. Designed as a scaled-down version of New York's Radio City Music Hall, it was opened in 1932 by film producer Jacques Haïk, with a sumptuous auditorium beneath a star-studded vault rising to a height of 30 metres. Its Mediterranean decor, the work of Maurice Dufrêne, features a rainbow of light framing the proscenium arch. **LES ÉTOILES DU REX** (tel 01 45 08 93 58), behind the big screen, is a visitor attraction, offering a forty-minute tour of the world of cinema, its tricks, illusions, and special effects. Star in your own disaster movie and discover the magic of film.

PALAIS GARNIER

8, rue Scribe, 9th, metro Opéra
Tel 0 892 89 90 90
www.operadeparis.fr
Box office open 11:30am to 6:30pm, closed Sunday, no performances on Monday

OPERA, BALLET

The Palais Garnier was the result of a commission from Napoleon III, who sought to create an opera house to dazzle all Europe and provide a fitting backdrop for the public appearances of Parisian high society, when the French capital was the continent's leader in matters of taste and elegance. In 1860, the competition to design the building was won by the young architect Charles Garnier – to the astonishment of all. The current director of the Palais Garnier is Stéphane Lissner, formerly of La Scala in Milan and known for the artistic chances he takes to attract young audiences. The programme is superlative, with Philippe Jordan as musical director and star dancer Aurélie Dupont in charge of the ballet. Together with the Opéra Bastille, Garnier undertook a creative digital project in 2015 with the 3e Scène platform, for which talents from the worlds of cinema and contemporary art – among them Bertrand Bonello, Fanny Ardant, Valérie Donzelli, Mathieu Amalric and Xavier Veilhan – create radical stagings and images. **Other location:** place de la Bastille, 12th, tel 08 92 89 90 90

PHILHARMONIE DE PARIS

221, avenue Jean Jaurès, 19th
Metro Porte de la Villette
Tel 01 44 84 44 84
www.philharmoniedeparis.com

CONCERT HALL

The Philharmonie is the splendid concert hall located in the La Villette musical complex. It opened in dire straits in January 2015 against the advice of its designer, the architect Jean Nouvel, and has stirred up emotions ever since. Yet with all its strife and troubles, this new-generation concert hall immerses the listener in shifting layers of music and light, just as its designer intended. It boasts outstanding, adjustable acoustics developed by Japan's Yasuhisa Toyota and New Zealand's Sir Harold Marshall, working alongside Jean Nouvel. The hall's organic forms, the warmth of its wood panelling and – a not insignificant point – the comfort of its seating add to the appeal of this admirable architectural feat that has won over the public. The Philharmonic, a temple for all types of music – Baroque, classical, contemporary, jazz and world – has succeeded in its goal of breaking down barriers and cultivating diversity. Its Music Museum hosts two exhibitions a year, one in spring and one in autumn: from David Bowie to Pierre Boulez, from Ludwig van Beethoven to Bob Dylan, along with Jamaican music, the offerings are eclectic. It has been a successful start for the Philharmonie, which attracted 1.15 million visitors in its first year and had 600,000 spectators in 2016.

"In general, Parisians can see nothing but their city; it's as if they are unaware that France has other cities."
Abbé Grégoire, *Mémoires*, 1808

SALLE CORTOT

78, rue Cardinet, 17th
Metro Malesherbes
Tel 01 47 63 47 48
www.sallecortot.com

CLASSICAL, RECITALS

In the late 1920s, the famous pianist Alfred Cortot decided to build a concert hall for students from the École Normale de Musique in Paris he had founded a few years earlier. He commissioned the architect Auguste Perret, who promised that he would create a place that would "sound like a violin", and delivered on it far beyond expectations. The concert hall was inaugurated in 1929, offering outstanding acoustics and a very modern Art Deco design, with a reinforced concrete structure covered with gilded bronze and okume wood panels on the walls, making it a very special venue for lovers of art and music. Listed as a historic monument in 1987, the Salle Cortot holds over 160 concerts a year. The lunchtime slot is reserved for students, all of them future international performers, who perfect their repertoire here. These 12:30pm concerts, conducted by prestigious masters like Felicity Lott, José van Dam, François-René Duchâble and Michel Dalberto, take place from October to April and are free.

SALLE WAGRAM

39-41, avenue de Wagram, 17th
Metro Ternes
Tel 01 58 05 56 23
www.orchestrecolonne.fr

CLASSICAL CONCERTS

The Salle Wagram, the legendary concert hall with nearly 750 seats, has been taken over by the Eurosites group. The company lost out in the competition to run the Salle Pleyel, taken over by Fimalac holding (where classical music is now "banned" so as not to compete with the Philharmonie de Paris). But no matter. The Wagram is where Maria Callas, Duke Ellington, Louis Armstrong and Django Reinhardt once performed to full houses. After the war, the Salle Wagram was also used for boxing matches (Marcel Cerdan triumphed there), wrestling matches (Lino Ventura got his start there before becoming a movie star), fashion shows and charitable events. Now more than 200 years old, it was opened in 1812 under a different name. Rebuilt in 1865 in the opulent Second Empire style and used for balls, the building is now a classified monument. It is home to the Colonne Orchestra, Paris's oldest still-active symphony orchestra, founded by Édouard Colonne in 1873, and known for its inexpensive prices. Under the artistic direction of Laurent Petitgirard, Colonne programmes forty concerts in this hall every season. Friday and Saturday concerts are for everyone, while Sunday performances are designed to introduce young audiences to music.

ART GALLERIES

ALMINE RECH

64, rue de Turenne, 3rd
Metro Filles du Calvaire
Tel 01 45 83 71 90
www.alminerech.com
Open 11am to 7pm,
closed Sunday and Monday

CONTEMPORARY ART

With galleries in Brussels, London and New York, and over forty-five artists, Almine Rech has established itself as a major international gallery. Good reason to check out the exhibitions in this beautiful space in the Marais, where the work of many emerging artists is shown, among them Brian Calvin, Erik Lindman, Ziad Antar and Tarik Kiswanson, as well as such big names as Jeff Koons, Richard Prince, Franz West, Julian Schnabel, Alex Israel and Joel Shapiro, and historical figures like Tom Wesselmann.

APPLICAT-PRAZAN

16, rue de Seine, 6th
Metro Saint-Germain-des-Prés
Tel 01 43 25 39 24
www.applicat-prazan.com
Open 11am to 1pm and 2:30pm to 7pm,
closed Monday

MODERN ART

For lovers of the 1950s and the École de Paris, Franck Prazan's gallery is the best in Paris. A former managing director of Christie's, this singular figure goes all out to promote his painters at a number of international fairs. He knows everything there is to know about Nicolas de Staël, Jean Fautrier, Serge Poliakoff and Zao Wou-Ki. Thanks to his impressive address book, he also has a knack for finding works unknown to the general public, which he shows in his Left and Right Bank galleries. **Other location:** 14, avenue Matignon, 8th, tel 01 43 25 39 24

ARTS FACTORY

27, rue de Charonne, 11th
Metro Ledru-Rollin, Bastille
Tel 06 22 85 35 86, www.artsfactory.net
Open 12:30pm to 7:30pm,
closed Sunday and Monday

CONTEMPORARY DRAWING

The Arts Factory gallery was founded in 1996 by Effi Mild and Laurent Zorzin and is the first large-scale venue devoted to the contemporary graphic scene. It incorporates a bookshop and exhibition spaces spread across four levels, and it still has a talent scout's appetite for making known and showcasing draughtsmen, illustrators and cartoonists through exhibitions, rare books and *Dans la marge*, their famous collection of workbooks. The artists include Blanquet, Blexbolex, Jean Lecointre, Sophie Dutertre, Pierre La Police, Anne Van Der Linden, Loulou Picasso and the American Daniel Johnston, plus Amandine Urruty.

BACKSLASH GALLERY

29, rue Notre-Dame de Nazareth, 3rd
Metro Temple
Tel 09 81 39 60 01
www.backslashgallery.com
Open 11am to 7pm,
closed Sunday and Monday

INTERDISCIPLINARY

The Rue Notre-Dame de Nazareth, just steps away from the Place de la République, has undergone radical change in recent years, with new galleries, restaurants and concept stores opening all the time. Young gallerists Séverine de Volkovitch and Delphine Guillaud (both ex-Daniel Templon) have created an atmospheric loft space in a former textile workshop, showing painting, photography, sound installations, video and sculpture. They organize productive multi-disciplinary shows involving publishers, the media and artists. Occasionally they call on external commissioners, such as Mathieu Mercier and Timothée Chaillou, who are given carte blanche to make their selections.

From many exhibitions, at least ten confirmed or promising talents have emerged: Tania Mouraud, a socially and politically committed installation artist and an important figure in contemporary French art, has joined the gallery, alongside Rero, Fahamu Pecou, Boris Tellegen, Michael Zelehoski, Charlotte Charbonnel, Xavier Theunis, France Bizot and Luc Schuhmacher.

BALICE HERTLING

47, rue Ramponeau, 20th
Metro Belleville
Tel 01 40 33 47 26
www.balicehertling.com
Open 2pm to 7pm and by appointment, closed Sunday to Tuesday

INTERNATIONAL CONTEMPORARY ART

Alexander Hertling and Daniele Balice's gallery in Belleville, a neighbourhood that now shows the most cutting-edge art in Paris, offers an insight into the international scene and often the first exhibitions of those who count or who will count in the contemporary art world, among them Oscar Tuazon, Neïl Beloufa, Julie Beaufils, Morgan Courtois and Camille Blatrix, as well as historic figures like Simone Fattal. The German and Italian partners believe that "committed" art still means something and prove it with their exhibitions, some of which are entrusted to independent curators.

BERNARD DULON

10, rue Jacques Callot, 6th
Metro Saint-Germain-des-Prés
Tel 01 43 25 25 00
www.dulonbernard.fr
Open 10:30am to 1pm and 2pm to 6:30pm, closed Sunday and Monday

TRIBAL ARTS

Immersed since childhood in the world of art and stimulated by his collector parents, Bernard Dulon never envisaged being anything other than an art dealer. His enthusiasm and knowledge and his deceptively disillusioned and laidback manner make him quite a character to meet. A renowned expert in his field, he does not define himself as an initiate of African symbolism and spirituality, but rather as an art historian enamoured of beauty. The objects he has brought together in his gallery are sufficient proof of this, even if all of them are laden with meaning and bearers of messages. Such is the case with the terrifying *nkisi* fetish with nails from the Democratic Republic of the Congo, and the Kota-Obamba reliquary figure from Gabon, which is of great initiatory significance. The gallery takes part in major events like the Biennale and the annual Parcours des Mondes event held in September, which confirms the importance of Paris in the tribal arts field.

BRAME & LORENCEAU

68, boulevard Malesherbes, 8th
Metro Villiers
Tel 01 45 22 16 89, www.gbl.fr
Open 9:30am to 7pm, closed Saturday and Sunday

IMPRESSIONIST AND MODERN ART

Usually, only one painting is displayed in the window here. Visitors have to climb the steps to the first floor to discover the rest. That is the beginning of a journey into the history of French 19th- and 20th-century, with an emphasis on the Impressionist period. Indeed, you can often admire one or more works by Gustave Caillebotte, Edgar Degas and Georges Seurat, as well as by Alexander Calder, Otto Fried and Auguste Rodin. Today's gallery is the result of the merger of two galleries, founded in Paris in 1864 and located in this 500-square-metre space since 1921. The owner, François Lorenceau, is always happy to share his knowledge with visitors.

BUGADA & CARGNEL

7-9, rue de l'Équerre, 19th
Metro Belleville, Buttes Chaumont
Tel 01 42 71 72 73
www.bugadacargnel.com
Open 2pm to 7pm and by appointment,
closed Sunday and Monday

INTERNATIONAL PLATFORM

In their Belleville gallery, Frédéric Bugada and Claudia Cargnel present an ambitious programme that makes this unusual place, located in what was a garage in the 1930s, definitely worth a visit to see the work of up-and-coming artists and internationally renowned figures like Cyprien Gaillard, a past winner of the Prix Marcel Duchamp, whose work has been shown at the Centre Pompidou. Thanks to the size of the venue, he was able to stage a memorable concert here. Other artists include Wilfrid Almendra, Étienne Chambaud, Adrien Missika, Julian Charrière, Théo Mercier and Alfredo Aceto, alongside painters Claire Tabouret and Iris van Dongen. And then there is Julio Le Parc; when a gallery represents a "modern" artist like him, who is already part of art history, it is always a sign that it is gaining in importance.

CAHIERS D'ART

14, rue du Dragon, 6th
Metro Saint-Germain-des-Prés
Tel 01 45 48 76 73, www.cahiersdart.fr
Open 11am to 7pm,
closed Sunday and Monday

PUBLICATIONS, CONTEMPORARY ART

Now owned by Swedish collector Staffan Ahrenberg, Cahiers d'Art has been reborn in both the spirit and the letter of the institution that presided over the cultural world from 1926 to 1960. During this time Cahiers d'Art comprised a magazine, a publishing house and a famous gallery. Its founder, art critic Christian Zervos (1889–1970), managed to bring together the great names in modern art (Braque, Léger, Ernst, Giacometti) with the most famous authors of the period (Éluard, Char, Hemingway, Beckett). In 1932, Zervos started a project on Picasso, working together with the artist to create a reference publication containing more than 16,000 paintings and drawings reproduced over 6,000 pages in 33 volumes. Known as "the Zervos", this work was out of print for many years, but has now been reissued in French and English editions. Collectors, art dealers, researchers and students can also come here to consult the *Cahiers d'art* archives, the magazine's invaluable general index. Retracing the gallery's prestigious past, the space exhibits work by internationally influential artists such as Martin Kippenberger, Inge Mahn, Thomas Schütte, Hiroshi Sugimoto, Rosemarie Trockel, Ellsworth Kelly and Gabriel Orozco. These monographic exhibitions are accompanied by the publication of a portfolio of each artist's work, including a numbered collector's edition containing an original work of art. A second location, opposite the company's historic home, sells limited editions and prints. It is also possible to consult the vast archives by appointment.

CHANTAL CROUSEL

10, rue Charlot, 3rd
Metro Filles du Calvaire
Tel 01 42 77 38 87, www.crousel.com
Open 11am to 1pm and 2pm to 7pm,
closed Sunday and Monday

CONTEMPORARY ART

Since 1980 Chantal Crousel has been introducing her Parisian visitors to artists of very different backgrounds, each taking a highly individual look at society. Previously based near the Centre Pompidou, she has now moved to the Marais, home to most of the city's best contemporary art galleries. The artists she represents include Gabriel Orozco, Melik Ohanian, Anri Sala, Willem de Rooij and Thomas Hirschhorn. Crousel, who was joined several years ago by her son Niklas Svennung, still focuses on the cutting-edge contemporary art scene, showing such artists as David Douard, Wade Guyton, Seth Price, Clément

Rodzielski and Danh Võ, successfully balancing historical rigour and the most contemporary issues. Her gallery also has a fine bookshop, with 300 books on the artists it represents, and also offers a selection of limited editions and prints.

DENISE RENÉ

196, boulevard Saint-Germain, 7th
Metro Rue du Bac
Tel 01 42 22 77 57, www.deniserene.fr
Open 10am to 1pm and 2pm to 7pm,
closed Sunday and Monday

ABSTRACTION

In 1944, Denise René opened Paris's first gallery devoted to abstract art on the Rue La Boétie. Advised by Victor Vasarely, she was soon specializing in geometric and kinetic art. Mondrian, Hans Arp, Jésus-Rafael Soto, François Morellet, Carlos Cruz-Diez – all the masters in the field were shown in her gallery. Sadly, Denise René, to whom the Centre Pompidou paid tribute in 2001, died in July 2012. But although she will be sorely missed, the gallery lives on as a vital space for perpetuating and furthering her work. A second gallery, opened twenty years ago, presents young kinetic and sound artists like the Belgian group LAb [au] and Elias Crespin. **Other location:**
22, rue Charlot, 3rd, tel 01 48 87 73 94

ÉDITIONS DILECTA

49, rue Notre-Dame-de-Nazareth, 3rd
Metro Temple, Strasbourg-Saint-Denis
Tel 01 43 40 28 10
www.editions-dilecta.com
Open 2am to 7pm, closed Sunday

BOOKS AND MULTIPLES

This space is so big that you can use it to cross from one street to another, Rue Vertbois. Inside, you won't find large-format works, but editions of books – which are the speciality of the house and are highly appreciated by artists – increasingly accompanied by artists' books. There is something for every taste and every budget, from the micro-sculptures of Emmanuel Lagarrigue to a brooch designed by Yves Klein, and especially works that often show a great sense of humour.

GALERIE CAMERA OBSCURA

268, boulevard Raspail, 14th
Metro Denfert-Rochereau
Tel 01 45 45 67 08
www.galeriecameraobscura.fr
Open noon to 7pm, Saturday from 11am,
closed Sunday and Monday

PHOTOGRAPHY

Didier Brousse spent a long time in the darkroom, where he made prints of extremely high quality, a true passion for him. In 2003, he opened a gallery across from the Fondation Cartier, with relatively classical but highly aesthetic choices. Since the beginning the most famous photographers in the business trusted him as they had known him for many years – for example, Willy Ronis, Marc Riboud, Lucien Hervé, Paolo Roversi, Sarah Moon, Bernard Plossu and Masao Yamamoto. The younger generation also makes an appearance, notably Denis Dailleux, Jungjin Lee and Patrick Taberna, as well as the Finnish Pentti Sammallahti, whose magnificent photography so entranced Cartier-Bresson that he bought one of Sammallahti's works here. Unconditional fans of silver prints, daguerrotypes and inkjet prints will think they've died and gone to heaven.

GALERIE CRÈVECŒUR

9, rue des Cascades, 20th
Metro Ménilmontant, Gambetta
Tel 09 54 57 31 26
www.galeriecrevecoeur.com
Open 11am to 7pm,
closed Sunday to Tuesday

CONTEMPORARY ART

Run by Alix Dionot-Morani and Axel Dibie, Crèvecoeur has gradually become one of the galleries to follow, and even manages to get its collectors to go to this small street in the 20th arrondissement. Thanks to the quality of the work, no one

SPOTLIGHT

AN OPEN BOOK: THE BEST BOOKSTORES IN PARIS

TRAVEL The whole world can be found at the **LIBRAIRIE DES VOYAGEURS DU MONDE**, with guides, essays and novels selected by experts. 55, rue Sainte-Anne, 2nd, Metro Pyramides, Quatre Septembre, tel 01 42 86 17 38, www.voyageursdumonde.com

LATE-NIGHT BROWSING Literature, biographies, essays, crime novels and new books can be perused every day at **L'ÉCUME DES PAGES**. 174, boulevard Saint-Germain, 6th, metro Saint-Germain-des-Prés, tel 01 45 48 54 48, www.ecumedespages.com

OLDEST Just opposite the Comédie-Française, **DELAMAIN**, opened in 1770, belongs to Gallimard. The oldest still-operating bookstore in Paris attracts a discerning clientele. 155, rue Saint-Honoré, 1st, metro Palais-Royal–Musée du Louvre, tel 01 42 61 48 78, www.librairie-delamain.com

FLAVOURSOME Everything published about gastronomy, food, chefs, recipes, trends, etc., can be found at the **LIBRAIRIE GOURMANDE**. 96, rue Montmartre, 2nd, metro Sentier, tel 01 43 54 37 27, www.librairiegourmande.fr

ACADEMIC Reopened in 2016, the **LIBRAIRIE DES PUF** (social sciences, *Que Sais-Je?* series, etc.) has taken a step towards the future by installing the Espresso Book Machine®, which can print one of 5,000 titles on demand at a rate of 110 pages per minute. 60, rue Monsieur le Prince, 6th, metro Odéon, RER Luxembourg, www.puf.com

HIGHEST ALTITUDE The well-named bookshop **LE MONTE-EN-L'AIR** (aerialist) on the Ménilmontant hill offers a wide selection of books on illustration, graphics and more, and holds book signings. Also has a gallery, café and terrace. 2, rue de la Mare, 20th, metro Ménilmontant, tel 01 40 33 04 54, https://montenlair.wordpress.com

COMMUNITY-ORIENTED Located in the Goutte d'Or neighbourhood, **LA RÉGULIÈRE** has an urban atmosphere with its café and workshops. 43, rue Myrha, 18th, metro Château Rouge, tel 09 83 43 40 69

VERY PARISIAN With its display windows and bins under the glass roof of the Galerie Vivienne, the **LIBRAIRIE JOUSSEAUME**, a literary bookshop opened in 1826, is full of gems about Paris not found elsewhere. 45, 46 and 47, galerie Vivienne, 2nd, metro Bourse, tel 01 42 96 06 24, www.librairie-jousseaume.fr

INTELLECTUAL Founded in 1929 by Louis Tschann and Marie-Louise Castex, the **TSCHANN** bookshop has been frequented by all the denizens of Montparnasse and many more, all lovers of good literature. 125, boulevard du Montparnasse, 6th, metro Vavin, tel 01 43 20 04 68, www.tschann.fr

POLISH The **LIBRAIRIE POLONAISE** is an amazing historical vestige that has survived since 1833. A national treasure well worth a visit. 123, boulevard Saint-Germain, 6th, metro Odéon, Mabillon, tel 01 43 26 04 42, www.librairiepolonaise.com

RARITIES Antique and rare books, first editions and illustrated volumes unearthed by expert rare-book dealer Claude Blaizot can be found in the **LIBRAIRIE AUGUSTE BLAIZOT**, a family-run shop founded in 1840. 164, rue du Faubourg Saint-Honoré, 8th, metro Saint-Philippe-du-Roule, tel 01 43 59 36 58, www.librairieblaizot.com

NAUGHTY Nicole Canet's gallery **AU BONHEUR DU JOUR** has an erotica-curiosa section that is unique in Paris. 1, rue Chabanais, 2nd, metro Quatre Septembre, Pyramides, tel 01 42 90 58 64, www.aubonheurdujour.net

is disappointed by a visit to this large space with several rooms, which also makes it possible to show videos. Many artists have been represented by the gallery since the beginning of their careers, including Xavier Antin, Julien Carreyn, Florian & Michael Quistrebert, Erica Baum, Shana Moulton, Jorge Pedro Nuñez and Louise Sartor. The programming is astute, with just the right touch of eccentricity. The owners are also among the founders of Paris Internationale, the only art fair that has succeeded in acting as a real complement to FIAC.

GALERIE HOUG

22, rue Saint-Claude, 3rd
Metro Saint-Sébastien-Froissart
Tel 01 42 78 91 71, www.galeriehoug.com
Open 10am to 7pm, Saturday 11am to 1pm and 3pm to 7pm, and by appointment, closed Sunday and Monday

CONTEMPORARY ART

After working for ten years with his father, Olivier, a well-known gallery owner in Lyon, Romain Houg opened his own gallery in Paris in late 2014. Now located on the attractive Rue Saint-Claude in the former space of Anne Barrault (who has moved to a larger gallery on Rue des Archives), he attracts a young generation of collectors looking to discover new talent. In his gallery, they will find such artists as Jérôme Allavena, Marjolijn de Wit, Sun Cunming, Maxime Lamarche, Maxime Duveau and Ivan Fayard. They will also see exhibitions by such guest curators as Marie de Brugerolle, who put together "Le Petit A de O", a show featuring the rediscovered work of Olivier Mosset. The friendly, knowledgeable and enthusiastic discussions that take place there are also highly appreciated.

GALERIE KRAEMER

43, rue de Monceau, 8th, metro Monceau
Tel 01 45 63 31 23, www.kraemer.fr
Open 10am to 7pm, closed Sunday

ANTIQUES AND FURNITURE

This exceptional gallery offers visitors a journey to 18th-century France, enhanced by the inexhaustible knowledge of the Kraemer family, which has run it since it was founded in 1875 by Lucien Kraemer, who came to Paris because his native Alsace was occupied by Prussia. The Kraemers have passed on the torch from father to son and daughter, with each generation showing the enterprising spirit that now inspires the new generation, which has set out to conquer China. Furniture that has passed through their hands now belongs to the collections of the world's greatest museums, including the Louvre, Versailles, Fontainebleau, the Met and the Getty Museum. Visitors are always warmly welcomed, and if one of the Kraemers is available, he or she will be happy to tell the fascinating story of the house.

GALERIE RUEVISCONTI

17-19, rue Visconti, 6th
Metro Saint-Germain-des-Prés
Tel 01 44 41 19 60
www.ruevisconti-editions.com
Open 2pm to 7pm, closed Sunday and Monday

PUBLISHER, CONTEMPORARY ART

Balzac's former printing shop, which was also Delacroix's studio for a time and then a bookstore, has been transformed by publisher Jean-Noël Flammarion and set designer Olivier Etcheverry into an unusual publishing house and art gallery. Since 2010, it has hosted a number of projects, many of them offbeat, in collaboration with big-name artists like Claude Lévêque, Bertrand Lavier, Tania Mouraud and Andres Serrano. Memorable events have included "La Chambre d'Huile", for which Per Barclay spread oil over the floor; works by Peter Buggenhout made from waste; and, more recently, work by Berger&Berger, the architects who designed the extension for the Collection Lambert in Avignon. In an appealing minimalist setting, they showed works with a strong narrative background that combined architecture, design, sculpture and the visual arts.

GALERIE THOMAS BERNARD – CORTEX ATHLETICO

12, rue du Grenier Saint-Lazare, 3rd
Metro Rambuteau, Étienne Marcel
Tel 01 75 50 42 65
www.galeriethomasbernard.com
Open 10:30am to 7pm and by appointment, closed Sunday and Monday

CONTEMPORARY ART

Thomas Bernard was an instant hit in Bordeaux when his association-run gallery opened. A few years later, one of his artists – Andreas Fogarasi – won the Lion d'Or prize at the Venice Biennale. Buoyed up by his success, Bernard opened a gallery space near the Pompidou Centre in Paris in 2013, before moving into a new space in 2015. Cortex Athletico was quick to find its place on the circuit of must-see contemporary art galleries. Thomas Bernard is drawn to artists with a critical take on history, society, modernism and the environment. Here you can discover the work of the Uruguyan Luis Camnitzer, the Spaniard Angel Vergara, Frenchman Nicolas Descottes and the profoundly conceptual work of Frenchman Benoît Maire. For Bernard, it is important to maintain activity, flow and constant exchange. He also holds short exhibitions in foreign cities, sometimes in partnership with other organizations.

IN SITU – FABIENNE LECLERC

14, boulevard de la Chapelle, 18th
Metro La Chapelle
Tel 01 53 79 06 12, www.insituparis.fr
Open 11am to 7pm and by appointment, closed Sunday to Wednesday

YOUNG ARTISTS

Fabienne Leclerc regularly moves his gallery – he's been in the 6th arrondissement and the Marais – in search of new experiences. His latest base, a 450-square-metre space opened in January 2017, is sure to please collectors and new fans of the gallery with its architecture and the surprises it offers. The space has been left a bit rough to preserve its authenticity, and alternates large spaces with smaller areas that are perfect for showing videos. Upstairs is a showroom with a view over the tracks of the Gare de l'Est, an impressive sight from this viewpoint. The challenge of attracting collectors to a new neighbourhood seems to have been met, given the number of visitors who linger and, once there, like to stay and see everything. Faced with a growing number of proposals, Fabienne Leclerc has developed a new way of working and reaffirms her difference, while giving herself the opportunity to present excellent exhibitions in the large spaces. In 2019, the gallery plans to open another branch in Romainville (Seine-Saint-Denis), not far from the Fondation Fiminco, which has just settled there.

KAMEL MENNOUR

47, rue Saint-André des Arts, 6th
Metro Odéon
Tel 01 56 24 03 63, www.kamelmennour.fr
Open 11am to 7pm, closed Sunday and Monday

CONTEMPORARY ART

This gallery, originally exclusively focused on photography, showing work by Nobuyoshi Araki, Stephen Shore, Larry Clark and Martin Parr, has gradually embraced other media. Today it has two addresses in Saint-Germain-des-Prés and

a more recent one at 18 Avenue Matignon (8th), together with an outpost in London, opened in 2017. Kamel Mennour has become a formidable businessman but is still just as charming with everyone he meets. He has attracted emerging talents who have become highly acclaimed artists, among them Mohamed Bourouissa, Camille Henrot and Lili Reynaud-Dewar. From Ann Veronica Janssens to the Chapman Brothers, Martin Parr and Christodoulos Panayiotou, the eclecticism of the artists is always accompanied by the enthusiasm of the gallery owner.
See website for other locations

KARSTEN GREVE

5, rue Debelleyme, 3rd
Metro Saint-Sébastien-Froissart
Tel 01 42 77 19 37
www.galerie-karsten-greve.com
Open 10am to 7pm, closed Sunday and Monday

MODERN AND CONTEMPORARY ART

This famous German dealer, who also has galleries in Milan and St Moritz, moved into this Marais town house in 1990 and set about showing his heroes from the international scene of the last sixty years, among them Jean Dubuffet, Lucio Fontana and Jannis Kounellis. He has recently showcased the still-lives of Giorgio Morandi, the fragile sculptures of Fausto Melotti, the works on paper of Pierrette Bloch, the photographs of John Chamberlain and the recent works of Pierre Soulages, as well as Josef Albers, Louise Bourgeois and Cy Twombly.

LAURENT GODIN

36bis, rue Eugène Oudiné, 13th
Metro Olympiades
Tel 01 42 71 10 66, www.laurentgodin.com
Open 11am to 7pm and by appointment, closed Sunday to Wednesday

CONTEMPORARY ART

This Marais gallery owner has been well known for many years – Laurent Godin celebrated ten years in the business in 2016 – but his space in the 13th arrondissement, offering his artists a huge space with many nooks and crannies, is less well known. In early 2016, a stunning exhibition by Wang Du demonstrated the full scope of his work. Claude Closky and Delphine Coindet were also given this opportunity.
Other location: 5, rue du Grenier-Saint-Lazare, 3rd, tel 01 42 71 10 66

LOEVENBRUCK

6, rue Jacques Callot, 6th
Metro Odéon
Tel 01 53 10 85 68
www.loevenbruck.com
Open 11am to 7pm, closed Sunday and Monday

IRREVERENT CONTEMPORARY ART

Opened in 2001, the Loevenbruck gallery has long promoted French artists, notably Bruno Peinado, Virginie Barré, Morgane Tschiember, Édouard Levé, Dewar & Gicquel and Arnaud Labelle-Rojoux. In recent years, however, it has turned towards more historic artists like Michel Parmentier and Jean Dupuy, and rediscovered older works by Alina Szapocznikow, as Hervé Loevenbruck began to represent artists' estates, a widespread practice, especially in the United States. It often gives a gallery financial stability, enabling it to support more emerging artists, in this case including the already admired Thomas Teurlai.

MARIAN GOODMAN

79, rue du Temple, 3rd
Metro Rambuteau
Tel 01 48 04 70 52
www.mariangoodman.com
Open 11am to 7pm, closed Sunday and Monday

ESTABLISHED AND NEW ARTISTS

One of the most respected gallery owners in New York, Marian Goodman opened a space in the Marais in 1999, where she exhibits her stable of nearly fifty international artists, including Eija-Liisa Ahtila, Yang Fudong, John Baldessari,

Maurizio Cattelan, Gabriel Orozco and Lawrence Weiner. She has also opened a second space covering 100-square-metres at no. 66 (tel 01 42 77 57 44), not far from the original gallery, to show other works by these artists. It also has a shop selling books, foreign catalogues and editions of prints. In the 1960s, Marian Goodman founded Multiples and started publishing Sol LeWitt, Man Ray, Andy Warhol, Robert Rauschenberg and Claes Oldenburg, a business she left behind when she opened her New York gallery. These gems crop up now and then in the Marais, along with products made for various exhibitions, including cups and T-shirts for John Baldessari's show and tote bags for Annette Messager's exhibition.

MARTEL

17, rue Martel, 10th
Metro Château d'Eau
Tel 01 42 46 35 09
www.galeriemartel.fr
Open 2:30pm to 7pm,
closed Sunday and Monday

COMICS, CARTOONISTS

In the land of Asterix- and Tintin-ophiles, at the gallery of Rina Zavagli-Mattotti, wife of the cartoonist Lorenzo Mattotti, no introductions are needed for the ex-underground graphic novelists and stars Art Spiegelman (whose show at the Bibliothèque Nationale de France she curated), Charles Burns, Aline and Robert Crumb, Jean-Philippe Delhomme, Gary Panter, Javier Mariscal and the promising Éric Lambé.

MARTINE ABOUCAYA

5, rue Sainte Anastase, 3rd
Metro Saint-Sébastien-Froissart
Tel 01 42 76 92 75
www.martineaboucaya.com
Open noon to 8pm,
closed Sunday and Monday

ART, CINEMA, ARCHITECTURE, MUSIC

Martine Aboucaya worked for fourteen years for Yvon Lambert. Her preferred styles? Minimalist and Conceptual. She offers generous, wise support both to confirmed artists and young talents whose work is often linked to literature and cinema. It was Aboucaya who organized the artistic revivals of British artist Anthony McCall, German Hans-Peter Feldmann and Belgian-American Peter Downsbrough. As a space for experimental art, the gallery features the groundbreaking work of Brazilians Angela Detanico and Rafael Lain which encompasses the worlds of both graphic art and semiology.

MAX HERTZLER

57, rue du Temple, 3rd
Metro Hôtel de Ville, Rambuteau
Tel 01 57 40 60 80
www.maxhetzler.com
Open noon to 7pm, closed Sunday
and Monday

CONTEMPORARY ART

The arrival of this heavyweight from the German art world on the Parisian scene in 2014 was an encouraging sign for contemporary art in France. Since then, this dealer, who opened a gallery in Stuttgart in 1974 and another in Cologne and still has two galleries in Berlin, has presented artists who had previously not been seen much in France, such as Ai Weiwei, Michel Majerus, Glenn Brown and Bridget Riley.

MFC-MICHÈLE DIDIER

66, rue Notre-Dame-de-Nazareth, 3rd
Metro Temple, Strasbourg-Saint-Denis
Tel 01 71 27 34 41
www.micheledidier.com
Open noon to 7pm,
closed Sunday and Monday

ARTISTS' BOOKS, INSTALLATIONS

MFC-Michèle Didier, a publishing house founded in 1987, has an office in Brussels and a gallery in the Haut Marais. The exhibition space showcases original works by contemporary artists, including artists' books, prints, installations and multiples. The exhibitions and in-situ installations incorporating printed material are well worth checking out. Michèle Didier is also well worth chatting with, as she really knows her artists, who include the Americans Allan McCollum and Allen Ruppersberg, as well as Christian Marclay, Mathieu Mercier and Saâdane Afif.

MICHEL REIN

42, rue de Turenne, 3rd
Metro Saint-Paul
Tel 01 42 72 68 13
www.michelrein.com
Open 11am to 7pm, closed Sunday and Monday

CONTEMPORARY POLITICAL ART

Michel Rein offers an activist view of art. For Rein, "political" is a word that covers a lot. The installations, paintings, videos and photos he shows all have to have a bearing on the world. Here, "socially meaningful" is not an empty slogan. Didier Faustino's "misarchitectures" and Jordi Colomer's Situationist visions of the pampas are formal embodiments of the dialectic between reality and utopia. The gallery is also resolutely non-ageist, showing Saâdane Afif's musical sculptures and Raphaël Zarka's rhombuses alongside the large, magnificent abstract canvases of Jean-Pierre Bertrand and those of Armand Jalut, who is helping to revive French painting. The latest discoveries include the captivating photographs of LaToya Ruby Frazier.

NATHALIE OBADIA

18, rue du Bourg Tibourg, 4th
Metro Saint-Paul
Tel 01 53 01 99 76
www.galerie-obadia.com
Open 11am to 7pm, closed Sunday

CONTEMPORARY ART

For twenty years now the energetic Nathalie Obadia, known for having launched the careers of artists like Valérie Favre, Carole Benzaken (Marcel-Duchamp prize in 2004) and Pascal Pinaud in the early 2000s, continues to extend her circle of artists. They include Fabrice Hyber, Valérie Belin, Sarkis and Agnès Varda. In addition, she is proud to exhibit the work of abstract artist Martin Barré, who died in 1993. A passionate reader who keeps a beady eye on everything that is going on in the world, Nathalie Obadia has a knack of uncovering captivating non-Western artists such as Rina Banerjee, the Chinese Conceptual artist Xu Zhen with his MadeIn Company and the Egyptian photographer Youssef Nabil. **Other location:** 3 rue du Cloître Saint-Merri, 4th, tel 01 42 74 67 68

PERROTIN

76, rue de Turenne and
10, impasse Saint-Claude, 3rd
Metro Saint-Sébastien-Froissart
Tel 01 42 16 79 79
www.galerieperrotin.com
Open 11am to 7pm, closed Sunday and Monday

CONTEMPORARY ART

Emmanuel Perrotin moved his gallery in 2006 to a townhouse in the Marais, overhauled by architects Manser and Bourgeois. Two separate spaces are connected by a passageway, so visitors won't get lost. One is in the right wing of the townhouse and the second is in the Impasse Saint-Claude. Representing Takashi Murakami, Sophie Calle, Xavier Veilhan, Terry Richardson, Maurizio Cattelan, Bernard Frize and Jean-Michel Othoniel, Perrotin has a proven feel for trends on the contemporary art market. With galleries in Hong Kong, New York, Seoul and now Tokyo, Perrotin has further reinforced the gallery's position on the international market. In the courtyard of no. 76, a bookshop offers selected fine art volumes and objects by Othoniel, Calle and Murakami, as well as exclusive collaborative projects with *Toilet Paper* magazine by Maurizio Cattelan and Pierpaolo Ferrari.

PRAZ-DELAVALLADE

5, rue des Haudriettes, 3rd
Metro Rambuteau
Tel 01 45 86 20 00
www.praz-delavallade.com
Open 11am to 7pm,
closed Sunday and Monday

CONTEMPORARY ART

Californian contemporary art would be much less well known in Paris if it weren't for Bruno Delavallade and René-Julien Praz. This gallery, opened in Paris in 1989, has now taken the plunge and opened a second one in LA. In Paris, we can see the work of Angelenos Jim Shaw, Matthew Brandt, Matthew Chambers and Analia Saban, in addition to other American stars like the great Marnie Weber. The gallery also presents abstract art by such artists as the Swiss Philippe Decrauzat and the Frenchman Thomas Fougeirol, and installations by Pierre Ardouvin and drawings by Fabien Mérelle. The truculent gallerists, who have a handsome space in the Marais, have formulated a trenchant analysis of the art market.

SOLO GALERIE

11, rue des Arquebusiers, 3rd
Metro Saint-Sébastien-Froissart
Tel 01 42 77 05 44
www.solo-galerie.com
Open 1pm to 7pm and by appointment,
closed Sunday and Monday

WORKS BY ARCHITECTS

Christian Bourdais, a real-estate entrepreneur, and Eva Albarran, a contemporary art producer, opened this gallery to show art by both new-generation architects and Pritzker Prize winners. The exhibitions are staged with the same sophisticated, minimalist aesthetic of nearby galleries, and involve micro-architecture/sculptures, photography, mixed media, light works and installations. Moving away from traditional architecture exhibitions, the gallery holds shows offering a formal experience of the work in the way a contemporary art gallery would. The gallery's artists include Berger & Berger, Anne Holtrop, Bijoy Jain and Junya Ishigami, more or less a young international generation whose work is often on the edge of visual art or even criticism. One particularly notable project was Solo Houses (www.solo-houses.com), featuring architectural practice OFFICE Kersten Geers David van Severen and Christian Bourdais.

THADDAEUS ROPAC

7, rue Debelleyme, 3rd
Metro Saint-Sébastien-Froissart
Tel 01 42 72 99 00, www.ropac.net
Open 10am to 7pm, closed Sunday
and Monday

PRESTIGIOUS INTERNATIONAL ARTISTS

This well-known Austrian dealer, who also has a gallery in Salzburg, moved into an old workshop in the Marais in 1991. Since then, he's been showing – and publishing – a selection of work by leading international artists such as Georg Baselitz, Gilbert & George, Anselm Kiefer, Mimmo Paladino and Andy Warhol, but he also likes to surprise by exploring new horizons and hotbeds, such as the young scene in Iran, and inviting celebrities like Isabelle Huppert and Peter Marino to become curators of shows by photographer Robert Mapplethorpe. Not far from the Hermès and Chanel ateliers located in Pantin, the gallery has opened a magnificent space in a listed former boiler-making factory (69, avenue du Général Leclerc, Pantin, tel 01 55 89 01 10). Its 2,000 square metres

"To err is human, to loaf is Parisian."
Victor Hugo, *Les Misérables*, 1862

of exhibition rooms are ideal for showing monumental works of art. The gallery has recently held incredible shows of the work of James Rosenquist and Tony Cragg, as well as group exhibitions devoted to the international scene that have plenty of room to spread out here.

TRIPLE V

5, rue du Mail, 2nd, metro Sentier
Tel 01 45 84 08 36, www.triple-v.fr
Open 10am to 7pm, closed Sunday and Monday

CONTEMPORARY ART

Triple V now has two galleries, but it is the one opened in March 2016 that we recommend, first of all for its size, more than impressive for a contemporary art gallery in the centre of Paris. Then for its director, Vincent Pécoil, also an art critic; he is no hard-sell dealer but a fine connoisseur of today's art scene, which he can talk about for hours. Finally, for the artists, including David Malek, Servane Mary, Laurent Montaron, Blair Thurman and Pierre Vadi, a happy mix of American and French artists.
Other location: 24, rue Louise Weiss, 13th, tel 01 45 84 08 36

UNTIL THEN

Tel 01 85 58 40 22
www.untilthen.fr

EXPERIMENTAL NEW ART

This gallery, run by Olivier Belot and Mélanie Meffrer Rondeau, was located for a few years in Saint-Ouen, where it attracted many collectors and curators, as well as flea market fans not necessarily used to visiting contemporary art galleries. They have now been forced to leave the 500-square-metre space where they showed such artists as Robert Barry, Jonathan Monk, Joan Jonas, Jill Magid and Douglas Gordon. Their new, smaller space, located in the 10th arrondissement, not far from the Place de la République (check the website for the address), will force them to once again reinvent themselves.

VALLOIS

33 and 36, rue de Seine, 6th
Metro Saint-Germain-des-Prés
Tel 01 46 34 61 07
www.galerie-vallois.com
Open 10:30am to 1pm and 2pm to 7pm, closed Sunday

YOUNG ARTISTS

Opened in 1990, the Vallois gallery puts on often joyous displays featuring various themes. The most historical one is Nouveau Réalisme, with such artists as Jacques Villeglé, Niki de Saint Phalle and Jean Tinguely. The most eccentric works can be seen in shows on Los Angeles artists, including Paul McCarthy, Richard Jackson, Martin Kersels and Adam Janes – although the sculptures of the Frenchman Gilles Barbier and the Brazilian Henrique Oliveira can also be pretty surprising. The gallery has a strong penchant for sculpture as well as drawing. Its Project Room shows work by young artists who are not necessarily part of its stable of artists, such as Theo Michael and Lamarche-Ovize.

MUSEUMS AND CULTURAL CENTRES

CENTQUATRE (104)

5, rue Curial, 19th, metro Riquet
Tel 01 53 35 50 00, www.104.fr
Open noon to 7pm, Saturday and Sunday from 11am, closed Monday

MULTI-DISCIPLINARY

The Centquatre is a unique venue for innovation in the city's cultural scene. What makes it especially interesting is its commitment to nurturing diversity and breaking down barriers. In this hangar-like complex of monumental proportions, previously the doleful preserve of the municipal funeral services, hundreds of young people practise drama, dance, hip-hop and circus arts in the central concourse. The likes of actor Jacques Gamblin, choreographer Maguy Marin and director Jean-Michel Ribes rehearse or improvise alongside them. The programme of events is exuberant and eclectic, and includes exhibitions, performances and concerts. In **LA MAISON DES PETITS**, designed by Matali Crasset, children can play while their parents do *qigong, tao yin* (a.k.a. *do in*) or relaxation exercises. The place is also an incubator for start-ups, and houses the impressive **EMMAÜS DÉFI** thrift shop along with the welcoming **CAFÉ CACHÉ** (www.cafecache.fr) and the **GRAND CENTRAL** restaurant, an industrial-style loft where arts professionals and artists cross paths.

CENTRE NATIONAL D'ART ET DE CULTURE GEORGES POMPIDOU – MUSÉE NATIONAL D'ART MODERNE

Place Georges Pompidou, 4th
Metro Rambuteau
Tel 01 44 78 12 33
www.centrepompidou.fr
Open 11am to 10pm, Thursday until 11pm, closed Tuesday

MODERN AND CONTEMPORARY ART

Opened in 1977 and renovated in 2000 by Renzo Piano, one of the building's original architects, this huge cultural Erector-set of a building is home to Europe's largest collection of modern and contemporary art, a public library, temporary exhibition galleries, children's areas, a shop selling select design objects and a car park. The building may have been one of the first to launch the style that came to be known as "High-Tech", but it has aged gracefully into a classic. The centre celebrated its fortieth anniversary in 2017, a triumph considering how scorned its inside-out architecture was to begin with. Inside, the permanent collection is rehung every two years. Each visit is a learning experience and a delight, as we watch the evolution of art during the 20th century, a composite of schools, individuals and theories, enriching, reacting to, rejecting and succeeding each other. Good news: Picasso's *La Coiffeuse,* stolen in 2001, has been found and restored. Don't miss the design shop, which offers a coherent range of beautiful and useful objects, with a brilliant selection of lighting fixtures.

"Paradoxically, the freedom of Paris is associated with a persistent belief that nothing ever changes. Paris, they say, is the city that changes least. After an absence of twenty or thirty years, one still recognizes it." **Marguerite Duras, *Outside: Selected Writings*, 1981**

Every year, from October to January, the four contenders for the famous Marcel Duchamp prize are "exposed" to the public. And the rooftop restaurant **GEORGES** (www.restaurantgeorgesparis.com) offers an unforgettable view of Paris.

CITÉ DE L'ARCHITECTURE ET DU PATRIMOINE

Palais de Chaillot, 1, place du Trocadéro et du 11 Novembre, 16th
Metro Trocadéro
Tel 01 58 51 52 00, www.citechaillot.fr
Open 11am to 7pm, Thursday until 9pm, closed Tuesday

HISTORIC FRENCH MONUMENTS

The museum showcasing Paris's architectural heritage is housed in the left wing of the Palais de Chaillot. On the ground floor is a fascinating collection of plaster casts of various architectural features, from entire church portals and funerary statues to gargoyles and decorative reliefs. Upstairs, innumerable scale models and blueprints evoke the buildings that have marked more recent architecture. The upper rooms are devoted to reproductions of ceiling-high medieval and Renaissance murals that line a maze of empty spaces. Of particular interest is a life-size recreation of an apartment from Le Corbusier's Cité Radieuse in Marseille. The Galerie d'Actualités hosts free temporary exhibitions exploring contemporary subjects accompagnied by excellent catalogues.

DOC

26, rue du Docteur Potain, 19th
Metro Télégraphe
www.doc.work
Information and exhibition dates on the website or the Facebook page; appointments can be made via contact@doc.work

CONTEMPORARY ART

This associative art space is the latest place in Paris to discover emerging artists, and the most sophisticated collectors are already flocking there. It was originally an artists' squat in a former technical secondary school. Now supported by the Paris mayor's office, it has space for some thirty artists, including tutelary figures like Pierre Ardouvin and Philippe Decrauzat, along with others in residence. It is run by artists like César Chevalier and Rafaela Lopez. On some evenings, workshops follow the openings held in a large room and welcome international artists for enlightening discussions on the creative process. Plays, film screenings, performances, debates and technical workshops are also held there. Or you can just stop by to admire the garden.

FONDATION CARTIER POUR L'ART CONTEMPORAIN

261, boulevard Raspail, 14th
Metro Denfert-Rochereau, Raspail
Tel 01 42 18 56 50
www.fondation.cartier.com
Open 11am to 8pm, Tuesday until 10pm, closed Monday

CONTEMPORARY ART

Time has been good to the Cartier Foundation, which celebrated its 30th anniversary in 2014. It is one of the oldest corporate foundations and a shining example of a successful cultural centre. Multiple forms of expression have been honoured in this spacious edifice designed by Jean Nouvel on the former site of the American Center. Programming over the years has been an eclectic bonanza, ranging from cartoons by Moebius to the photos of Alair Gomes and sculptures by Ron Mueck. The cedar of Lebanon that Chateaubriand planted in the garden still reaches for the sky as it did in the early days of Romanticism. Following the uplifting "AutoPhoto" show, the foundation will hold an exhibition on the Japanese architect Junya Ishigami through February 2018, along with a tribute to the Malian photographer Malick Sidibé, whose first solo show was held there in 1995.

FONDATION JÉRÔME SEYDOUX-PATHÉ

73, avenue des Gobelins, 13th
Metro Gobelins
Tel 01 83 79 18 96
www.fondation-jeromeseydoux-pathe.com
Open 1pm to 7pm, Friday 2pm to 8pm, Saturday from 11:30am, closed Sunday and Monday

FILM HERITAGE

The facade of this theatre, which dates back to 1869, is an allegory of Tragedy and Comedy. Its creator was none other than a young sculptor who had graduated from the school of fine art: Auguste Rodin. He gave his name to the playhouse which became a cinema in 1934. Since 2014, the former Rodin – subsequently the Gaumont – has been the headquarters of the Fondation Jérôme Seydoux-Pathé, established in an incredible 2,200-square-metre building designed by Renzo Piano and housing projection rooms, exhibition spaces and a resource centre. Aside from the Pathé archives, dating back to 1896, the Foundation holds many collections of posters, films and costumes – the entire memory, in fact, of French cinema. Clapperboard, take one!

FONDATION LE CORBUSIER – MAISONS LA ROCHE ET JEANNERET

10, square du Docteur Blanche, 16th
Metro Jasmin
Tel 01 42 88 41 53
www.fondationlecorbusier.fr
Le Corbusier's atelier apartment
24, rue Nungesser-et-Coli, 16th
Tel 01 42 88 75 72
Open 10am to 1pm and 1:30pm to 5pm

MODERN ARCHITECTURE

A place of pilgrimage for Modernists, these two interconnected villas were designed in 1923 by the architect Le Corbusier for his brother Albert Jeanneret and the Swiss banker Raoul La Roche, who collected Cubist paintings. Since 1968 it has been home to the Foundation created by Le Corbusier himself to ensure that his archives would not be broken up, and the centre also holds temporary exhibitions. Nearby you can visit the apartment where Le Corbusier lived on the top two floors of the Molitor building between 1933 and 1965. Don't miss the terrace perched on the roof.

FONDATION LOUIS VUITTON

8, avenue du Mahatma Gandhi, 16th
Metro Les Sablons
Tel 01 40 69 96 00
www.fondationlouisvuitton.fr
Open noon to 7pm, Friday until 9pm (11pm on the first Friday of the month), Saturday and Sunday 11am to 8pm, closed Tuesday

CONTEMPORARY ART

On the edge of the Bois de Boulogne, between Neuilly and Paris, in the Jardin d'Acclimatation that kids have loved since the time of Napoleon III, a glass building cleaves the air and seems to take flight in a bid for freedom. This earthbound ship, flying the Louis Vuitton flag, is the work of the unconventional American architect Frank Gehry, winner of the Pritzker Prize, whose edifices are strewn across the world.

Bernard Arnault, president of the LVMH group and the person behind this unrivalled building, has offered Parisians an outstanding venue dedicated to the emblematic art and culture of the 21st century. In choosing Frank Gehry, Bernard Arnault opted for boldness, emotion and exhilaration. The architect has once again demonstrated his mastery of technology and the joy he takes in shattering forms, stretching the limits of harmony and bending building materials to obey the dictates of his unbridled imagination. Twelve superimposed sails composed of 3,600 glass panels swell out, unfurl and soar up to conquer the heavens, giving the building its unique impetus and energy. Around it, the Jardin d'Acclimatation invites visitors to rediscover their inner child and enjoy the Rousseauesque pleasures of strolling outdoors, enjoying centuries-old trees, ancient pines and young lime trees, rocks, waterfalls and other water works. The building leaps up in the middle of a meadow without warning – at first concealed, then suddenly revealed. It is both near-invisible with its glass structure and strikingly modern. Frank Gehry seems to say, "Come on in! Give free rein to your dreams!" Visitors are greeted by a work created specially for the building: *Inside the Horizon* by Danish-Icelandic artist Olafur Eliasson. Its forty-three columns create an infinite play of reflections and a calming sensory experience. Further inside, the building houses a 350-seat auditorium and eleven galleries designed to display the permanent collections, including one devoted to Gerhard Richter which features fourteen stunning works. There's also a bookstore, a café, a gourmet restaurant called **LE FRANK**, and huge panoramic terraces where you can view Paris from angles unlike any before. The Foundation focuses on contemporary art, which it juxtaposes with modern art. The outstanding permanent collection features, among others, works by Maurizio Cattelan, Tacita Dean, Alberto Giacometti, Annette Messager, Nam June Paik, Giuseppe Penone and Sigmar Polke. Further highlights include specially commissioned works by artists such as Ellsworth Kelly, Adrián Villar Rojas and Daniel Buren. Buren had applied an array of coloured filters in a chequered pattern to the glass sails, creating an in situ installation called Observatory of Light. In 2016–17, the exhibition devoted to the Shchukin Collection was one of the most popular in Paris, attracting over 1.2 million visitors.

GAÎTÉ LYRIQUE

3 bis, rue Papin, 3rd
Metro Réaumur-Sébastopol
Tel 01 53 01 52 00, www.gaite-lyrique.net
Open 2pm to 8pm, Sunday until 6pm, closed Monday

DIGITAL REVOLUTION

The Ville de Paris's centre for digital arts and contemporary music is located in the famous Gaîté Lyrique theatre, once devoted to operetta and where Offenbach reigned supreme. Transformed by the architect Manuelle Gautrand, this relic of *opéra bouffe* is now devoted to new forms of expression under the stewardship of Marc Dondey. On the programme are exhibitions like "Arrrgh! Monstres de Mode" ("Arrrgh! Fashion Monsters"), presentations, screenings and video games based on new technologies.

INSTITUT DU MONDE ARABE

1, rue des Fossés Saint-Bernard, 5th
Metro Sully-Morland
Tel 01 40 51 38 38, www.imarabe.org
Open 10am to 6pm, Saturday and Sunday until 7pm, closed Monday

ARAB CULTURES

The spectacular south facade of this unique building designed by Jean Nouvel and Architecture-Studio is made up of 240 high-tech *mashrabiyas* fitted with slats that can be opened, closed and adjusted at all times of the day depending on light conditions outside, thus creating a play of light within the building. The IMA's collections are displayed over four floors comprising around 2,400 square metres, and feature 380 pieces which also include loans from the Arab world and French institutions. In an attempt to attract the younger generation, today the IMA is involved in many disciplines, including contemporary art, graphic novels, theatre, dance, film festivals, music events where hip-hop meets techno and jazz with influences from the Arab world. Plus there are numerous colloquia and events held jointly with major foreign and French institutions.

JEU DE PAUME

1, place de la Concorde, 8th
Metro Concorde
Tel 01 47 03 12 50, www.jeudepaume.org
Open 11am to 7pm, Tuesday until 9pm, closed Monday

PHOTOGRAPHY

Since 2004, the focus of the Jeu de Paume has been on photography and images in general (cinema, video, installation). This superb building between the Jardins des Tuileries and the Place de la Concorde dates from 1862 and has been restored in minimalist style by architect Antoine Stinco. It is a dynamic venue that organizes exhibitions, conferences, seminars and screenings devoted to rising young talents as well as established artists. In recent years, the Jeu de Paume has organized exhibitions of work by Garry Winogrand, Germaine Krull, André Kertész, Philippe Halsman and Erwin Blumenfeld. In 2018, the programme includes retrospectives of Turkish photographer Ali Kazma and German photographer Albert Renger-Patzsch.

LA MAISON ROUGE

Fondation Antoine de Galbert,
10, boulevard de la Bastille, 12th
Metro Bastille, Quai de la Rapée
Tel 01 40 01 08 81
www.lamaisonrouge.org
Open 11am to 7pm, Thursday until 9pm, closed Tuesday

CONTEMPORARY ART CENTRE

Only a few months remain to visit the Maison Rouge, an exhibition space created by Antoine de Galbert, who has officially announced its closure in October 2018. A great collector, this former gallerist turned a disused industrial site into an art centre (with reception spaces designed by Jean-Michel Alberta) in 2004. His aim was to promote contemporary art through artists and collectors who are off the beaten track. The exhibitions were – and will continue to be for a short time – always visual shocks. Unfortunately, things change…

LE BAL

6, impasse de la Défense, 18th
Metro Place de Clichy
Tel 01 44 70 75 50, www.le-bal.fr
Open Wednesday noon to 9pm, Thursday until 10pm, Friday until 8pm, Saturday 11am to 8pm and Sunday 11am to 7pm, closed Monday and Tuesday

PHOTOJOURNALISM

This huge, all-white space where photos and books are exhibited is located in the up-and-coming neighbourhood around the Place de Clichy, behind the Brasserie Wepler. The building was originally a dance hall during the Roaring Twenties and then after the war, a betting shop. It was bought by the Ville de Paris following a proposal by the Association des Amis de Magnum Photos, whose president is photographer Raymond Depardon. It can be seen as an attempt to restore some of the lustre Paris had in the 1970s and 1980s, when it was still the capital of photojournalism. Walker Evans, Jeff Wall, Eugène Atget and Gilles Peress take pride of place here.

SPOTLIGHT

SMALL MUSEUMS

The city of Paris boasts an abundance of small museums, from writers' houses to artists' studios. A walk around each district will reveal lots of treasures.

MAISON DE VICTOR HUGO **The Hôtel de Rohan-Guéménée, where Victor Hugo lived from 1832 to 1848 on the second floor with his family, was turned into a museum in 1903. It was here that Hugo wrote *Marie Tudor, Ruy Blas,* and the majority of *Les Misérables*.** 6, place des Vosges, 4th, metro Saint-Paul, tel 01 42 72 10 16, www.maisonsvictorhugo.paris.fr, open 10am to 6pm, closed Monday

MUSÉE BOURDELLE **This studio-residence, which houses the works of Rodin's pupil, Antoine Bourdelle, is a real haven of peace. Here you'll find 3,000 sculptures, 4,000 drawings and watercolours, 150 paintings and pastels, and much more. A wing designed by architect Christian de Portzamparc hosts exhibitions of contemporary sculpture.** 18, rue Antoine Bourdelle, 15th, metro Montparnasse-Bienvenüe, tel 01 49 54 73 73, www.bourdelle.paris.fr, open 10am to 6pm, closed Monday

MUSÉE COGNACQ-JAY **The Hôtel Donon, a rare example of a late 16th-century Paris residence, is home to the art collection of Ernest Cognacq and Marie-Louise Jäy, connoisseurs of the 18th century.** 8, rue Elzévir, 3rd, metro Saint-Paul, tel 01 40 27 07 21, www.museecognacqjay.paris.fr, open 10am to 6pm, closed Monday

MUSÉE NATIONAL EUGÈNE DELACROIX **Painter Eugène Delacroix once said: "The view of my little garden and the cheerful appearance of my studio always make me happy." Since 1954 this state-run museum has displayed masterpieces such as *Mary Magdalen in the Wilderness* and *The Education of the Virgin*, as well as engravings by this great Romantic artist.** 6, rue de Furstemberg, 6th, metro Saint-Germain-des-Prés, tel 01 44 41 86 50, www.musee-delacroix.fr, open 9:30am to 5:30pm, closed Tuesday

MUSÉE DE LA VIE ROMANTIQUE **Originally the home of the painter Ary Scheffer, this handsome house in the Nouvelle Athènes neighbourhood became a meeting place for Parisian intellectuals and artists in 1830. It was sold to the French state in 1956 and turned into a branch of the Musée Carnavalet. It was renamed Musée de la Vie Romantique in 1987. It offers full immersion in the world of that time, still haunted by the spirit of George Sand.** 16, rue Chaptal, 9th, metro Blanche, tel 01 55 31 95 67, www.vie-romantique.paris.fr, open 10am to 6pm, closed Monday

MUSÉE ZADKINE **A shrine to the artistic community of Montparnasse, this museum has recently been completely overhauled. A Post-Cubist sculptor of Russian origin, Ossip Zadkine worked here between 1928 and 1967. The garden is a delight, and in the entrance hall a samovar provides visitors with a welcoming cup of tea.** 100 bis, rue d'Assas, 6th, metro Vavin, tel 01 55 42 77 20, www.zadkine.paris.fr, open 10am to 6pm, closed Monday and some holidays

MUSÉE DU PARFUM FRAGONARD **Designed by architect François Muracciole, with exhibition design by the agency Arter, the museum is located in a former velodrome and covers three thousand years of the history of perfume as well as the story of the brand and its production secrets. The display cases hold over 300 rare objects: bottles, kohl jars, unguents and more.** 3-5, square de l'Opéra Louis Jouvet, 9th, metro Opéra, tel 01 40 06 10 09, www.nouveaumuseefragonard.com, open 9am to 6pm, closed Sunday

The exhibitions, film screenings, performances and talks focus on both the classics and the latest developments. You can brunch at the Bal Café on scones, pancakes, bacon and eggs, sweet-potato gratin with sage, and black pudding terrine.

LES ARTS DÉCORATIFS

107, rue de Rivoli, 1st
Metro Palais-Royal–Musée du Louvre
Tel 01 44 55 57 50
www.lesartsdecoratifs.fr
Open 11am to 6pm, until 9pm some Thursdays, closed Monday

DESIGN, FASHION, ADVERTISING

The museum of decorative arts is located in the Marsan wing of the Louvre palace and houses collections of decorative arts, design, fashion, textiles, advertisements and graphic art that stretch from the Middle Ages to the modern day. Some of these works are presented in the settings of period rooms whose decors have been recreated. The most intimate of these recreations is no doubt Jeanne Lanvin's bedroom and bathroom, both the work of Armand-Albert Rateau. The new director, Olivier Gabet, is particularly keen to showcase the richness of the older collections. Following exhibitions on the Bauhaus and the designer Roger Tallon, the museum will present "Christian Dior, Couturier du Rêve" until 7 January 2018. The restaurant **LOULOU** (www.loulou-paris.com), decorated by Joseph Dirand, offers various dining rooms and a huge terrace. The **107RIVOLI** gift and bookshop (tel 01 42 60 64 95) is managed by the dynamic Arteum company, which has also been entrusted with the management of the shops of the Musée de l'Armée, the Musée Carnavalet and the Paris catacombs.

MAISON EUROPÉENNE DE LA PHOTOGRAPHIE

5-7, rue de Fourcy, 4th, metro Saint-Paul
Tel 01 44 78 75 00, www.mep-fr.org
Open 11am to 7:45pm, closed Monday and Tuesday

PHOTOGRAPHY

All the greats, from Raymond Depardon and Robert Frank to Sebastião Salgado and Martin Parr, can be found here, in thematic or solo shows of works from the museum's permanent collections. The multiplicity of individual spaces, the combinations of artists and the variety of formats and points of view set up an interesting interaction among the works presented, facilitating comparison, confirming affinities and divergences. This is prime territory for the photography critic, whether professional or amateur. Make a detour to the excellent little café. Not to be missed: from November 2017 to late January 2018, "Claude Mollard", "Chengdu et la photographie" and "Marlene Dietrich".

MUSÉE CERNUSCHI

7, avenue Vélasquez, 8th
Metro Monceau
Tel 01 53 96 21 50
www.cernuschi.paris.fr
Open 10am to 6pm, closed Monday

ASIAN ART

A wonderful sanctuary, this is France's second-largest museum of Asian arts, with the fifth-largest collection of Chinese art in Europe. A gigantic, bronze, 18th-century Japanese Buddha forms the centrepiece. Besides enjoying the many splendours here, you can meditate on the life of Henri Cernuschi, an Italian banker, globetrotter and art collector who set off in 1871 to tour the world with the art critic Théodore Duret. He returned home two years later, his trunks filled with a fantastic collection of artworks, and commissioned the Dutch architect William Bouwens van der Boijen to build him this town house near the Parc Monceau.

MUSÉE D'ART ET D'HISTOIRE DU JUDAÏSME

71, rue du Temple, 3rd
Metro Rambuteau, Hôtel de Ville
Tel 01 53 01 86 60, www.mahj.org
Open 11am to 6pm, Saturday and Sunday from 10am, closed Monday

JEWISH HISTORY

Dating from the 17th century and boasting a garden designed by André Le Nôtre, the former town house of the Duc de Saint-Aignan became a museum of Jewish art and history in 1998. The original collection of religious objects and documentary material was assembled in 1948 by the Musée d'Art Juif de Paris and has been supplemented by loans from the Musée National du Moyen Âge, the Musée Carnavalet and various Paris synagogues. These collections trace the history of the Jewish community, essentially in France, viewed chronologically and according to theme. They offer a clear overview of the religious rites and diverse local traditions of the diaspora. Paintings, sculptures, objects in gold and silver, costumes and scale models illustrate the social, religious and artistic heritage of a community for which Scripture is a source of both identity and aesthetics.

MUSÉE D'ART MODERNE DE LA VILLE DE PARIS

11, avenue du Président Wilson, 16th
Metro Iéna
Tel 01 53 67 40 00
www.mam.paris.fr
Open 10am to 6pm, Thursday until 10pm for exhibitions, closed Monday

MODERN AND CONTEMPORARY ART

The Ville de Paris's very own museum of modern art was created back in 1961 in a wing of the Palais de Tokyo (originally built for the World's Fair of 1937). It houses a fine collection of modern art, much of which was given to the city by private donors, including the art dealer Ambroise Vollard. There are works by Braque, Léger, van Dongen and Picasso, among others. Modern art goes hand in hand with cutting-edge contemporary art here (Alexander Rodchenko, Bridget Riley, Sonia Delaunay, photography in Düsseldorf). The museum pursues its avant-garde vocation through its ARC (Animation-Recherche-Confrontation) department, established in 1966.

MUSÉE DE L'HISTOIRE DE L'IMMIGRATION PALAIS DE LA PORTE DORÉE

293, avenue Daumesnil, 12th
Metro Porte Dorée
Tel 01 53 59 58 60
www.histoire-immigration.fr
Open 10am to 5:30pm, Saturday and Sunday until 7pm, closed Monday

HISTORY OF IMMIGRATION

Paris's most beautiful Art Deco monument, built by Albert Laprade for the 1931 Paris Colonial Exhibition with outstanding reliefs by Alfred Auguste Janniot, is today home to the Musée de l'Histoire de l'immigration. It's the main French heritage project aiming to highlight the contributions immigrants have made to French culture, in an attempt to build social cohesion and better community relations. Paris's ambition is to bestow upon second- or third-generation immigrants a feeling of legitimacy and belonging to their country. One French person in four has at least one immigrant parent or grandparent. The story began in 1820 with the arrival of the Spanish, the Belgians, the Kabyles (Berber Algerians), the Poles and the Italians to take part in France's industrial boom. The permanent exhibition, "Repères", comprises the original "new gallery of donations". The museum also organizes outstanding temporary exhibitions, as well as an extraordinary photographic collection. Finally, the museum is home to other little-known treasures. At each end of the main hall, two magnificent oval salons feature furniture by Jacques-Émile Ruhlmann (in one) and Eugène Printz (in the other), both important Art Deco designers. On the ground floor, don't miss the **AQUARIUM TROPICAL** (www.aquarium-portedoree.fr), built in 1931 by Marshal Hubert Lyautey using seawater imported from Normandy on special trains. The aquarium's magical setting features 5,000 examples of 300 species. The garden has been replanted with 130 plant varieties.

MUSÉE DE L'HOMME

17, place du Trocadéro, 16th
Metro Trocadéro
Tel 01 44 05 72 72
www.museedelhomme.fr
Open 10am to 6pm, closed Tuesday

ANTHROPOLOGICAL SCIENCES

The Moorish-style Trocadéro Palace, located on the Chaillot Hill, part of the Exposition Universelle site, was designed in 1878 by architect Gabriel Davioud in the eclectic style of the period. Fifty-eight years later, the building no longer conformed to the reigning architectural tastes, and for the Exposition Universelle of 1937 it was partially torn down, camouflaged and renovated. Under the direction of architect Jacques Carlu, the monumental Palais de Chaillot, an icon of 1930s architecture, emerged, facing the Seine and the Eiffel Tower. Today, it houses four institutions: the Musée de la Marine, the Cité de l'Architecture et du Patrimoine, the Théâtre National de Chaillot and, in the Passy wing, the Musée de l'Homme, which reopened on 17 October 2015 after a six-year renovation, enabling the public to once again see its fabulous collections, with no fewer than 700,000 objects. This 21st-century museum defines itself as a home for science and society, interactivity and knowledge sharing. It aims to answer such essential questions as who are we, where we come from, and where we are going. The ambitious collections and events are magnificently presented in the museum's bright, flexible spaces, from the Gallery of Humans and the Balcony of Science to the auditorium, library and Café Lucy. This laboratory-museum makes anthropology, ethnology and prehistory more accessible, linking the imagination to the latest science in a contemporary setting, where glass, stainless steel and wood play with volumes and empty and full spaces, a wonderful setting for spectacular new curiosity cabinets. The **CAFÉ DE L'HOMME** (www.cafedelhomme.com), with the 1930s style of the interiors by Gilles & Boissier, is a fashionable spot on the Paris food scene. The 300-square-metre terrace, where you can just have a drink in the afternoon, has a beautiful view of the Eiffel Tower.

MUSÉE DE L'ORANGERIE

Jardin des Tuileries, 1st, metro Tuileries
Tel 01 44 77 80 07
www.musee-orangerie.fr
Open 9am to 6pm, closed Tuesday

ART AND TECHNOLOGY

This museum is world famous for housing Claude Monet's *Water Lilies*, eight compositions made up of twenty-two panels, donated to the nation by the artist after the Armistice of 1918. Sadly, however, the works weren't hung until 1927 – five months after the artist's death. The 144 other paintings on display are from the collection of art dealer Paul Guillaume.

MUSÉE D'ORSAY

62, rue de Lille, (entrance at 1, rue de la Légion d'Honneur), 7th
Metro Solferino
Tel 01 40 49 48 14, www.musee-orsay.fr
Open 9:30am to 6pm, Thursday until 9:45pm, closed Monday

19TH-CENTURY ART

The Orsay railway station, abandoned in the 1930s, was long threatened with demolition before being transformed into a museum of 19th-century art. It now houses 1,850 works of art in an area covering 7,200 square metres. The result conforms to the original purpose of the museum, namely to show Western art dating from 1848 to 1914, from Realism to Fauvism, and including academic art and

Symbolism. The museum is home to the world's largest collection of Impressionist works, which is continually augmented by donations and an energetic acquisitions policy, including paintings, furniture and objets d'art (in 2016, the museum received the Hays donation, with more than 600 works, including many by the Nabis). If hunger strikes, try the **RESTAURANT DU MUSÉE D'ORSAY** open on Thursday night, with its Belle Époque decor and menu by chef Yann Landureau, or the **CAFÉ CAMPANA**, with its exuberant design.

MUSÉE DU LOUVRE

34, quai du Louvre, 1st
Metro Palais-Royal–Musée du Louvre
Tel 01 40 20 53 17
www.louvre.fr
Open 9am to 6pm, Wednesday and Friday until 9:45pm, closed Tuesday

INSTITUTION, FINE ARTS

Cézanne spent hours here, as did Matisse; all the great painters frequented this temple of the arts and of taste to admire and study the Old Masters and absorb some of their genius. The Louvre, the largest building in Europe open to the public, welcomes ten million visitors per year. After two years of work, which was completed in July 2016, the reception area has been reorganized to facilitate access and restore serenity to the Hall Napoléon. A new space in the Pavillon de l'Horloge tells the story of the palace, shows the diversity of the works displayed in it and maps out various routes for visitors. The museum's major concern today is to improve the presentation of its collections and get them out of the storerooms and back into the light of day. Examples are the rooms devoted to the 18th century, designed by decorator Jacques Garcia, which alternate reconstituted period rooms with display cases filled with masterpieces. The Islamic art collection, one of the finest in the world, is now on show in the Visconti courtyard under an undulating golden-mesh roof. Some of the exhibitions planned for 2018 include "Drawing in the Open Air: Variations on Drawing from Nature in the First Half of the 19th Century", "François I and Dutch Art" and "Power Plays", an analysis of art and political power.

MUSÉE DU QUAI BRANLY – JACQUES CHIRAC

37, quai Branly and
222, rue de l'Université, 7th
RER Pont de l'Alma
Tel 01 56 61 70 00, www.quaibranly.fr
Open 11am to 7pm, Thursday to Saturday until 9pm, closed Monday

AFRICA, ASIA, OCEANIA, AMERICAS

Architect Jean Nouvel was much criticized for this ambitious building for the complex layout and less-than-academic presentations. Yet the establishment, which celebrated its tenth birthday in 2016, has created something unusual: a universal museum that encourages dialogue and exchanges between cultures. The works on show are especially fascinating. Visitors encounter, among others, Aztec, Aborigine, Dogon, Ifugao, Tolai, Bamiléké and Haida sculptures. Two new spaces have been opened amidst the permanent collections to present installations and the photography and graphic arts collections. Upstairs, unusual bean-shaped rooms host temporary exhibitions. The whole building is traversed from top to bottom by a cylindrical glass tower containing 9,700 tribal musical instruments. Like many tribal buildings, the museum is built on stilts. The administrative offices nestle behind a "green wall" by the French botanist Patrick Blanc, featuring a rich assortment of plants. The "exotic" gardens designed by Gilles Clément feature winding stone pathways, a waterfall with a bed of glass pebbles and a "treasure trail" of large stone insects and seashells.
At night, everything is illuminated thanks to lighting by Yann Kersalé. The gift shop, bookstore and café are invariably packed, and the fifth-floor restaurant **LES OMBRES** (www.lesombres-restaurant.com), where reservations are required, boasts a roof

terrace dominated at night by the silhouette of the Eiffel Tower, while the café and the shop, designed by Projectiles and opened in March 2017, are packed.

MUSÉE GUIMET

6, place d'Iéna, 16th, Panthéon Bouddhique at 19, avenue d'Iéna, metro Iéna
Tel 01 56 52 54 33, www.guimet.fr
Open 1am to 6pm, closed Tuesday

ASIAN ARTS

Lyon-based industrialist Émile Guimet was an obsessive art collector. He brought back some 300 paintings and 600 sculptures from his travels in China and Cambodia, and assembled them into a museum of religions, which opened in Lyon in 1879 and moved ten years later to Paris. Designed and built by architect Charles Terrier, the museum, with its trademark rotunda, was enriched in 1928 by the addition of the Khmer art collection from the former museum of Indochina at Trocadéro. The Musée Guimet was completely renovated, modernized and reorganized between 1996 and 2000 by architects Henri and Bruno Gaudin, and is the leading museum of Asian art in Europe. In a neighbouring mansion, a garden and Japanese tearoom offer an experience of complete escapism.

MUSÉE JACQUEMART-ANDRÉ

158, boulevard Haussmann, 8th
Metro Miromesnil, Saint-Philippe-du-Roule
Tel 01 45 62 11 59
www.musee-jacquemart-andre.com
Open daily 10am to 6pm, Monday and Saturday during exhibitions until 8:30pm

PRIVATE COLLECTION

The Jacquemart-André is the home of a collection built up over the years by portraitist Nélie Jacquemart and her husband Édouard André, a banker. Both loved filling their Paris home with fine works of art: Dutch and Flemish painting in the library, French works in the study, Italian in Nélie's atelier, English portraits in the smoking room, and, above the staircase, a Tiepolo fresco from a villa near Venice. Taken together, it is breathtaking. The collection and the luxurious mansion that houses it were donated to the Institut de France in 1912. Since that time, little has changed, so the museum bears witness not only to the timeless grandeur of artistic genius. Don't miss the exhibition "Les Impressionnistes de la collection Ordrupgaard", which ends on 22 January 2018. Don't miss the **CAFÉ JACQUEMART-ANDRÉ** with its exquisite setting. Housed in the André couple's former dining room, it boasts a ceiling fresco by Tiepolo and is ideal for teatime thanks to the excellent pastries from Stohrer. In fine weather, lunch can be taken on the terrace with a lovely stone railing overlooking the courtyard.

MUSÉE MARMOTTAN-MONET

2, rue Louis Boilly, 16th, metro La Muette
Tel 01 44 96 50 33, www.marmottan.fr
Open 10am to 9pm, Thursday until 8pm, closed Monday

IMPRESSIONIST PAINTING

This town house was once home to the Marmottans, a family of coal-mining industrialists and art collectors. Following the bequest of 120 of Monet's works by the painter's son, Michel, it became the museum of Impressionist works in 1966. It houses the world's largest collection of paintings by Monet, including the celebrated *Impression: Sunrise.* Stolen in 1985 and found five years later in a Corsican sheep shed, the painting had an unusual existence and gave its name to the world's most popular art movement. The museum also displays collections of decorative art going back to the First Empire, Paul Marmottan's favourite period.

MUSÉE NATIONAL GUSTAVE MOREAU

14, rue de la Rochefoucauld, 9th
Metro Saint-Georges
Tel 01 48 74 38 50, www.musee-moreau.fr
Open 10am to 12:45pm and 2pm to 5:15pm, Friday, Saturday and Sunday nonstop, closed Tuesday

SYMBOLIST PAINTING

At the age of sixteen André Breton visited the studio residence of Gustave Moreau, the great Symbolist painter and fine arts teacher to Matisse and Rouault, which Moreau had bequeathed to the French state. The aesthetic impact on the future Surrealist guru was so great that he claimed his visit "had influenced forever my idea of love". He said he dreamed of "breaking into it at night". He had doubtless been impressed by Moreau's own romantic gesture: on his deathbed Moreau decided to burn all his correspondence with Alexandrine Dureux, the only woman he had loved in his entire life. After a year of renovations, the museum, a paean to Symbolism, reopened in 2015. During his lifetime Moreau decided to convert his house into a museum to prevent the collection of his own paintings from being broken up. The renovation process recreated the museum in its original image. What is striking is the sheer number of paintings, photos and sketches of the house itself: 25,000 works are on show here, including 15,000 by Moreau himself. This amazing mass of paintings, photos and drawings is a delight. This fantastic collection of paintings and photos is supplemented by watercolours and some 4,000 drawings. And the most spectacular sight is the spiral staircase leading to the studios. In the basement, a space allows students to consult 10,000 sketches and 3,000 photos and engravings in order to trace the origins of this unique artist's paintings.

MUSÉE NATIONAL PICASSO

5, rue de Thorigny, 3rd
Metro Saint-Sébastien-Froissart
Tel 01 85 56 00 36, www.musee-picasso.fr
Open 10:30am to 6pm, Saturday and Sunday from 9:30am, closed Monday

20TH-CENTURY PAINTING

The refurbishment of the interiors of the Hôtel Salé, one of the most beautiful mansions in the Marais, has been particularly successful. Architect Jean-François Bodin doubled the exhibition area by opening up attic space and reclaiming rooms previously devoted to storage, offices or workshops. Two staircases, featuring stripes of iridescent aluminium, lead in one direction to the café, in another to the garden. Furniture and light-fittings are by Diego Giacometti. The overall effect is beautiful, elegant and cheerful. The public flock here to see the world's most important collection of Picasso's work, the product, among other things, of two priceless donations, first by Picasso's heirs granted to the French state in 1979, and second by his last wife Jacqueline Roque in 1990. The permanent displays offer a tour of almost 400 works displayed according to form or theme. In charge is Laurent Le Bon, former director of the Centre Pompidou in Metz and curator of the Jeff Koons and Takashi Murakami exhibitions at the Château de Versailles, who brings with him a unique, somewhat provocative approach, and great ambitions for the entire Picasso project. For example he's proposing to take a fresh look at the underrated paintings of the 1970s, and to shine a light on Picasso's work as a writer and as a curator of mini-exhibitions in his studio. Laurent Le Bon's other big idea is to open the Picasso Museum to the world and augment the programme by including contemporary art. The museum has announced it will be mounting no fewer than nine temporary exhibitions every year.

THE IMAGINARY MUSEUM

A selection of works reflecting the artistic richness and diversity of Paris that would make great additions to your own private museum.

NIJINSKY (1912), a plaster sculpture by Auguste Rodin at the Musée Rodin. The Russian dancer and choreographer is captured just as he is about to leap into the air. www.musee-rodin.fr

CLAUDE RENOIR IN A CLOWN COSTUME (1909), a full-length portrait of the painter's third child. Oil on canvas by Auguste Renoir, Musée de l'Orangerie. www.musee-orangerie.fr

STARRY NIGHT (1888), a fantastical night vision of the Rhône River in Arles. Oil on canvas by Vincent Van Gogh, Musée d'Orsay. www.musee-orsay.fr

LE TALISMAN, L'AVEN AU BOIS D'AMOUR (1888), a small gem by Paul Sérusier and a key work in the Nabis movement. www.musee-orsay.fr

L'ENFANT PRODIGUE (ca.1890), oil on canvas, by Gustave Moreau, Musée Gustave Moreau. www.musee-moreau.fr

THE CHEAT WITH THE ACE OF DIAMOND (c. 1636–38), one of the rare diurnal scenes of this master of chiaroscuro. Oil on canvas by Georges de La Tour, Musée du Louvre. www.louvre.fr

BULL'S HEAD (1942), bicycle handlebars attached to a leather bicycle seat form the animal's head. Sculpture by Pablo Picasso, Musée National Picasso Paris. www.musee-picasso.fr

THE UNFINISHED DANCE (1931–33), oil on canvas by Henri Matisse, found during an inventory of the artist's estate in 1992 and today in the Musée d'Art Moderne de la Ville de Paris. www.mam.paris.fr

CELESTRIAL MUSICIAN PLAYING THE PIPA (pre-480 AD), small sandstone relief, Northern Wei Dynasty, Shanxi Province, China, Musée Cernuschi. www.cernuschi.paris.fr

PAIR OF JAPANESE SCREENS WITH SIX PANELS, "FANS FLOATING ON THE RIVER" (Edo period, 1603–1868), anonymous, pigment and gold-leaf on paper. www.guimet.fr

MUSICIANS, SOUVENIR OF SIDNEY BECHET (1953), oil on canvas by Nicolas de Staël, Centre National d'Art et de Culture Georges Pompidou, Musée National d'Art Moderne. www.centrepompidou.fr/en/the-centre-pompidou

MUSÉE NISSIM DE CAMONDO

63, rue de Monceau, 8th
Metro Monceau
Tel 01 53 89 06 50
www.lesartsdecoratifs.fr
Open 10am to 5:30pm,
closed Monday and Tuesday

DECORATIVE ARTS

Built by architect René Sergent in the early 20th century in the style of the Petit Trianon at Versailles, on the edge of the chic Parc Monceau, this mansion-museum is home to an extraordinary collection of 18th-century paintings, furniture, porcelain, silver- and goldwork and tapestries. It was bequeathed in 1935 to the Union Centrale des Arts Décoratifs by Count Moïse de Camondo, born in Constantinople into a Sephardic Jewish family of bankers, in memory of his son, Nissim, shot down during the First World War. As renovations continue, this incredible museum reveals more and more treasures. Nissim de Camondo's apartment has been reopened, as have the kitchens, however not the garage where Camondo once kept his Voisin, Talbot and Bugatti cars (the storerooms are unfortunately not open to the public). The small **CAMONDO** café and restaurant (61 bis, rue de Monceau, 8th, tel 01 45 63 40 40) is not only charming and elegant, but also has a miraculous shady, flower-filled garden.

MUSÉE RODIN

77, rue de Varenne, 7th, metro Varenne
Tel 01 44 18 61 10
www.musee-rodin.fr
Open 10am to 5:45pm, Wednesday until 8:45pm, closed Monday

SCULPTURE

In 1908, the poet Rainer Maria Rilke invited August Rodin, his mentor and boss (Rilke was Rodin's secretary), to visit him where he lived in a rented apartment in the Hôtel Biron. Rodin, the genius of 19th-century French sculpture, fell in love with the big French windows and the neglected garden where rabbits frolicked. He moved once again. Two years after his death, thanks to a donation, the state turned the building into a museum in his honour. Unchanged since 1919, the museum had started to become decrepit, but shutting it down for restoration was unthinkable since it has 700,000 visitors a year. Instead, the work was staggered over a three-year period. The result is a masterful renovation that returns the classical- and Rococo-style building to its 18th-century splendour. Extraordinary attention has been paid to detail. Farrow & Ball, a partner in the renovation, helped choose the colours for the eighteen rooms. The first floor is painted in grey-green tones and the ground floor an original taupe-grey called Biron grey, which contrast with the plaster casts, whose whiteness fascinated Rodin and dazzles visitors. Each room contains a major work, whether *The Kiss*, *The Age of Bronze* or *The Walking Man*. The sculptures are striking in their sensuality, raw power and movement, even though they are made of hard materials. Several rooms are devoted to Rodin's personal and artistic environment, with his antiques collection and his paintings – among them Van Gogh's *Père Tanguy* and Munch's *The Thinker* – on display. The master's studio has been recreated based on period photographs. The sophisticated, much-needed new lighting for the works varies with the natural light. Another great outcome of the renovation is the revival of the collection: 20 percent of the works hidden away in the reserves have been put on display, including plasters, terracottas and preparatory models that show the genesis of some sculptures.
In the museum's garden – one of the finest in Paris – thirty monumental bronze masterpieces stand on three wooded hectares, among them *The Burghers of Calais*, *The Gates of Hell*, *The Thinker* and *Balzac*, which caused such controversy in its time.

PALAIS DE TOKYO

13, avenue du Président Wilson, 16th
Metro Alma Marceau, Iéna
Tel 01 81 97 35 88
www.palaisdetokyo.com
Open noon to midnight, closed Tuesday

CONTEMPORARY ART CENTRE

Built in 1937 for the Paris World's Fair, this building, which extends for 22,000 square metres, three times its original area, now houses the largest centre for contemporary art in Europe. Installations, performances, videos and music are presented here in an informal atmosphere. Breaking with the "white cube" gallery cliché, some areas have been arranged to resemble grottos. The Palais de Tokyo is now dedicated to French art, but without a permanent collection, is only open for temporary exhibitions. Emerging talents and established figures are juxtaposed with international artists. This new showcase for 21st-century art has an irreverent air about it, focusing on French works and open to all sorts of contrasts and encounters: visual arts, design, music and fashion. The restaurant **TOKYO EAT** (tel 01 47 20 00 29) – with a pop decor, world-food cuisine and hip diners – is particularly popular on Sunday night.

PALAIS GALLIERA – MUSÉE DE LA MODE DE LA VILLE DE PARIS

10, avenue Pierre Ier de Serbie, 16th
Metro Iéna
Tel 01 56 52 86 00
www.palaisgalliera.paris.fr
Open 10am to 6pm, Thursday until 9pm, closed Monday and outside exhibition periods

FASHION AND ACCESSOIRES

The collections in the Musée de la Mode de la Ville de Paris are considered some of the most beautiful in the world, with one hundred thousand items of clothing and accessories held in secret storerooms. The collection grew out of donations by the rich customers of grand couturiers, such as the Countess Greffulhe, the model for Oriane, duchess of Guermantes, in Proust's *In Search of Lost Time*. Items are put on public display only on special occasions during temporary exhibitions that take place two or three times a year. At all other times, the Musée de la Mode is closed. The Palais Galliera has been restored to the "eclectic Renaissance" style it enjoyed when it was built in 1894, with ironwork designed by Gustave Eiffel. The building is worth visiting for the latter alone.

PETIT PALAIS – MUSÉE DES BEAUX-ARTS DE LA VILLE DE PARIS

Avenue Winston Churchill, 8th
Metro Champs-Élysées-Clemenceau
Tel 01 53 43 40 00
www.petitpalais.paris.fr
Open 10am to 6pm, Friday until 9pm during temporary exhibitions, closed Monday

ARTS, TEMPORARY EXHIBITIONS

Little brother of the Grand Palais and, like its counterpart, built for the 1900 World's Fair, the Petit Palais is a light-drenched architectural marvel by Charles-Louis Girault. In 1900, the Ville de Paris chose it as the home of its museum of fine arts, with collections running from antiquity to the early 20th century. Temporary exhibitions are regularly held. End your visit with a tasty bite from the café, located beneath the elegant peristyle of the inner courtyard, which is filled with palm trees and fountains.

ARCHITECTURE AND GARDENS

CINÉMATHÈQUE FRANÇAISE

51, rue de Bercy, 12th
Metro Bercy, Cour Saint-Émilion
Tel 01 71 19 33 33
www.cinematheque.fr
Open noon to 7pm, Thursday until 9pm, closed Tuesday

CONTEMPORARY

Designed in 1994 by architect Frank Gehry to accommodate the American Center, this building has since been given over to the history of cinema. It is faced in stone, an unusual material for the architect, blending respectfully into the Bercy neighbourhood. The Rue de Bercy facade, dutifully aligned with the surrounding buildings, is relatively restrained. The park-side frontage, however, is an exuberant juxtaposition of angles and forms. The name of the building, "The Dancer Raising Her Tutu", is yet another enticement to enter and see what's inside. Laid out around an atrium, the interior offers spectacular points of view and sun-drenched nooks. While these sculptural spaces can't rival the Guggenheim Museum in Bilbao, the effect is nonetheless surprising and inviting. The Cinémathèque is an ongoing celebration of film, with a collection of 40,000 of them, to which 800 more are added each year. The programme is action-packed, with regular screenings, exhibitions and debates.

CIRQUE D'HIVER

110, rue Amelot, 11th
Metro Filles du Calvaire
Tel 01 47 00 28 81
www.cirquedhiver.com

SECOND EMPIRE

German-born French architect Jakob Ignaz Hittorff (1792–1867) contributed hugely to the embellishment of central Paris. Among other things, he redesigned the Place de la Concorde and the Place de l'Étoile, and built the Gare du Nord as well as the dozen buildings, known at the time as the "hôtels des Maréchaux", whose curved facades encircle the Arc de Triomphe. At the behest of Louis Dejean, owner of the Cirque d'Été on the Champs-Élysées, Hittorff pulled off a tremendous feat in building the Cirque d'Hiver in the space of only nine months. It was opened by Napoleon III in 1852. What is most striking about this icosagon (twenty-sided polygon) of Greco-Roman inspiration is its polychrome exterior. Hittorff campaigned for colour here: blue for the forty stained-glass windows, red and yellow for the two friezes by Francisque Duret and Astyanax Scévola Bosio encircling the facade, recalling the frieze of the Panathenaic Procession on the Parthenon. The two cast-iron statues framing the main door, an Amazon and a Greek warrior, allude to the venue's intended function: to hold "hippodramas", or equestrian events. Red predominates inside the edifice: crimson blazes beneath the spotlights. The ceiling, faithful to the tradition of ancient circuses, is tented over with painted vellum, and if you walk along the marble passageways you'll discover the Bar de l'Impératrice, with its freshly restored frescos. The Cirque d'Hiver is listed as a historic monument and has belonged to the Bougliones since 1936.

CITÉ INTERNATIONALE UNIVERSITAIRE

17, boulevard Jourdan, 14th
Metro Porte d'Orléans
Tel 01 44 16 64 00, www.ciup.fr

EARLY 20TH CENTURY

The Cité Internationale Universitaire, located in a 34-hectare landscaped park in the southernmost part of Paris, is worth exploring if only for its panoply of architectural curios. The brainchild of French industrialist and patron of the arts Émile Deutsch de la Meurthe (co-founder of Shell Oil), it was built to provide accommodation and facilities for international students. Between 1923 and 1969, several countries and schools financed and built a total of forty buildings, resulting in a kind of compendium of 20th-century styles. The Dutch College is a masterpiece of the Modern Movement, completed in 1938 by Dutch Modernist master Willem Marinus Dudok. At the opposite end of the park is another gem: the Swiss Foundation (1932) designed by Le Corbusier and his cousin Pierre Jeanneret. The Swiss architect's first foray into collective housing, this avant-garde edifice already combined all the distinctive elements of his idiosyncratic architecture. In a model room here you can also see the furnishings designed by Charlotte Perriand. A tour of the "Cité U" is good for other surprises as well: murals painted by Tsuguharu Fujita in the Japan House; the very Oxfordian oriels and red bricks of the Franco-British College; the Italy House's 15th-century entryway and the ancient ruins in front of the building; and a replica of the Sun Stone, an Aztec calendar 3.6 metres in diameter, which was discovered in Mexico City's main square in 1790 and acquired by the Mexico House.

INSTITUT DE FRANCE

23, quai Conti, 6th
Metro Odéon, Pont Neuf
Tel 01 44 41 44 41
www.institut-de-france.fr

FRENCH BAROQUE

Facing each other across the Seine, the Louvre and the Institut de France present one of the most majestic and admired panoramas Paris has to offer, with the rigid classicist ideal apparent in the Colonnade on the Right Bank and the tempered French Baroque style on the Left. One and the same man, Louis Le Vau, designed both. The Collège des Quatre-Nations, under the patronage of Cardinal Mazarin, became a vehicle for his creative exuberance. The riverside composition is framed by two French-style pavilions topped with high-pitched roofs. In the middle is the chapel, crowned with a dome completed by François d'Orbay.
The two wings, curving inwards to form a semi-circular facade, make the ensemble even more stunning, quietly evoking the Italian Baroque of Bernini and Borromini. Closed during the Revolution so that it could be converted into a prison, the building was restored to its learned purpose by Napoleon, who made it the seat of the Institut de France, heir to the royal academies of the Ancien Régime.
Behind the main entrance lies an octagonal courtyard, which leads to the Salle des Séances (council chamber for plenary sessions) and the Mazarine Library. Today, the Institut de France hosts the meetings of the Académiciens, the illustrious "immortals" elected to the Académie Française for life.

JARDIN DES PLANTES

Place Valhubert,
entrances at 57, rue Cuvier, 2, rue Buffon,
36, rue Geoffroy Saint-Hilaire, 5th
Metro Gare d'Austerlitz, Jussieu
Tel 01 40 79 56 01
www.jardindesplantes.net
Open daily 8am to 5:30pm in winter,
7:30am to 8pm in summer

FLORA AND FAUNA

This former royal garden was created by Louis XIII and opened to the public in 1640. It is home to the **MUSÉUM NATIONAL D'HISTOIRE NATURELLE** (tel 01 40 79 30 00). Continually enhanced over the centuries by botanists and naturalists, including the eminent Georges-Louis Leclerc, Comte de Buffon, the garden now offers a unique natural setting in Paris, with hundreds of different varieties of flowers and plants, as well as beehives, an ecological garden, an Alpine garden, a labyrinth, a small zoo and a metal gazebo dating from 1788, just before the Revolution. But the most extraordinary attraction remains the greenhouses, which were renovated in 2010 by the Monuments Historiques department. The spectacular tropical hothouse is especially worth seeing. You walk in through a superb Art Deco peristyle to find yourself submerged in an atmosphere of rare and luxuriant vegetation, then follow paths lined with palm trees, banana trees, ferns and orchids to reach a concrete "rock", where the exoticism of the place is even more impressive. After leaving this enchanting hothouse, which inspired Henri Rousseau, amble over to the Hôtel de Magny built by Pierre Bullet, one of the leading architects at the close of Louis XIV's reign. The exhibitions here tell the story of the Jardin des Plantes and the scientists who planned it. Don't miss the Galérie de Paléontologie et d'Anatomie Comparée, which graphically recounts the whole story of the evolution of animal species.

JARDIN DES TUILERIES

Entrances at place de la Concorde,
place du Carrousel, rue de Rivoli,
quai des Tuileries, 1st
Metro Tuileries, Concorde
Open April to September 7am to 9pm,
October to March 7:30am to 7:30pm

ROYAL GARDEN

The Tuileries palace was razed to the ground in 1871, in the flames of the Commune. Yet if it were not for this, there would have been no Jardin des Tuileries. The first flowerbeds were designed for Marie de Médicis. In 1666, André Le Nôtre put his classical stamp on the garden. Ornamental ponds and copses were arranged around the central alley, which terminates at the Place de la Concorde, framed by two horseshoe-shaped ramps that emphasize the perfect symmetry of the place. From here, there is a splendid view down the Champs-Élysées. In summer, it is ablaze with light as the sunset aligns with the Place de l'Étoile. When the red light sinks under the Arc de Triomphe it is a moment of pure magic. The Jardin des Tuileries maintains a tradition that is a 19th-century legacy: nestling beneath the foliage are wooden pavilions that serve refreshments. With the first days of spring, their tables are taken by storm. And, once the fine weather sets in, model sailing boats can be hired from a stand near the round pond (on the Louvre side). Many generations of young Parisians have tried their hand at sailing these small wooden craft. Sculptures decorate the garden, from the Henry Moore bronze at the foot of the Orangerie steps, to the Alberto Giacometti and Giuseppe Penone bronzes, in the shade of the horse-chestnut trees.

JARDIN DU LUXEMBOURG

Entrances at place Edmond Rostand,
place André Honnorat, rue Auguste Comte,
rue Guynemer, rue de Vaugirard,
rue de Médicis, 6th
Metro Odéon, Notre-Dame-des-Champs,
RER Luxembourg
Tel 01 42 34 20 00, www.senat.fr
Opening hours vary, check the website

LEFT BANK CHIC, TIMELESS

The charms of the Jardin du Luxembourg are inexhaustible. There are statues scattered all over the park, the Médicis fountain, a serene Baroque masterpiece, 100-year-old horse-chestnut trees, chairs in which students flirt and seniors chat, a kids' playground for little Parisians and their elegant mothers, impeccably groomed lawns, tennis courts and a dance of model sailing boats in the basin, not to mention the open-air refreshment stalls: all are an expression of a timeless charm. Affectionately known as the "Luco", the 23-hectare garden holds memories for many Parisians of their first romps and the subsequent agitations of adolescence – a green idyll, in short, of youth. It's Parisian, to be sure, but Florentine, too, because Marie de Médicis had it built in 1612 and modelled on the Boboli Gardens in her native Florence. It is something of a dale dug into the heart of the Left Bank, bordered with Italian-style outdoor cafés and enclosed on the north side by the imposing Palais du Luxembourg (the French Senate), to which it belongs. For nature enthusiasts, there's a botanical garden and beehives offering an introduction to apiculture. For children, there are donkey rides, swings, an old carousel designed by architect Charles Garnier and built in 1879, and a puppet theatre that has been running since 1933. The "Luco" is also the haunt of Saint-Germain-des-Prés intellectuals and joggers, who mix here with stylish families taking a stroll or enjoying a casual get-together.

PARC ZOOLOGIQUE DE PARIS

Intersection of avenue Daumesnil
and the route de la Ceinture du Lac, 12th
Metro Porte Dorée
Tel 0 811 224 122
www.parczoologiquedeparis.fr
Opening times vary according to the season, see website

ANIMAL BIODIVERSITY

The zoological garden at the Bois de Vincennes has recently reopened after years of work to transform it into a modern, more animal-friendly place. More than 180 species now live in environments that are as close as is reasonably possible to their original habitats. The zoo covers 14.5 hectares and is divided into five biozones: Patagonia, the Sudanese Sahel, Europe, Amazonian Guiana and Madagascar, each planted with the appropriate vegetation. You'll see South American sea lions basking on the rocks, Grévy's zebras, West African lions, and the lemur of Madagascar, which finds shelter in the tropical forest recreated in the big hothouse. The aviaries are filled with thousands of birds creating a spectacular display of coloured plumage. Everything is designed to ensure the best experience for both visitors and the permanent residents. The other objective of the Parc Zoologique de Paris is to preserve endangered species, such as the lemurs and the European otter: here they enjoy the conditions they require for survival and reproduction.

CULTURAL PURSUITS WITH DOMINIQUE PERRAULT

In my mind there are no boundaries between the arts. This has been the case since I started, whether it was Christo, Louise Bourgeois or Denise René, who was the first gallery owner in Paris to understand and support the French National Library, even holding an exhibition of the models in her gallery on the Boulevard Saint-Germain. In addition, I often visit the Kreo design gallery, for which, in 2012, Gaëlle and I designed the Brisé necklace made of concrete and solid silver. I recently came across a curious gallery of Japanese ceramics, 1 to 7, run by a publisher of Japanese mangas, and whose creations seem straight out of an archaeological dig. I am also dazzled by the richness of the collections of the National Library, especially its rare and valuable works.

As for my own books, I'm a voracious reader of Scandinavian and American detective fiction and biographies. I frequently go on buying sprees at the La Friche bookshop. And I mustn't forget the bookshop owned by publisher-bookseller Yvon Lambert (www.yvon-lambert.com), which we are designing near the Cirque d'Hiver. When I want architecture books, I go to museum bookshops, and always look out for books related to an exhibition.

Françoise and Jean-Philippe Billarant, contemporary art collectors and close friends, were seeking the ideal space for their collections. It turned out to be a disused grain silo in Marines, in the Val-d'Oise, in the heart of the Vexin (www.lagoradesarts.fr/le-silo-collection-billarant). We designed the project together to house their collection of works by Daniel Buren, François Morellet, Richard Serra, Felice Varini, Bertrand Lavier, Carl Andre, Donald Judd and Michel Verjux is open to the public free of charge by appointment. As an artistic destination it's well worth the trip.

DENISE RENÉ RIVE DROITE

22, rue Charlot, 3rd, metro Rambuteau, tel 01 48 87 73 94, www.deniserebe.com

GALERIE KREO

31, rue Dauphine, 6th, metro Odéon, tel 01 53 10 23 00, www.galeriekreo.comm

1 TO 7

11, rue des Grands Augustins, 6th, metro Saint-Michel, www.1to7.fr

BIBLIOTHÈQUE NATIONALE DE FRANCE FRANÇOIS MITTERRAND (BNF)

Quai François Mauriac, 13th, metro Bibliothèque François Mitterrand, tel 01 53 79 59 59, www.bnf.fr

YVON LAMBERT

www.yvan-lambert.com

LA FRICHE

36, rue Léon Frot, 11th, metro Charonne, tel 01 78 11 80 40, www.la-friche.org

THE SCENIC ROUTE

FIVE WALKING TOURS AROUND THE CITY

With its narrow cobblestone streets, hidden alleys, broad boulevards, covered passageways, shady avenues, busy shopping streets, arcades, parks, gardens, bridges and quaysides, its Left and Right Banks, Paris is made for walkers. It is filled with little secrets, interesting angles and perspectives, terraces and esplanades, inviting the stroller to stray off the beaten path. When you pick a theme for your walk, suddenly the city changes personality, taking on an unusual, often totally surprising character.

There is no better way to discover the city than on foot. The following Parisian walks explore the haunts of famous people, unsuspected architectural treasures, cool waterways, verdant urban parks and the city's most interesting or elegant stores. Five delightful itineraries for inquisitive walkers.

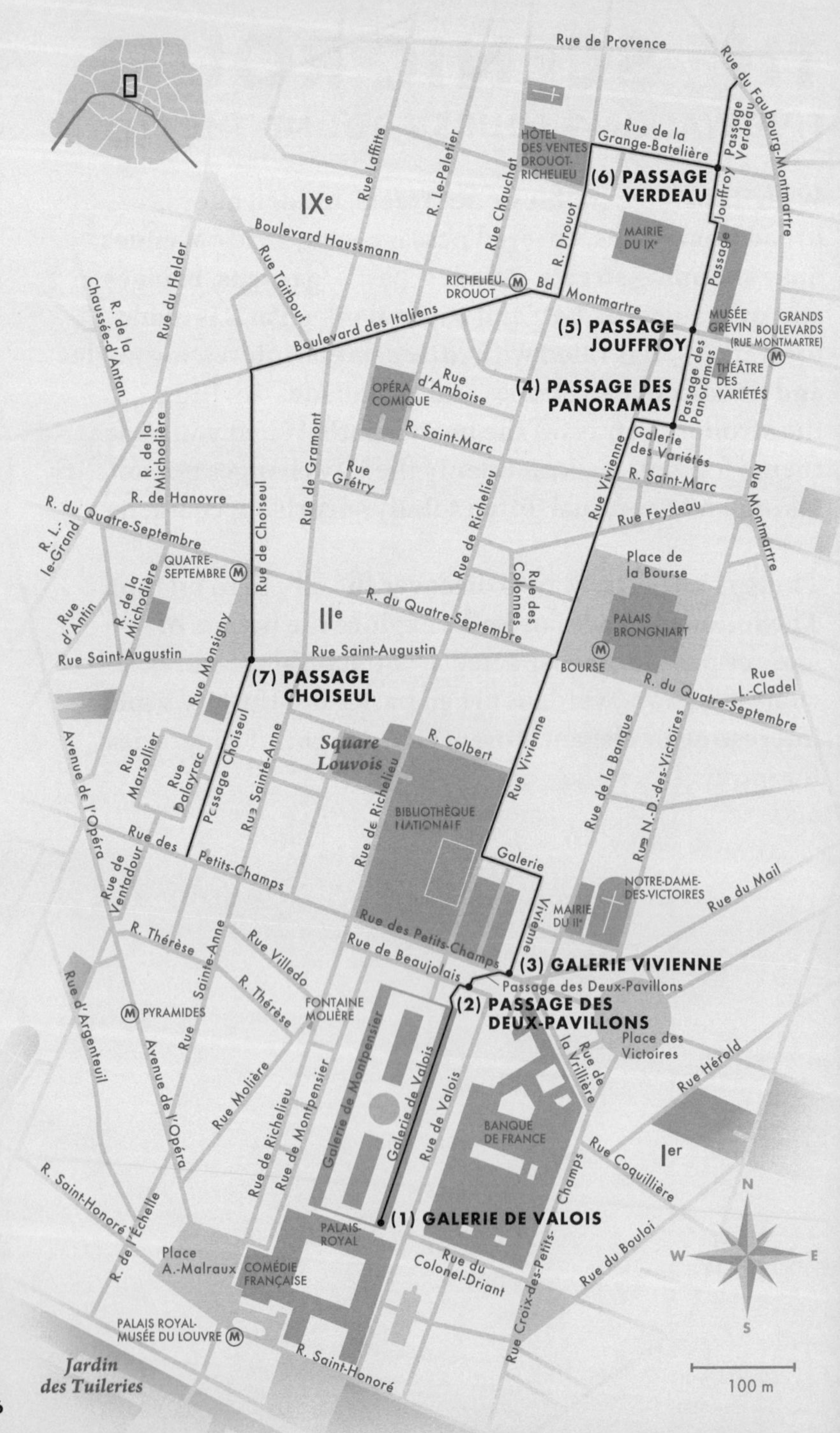

Rue de Provence
Rue du Faubourg-Montmartre
Passage Verdeau
Rue de la Grange-Batelière
HÔTEL DES VENTES DROUOT-RICHELIEU
(6) PASSAGE VERDEAU
MAIRIE DU IXe
IXe
Rue Laffitte
R. Le-Peletier
Rue Chauchat
R. Drouot
Boulevard Haussmann
Rue Taitbout
Rue du Helder
R. de la Chaussée-d'Antin
RICHELIEU-DROUOT
Bd Montmartre
Passage Jouffroy
MUSÉE GRÉVIN
GRANDS BOULEVARDS (RUE MONTMARTRE)
(5) PASSAGE JOUFFROY
Boulevard des Italiens
Passage des Panoramas
THÉÂTRE DES VARIÉTÉS
(4) PASSAGE DES PANORAMAS
OPÉRA COMIQUE
Rue d'Amboise
R. Saint-Marc
Galerie des Variétés
R. Saint-Marc
Rue Grétry
Rue de Gramont
R. de la Michodière
R. de Hanovre
Rue de Choiseul
Rue de Richelieu
Rue Vivienne
Rue Feydeau
Rue Montmartre
R. du Quatre-Septembre
R. L.-le-Grand
QUATRE-SEPTEMBRE
Rue des Colonnes
Place de la Bourse
PALAIS BRONGNIART
BOURSE
R. du Quatre-Septembre
Rue d'Antin
R. de la Michodière
IIe
Rue Saint-Augustin
Rue Saint-Augustin
(7) PASSAGE CHOISEUL
Rue L.-Cladel
R. du Quatre-Septembre
Rue Monsigny
Square Louvois
R. Colbert
Rue Vivienne
Rue de la Banque
Rue N.-D.-des-Victoires
Avenue de l'Opéra
Rue Marsollier
Rue Dalayrac
Passage Choiseul
Rue Sainte-Anne
Rue de Richelieu
BIBLIOTHÈQUE NATIONALE
Rue des Petits-Champs
Galerie Vivienne
NOTRE-DAME-DES-VICTOIRES
MAIRIE DU IIe
Rue du Mail
Rue de Ventadour
R. Thérèse
Rue Villedo
Rue des Petits-Champs
Rue de Beaujolais
(3) GALERIE VIVIENNE
Passage des Deux-Pavillons
(2) PASSAGE DES DEUX-PAVILLONS
Rue d'Argenteuil
PYRAMIDES
Rue Sainte-Anne
R. Thérèse
FONTAINE MOLIÈRE
Place des Victoires
Rue de la Vrillière
Rue Hérold
Avenue de l'Opéra
Rue Molière
Rue de Richelieu
Rue de Montpensier
Galerie de Montpensier
Galerie de Valois
Rue de Valois
BANQUE DE FRANCE
Ier
Rue Coquillière
R. Saint-Honoré
R. de l'Échelle
PALAIS-ROYAL
(1) GALERIE DE VALOIS
Rue Croix-des-Petits-Champs
N
W
E
S
Place A.-Malraux
COMÉDIE FRANÇAISE
Rue du Colonel-Driant
Rue du Bouloi
PALAIS ROYAL-MUSÉE DU LOUVRE
R. Saint-Honoré
Jardin des Tuileries
100 m

ART AND ARCHITECTURE
COVERED PASSAGES

Time: 2 hours

Covered passages appeared on the Right Bank in the first half of the 19th century around the Palais-Royal and as far as the suburbs at a time when Paris was growing northward and trade was developing in the area. Fortunately, a few such shopping galleries survived Baron Haussmann's major overhaul of Paris.

(1) GALERIE DE VALOIS (Palais-Royal, 1st). With its fine restaurants and shops, this arcade might be considered the ancestor of the passages built later. Take the time to admire its regular arches, the garden and the handsome facades lit by the sun.
(2) PASSAGE DES DEUX PAVILLONS (10, rue de Beaujolais, 1st). As you leave the Palais-Royal, climb a few steps to this cute little passage that links Rue de Beaujolais to Rue des Petits Champs. It is home to Maison Bonnet, which makes bespoke glasses for a number of celebrities.
(3) GALERIE VIVIENNE (4, rue des Petits Champs, 1st). Built in 1823 to a design by the architect François-Jacques Delannoy, it has an elegant glass roof, a cupola and a Pompeii-inspired mosaic floor. The gallery has always housed a range of prestigious shops. A wine merchant (Caves Legrand), fashion designers, fashionable restaurants, bookshops (Jousseaume has been there since it opened) line the passage: there's plenty to detain you.
(4) PASSAGE DES PANORAMAS (38, rue Vivienne, 2nd). Built in 1800, this passage receives daylight through a high glass roof and in some ways resembles an Oriental souk. In fact, it was created for the same reason as the souks: at a time when Paris was dirty, muddy and poorly lit, it was more pleasant to shop indoors. It still has its picturesque postcard, coin and stamp shops, but has been somewhat gentrified by the hip Caffè Stern (which replaced the famous engraver of the same name) and the chic restaurant Passage 53.
(5) PASSAGE JOUFFROY (10, boulevard Montmartre, 9th). This gallery is the continuation of the Passage des Panoramas on the other side of Boulevard Montmartre. It is topped with a glass and metal structure that was innovative at the time of its construction. Once full of life with its many eateries and an opera cabaret, it attracted a population of courtesans and upper-class Parisians eager to find the latest novelties in its shops. Since 1882, it has housed the exit from the Musée Grévin, with its truer-than-life wax figures, and – just under the clock – the charming Hôtel Chopin, not at all a bad place to stay.
(6) PASSAGE VERDEAU (6, rue de la Grange Batelière, 9th). More discreet but just as charming as the Passage Jouffroy across the road, Passage Verdeau is topped with a high glass roof that lets the daylight stream in. Filled with the shops of antiques and antiquarian book dealers, it has a charming atmosphere.
(7) PASSAGE CHOISEUL (23, rue Saint-Augustin, 2nd). Before entering the passage, stop in at Ultramod (4, rue de Choiseul, 2nd), a notions store selling buttons, ribbons and braid the likes of which are hard to find these days, then continue to the entrance of the passage, with its pretty stone pediment. Inside you will find the engraver Boisnard et Lavrut, a favourite supplier of art students. When you get to the store La Belle Époque (38, rue des Petits Champs, 2nd), have a well-deserved drink on the Rue des Petits Champs.

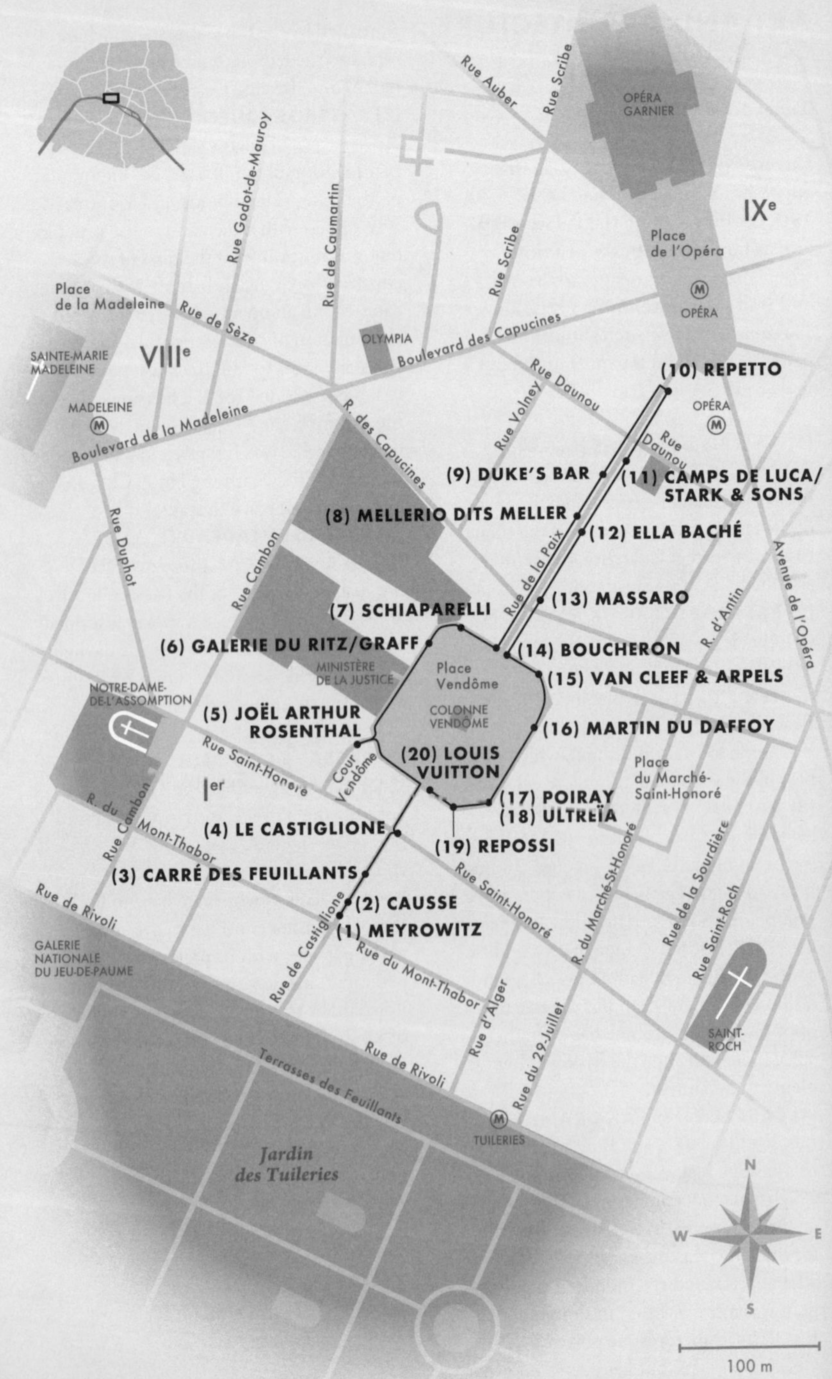
OPÉRA GARNIER
IXe
Place de l'Opéra
OPÉRA
Rue Auber
Rue Scribe
Rue Godot-de-Mauroy
Rue de Caumartin
Place de la Madeleine
Rue de Sèze
SAINTE-MARIE MADELEINE
VIIIe
OLYMPIA
Boulevard des Capucines
MADELEINE
Boulevard de la Madeleine
Rue Daunou
Rue Volney
R. des Capucines
(10) REPETTO
(9) DUKE'S BAR
(11) CAMPS DE LUCA/ STARK & SONS
(8) MELLERIO DITS MELLER
(12) ELLA BACHÉ
Rue Duphot
Rue Cambon
Rue de la Paix
(13) MASSARO
Avenue de l'Opéra
R. d'Antin
(7) SCHIAPARELLI
(6) GALERIE DU RITZ/GRAFF
(14) BOUCHERON
MINISTÈRE DE LA JUSTICE
Place Vendôme
(15) VAN CLEEF & ARPELS
NOTRE-DAME-DE-L'ASSOMPTION
COLONNE VENDÔME
(5) JOËL ARTHUR ROSENTHAL
(16) MARTIN DU DAFFOY
Rue Saint-Honoré
Cour Vendôme
(20) LOUIS VUITTON
Place du Marché-Saint-Honoré
Ier
(17) POIRAY
(18) ULTREÏA
R. du Mont-Thabor
(4) LE CASTIGLIONE
(19) REPOSSI
(3) CARRÉ DES FEUILLANTS
Rue Saint-Honoré
R. du Marché-St-Honoré
Rue de la Sourdière
Rue de Rivoli
(2) CAUSSE
(1) MEYROWITZ
Rue Saint-Roch
GALERIE NATIONALE DU JEU-DE-PAUME
Rue de Castiglione
Rue du Mont-Thabor
Rue d'Alger
SAINT-ROCH
Rue du 29-Juillet
Rue de Rivoli
Terrasses des Feuillants
TUILERIES
Jardin des Tuileries
N
W
E
S
100 m

LUXURY AND FASHION
RUE DE CASTIGLIONE, PLACE VENDÔME AND RUE DE LA PAIX

Time: 4 hours

Connecting the Tuileries to the Opéra Garnier, the route along the Rue de Castiglione-Place Vendôme-Rue de la Paix was once emblematic of the opulent fashions and jewellery of the Second Empire. The walk takes you along the covered arcades of the Rue de Castiglione, named after the spying countess and mistress of Napoleon III, who ended her days as a recluse in a mansion on the Place Vendôme with all the mirrors veiled in black.

(1) MEYROWITZ (5, rue de Castiglione). Since 1875, this famous optician has been correcting short and long sight in the most stylish eyes in Paris. Original decor.
(2) CAUSSE (12, rue de Castiglione). For gloves, skilfully handmade since 1892.
(3) CARRÉ DES FEUILLANTS (14, rue de Castiglione). The in-demand restaurant helmed by chef Alain Dutournier.
(4) LE CASTIGLIONE (235, rue Saint-Honoré). Stop for a coffee and croissant or a glass of Chablis depending on the time of day. The most popular small café in the neighbourhood. "Le Casti'" to its regulars.
(5) JOËL ARTHUR ROSENTHAL (cour Vendôme, at 7, place Vendôme). Nicknamed the Greta Garbo of jewellery.
(6) GALERIE DU RITZ (15-17, place Vendôme). Home to Heroes and Maison Ullens. Also accessible from the Ritz: **GRAFF** jewellers. To recover from this luxury overload, drop into the Ritz spa, refresh your blond Ritz highlights at hairdresser David Mallett or enjoy a Proustian madeleine in its tearoom.
(7) SCHIAPARELLI (21, place Vendôme). Same address since 1935, now upstairs. You'll need credentials to get in and see the spectacular decor.
(8) MELLERIO DITS MELLER (9, rue de la Paix). *The* historic jeweller in Paris!
(9) DUKE'S BAR (Hôtel Westminster, 13, rue de la Paix). English-style bar with food, and the best club sandwich in Paris.
(10) REPETTO (22, rue de la Paix). The world famous ballet shoes made by Rose Repetto, worn by Brigitte Bardot, Charlotte Gainsbourg and the entire corps de ballet of the Opéra Garnier.
(11) CAMPS DE LUCA / STARK & SONS (16, rue de la Paix, upstairs). Bespoke tailoring for men.
(12) ELLA BACHÉ (8, rue de la Paix). French beauty salon, family run, still at its original address (1936).
(13) MASSARO (2, rue de la Paix). Founded right here in 1894, this celebrated shoemaker who worked for Marlene Dietrich has joined the galaxy of artisan stars run by Chanel.
(14) BOUCHERON (26, place Vendôme). Sparkling occupant since 1893 of the former home of the Comtesse de Castiglione.
(15) VAN CLEEF & ARPELS (22, place Vendôme). The famous jeweller, which has occupied this address since 1906, also offers classes in the art of fine jewellery at 3 rue Danielle Casanova (booking on 01 70 70 36 00).
(16) MARTIN DU DAFFOY (16, place Vendôme, 1st floor). A unique figure in the jewellery business. Seeker of antique treasures for the world's wealthiest.
(17) POIRAY (8, place Vendôme). Founded in 1972 by François Hérail and Michel Hermelin is the "youngster" of Place Vendôme. Aurélie Bidermann is the artistic director.
(18) ULTREÏA (8, place Vendôme, 1st floor). Caviar tasting salon founded by Véronique Y-K Martin. For a change from all the carats.
(19) REPOSSI (6, place Vendôme). Italian jeweller (1920) in a postmodern setting designed by Rem Koolhaas.
(20) LOUIS VUITTON (23, place Vendôme). The new flagship store, designed by Peter Marino.

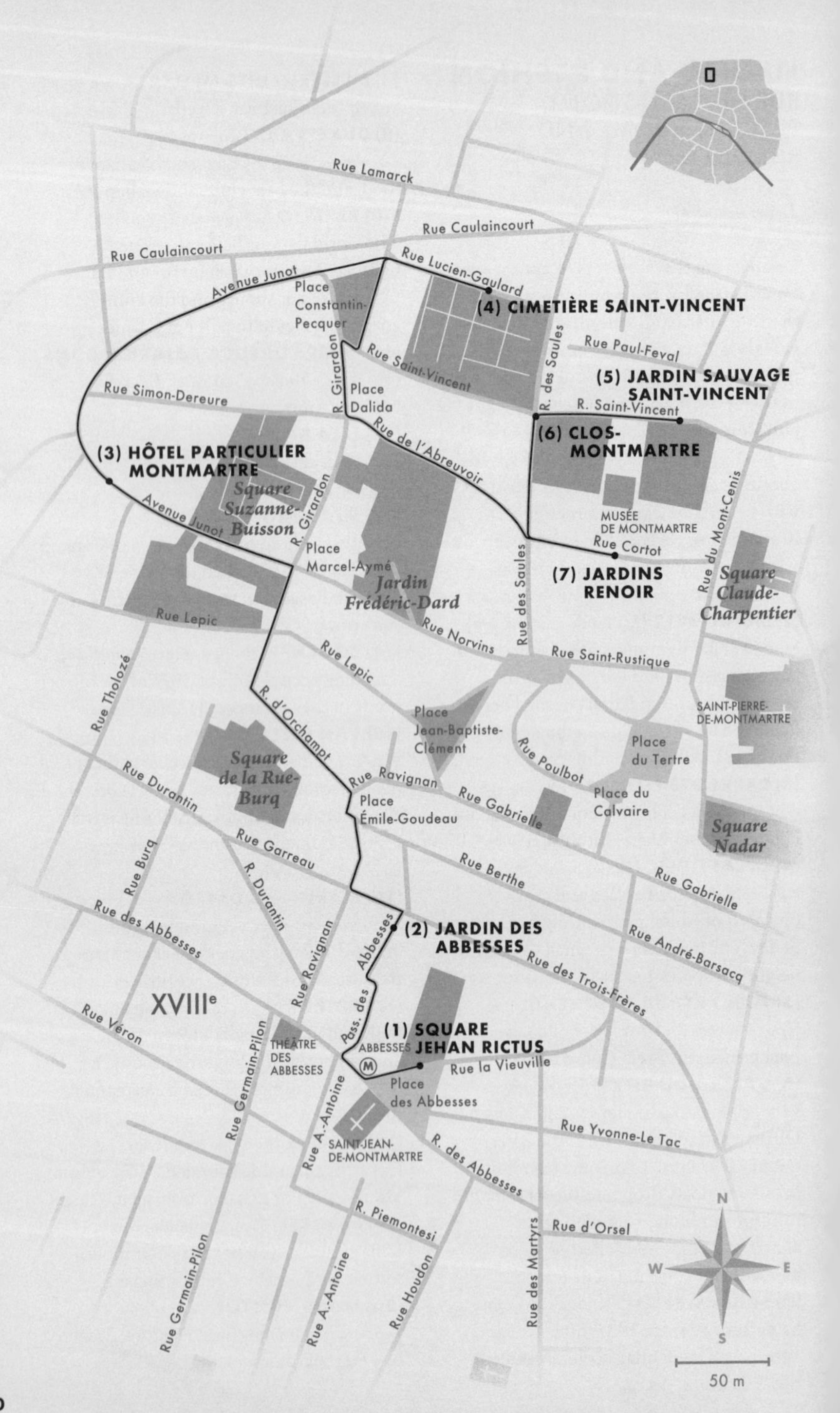

(1) SQUARE JEHAN RICTUS
(2) JARDIN DES ABBESSES
(3) HÔTEL PARTICULIER MONTMARTRE
(4) CIMETIÈRE SAINT-VINCENT
(5) JARDIN SAUVAGE SAINT-VINCENT
(6) CLOS-MONTMARTRE
(7) JARDINS RENOIR

Rue Lamarck
Rue Caulaincourt
Rue Caulaincourt
Avenue Junot
Rue Lucien-Gaulard
Place Constantin-Pecquer
R. Girardon
Rue Saint-Vincent
Rue Paul-Feval
Rue Simon-Dereure
Place Dalida
R. des Saules
R. Saint-Vincent
Rue de l'Abreuvoir
Square Suzanne-Buisson
Avenue Junot
R. Girardon
MUSÉE DE MONTMARTRE
Rue du Mont-Cenis
Rue Cortot
Place Marcel-Aymé
Jardin Frédéric-Dard
Rue des Saules
Square Claude-Charpentier
Rue Lepic
Rue Norvins
Rue Saint-Rustique
Rue Lepic
Rue Tholozé
R. d'Orchampt
Place Jean-Baptiste-Clément
SAINT-PIERRE-DE-MONTMARTRE
Rue Poulbot
Place du Tertre
Square de la Rue-Burq
Rue Durantin
Rue Ravignan
Place Émile-Goudeau
Rue Gabrielle
Place du Calvaire
Square Nadar
Rue Garreau
Rue Burq
R. Durantin
Rue Berthe
Rue Gabrielle
Rue des Abbesses
Pass. des Abbesses
Rue Ravignan
Rue André-Barsacq
Rue des Trois-Frères
XVIIIe
Rue Véron
Rue Germain-Pilon
THÉÂTRE DES ABBESSES
ABBESSES
M
Rue la Vieuville
Place des Abbesses
Rue A.-Antoine
SAINT-JEAN-DE-MONTMARTRE
Rue Yvonne-Le Tac
R. des Abbesses
R. Piemontesi
Rue d'Orsel
Rue Germain-Pilon
Rue A.-Antoine
Rue Houdon
Rue des Martyrs
N
W
E
S
50 m

NATURE
BUCOLIC MONTMARTRE

Time: 2 hours

A world away from the busy Place du Tertre, tiny squares, village houses, gardens and a vineyard border the Butte, a reminder that the Commune de Montmartre, absorbed by Paris in 1860, remains a place apart. Make sure you wear comfortable shoes.

(1) SQUARE JEHAN-RICTUS (14, place des Abbesses, 18th). This little square has a provincial charm, with its old roses, Japanese cherry trees, medicinal plants and benches where the locals enjoy relaxing. A wall of glazed lava tiles, designed in 2000 by Frédéric Baron and Claire Kito, bears the words "I love you" written 311 times, each in a different language.

(2) JARDINS DES ABBESSES (passage des Abbesses, 18th). Devoted to calm, meditation and environmental education, the Jardin des Abbesses commemorates the nuns of Montmartre, whose 12th-century convent stood here until the Revolution. The garden in this serene place is laid out like a cloister. Enclosed by wooden pergolas and huddled against high walls, it is organized into square plots defined by box hedges and planted with herbs and other plants with medicinal properties.

(3) HÔTEL PARTICULIER (23, avenue Junot, Pavillon D, 18th). To enjoy a drink or brunch in the garden of this house-hotel away from the city bustle is a delight. An oasis of green, its 900 square metres have been carefully landscaped by Louis Benech to offer a refreshing burst of chlorophyll.

(4) CIMETIÈRE SAINT-VINCENT (6, rue Lucien Gaulard, 18th). Opened in 1831, this romantic cemetery, a haven of (eternal) peace, is on the northern flank of the Butte. Nevertheless it gets enough sun to maintain a number of Mediterranean trees, including cypress, olive, fig, almond, pomegranate, cork oak and myrtle. The film director Marcel Carné, and the painters Eugène Boudin and Maurice Utrillo are buried here.

(5) JARDIN SAUVAGE SAINT-VINCENT (17, rue Saint-Vincent, 18th). This place has deliberately been left to run wild as a sort of conservatory of local biodiversity. Weeds, grasses, ivy, foxgloves, nettles and other plants typical of natural areas in the Paris region grow unhindered here. Birds, butterflies and insects have also found shelter here; there's even a pond for frogs and toads to breed. In order to protect this ecological refuge, public access is restricted. Guided tours from 1 April to 31 October: on the first Sunday of every month at 10:30 am and the third Wednesday of the month at 2:30 pm.

(6) CLOS MONTMARTRE (corner of rue des Saules and rue Saint-Vincent, 18th). This vineyard was planted in 1933 on the northern slope of the Butte. It now has some 2,000 vines of various varieties – mainly pinot noir and gamay – and produces a beautifully coloured rosé wine, improving in quality every year. Though the vineyard is not open to the casual visitor, there is a good view of it from the street and an even better one from the back of the Musée de Montmartre, which overlooks it.

(7) JARDINS RENOIR (Musée de Montmartre, 12, rue Cortot, 18th). The oldest house in Montmartre, the Bel Air dates from the 17th century. A little gem, with shutters and a pretty tiled roof, it stands in a beautiful garden with roses climbing over old arches and is home to the museum collections. An ancient pear tree dips its branches onto the lawn, the flowers release their fragrance, a blackbird sings. You're in the countryside. Just like long ago, when Renoir had his studio here and painted gentle scenes from *la vie heureuse.* Behind the house there's an excellent view of the Montmartre vineyard and the Saint-Vincent wild garden. The left side leads into the garden of the Hôtel Demarne, where temporary exhibitions are held.

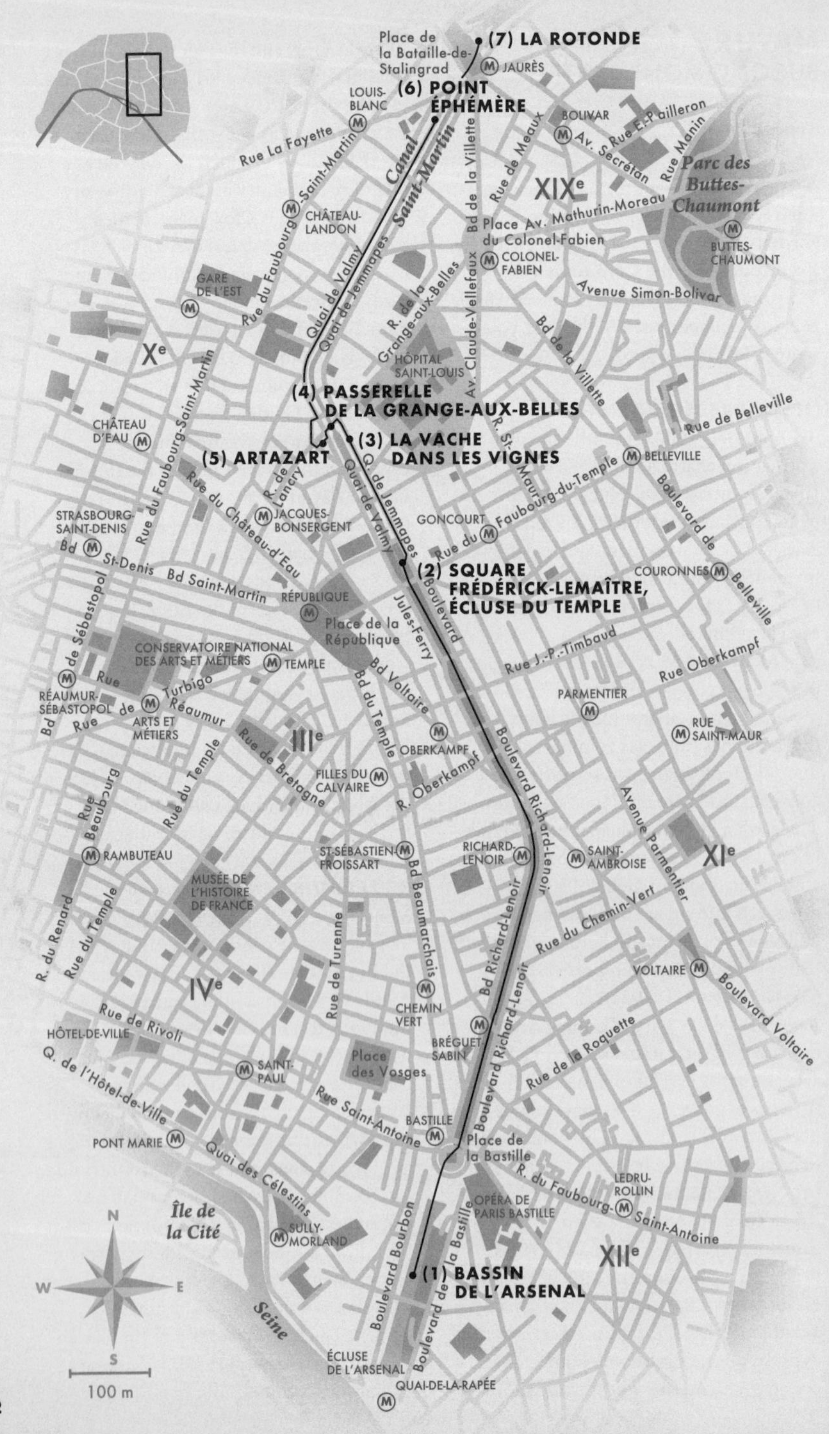
(7) LA ROTONDE
(6) POINT ÉPHÉMÈRE
(4) PASSERELLE DE LA GRANGE-AUX-BELLES
(3) LA VACHE DANS LES VIGNES
(5) ARTAZART
(2) SQUARE FRÉDÉRICK-LEMAÎTRE, ÉCLUSE DU TEMPLE
(1) BASSIN DE L'ARSENAL
Canal Saint-Martin
Parc des Buttes-Chaumont
Place de la République
Place des Vosges
Place de la Bastille
Île de la Cité
Seine
100 m

WATERSIDE TRAILS
CANAL SAINT-MARTIN

Time: 2 hours

The Canal Saint-Martin was built in the early 19th century to supply Paris with drinking water from the Ourcq River, a tributary of the Marne. It was used intensely, with heavy barge traffic, until the 1950s. Today it lazes along romantically between Quai de Jemmapes and Quai de Valmy, interrupted only by its locks and bridges.

(1) BASSIN DE L'ARSENAL (boulevard de la Bastille, 12th, boulevard Bourdon, 4th). This basin connects the Canal Saint-Martin with the Seine through the Arsenal lock. Once an important cargo port, it became a marina in 1983. It is bordered on one side by a garden adorned with a collection of climbing plants, including clematis and roses. The cruise boats that leave from the Arsenal port offer an unusual way to see the canal. (Canauxrama, www.canauxrama.com)
(2) SQUARE FRÉDÉRICK LEMAÎTRE, ÉCLUSE DU TEMPLE (rue du Faubourg du Temple, quai de Valmy, quai de Jemmapes, 10th). At the Port de l'Arsenal, the Canal Saint Martin disappears under a wide arch and reappears 2 kilometres away. Travelling along this underground section by boat is a delight. Walking it on the surface is less exciting, with its wide boulevards punctuated by unattractive squares and patches of greenery protecting the skylights that illuminate and ventilate the canal. At Square Frédérick Lemaître, the canal resurfaces and reveals all its charm. Lean on the railing of one of the footbridges and take the time to watch the boats go through the Temple Lock while admiring the alignment of the bridges in the distance.
(3) LA VACHE DANS LES VIGNES (46, quai de Jemmapes, 10th). A wine bar where you will find the best pairings of Roquefort and Sauterne, Camembert and champagne, dry goat cheese and white wine from the Loire, old Comté and robust Gigondas. The perfect complement to a walk along the waterfront.
(4) PASSERELLE DE LA GRANGE AUX BELLES (rue de Lancry, rue de la Grange aux Belles, 10th). From the top of the footbridge, admire the pivoting of the swing bridge when a barge passes. On Quai de Jemmapes, you'll see the Hôtel du Nord, which for every French film lover automatically calls to mind the actress Arletty's famous line, *"Atmosphère! Atmosphère! Est-ce que j'ai une gueule d'atmosphère!?"*, from Marcel Carné's eponymous 1938 film, also starring Louis Jouvet.
(5) ARTAZART (83, quai de Valmy, 10th). A wonderful bookstore-gallery specializing in graphic arts and contemporary books. It also offers a number of creative publications, children's books, pop-ups and updated reissues.
(6) POINT ÉPHÉMÈRE (200, quai de Valmy, 10th). In 2004, this former building materials store was converted into a concert hall presenting cutting-edge music. It also has an exhibition space, a bar, an Asian-influenced restaurant and even ping-pong tables that anyone can use.
(7) LA ROTONDE (6-8, place de la Bataille de Stalingrad, 19th). This majestic building is one of the last vestiges of the fifty tollhouses designed by architect Claude-Nicolas Ledoux and built shortly before the Revolution. Spaced out along the Fermiers Généraux wall surrounding Paris, the buildings were centres for tax collection on goods entering the city. The wall and the handsome tollhouses, built at great expense, immediately raised popular indignation. La Rotonde, currently home to a restaurant, garden, wine bar, club and gallery, now collects only cool cred.

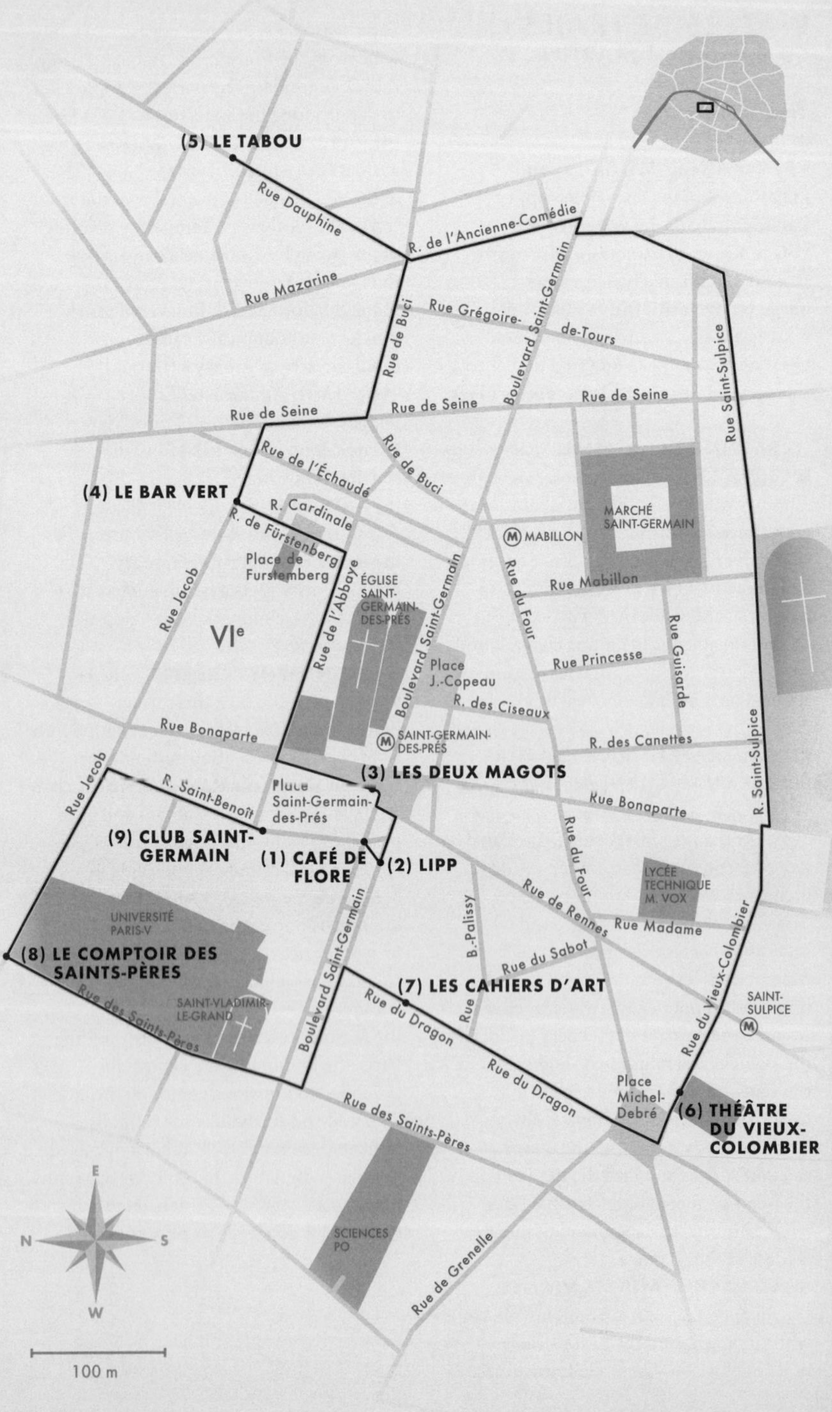

(5) LE TABOU
(4) LE BAR VERT
(3) LES DEUX MAGOTS
(9) CLUB SAINT-GERMAIN
(1) CAFÉ DE FLORE
(2) LIPP
(8) LE COMPTOIR DES SAINTS-PÈRES
(7) LES CAHIERS D'ART
(6) THÉÂTRE DU VIEUX-COLOMBIER

Rue Dauphine
R. de l'Ancienne-Comédie
Rue Mazarine
Rue de Buci
Rue Grégoire-de-Tours
Boulevard Saint-Germain
Rue Saint-Sulpice
Rue de Seine
Rue de Seine
Rue de Seine
Rue de l'Échaudé
Rue de Buci
R. Cardinale
R. de Fürstenberg
Place de Furstemberg
MARCHÉ SAINT-GERMAIN
MABILLON
Rue Jacob
VIe
Rue de l'Abbaye
ÉGLISE SAINT-GERMAIN-DES-PRÉS
Boulevard Saint-Germain
Rue du Four
Rue Mabillon
Rue Guisarde
Place J.-Copeau
Rue Princesse
R. des Ciseaux
Rue Bonaparte
SAINT-GERMAIN-DES-PRÉS
R. des Canettes
R. Saint-Sulpice
Rue Jacob
R. Saint-Benoît
Place Saint-Germain-des-Prés
Rue Bonaparte
Rue du Four
LYCÉE TECHNIQUE M. VOX
Rue de Rennes
Rue Madame
UNIVERSITÉ PARIS-V
Boulevard Saint-Germain
Rue B.-Palissy
Rue du Sabot
Rue du Vieux-Colombier
SAINT-SULPICE
SAINT-VLADIMIR-LE-GRAND
Rue des Saints-Pères
Rue du Dragon
Rue du Dragon
Place Michel-Debré
Rue des Saints-Pères
SCIENCES PO
Rue de Grenelle
E
N
S
W
100 m

IN THE FOOTSTEPS OF BORIS VIAN

Time: 3 hours

In the immediate post-war years, the bars of Saint-Germain-des-Prés thronged with wits and intellectuals, and their smoky basements were monopolised by the Existentialists. A true polymath – engineer, writer, poet, songwriter and trumpeter – Boris Vian wrote an amusing takedown of the area, the *Manuel de Saint-Germain-des-Prés*, where it seems true life also lies beneath.

(1) CAFÉ DE FLORE (172, boulevard Saint-Germain, 6th). It was bought by the Auvergnat Paul Boubal in 1939. It attracted a whole herd of intellectuals, including Sartre and Beauvoir, of course, as well as Camus, Queneau and Prévert. It still has a vibrant atmosphere. Boubal, whom Vian admired all the more because he was a regimental trumpeter, still seems to be watching over his flock.

(2) LIPP (151, boulevard Saint-Germain, 6th). This is a restaurant where civilized people can discuss culture and politics over a slice of foie gras without being bothered by pretentious poseurs.

(3) LES DEUX MAGOTS (6, place Saint-Germain, 6th). Famous "since forever", this legendary place is a favourite with literary and artistic figures, as well as people from fashion and politics. The waiters have a reputation for grumpiness. Vian loved its strategic location.

(4) LE BAR VERT (10, rue Jacob, 6th). Opened in 1944, it was the capital's first American bar. Unusually, you could get café au lait here, and Prévert's crowd, with Vian to the fore, came for theirs at precisely 2:30 pm. Taken over shortly after by Bernard Lucas, the bar attracted a fashionable crowd who frittered away their time there. The site is now a gallery owned by David Ghezelbash (www.davidghezelbash.com), specializing in Mediterranean archaeology.

(5) LE TABOU (33, rue Dauphine, 6th). A simple bar at street level, Le Tabou's basement was the ultimate Existentialist cellar. Opened by Bernard Lucas in April 1947, it sucked in young "hepcats" thirsty for freedom, alcohol and music. Wreathed in cigarette smoke, they danced crazy boogie-woogie to wild jazz combos, with Boris on trumpet. These days, the site is occupied by the Hôtel d'Aubusson (www.hoteldaubusson.com) and its Café Laurent. It's still a jazz bar, but much more plush.

(6) THÉÂTRE DU VIEUX-COLOMBIER (21, rue du Vieux Colombier, 6th). Two in one: it was a theatre on the ground floor, a club in the cellar. Upstairs, *Lucienne et le boucher*, a play by Marcel Aymé. Downstairs, Claude Luter and his band improvising. Not far away, Les Frères Jacques starred at the Rose Rouge cabaret, while Juliette Gréco electrified her audience with lyrics by Queneau and songs by Mouloudji. Later it would become a lesbian club, the Katmandou.

(7) LES CAHIERS D'ART (14, rue du Dragon, 6th). Still active today, this publisher, gallery and arts magazine was founded in 1926 par Christian Zervos. Here, Vian saw works by Picasso, Braque, Léger and Kandinsky, among others.

(8) LE COMPTOIR DES SAINTS-PÈRES (29, rue des Saints-Pères, 6th). Formerly the Restaurant Michaud, where Boris Vian was a regular. It still has most of its original decor and a very Parisian ambience.

(9) CLUB SAINT-GERMAIN (13, rue Saint-Benoît, 6th). In June 1948, Vian settled in Rue Saint-Benoît where Freddy Chauvelot had converted the high-ceilinged basement rooms beneath the Société d'Encouragement pour l'Industrie Française. The chic club was frequented by elegantly dressed people and charged high prices. One particular evening of jazz with Duke Ellington drew an audience of over 1,000. Charlie Parker and Kenny Clark also played there. Its famous theme nights were an in-crowd favourite.

LOUIS VUITTON'S GUIDE FOR TRAVELLERS

Travellers are not ordinary people. Curious, cultivated and demanding, they know that a journey is never insignificant. Such adventures can be fascinating, but also disastrous. We rarely travel luggage-free. Suitcases, bags and trunks accompany the globetrotter on long journeys, while the business traveller is never without a bolster bag containing a fresh outfit, nor a briefcase into which he or she has slipped a good read. We always put something of ourselves in our bags. Everything that touches on our personal world is there and needs to be well protected.

Cities, countries, people, landscapes, monuments, lifestyles, cultures – even on short trips, the traveller is driven by curiosity and a desire for new discoveries. A similar spirit guides his reading. Art, literature, images, stories – he wants to be transported far, far away. Ever since it was founded in 1854, Louis Vuitton has been in tune with the desires and aspirations of those who travel, whether physically or mentally. Today, it continues to help them fulfil their expectations, their wishes and their dreams.

THE ART OF PACKING

BACK IN THE DAY

Before going it alone and founding his own House, Louis Vuitton was a trunk maker and packer to the French court. For not only did he craft trunks that were as light as they were tough, but he was himself responsible for carefully packing his clients' effects in these chests, using a tried and tested procedure. Today, while the containers are no longer quite the same, the spirit is identical: practicality, lightness, comfort – everything that has been stored in the baggage must come out in perfect condition.

HOW TO PACK YOUR CLOTHES

Folding, rolling, turning down collars, slip-casing suits, stuffing shoes with tissue paper, doing up every second button – nothing is left to chance and nothing is improvised. Properly understood, packing is an art in which each item of clothing is folded and stored in a particular way.

SHOES

1. Put shoe trees in men's shoes.
2. Fill women's shoes with tissue paper.
3. Slip each shoe into its own pouch.

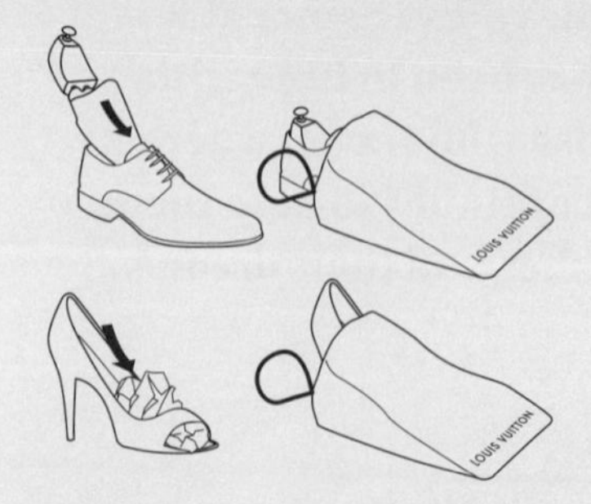

JEANS

1. Lay the jeans flat, legs apart, seams facing outwards, pockets face down.
2. Place one leg over the other.
3. Fold the jeans two or three times, or roll them up.

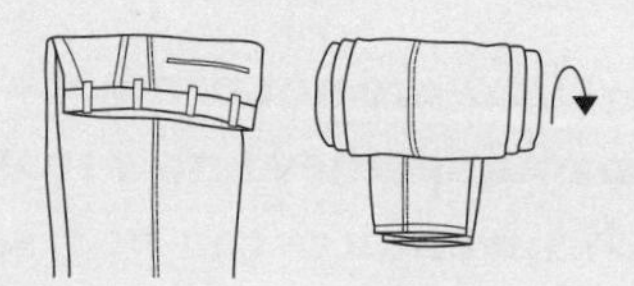

FINE SWEATER

1. Lay the fine sweater flat, neck at the top. Fold the sleeves inwards.
2. Roll it up from collar to base.
3. If necessary, roll it again, from left to right.

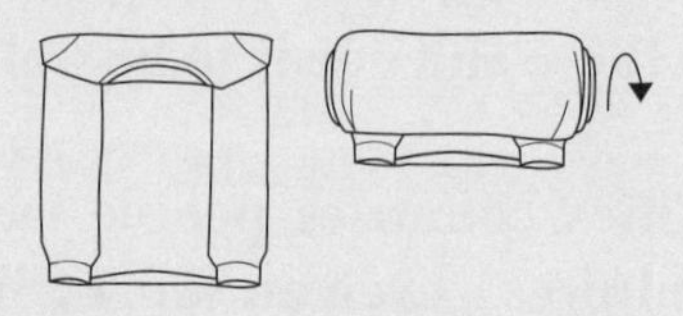

SHIRT

1. Raise the shirt collar in order to protect it.
2. Fasten every second button.
3. Fold it in two in the classic way, lengthways, with the collar visible and the sleeves folded behind.
4. Place one shirt over another, "head to toe", in order to avoid unwanted creases.

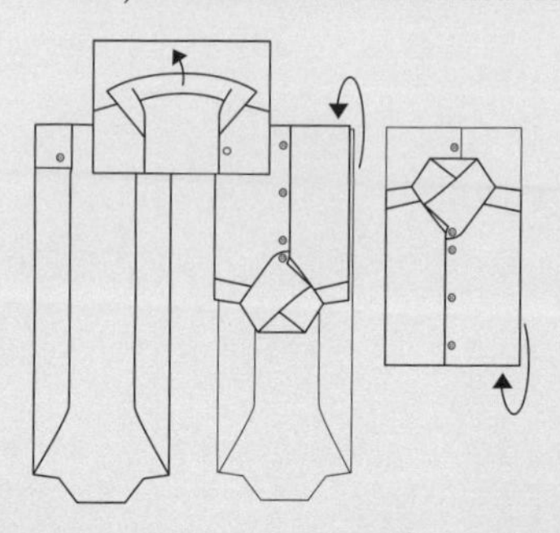

DELICATE DRESS

1. Place a t-shirt face down on the dress.
2. Fold the sides of the dress over the t-shirt.
3. Carefully fold the dress in three, starting at the top.

JACKET

1. First, raise and flatten the collar.
2. Fold in each sleeve, leaving the shoulders straight.
3. Carefully fold the jacket to fit the length of the bag.

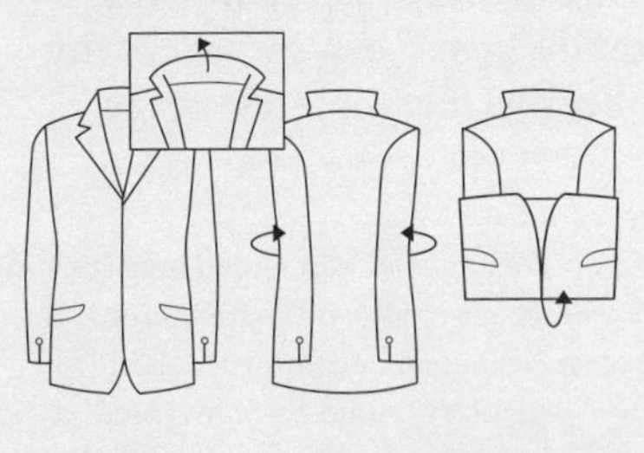

SKIRT SUIT

1. Fold the skirt in two vertically.
2. Raise and flatten the jacket collar.
3. Place the skirt inside the jacket.
4. Button up the jacket to protect the skirt.

TEXTILES, TIES AND BELTS

Roll up ties and belts, also scarves, which should be tightly rolled.

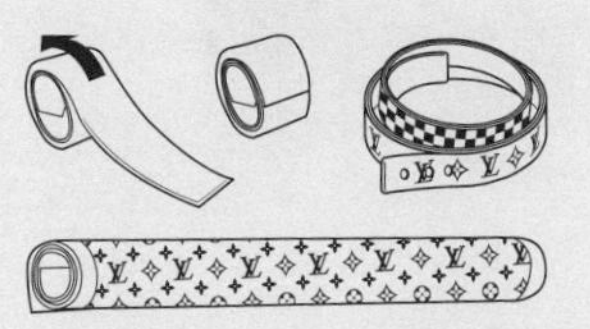

MAN'S SUIT

1. Lay the trousers flat, the legs folded in the usual way.
2. Pass the outer leg of the trousers through the hanger. Fold it in two over the inner leg.
3. Pass the inner leg through the same hanger, fold it in the same way, towards the trouser waist.
4. Place the jacket on the hanger.
5. Put the complete suit in its bag.

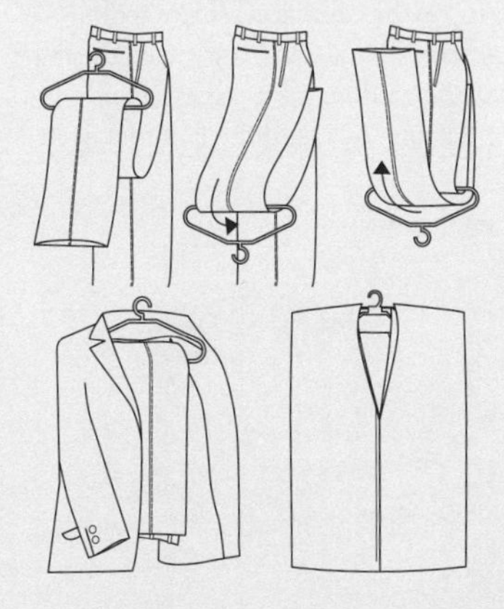

THE TEN ICONS OF TRAVEL

The history of the House of Louis Vuitton is measured out in landmark creations. These are hard-wired into the brand's genes and are part of the collective memory of luggage.

WARDROBE

The quintessence of hard-sided luggage, the wardrobes are the ultimate example of a practical form becoming a cult object. These legendary trunks were invented in 1875 to allow travellers to carry all their effects in a single container, a matchlessly robust combination of wooden structure and coated leather or canvas exterior. The two parts of this prodigious wardrobe-trunk have a hanging space on one side and drawers on the other. The woman's model has racks for hanging long dresses, while some of the drawers are spacious enough to hold voluminous hats. Even today, demanding travellers refuse to do without this accessory, which ensures that their clothes and accessories will remain perfectly safe and organized during their journey. Other advantages include the unpickable lock, and the fact that each client has a unique, single key for all his or her Louis Vuitton bags. And, finally, there's the pleasure of finding your mobile wardrobe at each destination. Travellers who travel lighter use these wardrobes as the centrepiece of their living space, setting the trunk in the hall, lounge or bedroom.

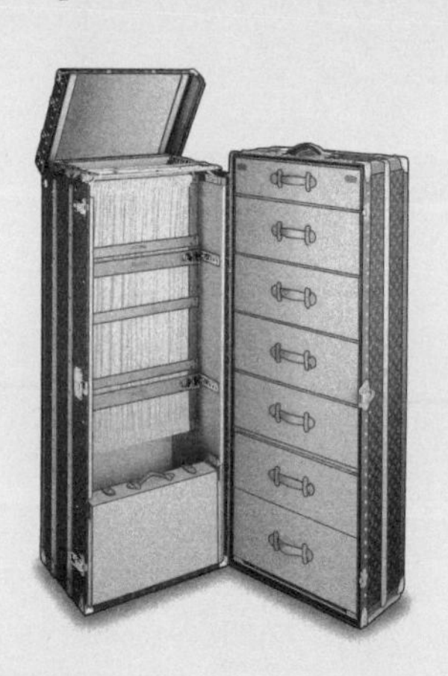

STEAMER BAG

Created in 1901, the Steamer Bag was originally one of those extra bags in canvas and leather offered with the trunk, made simply as an elegant receptacle for the personal laundry worn by travellers during a long ocean crossing. Hence its name. As for its nickname, "the inviolable", this was due to its reassuring reputation for never divulging those personal details, thanks to a highly sophisticated locking system. Tough, thanks to its hard-edged rectangular base, and exceptionally capacious, its versatility as a container made this complementary baggage a permanent favourite. Like the Keepall, the Steamer Bag benefited from the invention of the supple Monogram canvas in 1959, establishing itself as an item of luggage in its own right. Entirely hand-sewn, this bag still requires fifteen hours of crafting in the workshop.

KEEPALL

For many years, travellers who ordered a trunk or hard-sided luggage from Louis Vuitton were offered auxiliary bags in canvas with leather straps. One was the Keepall, designed in 1930. It is the ancestor of all the bolster-shaped duffel bags which, with changing lifestyles and means of transport, have become separate items in their own right. The invention of the supple Monogram canvas in 1959 made the Keepall the perfect answer to the demands of New Wave stars. A treasured personal signature, it was ideal for a weekend dash to Saint Tropez or Deauville at the wheel of a sports car. This spirit of freedom emanates from the films shot at the time on the beach at Pampelonne – ah, those sublime blond actresses! – or in the Saint-Germain-des-Prés of Jean-Luc Godard, François Truffaut and Jacques Rivette.

SPEEDY

Archetype of the versatile soft bag, the Speedy was conceived in the 1930s. Its extremely simple, generous form, easily identifiable for those familiar with its older brother, the Keepall, immediately established itself as the obvious partner of modern travel, where its lightness and versatility were a key advantage. In the 1960s, a new size was created for Audrey Hepburn. An easygoing city bag, it became one of the prime accessories of the modern woman. It plays a role in several histories – the history of Louis Vuitton, of course, but also within movies and fashion.

NOÉ

Designed in 1932 by Gaston-Louis Vuitton, grandson of Louis, when a champagne producer asked him to devise a robust but elegant bag capable of carrying five bottles of champagne (four upright and one in the middle, top-down), the Noé has become one of the House's cult objects. It too benefited from the invention of supple canvas, becoming a favourite of free, active women for whom distinction is a given. Today, the proportions have been modified and the bag is available in several sizes and finishes. Popular with female clients worldwide, the Noé is one of the great Louis Vuitton classics.

ALMA

The Alma was inspired by the Squire Bag, which was designed in 1934, and one of its first enthusiasts was an illustrious fashion designer. Reinvented in 1992, this pure Art Deco form naturally became a Louis Vuitton emblem, with its combination of roominess and obvious elegance. The quintessential multipurpose city bag comes in a range of sizes and materials and its design is constantly reworked through artist collaborations and following seasonal runway shows.

NEVERFULL

Resolutely contemporary, the Neverfull has been living up to its name since 2007. Its striped lining recalls the finest luggage of yesteryear, but this tote offers far more than mere history: it is superbly functional. Its slim, vegetable-tanned leather handles make the Neverfull tough enough for any occasion, and it is light and supple. Printed in Palm Beach or Porto Cervo colours, covered in Stephen Sprouse roses or awash with Yayoi Kusama waves, the Neverfull is perfect for the beach or the city and will carry back the best memories of either. Forever.

ICON OF ICONS

MONOGRAM CANVAS

The Monogram canvas was designed by Georges Vuitton in 1896. Initially conceived to thwart the fakers who copied striped and chequered canvases, it soon became the house symbol. At once bold and harmonious, the motif has always been utterly modern. LV, the initials of the house, are simply intertwined so that they remain perfectly visible, and three stylized flowers worked in different themes and variations mirror these. The elegance and restraint of these repeated ornaments create an image of graphic perfection, which is underscored by the positioning of the motifs.

PORTE-DOCUMENTS VOYAGE

Like the Steamer Bag and the Keepall, the Porte-Documents Voyage was one of the auxiliary bags offered with the hard-sided trunks. It was used for keeping travel pillows, but has now been diverted from this original function and, clad in Épi leather, as here, or Monogram canvas,

its new function, greatly appreciated by business travellers, is to carry documents, dossiers, papers and notes, which emerge without a crease or dog-ear from their journey. Neither a satchel nor a briefcase, the Porte-Documents Voyage is a sure way of keeping pages from scattering.

ALZER

The suitcase's traditional appearance masks a deceptively spacious, robust interior. The Alzer is like a chest, or even a strong box, with its reinforced locks, separate compartment and inner straps. A reassuring holder of treasured clothes that must be impeccable on arrival, its dimensions are ideal for optimum storage of everything you need when travelling for a few days. Its Monogram canvas exterior lends itself to personalization, helping to make this protective case unique, the must-have for refined travellers with a sense of what's best about tradition.

HORIZON

The Maison Louis Vuitton has called on renowned designer Marc Newson to create the luggage of the future. A great traveller himself, Newson designed Horizon with his own travel needs and experiences in mind. He used the most sophisticated technologies and materials available to make a superlative suitcase that is ultra-light, ultra-resistant and ultra-easy to handle. It has miniature wheels, moves silently and rotates 360 degrees. Its telescoping trolley handle is on the outside of the case, providing extra space inside and a flat interior surface for ease of packing. Equipped with accessories and storage pockets, it is sealed with a clever lightweight aluminium zipper. It took almost eighteen months to develop this "smart" suitcase, a technological marvel that can even be connected to other devices. Available in two sizes, with a choice of several surface styles, the perfectly elegant Horizon suitcase demonstrates once again Louis Vuitton's constant concern for innovation.

LOUIS VUITTON: AN OPEN BOOK

Books have always played a special role in the history of Louis Vuitton. The literary adventure begun by Gaston-Louis continues today with several authoritative series.

AN ENLIGHTENED BIBLIOPHILE

Gaston-Louis Vuitton (1883–1970), the founder's grandson, was a great lover of art books and literature. The founder of three bibliophile clubs, he corresponded with publishers, illustrators and authors, cultivating privileged relations with many writer-travellers. These unique bonds are reflected in the documents and objects kept in the House archives, such as Ernest Hemingway's bookshelf-trunk, which still contained handwritten notebooks, and the desk-trunk of Savorgnan de Brazza, the hidden compartment of which housed a top-secret report.

RENEWING THE LITERARY TRADITION

Today, the House of Louis Vuitton has its own publications, with three travel-related collections.

THE CITY GUIDES

Eagerly awaited every year, acclaimed by opinion leaders, they capture with glorious subjectivity the essence of urban experience in an up-to-the-minute selection of addresses, from the latest designer hotel to a gourmet restaurant, from the hottest fashion designer to the best organic market, from a photography gallery to a secret museum, from a refined spa to a late-night watering hole, or a surprising antiques dealer to a maker of scrumptious chocolate. Their mix of fascinating insider information covers every aspect of metropolitan life. This expert local knowledge is made even more vivid by the viewpoints of distinguished residents.

THE TRAVEL BOOKS

First published in 2013, this collection revisits the travel notebook collection. Louis Vuitton asked artists, illustrators, graphic designers, painters and *mangaka* to produce images that sum up their vision of a city or country they don't know, or know only slightly, in 120 original plates. The Japanese Jirô Taniguchi goes into exile in Venice, the Belgian Brecht Evens arrives in Paris, the Frenchman Jean-Philippe Delhomme sketches New York, the Chinese Liu Xiaodong flies to South Africa, the Arctic is captured by the Irishman Blaise Drummond and Mexico is charted by Nicolas de Crécy.

Colourful, personal and packed with detail, this collection handsomely combines Louis Vuitton's various initiatives in art and publishing.

VOYAGER AVEC...
This collection, prized by literature lovers, comprises over thirty titles in which excerpts from the works of distinguished writers offer fresh perspectives on travel. The collection has invited readers to "travel with" Marcel Proust, Le Corbusier, Joseph Conrad, Nicolas Bouvier and Friedrich Nietzsche. This collection, published in French, is illustrated.

FASHION EYE
Each book in this photography series, launched in 2016, focuses on one location seen through the lens of a fashion photographer. Some places are well-known, others less so. There are famous photographers – some living, others long gone – and emerging talents. Paris by Jeanloup Sieff, Shanghai by Wing Shya, New York by Saul Leiter, California by Kourtney Roy, British Columbia by Sølve Sundsbø, Monte Carlo by Helmut Newton and Miami by Guy Bourdin. Some works are from the archives, others are contemporary shots. This is travel photography at its aesthetic best, a welcome return to the genre.

ART BOOKS
Louis Vuitton also collaborates on the publication of lavish books about the House and its heritage distributed worldwide. Co-edition titles include *Louis Vuitton: Art, Fashion and Architecture*, *Louis Vuitton City Bags: A Natural History*, *Louis Vuitton Fashion Photography* and *Volez Voguez Voyagez – Louis Vuitton* with Rizzoli, New York; *Louis Vuitton: The Birth of Modern Luxury* with Éditions de La Martinière; *I've just arrived in Paris* and *For Friends* with Steidl; *Louis Vuitton: The Spirit of Travel* with Éditions Flammarion; *Cabinet of Wonders: The Gaston-Louis Vuitton Collections* with Thames and Hudson and *World Tour* with Éditions Xavier Barral.

Limited, numbered artists' editions are also available, such as those by photographer Jean Larivière and illustrator Ruben Toledo, echoing their creations for the House. Furthermore, in 2012, Louis Vuitton celebrated its savoir-faire and the art of travel by offering the House's first app for iPad, *Louis Vuitton: 100 Legendary Trunks*, conceived in association with Éditions de La Martinière, who edited the paper version.

THE ART OF WRITING
Moving forward from an outstanding heritage, Louis Vuitton journeys through the world of writing. Writing instruments, exclusive inks, crystal inkwells, writing kits, collector's trunks and boxes, as well as stationery, make up a highly symbolic art of writing which reinforces links with the House's history, as embodied in rare historic objects, and enables its clients to encounter some remarkable artists and artisans.

TRAVELLERS' BOOKSTORES
This tradition of the book initiated by Gaston-Louis Vuitton nearly a hundred years ago is now maintained and spread throughout the world. Several Maison Louis Vuitton have their own bookstore where Louis Vuitton publications are offered alongside a careful, pertinent selection of books on art, fashion, design and travel, helping to complete and enrich the heritage of knowledge, art and culture.

LOUIS VUITTON TIMELINE

1854
Louis Vuitton opens his first store at 4, rue Neuve-des-Capucines, Paris, and develops his first trunk, covered with grey Trianon canvas.

1859
Louis Vuitton moves his production workshops to Asnières, by the Seine, west of Paris.

1880
The newly married Georges Vuitton becomes co-director of the House with his father.

1883
Birth of Gaston-Louis Vuitton, son of Georges and Joséphine Vuitton.

1885
Opening of a Louis Vuitton store at 289 Oxford Street, in the heart of London. Four years later it moves to 454 Strand.

1888
Creation of the Damier canvas. For the first time in the history of the House, the words "Marque L. Vuitton déposée" appear on the canvas.

1890
Creation of the patented unpickable and individualized tumbler lock.

1892
Death of Louis Vuitton, aged 71.
Georges Vuitton works on his book *Le Voyage depuis les temps les plus reculés jusqu'à nos jours,* which would be published in 1894 and earns him the rank of Officier d'Académie.

1896
Creation of the Monogram canvas.

1905
Among other items, Pierre Savorgnan de Brazza orders two large bed-trunks from Louis Vuitton.

1914
Louis Vuitton opens the world's biggest store of travel items at 70, avenue des Champs-Élysées.

1920
A passionate collector and reader, Gaston-Louis Vuitton publishes *Voyage iconographique autour de ma malle.*

1923
The workshops in Asnières prepare 150 objects for Citroën's "Croisière Noire" African expedition.

1930
Launch of the Keepall soft bag.

1931
After the Croisière Noire, the House equips the Citroën Croisière Jaune (to China) and takes part in the Exposition Coloniale Internationale in Paris, where the Modernist Louis Vuitton Pavilion is entirely designed by Gaston-Louis Vuitton.

1959
Development of a new technique for coating the Monogram canvas, which will enable the conception of the whole soft baggage range and assure its success.

1978
Opening of the first Japanese stores in Tokyo and Osaka.

1983
Launch of the Louis Vuitton Cup, the winner of which challenges for the America's Cup. First edition at Newport, Rhode Island.

1985
Launch of the Épi leather line, now a House classic.

1992
Opening of the first store in China, in Beijing.

1996
Centenary of Monogram canvas.

1998
Louis Vuitton steps into the world of fashion with its debut ready-to-wear collection by Artistic Director Marc Jacobs.

2001
Creation of the Monogram Graffiti canvas, designed by Marc Jacobs in collaboration with American artist Stephen Sprouse.

2003
Launch of the Monogram Multicolore line, designed in collaboration with Japanese artist Takashi Murakami.

2004
Louis Vuitton celebrates its 150th birthday by opening the Maison Louis Vuitton on New York's Fifth Avenue.

2005
Opening of the Maison Louis Vuitton at 101, Avenue des Champs-Élysées, the brand's biggest store anywhere in the world, with interior architecture by Peter Marino.

2008
Collaboration between the American artist Richard Prince and Marc Jacobs for the spring-summer women's ready-to-wear collection. Launch of the Louis Vuitton Sofia Coppola collection of leather goods.

2010
Louis Vuitton takes part in Expo 2010 in Shanghai. "Voyage en capitale, Louis Vuitton et Paris": exhibition at the Musée Carnavalet in Paris.

2011
Opening of the Maison Louis Vuitton Marina Bay in Singapore, and of the first Australian Maison in Sydney. "Louis Vuitton. Voyages", an exhibition at the National Museum of China, Beijing.

2012
Louis Vuitton partners Japanese artist Yayoi Kusama in a series of artistic projects and products sporting her signature dots. "Louis Vuitton Marc Jacobs" exhibition at the Musée des Arts Décoratifs, Paris.

2013
The House collaborates with French artist Daniel Buren on the advertising campaign and store windows for its spring/summer women's ready-to-wear collection.

2014
The first Louis Vuitton ready-to-wear collection by Artistic Director Nicolas Ghesquière. Opening of the Fondation Louis Vuitton, designed by architect Frank Gehry. Celebration of the Monogram by Frank Gehry, Rei Kawakubo, Karl Lagerfeld, Christian Louboutin, Marc Newson and Cindy Sherman.

2015
Opening of the exhibition space adjoining the Louis Vuitton family home in Asnières-sur-Seine. Exhibition *Volez Voguez Voyagez – Louis Vuitton* at the Grand Palais, Paris.

2016
Louis Vuitton joins up with Unicef to help children in peril. Launch of Les Parfums Louis Vuitton

2017
Launch of the Masters collection, a series of bags and accessories created in collaboration with the New York artist Jeff Koons which revisits the emblematic works of the great masters of art.

NOTES

GENERAL INDEX

M

N

O

P

Q

R

S

T

U

V

W

Y

INDEX BY NEIGHBOURHOOD

LOUVRE, TUILERIES, PALAIS-ROYAL, LES HALLES
1ST & 2ND ARRONDISSEMENTS

FAUBOURG SAINT-HONORÉ, CHAMPS-ÉLYSÉES, MADELEINE, MONCEAU

8TH ARRONDISSEMENT

LES GOBELINS, DENFERT-ROCHEREAU, MONTPARNASSE
13TH, 14TH & 15TH ARRONDISSEMENTS

AUTEUIL, PASSY, TROCADÉRO, ÉTOILE
16TH & 17TH ARRONDISSEMENTS

MONTMARTRE, LA VILLETTE, BELLEVILLE, MÉNILMONTANT
18TH, 19TH & 20TH ARRONDISSEMENTS

ELSEWHERE

AUTHORS, PHOTOGRAPHERS AND EDITORIAL TEAM

AUTHORS

Marie-Hélène Brunet-Lhoste
Managing Editor of the Louis Vuitton City Guides since their inception, she never fails to be impressed with the incredible beauty of the city whose secrets she continues to explore.

Alfred Escot
A specialist in interior decoration and design, journalist Alfred Escot contributes to the "Mode de Vie" column in *Grazia* magazine and to the "News" pages of *Ideat* magazine. Hailing from the South of France and now based in Paris, he seeks out the movers and shakers who are influencing lifestyle choices today.

Pierre Groppo
Head of *Vanity Fair*'s fashion and lifestyle section, Pierre Groppo cut his teeth working at *Vogue*. For over ten years he has been reporting and commenting on the comings and goings in the world of fashion, from the front row of the catwalks to backstage in the dressing rooms and the hair salons.

Katia Kulawick-Assante
Journalist and cool-hunter, she writes the "Vanity Confidential" newsletter for French *Vanity Fair*. For this edition of the Paris City Guide, she takes us behind the scenes in Paris's hotels.

Pierre Léonforte
Pierre Léonforte writes a monthly column for French *Vanity Fair* magazine and contributes to *Marie Claire Maison, Beaux-Arts Magazine* and *Schnock*. He has worked as Editor-in-Chief of the Louis Vuitton City Guides, which he helped to create in 1998. He is the author of several books, including *Jean-Paul Hévin : Délices de Chocolat, Paris des Hommes* and *Louis Vuitton: 100 Legendary Trunks*, some of which have been published in Italian and English.

Marie Maertens
The ultimate Parisienne, she has her finger on the pulse of the museum and gallery world. She is also a journalist, art critic and independent exhibition curator, notably for "Desdémone, entre désir et désespoir" (Institut du Monde Arabe). She writes regularly for *Connaissance des arts magazine* and *AMA* (Art Media Agency), contributes to collective works, and has served as a jury member.

Laurence Marot
Specializing in the world of beverages, she seeks out the best drinking dens, the new trends and tomorrow's star mixologists for both mass-media and professional publications. She has also authored a collection of books on rum, whisky and gin cocktails (Éditions Tana).

Hugo de Saint-Phalle
Hugo de Saint-Phalle spends his life dashing between restaurants and cinemas. For TV magazines of the Prisma Media group, he covers all the latest news in the world of film, while for *Figaroscope* and *Fooding*, among others, he reviews Parisian restaurants – anonymously, of course.

François Simon
Gault&Millau, Cuisines et Vins de France, Figaroscope. Wielding his formidable expense account, he has written for *M Le Monde* and *Air France magazin*, while freelancing for TV, before hosting the cult TV show *Paris Dernière*. As an anonymous restaurant reviewer he contributes to many platforms, including his own website (simonsays.fr), and has published over forty books.

PHOTOGRAPHY

Tendance floue
Founded in 1991, Tendance floue (literally, a tendency to be out of focus) is a group of thirteen photographers who have created a collective with the aim of working together to open up new perspectives and diversify the ways that contemporary photography can represent the world.
In addition to their personal projects, these photographers nurture their collective photographic work by comparing images, assemblages and combinations, their pooled results giving rise to completely new material.
www.tendancefloue.net

Bertrand Meunier
With its cinematic dimension, his work is deliberately freed from raw information. After years of building up his "Erased" series on post-industrial China, Bertrand Meunier is currently working on a survey of people in France who suffer in various ways. He is also developing a parallel "psycho-geography" photographic project about Asian megacities.

PRESIDENT
Michael Burke

EDITORIAL DIRECTOR
Julien Guerrier

MANAGING EDITOR
Marie-Hélène Brunet-Lhoste

EDITORIAL CONSULTANT
Pierre Léonforte

MANAGING EDITOR
ENGLISH EDITION
Nicola Mitchell

COPY EDITOR
Bernard Wooding

PROOFREADERS
Rebecca Brite
Erin Conroy

TRANSLATORS
Heidi Ellison
Philippa Hurd

ARTISTIC DIRECTION
Lords of Design™:
Frédéric Bortolotti
Frédérique Stietel

LAYOUT ARTISTS
Marie Barbelet
Sophia Mejdoub
Catherine Riand

MAPS
EdiCarto

PRINT PRODUCTION
Desgrandchamps:
Karine Rejon Midas
François Ollivier

THANKS
To everyone who has helped with this edition, in particular: Audrey Belescot, Nicolas Bussière, Gwenaëlle Carruth, Caroline Charles, Julien Charles, Bénédicte Colpin, Rosita Fanelli, Clémentine Herbinet, Édith Jarboua, Chantal Muller, Pascale Tinozzi, Anthony Vessot, Valérie Viscardi.

We decline all responsibility with regard to any errors or omissions that have occurred despite the careful editing and proofreading of the guide.

19th edition of the collection

Published by
Louis Vuitton Malletier
Louis Vuitton City Guide
2, Rue du Pont-Neuf
75001 Paris
cityguide@frvuitton.com
www.louisvuitton.com

A limited corporation with a board of directors and capital of €21,119,700
318 571 064 RCS Paris
APE: 514S
TVA: FR 43 318 571 064

The Louis Vuitton City Guide is a collective work published by Louis Vuitton Malletier. It is produced by authors, illustrators, layout artists, copy editors, translators and proofreaders working in collaboration with the company BETC, under the direction of the company Louis Vuitton Malletier and its President and Editorial Director.

The Louis Vuitton City Guide is printed on Primalux 65g FSC made with pulp from sustainable forests. It is set in the Futura typeface designed by Paul Renner in 1932, digitalized and distributed by URW++ (Germany), and in the Arno Pro typeface designed by Robert Slimbach in 2007 for Adobe (US).

All rights reserved worldwide.
© Louis Vuitton Malletier, 2018
ISBN: 978-2-36983-117-4
ISSN: 1968-1941
Registration: 4th trimester 2017
Printed in Italy

R08376